IN PURSUIT
OF A
WELSH EPISCOPATE

Appointments to Welsh Sees, 1840–1905

Roger Lee Brown

UNIVERSITY OF WALES PRESS
CARDIFF
2005

British Library Cataloguing-in-Publication Data
A catalogue for this book is available from the British Library.

ISBN 0-7083-1939-4

Published with the financial support of the Marc Fitch Fund.

Printed in Great Britain by Dinefwr Press, Llandybïe

Bishops, just like the very poor and the uneducated,
should be treated with special prudence.

Graham Green, *Monsignor Quixote*

Contents

CONTENTS

General Editor's Foreword

During the late nineteenth and early twentieth centuries, Wales was renowned for its strong Nonconformist tradition, and so dramatic was its growth and development that it eclipsed for a while the contributions made by other Christian traditions that ministered to the needs of the people at that time.

To a degree, this has been reflected in the themes of the volumes which have appeared to date in this series. With works on the Nonconformist social gospel, the beginnings of Welsh Calvinistic Methodism, the history of Congregationalism and the faith and crisis of the nation between 1890 and 1914, a distinct emphasis has been in evidence. At the same time, an effort has been made to strike a balance, firstly through the publication of Trystan Hughes's volume on the re-emergence of Catholicism during the twentieth century, and now through this volume by Roger Lee Brown representing, as it does, the Anglican tradition in Wales.

For many years Roger Lee Brown has been associated with the Centre for the Advanced Study of Religion in Wales as a Research Fellow and has written numerous books and articles focusing mainly on topics associated with the history of the Anglican Church. In this current volume he investigates the appointment of bishops to Wales during the period 1840 to 1905, that is, from the time of the parliamentary reforms of the 1830s to the last political appointment to a Welsh see before the disestablishment of the Church in 1920 permitted the Church in Wales to choose its own bishops.

As has been pointed out in other volumes in this series, the Centre was established in 1998 to encourage scholarly research and to contribute towards a better and wider understanding of the history of religion among the Welsh people. Like the previous publications, it is believed that this book contributes towards the fulfilling of that aim by allowing us a view of yet another aspect of the subject, and by casting new and interesting light on decisions and appointments which were to have a far-reaching effect both on the witness of the Church in general and on the lives and experiences of the people who belonged to it.

Geraint Tudur
The Centre for the Advanced Study of Religion in Wales,
University of Wales, Bangor

Acknowledgements

I am most grateful to the many librarians and archivists without whose cooperation this book would never have been completed. Mr Robin Harcourt-Williams, the marquess of Salisbury's librarian, not only drew my attention to material at Hatfield House, but also kindly checked some references for me. The Queen's librarian at Windsor Castle and the archivists of Flintshire and Liverpool Record Offices provided photostat copies of correspondence. In particular I am most appreciative of the help given me by the librarians and their staff at Lambeth Palace Library and the Royal Archives at Windsor.

I am indebted to Her Majesty Queen Elizabeth II for permission to quote from the papers of Queen Victoria and the Melbourne Correspondence held at Windsor Castle, to the marquess of Salisbury for permitting me to quote from the correspondence of the third marquess, to the earl of Derby for similar permission regarding the correspondence of the fourteenth earl, and to the National Trust for being able to quote from the letters of Benjamin Disraeli. Sir William Gladstone was equally kind in permitting me to quote from the Gladstone papers at the British Library. The copyright of manuscript material is a notoriously difficult subject, and if I have infringed anybody's copyright I beg their forgiveness.

One of my main sources for this study has been newspapers and periodicals. Thankfully, most newspapers of this period quoted one another extensively and sometimes verbatim. The Nonconformist periodicals tended to avoid speculation about these episcopal elections, mainly because they had taken place by the time of their publication. The Welsh Nonconformist press has proved to be a poor source of material. Thomas Gee's *Baner ac Amserau Cymru* might be thought to have been an exception, but even this paper was muted in its reporting of these elections. Though it could describe Llandaff as an 'empty diocese' in 1883, and as a 'sinecure' in 1905, its main concern was for the appointment of Welsh-speaking bishops, though it expressed continual annoyance at Lord Salisbury's Tory appointments. Where one might have expected the editors of this paper to use these elections as a means of attacking the Church, especially when Dean Edwards or his brother were the favoured candidates, one finds instead a certain degree of sympathy. Bishop Lewis of Llandaff, for example, was described in his obituary as one of the hardest working bishops on the entire bench. Surprisingly, the Welsh Church press was also muted in its comment. *Yr Haul*, a monthly journal, was understandably so, for the elections might have come and gone before an issue could appear, but *Y Llan*, a weekly paper, only came to life during the 1898 Bangor election. Its coverage prior to this was very restrained, and even in 1905 it was hardly excessive. Possibly episcopal pressure, either in actuality or the fear of such interference, was able to prevent any free comment.

This book has been written among the pressures of parochial life, often utilizing holiday time for research work and spare moments for its writing. Without the cooperation and assistance of my wife Phyllis it could never have been completed. Many others assisted me by reading and commenting on various chapters as they were written. Archdeacon Bill Prichard was especially helpful in this respect as was Mr Bill Gibson, who had already published an article on the 1882 Llandaff vacancy, and who readily and graciously accepted that I was working in this field from a prior date. I am especially grateful to those who acted as assessors for this work on behalf of the Centre for the Advanced Study of Religion in Wales and in particular to Dr Robert Pope. I would also wish to thank the personnel of the University of Wales Press, and in particular Sarah Lewis and Nia Peris, for their kindness and their skill in preparing this work for the press.

The origin of this book lay in my study of David Howell, published in 1998. His candidature for episcopal office led me to study the wider field. Since the publication of the above work I had had access to the Royal Archives at Windsor and to Bishop John Owen's papers at the National Library of Wales. These were previously unavailable to me.

I ought to state that I have used the word 'candidate' in the widest possible sense. It includes those men whose claims to episcopal office were seriously considered by the various prime ministers, and those who were considered by their friends, and in some cases by themselves, to have such claims. In constitutional practice the election of a bishop in the pre-disestablished Church in Wales was made by the dean and chapter of the cathedral of the vacant see; in practice, however, the prime minister would send a writ to that chapter containing the name of the candidate selected by him and approved by the monarch, whom the chapter was required to elect. For convenience I have suggested that the prime minister appointed or nominated to the see, without reference to the actual but formal election by the dean and chapter concerned.

The abbreviations used in quotations have been extended, and the folio number given as a reference for a letter relates to its opening page.

Abbreviations

Baner	*Baner ac Amserau Cymru* [of Thomas Gee]
CDH	*Carnarvon and Denbigh Herald*
CJ	*Carmarthen Journal*
CMG	*Cardiff and Merthyr Guardian* (originally called *The Glamorgan, Monmouth and Brecon Gazette and Merthyr Guardian*)
BP	Benson Papers at Lambeth Palace Library
CT	*Church Times*
DNB	Dictionary of National Biography
DP	Davidson Papers at Lambeth Palace Library
DerP	Letter Books of the 14th earl of Derby at City of Liverpool Library [class number: 920/DER (14)]
DisP	Disraeli Papers at the Bodleian Library, Oxford [class number: Dep Hughenden 157/4]
GGC	Glynne-Gladstone Correspondence held at St Deiniol's Library, Hawarden, but available at Flintshire Record Office, Hawarden
GP	Gladstone Papers at the British Library
JOP	Bishop John Owen papers at the NLW (at present uncatalogued)
Letters	*Letters from Llanbadarnfawr Parish Chest*, typescript at the National Library of Wales
LJRP	Lord John Russell Papers at the Public Record Office, Kew [class number 30/22]
LPL	Lambeth Palace Library
NLW	National Library of Wales, Aberystwyth
NWG	*North Wales Guardian*
PLD	Powis Letters and Documents relating to the Proposed Union of the Dioceses of St Asaph and Bangor [NLW]

ABBREVIATIONS

RA MP   Royal Archives, Windsor, Melbourne Papers
RA VIC Royal Archives, Windsor, papers of Queen Victoria
Report   *Report of the Association of Welsh Clergy in the West Riding of Yorkshire*
SP   The papers of the 3rd marquess of Salisbury at Hatfield House
SPCK   Society for Promoting Christian Knowledge
SPG   Society for the Propagation of the Gospel
TP   Tait Papers at Lambeth Palace Library
TemP   The papers of Archbishop Temple at Lambeth Palace Library
WA   *Wrexham Advertiser*
WM   *Western Mail*

~ 1 ~

In Pursuit of a Welsh Episcopate: Appointments to Welsh Sees, 1840–1905

The subject of this book is the appointment of bishops, by the prime ministers of the day, to Welsh sees during the period 1840–1905. The year 1840 marked the first appointment to a Welsh see made after the parliamentary reforms of the 1830s which inaugurated the Ecclesiastical Commission. Thereafter bishops, and not only Welsh bishops, were provided with adequate incomes, episcopal residences and an administrative machinery. There was no need, therefore, for bishops to hold livings or deaneries *in commendam* in order to make their incomes respectable, or for their rapid transfer, depending upon their political allegiance and loyalty in the House of Lords, to other and more lucrative sees elsewhere. This had been the bugbear of the Welsh Church for generations. All the Welsh dioceses save one, St Asaph, possessed an inadequate income, and one, Llandaff, was at the bottom of the league table of episcopal incomes. To give one example of these rapid episcopal translations: between 1724 and 1825 the diocese of St Davids had sixteen bishops, but during the next hundred years it had only five.

The ecclesiastical reforms of the 1830s ended such episcopal journeyings, with the result that the bishops became less subservient to their human makers. After 1840 no Welsh bishop was translated to another diocese until C. A. H. Green, bishop of Monmouth, was elected bishop of Bangor in 1928. But the Church in Wales was by then a disestablished Church and a separate province of the Anglican Communion, and was thus able to appoint its own bishops. Presumably it knew its own business.

The terminal date of the study is that of the last political appointment to a Welsh see before the disestablishment of the Church in 1920 permitted the Church in Wales to choose its own bishops. But perhaps it is salutary to note that the last survivor of the pre-disestablishment bishops, A. G. Edwards, continued as bishop until 1934, and the widow of his successor, William Thomas Havard, died as late as 1986.

The right of appointment to a bishopric in the Church of England was clearly vested in the Crown by the time of the Reformation, although, in order to maintain some concept of subservience to Christian tradition, the dean and chapter of the vacant see were required to elect the person nominated by the Crown. Under George 1 (1714–27) the nomination was made by the prime minister, who recommended a name to the Crown. Canonical order required that a person elected and thereafter consecrated as a bishop should be at least thirty years of age, had spent a certain time in priest's orders, and be of good character and sound doctrine. Because bishops also sat in the House of Lords and were officers of state, additional social qualifications were also required.

Until the mid-nineteenth century bishops were appointed for the four Welsh dioceses from the same social class as those appointed for English sees. This background was often aristocratic and their appointments also had political overtones. The cry for Welsh-speaking bishops for the four dioceses in Wales was given serious attention by the late 1840s, at least, not only because of the lobby being organized among the Welsh but because of a fear at the worse, or an understanding at the best, that the selection of non-Welsh speakers to these sees might have caused the spread of Nonconformity in Wales. Nonconformity was seen in many quarters as socially divisive and as a cause for alarm, so there was an expectation that the appointment of Welsh speakers to the Welsh dioceses would strengthen the established Church and help diminish the impact of Nonconformity in Wales.

Thus from the 1840s onwards there was an additional requirement for bishops of Welsh sees, namely that they spoke Welsh. At first it was assumed that men who had acquired some knowledge of Welsh as a second language came into this category, but it was soon accepted that native Welsh speakers were required. For reasons noted later this meant that these men might not be of the same social and educational calibre of their English colleagues. Consequently, many of those appointed during the period under review were appointed under circumstances and for requirements quite different to those for an English see.

This study reveals not only the methods used by the various

prime ministers to find the right candidates, but also seeks to understand why others were rejected. It indicates the enormous pressures put on the premiers, by their own political partisans, by supporters of particular candidates, or by other members of the bench. This was especially true of Bishop Edwards, who became an increasingly influential figure in many of the later Welsh appointments during the period here under review. There was also Queen Victoria, who insisted on having a very real say in these appointments. In this respect she was assisted by her unofficial but extremely influential advisors, Lord Gerald Wellesley and Randall Davidson, both deans of Windsor. But above all there was the clamour of the Welsh press and the so-called patriotic clergy for Welsh speakers to be appointed to the Welsh dioceses. All endeavoured to get their man elected, though in Wales again there was a phenomenon not seen in England, namely the open canvassing of office by would-be candidates. This outraged the establishment, although in all probability the complaint was that it was openly done, rather than taking place in the more dignified and convivial atmosphere of club rooms, stately homes and college common rooms.

The study also reveals the enormous difficulties faced by the various prime ministers in selecting the right man for a Welsh see. He had to balance finely the requirements of the see and the claims of individuals, and between the need for a Welsh-speaking and native appointment, as against the contrasting claim of the establishment that a bishop was also a peer of the realm and needed to be a gentleman and a scholar. It was a conflict that was never satisfactorily resolved, mainly because the political authorities of the day never really asked the crucial question, 'What is a bishop?' Was he primarily a diocesan official or a functionary in the House of Lords, and which was the more important role of the two?

One tentative conclusion of this study may be that prime ministers have made a better choice of men for the episcopal office than electoral colleges. The choice of one man, even if somewhat hesitant, but made after much anxious deliberation and examination of the various claims of others, and with the advice of both local and national figures, may often be better than that of an electoral college which may not be in possession of the full facts regarding a person's life, and subject, as Peart-Binns has pointed out in his study of Edwin Morris, to organized pressure groups and 'funny business'.[1] Can it be claimed that the post-disestablishment Church has had many such men as Ollivant, John Owen, or even Edwards, misguided as he was in many instances, among its bishops? None could be regarded as 'safe men', but all gave strong leadership in their dioceses and to the Church at large. Their like is sorely needed once more. Bishop Bell of Chichester, consulted about the kind of men who should be appointed bishops in 1946, suggested 'the need to take some risks rather than continually appoint "safe" men. We can afford a few mistakes. What, in my humble opinion, is wanted is the infusion into the bench of bishops of a few men of imagination and daring.'[2] A disestablished Church probably feels it cannot afford such risks, and its election procedures avoid such calamities! It has become a safe Church with the result, as Bell went on to say, that such a bench inevitably affects the kind of men who seek ordination.

The Welsh Language

The number of Welsh speakers in nineteenth-century Wales is a much-debated subject. Even the 1891 census, which for the first time asked about linguistic ability, is notoriously difficult to interpret. W. T. R. Pryce, in a study of Welsh visitation returns between 1801 and 1881, suggests that throughout Wales and Monmouthshire in 1801, 44 per cent of the people lived in Welsh-speaking areas, 10.4 per cent in a mainly Welsh-speaking area, 17.2 per cent in a bilingual area, and 26.2 per cent in English and mainly English areas. In 1851 the percentages were 27.5 per cent, 14.2 per cent, 27.3 per cent and 31 per cent respectively, and in 1881, 7.3 per cent, 14.5 per cent, 15 per cent and 63.2 per cent, indicating a large shift in the use of the Welsh language during those eighty years. Ravenstein's language survey of 1871 indicated a rather different picture with 22.4 per cent of people in Wales being monoglot Welsh, 48.8 per cent being bilingual and 28.8 per cent being English speakers.[3]

The state of the Welsh language was ambiguous. Its only official recognition was in an ecclesiastical setting, and even this, the 1562 act which enabled the Bible and Book of Common Prayer to be translated into Welsh, had a sting in its tail. The act made clear that this concession to the Welsh language was in order to extend the knowledge and use of the English tongue in Wales by allowing a comparison between the English and Welsh versions of these books.

In reality, the Welsh language was effectively outlawed from law and administration, as Geraint H. Jenkins points out, adding that 'it was judged to be a language of no real importance in the educational curriculum'.[4]

This situation was even more apparent after the celebrated 1847 'Blue Books' report into the provision of Welsh education. A number of Anglican correspondents identified Nonconformity with the Welsh language and a primitive and immoral lifestyle. If the report helped to create an inferiority complex among Welsh speakers, it also encouraged a growing trend which saw English as the 'high prestige language' (to use Geraint H. Jenkins's phrase), that is, a language more fitting for use in the wider commercial and scientific world. As a result not only the requirements of social control but also the demands of parents encouraged the majority of day schools to teach through the medium of the English language. It is not surprising, therefore, that many influential Welsh speakers expressed critical views of their own language. Thomas Nicholas, a prominent Welsh Nonconformist, may be quoted as an example. He suggested that it would be better for Wales to 'share in the honour and dignity, the intelligence and enterprise, of England', by forsaking its 'antiquated customs' and speech, and so allow the English language to infuse into Wales 'the life and civilization of England'.[5] Such comments as these, echoed by many other influential leaders of Welsh opinion, including the Nonconformist divines J. R. Kilsby Jones, Lewis Edwards and Thomas Rees, and the Anglican leaders Dean H. T. Edwards and Bishop Joshua Hughes, helped persuade many Welsh speakers that the English language was the passport for success and the Welsh language an impediment to that success.[6] The industrialist David Davies summed up the position neatly in his comment that Welsh was the language of brown bread but English that of white bread and the luxuries of life.[7]

We need to remember, however, that in spite of all these pressures the Welsh language remained in many areas the language of the hearth and the workplace, and especially of the heart and religion, both Nonconformist and Church. It was nourished by the Welsh press and the Sunday School, and Brinley Thomas has argued that the industrialization of the Welsh valleys gave the language a new lease of life.[8]

The attitude of the Established Church to the Welsh language was equally ambivalent. The Church in Wales was, in reality, but four dioceses in the province of Canterbury, and was much influenced by the assumptions and prejudices of this wider constituency. In the nineteenth century its dilemma was the same as the Tudor reformers of 1562 who wished to encourage the use of English as the common language of the realm, but realized the spiritual need to minister in the language used by the people. If this was seen by some as an evangelical task, others saw it as a social necessity, the Church being regarded as an agent of the state in promoting the peace of the nation. The attitude of the Anglo-Welsh leaders of the Church might be summed up by Bishop Copleston of Llandaff (1828–49) who was concerned that no attempt should be made to revive this 'provincial language', but rather that it should be allowed to die a natural death and be supplanted 'by the more modern and useful tongue'.[9] Yet Copleston was deeply concerned to ensure that parishes which had a Welsh-speaking population should have Welsh-speaking incumbents.[10] This position was followed by the other bishops of his time.[11]

The pressures against the Welsh language became more acute after the 1850s, and it is tempting to suggest that the growing concern for Welsh-speaking bishops and for appointing Welsh-speaking clergymen to parishes where Welsh was generally spoken was a result of the reaction by a large number of nationalists and patriots against the Anglicization of Wales. This was true, but there was also a spiritual element. The Church in Wales had been profoundly shocked by Mann's religious census of 1851, not so much by the number who attended no place of worship, but rather by the strength of Nonconformity that the census revealed. As a result those who wished to disestablish the Welsh Church were able to speak of an 'alien' Church, alien not only in sentiment from the Welsh language and culture, but alien in a statistical sense, for Mann's census allowed Nonconformists to claim that dissent was the religion of Wales. Welsh Church people, in their defence, found themselves obliged to stress the need for Welsh-speaking bishops and pastors in order to claim once more the high ground of being an indigenous body.

A Welsh Episcopate

'Do you ever expect to see a Welshman a Bishop?' asked Goronwy Owen in a letter of 1753. It was a rhetorical question, for he answered himself: 'Sooner would I give credence to the Brut which promises the second coming of Owain Lawgoch than expect ever to see a Welshman holding an office of the least distinction in either Church or State.'[12]

No Welsh speaker had been appointed to a Welsh see since 1702 when John Evans was appointed to Bangor. He was later translated to Meath in Ireland. In 1721 Evans unsuccessfully requested Archbishop Wake to ensure that the vacancy in Bangor caused by Bishop Hoadly's translation was filled by a Welsh speaker.[13] Bishop Wynne of St Asaph (1715–27) may have understood Welsh but probably did not speak it. John Harris of Llandaff (1729–38), a Pembrokeshire man, and Richard Trevor of St Davids (1744–52), though born in Wales, did not speak the language. However, Richard Smalbroke, though of English birth, is alleged to have mastered the Welsh language and is said to have officiated in it while he was bishop of St Davids, between 1724 and 1731.[14]

It has been claimed that the reason for this refusal to appoint Welsh speakers to Welsh dioceses was that the Welsh were Jacobite in sympathy. The government of that day, concerned that such sentiments were linked with a language they regarded as archaic, thus determined to appoint English bishops in order to promote the English tongue and English ways in their dioceses. While it is probably true that the SPCK charity schools were discontinued because of the alleged involvement of the Welsh SPCK leaders in Jacobite activities, the claim that English-speaking bishops were appointed in order to promote the English language is probably a nineteenth-century myth. However, it is not difficult to see how it arose when one considers the statements made by some of these bishops and their supporters. In the celebrated case of Dr Bowles versus the wardens of Trefdraeth in Anglesey it was maintained for Bowles, as rector, that it was in order for him to remain as an English-speaking incumbent of a Welsh parish because it was his task to introduce that language to his parish.[15] Statements made by Bishops Copleston (already quoted), Bethell, Short, Campbell and Basil Jones reflected Bowles's comments, although they were made with more pastoral sensitivity.

The position in Wales needs to be seen against the backcloth of the wider established Church. After George I's accession, the prime minister of the day controlled appointments to the bench, and that bench was of vital importance in the voting power of an often

independently minded House of Lords. Consequently the politicians, commencing with Walpole, regarded episcopal appointments as political nominations, and thus appointed 'safe' men as
bishops who would serve their party's interests in Parliament. A
system thus evolved by which bishops were promoted to better and
more lucrative sees according to their political stability. This system
gained its strength from the fact that the incomes of the various
sees varied enormously. Llandaff and St Davids were at the bottom
of the financial league, so that they were generally regarded as first
or even as 'trial' appointments. Bishop Watson of Llandaff remained bishop of that see from 1782 to 1816 because he believed,
probably correctly, that as he refused to follow the political line
expected by his political makers, he was refused 'promotion' to a
better see.[16] St Asaph, being a more lucrative see, tended to attract
men translated from other dioceses, who thereafter rewarded their
families with the fruits of their diocesan patronage, as Johnes so
eloquently recorded in his book on the reasons for Welsh dissent.[17]

Nevertheless, it should be remembered that in these appointments
there was no real antipathy towards Welshmen, who were appointed to sees elsewhere. In fact, as the Welsh gentry became
Anglicized, those who spoke Welsh tended to belong to a class of
people who were generally unable to obtain a university education
or gain political patronage. Furthermore, most of the bishops
appointed carried out their duties conscientiously according to the
standards of their own day, attending their dioceses during the parliamentary vacation year by year. Indeed some of them, such as
Burgess and Copleston, were conspicuous for their insistence that
Welsh-speaking clerics should be appointed to Welsh parishes.

The opposition to this state of affairs within the Church in Wales
was established on nationalistic grounds. Although the nineteenth
century saw an explosion in Welsh national consciousness and a
revival of Welsh culture, often incubated by clergymen, this movement had eighteenth-century origins. It may well have arisen as a
result of the concern over parochial appointments made by the
Anglo-Welsh episcopate (as the non-Welsh English-speaking bishops
of Wales were described), one of the first manifestations of which
was the Bowles case. The claim was thus made that as most Welsh
people spoke Welsh it was important that they should have leaders
who could speak to them in their own language, and do so with
fluency and ability. It was not simply an ecclesiastical argument. At

the same time as the demand for Welsh-speaking bishops reached its height, there was an equal outcry against the appointment of English-speaking judges in Welsh-speaking areas as well as for Welsh-speaking chaplains in Welsh prisons. In the 1880s, for example, the English-speaking Homersham-Cox was appointed to the Welsh judicial bench. The protests were so clear and strong that in 1884 Lord Selbourne, as lord chancellor, appointed Gwilym Williams of Miskin as the first Welsh-speaking stipendiary judge in Wales for several generations.[18]

This demand for Welsh-speaking bishops, as well as clergy, was sufficiently strong to obtain a specific clause in the Ecclesiastical Church Bill of 1836. This occurred three years after the alleged first speech in the House of Commons in favour of Welsh-speaking bishops. Lord Robert Grosvenor was the speaker.[19] This clause directed the newly appointed Ecclesiastical Commissioners to ensure that all those appointed to Welsh dioceses and Welsh-speaking parishes were Welsh speakers themselves. Unfortunately the clause regarding this requirement for episcopal appointments was rejected by the House of Lords. The omission was moved by the archbishop of Canterbury on the grounds 'that it was not requisite for a Welsh bishop to possess the knowledge of the Welsh language, as the duty of a bishop was *not* to act as the shepherd of the flock, but as the superintendent of the pastors'.[20] A motion to reintroduce this clause was lost by six votes in the Commons. The arguments used to defeat it included the assertions that Welsh was not spoken in the diocese of Llandaff to any great extent, and that a considerable proportion of the population of Wales spoke English. Lord John Russell argued that the clause 'would be an improper restriction on the prerogative of the Crown', and in some cases it 'would be found to operate in a most inconvenient manner'. Others assumed that a person nominated to a Welsh diocese could easily acquire a knowledge of the Welsh language in the course of a few months. Even a Welsh member, Mr Trevor, though he partly supported the motion, did not consider it necessary to make such a knowledge a *sine qua non* for Welsh episcopal appointments.[21] The act was later modified to give bishops the right to decline to institute clergymen unable to speak Welsh to Welsh benefices where the majority of the inhabitants did not speak English.[22]

It may be that it was the failure of this clause regarding episcopal appointments to Welsh dioceses that brought into being the movement to obtain Welsh-speaking bishops for Wales. It is hardly surprising that this movement gained rapid ground in those centres of substantial Welsh settlement in England, such as London, Liverpool and Yorkshire, for at that time there was no regional centre of influence in Wales. Benjamin Hall alleged that he had presented two petitions during the debates on this clause which, regretting its loss, prayed that rather than have a continuation of English bishops in Wales, they might have no bishops at all.[23] There was also a general belief that Lord John Russell had pledged himself and his party to honour that clause in any future vacancy.[24] Thereafter, the Welsh people clearly assumed that Lord John Russell needed to be reminded of this pledge at frequent intervals.

One of the first meetings called to promote this cause of Welsh-speaking bishops for the Welsh dioceses was held in 1837 by the Liverpool Welsh (always an articulate group) under the chairmanship of Evan Evans of Chester. Better known by his bardic name, 'Ieuan Glan Geirionydd', he was then the Welsh chaplain at Chester. It was later alleged that his activities as a Welsh patriot debarred him from preferment in his native land. Addresses requesting Welsh bishops for Welsh dioceses were sent to both king and parliament.[25]

Probably the most persistent of all the campaigners for Welsh-speaking bishops was the Association of Welsh Clergy in the West Riding of Yorkshire. The association was founded in 1821 through the influence of Lewis Jones, rector of Almondbury. Jones had brought into this vast and industrialized Yorkshire mill parish a considerable number of his fellow Welsh clerics to serve as his curates, and then preferred them to the new districts carved out of it. These men whose love of their country was not diminished by their absence from it formed the society with him, along with various other Welsh clerics living in those parts. The association's members claimed that they could speak freely about the position in Wales, unlike their fellow countrymen living in Wales who were often afraid to speak openly for fear of episcopal disapproval and disfavour.[26]

The association's first known attempt in this direction was a petition of 1835 sent to Sir Robert Peel, which related to the legislation noted above. It was drafted by David James, later rector of Panteg and a future warden of Llandovery college. He was then at Almondbury. The association, always skilled in publicity, communicated this petition to the press, and it is said to have created a great stir as it pointed out in dramatic terms the abuses that had occurred in the past.[27]

The petition's preamble was as follows:

THE HUMBLE MEMORIAL OF THE UNDERSIGNED CLERGY, NATIVES OF THE PRINCIPALITY OF WALES, RESIDING IN THE WEST RIDING OF THE COUNTY OF YORK, SHEWETH, – That we, your Memorialists, being sincerely attached to the Institutions of this highly favoured Country, and especially to that ancient and venerable Church of which we are Ministers, are anxious to express the satisfaction with which we have learned, by His Majesty's Speech from the Throne, that measures will shortly be submitted to the Legislature for the removal of all proved abuses connected with the Temporalities and Discipline of the Established Church: and that we look with deep interest for the development of those Measures, in confident hope that we shall find them based on sound principles, and at the same time sufficiently extensive, and well calculated to remedy the defects, and extend the usefulness of our National Church, and thus to render it, as far as human legislation can effect, what every National Church ought to be – eminently pure, and universally efficient; which characteristics alone, we conceive, can procure for it in future, under the blessing of God, that degree of respect from all classes of His Majesty's subjects, that will secure its existence, and maintain unimpaired its constitutional rights and privileges.

The association now requested that the old policy, 'so ancient and just, and which was productive of such unquestionable benefits to the Principality', be restored:

We therefore humbly beg to suggest, that in your contemplated measures of Church Reform, a provision be graciously made to secure in future the appointment of pious and approved Welsh Scholars to each of the Welsh Bishoprics, as long as the Welsh tongue shall remain the vernacular language of that Country: to the intent that every Bishop may be able to decide for himself, and not by proxy, on the competency of Candidates for Orders and Applicants for Preferments, 'to preach the Word and administer the Sacraments' in the Welsh language; and that at 'the laying on of hands', in the solemn and Apostolic Rite of Confirmation, he may be able to bless the Welsh Children in the only language they understand . . .[28]

Between the years 1852 and 1856 the association produced annual printed reports, and in all these reports the same concern for a Welsh-speaking episcopate was exhibited. The ludicrous statements made by the Anglo-Welsh bishops in their attempts to speak Welsh were frequently noted. In 1855 David James claimed that the association had never lost its concern in this matter since the date of its foundation.[29] In the 1852 report it was suggested that as a result of the 1835 petition 'many members of parliament felt the force of the representations then made', and their votes enabled the clause in the Established Church Bill of 1836, requiring Welsh-speaking clergymen to be appointed to Welsh-speaking parishes, to be passed. Though the clause extending this requirement to bishops in Welsh sees was lost it produced a 'tide of feeling' which forced Thirlwall to learn Welsh and Lord John Russell to nominate Ollivant for Llandaff in 1849 because 'he was understood to be conversant with the Welsh tongue'.[30]

A further petition in favour of Welsh-speaking bishops was presented to Parliament in that same year of 1852, probably as it was clear by that time that Ollivant's Welsh was none too good. This petition claimed that the Welsh Church 'under the government of English Bishops, has long ago ceased to be an instrument for good to the great body of the Welsh people'. It therefore prayed 'that no individual unacquainted with the language of the Welsh people be henceforth promoted to a bishopric in Wales. And that such measures be adopted, as in the wisdom of your right honourable house may be deemed most effective, for securing to the Principality of Wales the benefit of native bishops.'[31] The same petition was repeated in the following year,[32] and the matter was still under discussion in the last printed report of 1856. By this time the Welsh antagonists had received some limited support from the archbishop of Canterbury. Archbishop Sumner had replied to a letter pointing out the problems of such Anglo-Welsh episcopates by stating he did not expect to be consulted about these appointments. Rather he advised all those interested to make the facts known to the prime minister.[33]

Daniel Jones, vicar of Caerleon, wrote a pamphlet entitled *Welsh Bishops for Wales: An Essay on the National and Scriptural Claims of the Established Church in Wales to be Governed by Welsh Bishops*. The pamphlet was published at Llandovery in 1851, being the revision of an essay submitted for a prize given by one John

Richards of Treiorwerth [*sic*] in Anglesey on that particular subject, even though it had only been awarded a consolation prize. Though Jones claimed that his views had been sanctioned by clerical and lay speakers at various meetings, especially of the Llandaff Church Extension Society, his arguments were mainly antiquarian and rather compromised by his willingness to accept men as bishops who had learnt Welsh as a second language as Thirlwall and Ollivant had done. As Ollivant had presided over some of these meetings it appears that Jones had little choice but to accept that argument or to incur episcopal disfavour! He argued, for example, that as the British or Welsh Church had been preserved by providence as a memorial 'of God's designs of love in Christ towards all men . . . *it is therefore clear that we should have expected such a Church to be led and ruled by her own faithful sons*'. Furthermore, he suggested that because there were no Welsh-speaking bishops able to interpret the Welsh people to the government, the government was ignorant about the feelings and habits of the Welsh people and inclined to regard them as barbarians. What power for good, he asked, would Bruce Knight have yielded had he been a bishop and not simply the bishop's chaplain? Nevertheless, Jones believed that the present Welsh bench was desirous of better things, and having learnt the Welsh language, wished to 'encourage and perfect what they find good and useful among them'.[34]

The Church's Welsh-language newspaper, *Yr Haul*, also joined in the campaign. In 1844 'Cymro', writing in its pages, regarded the appointment of non-Welsh-speaking bishops as part of the 'Welsh Church spoilation',[35] while in 1852 the editor published a petition of the Bath Church of England Lay Association which read, in part, as follows:

> That by the 24th Article of our Church, it is expressly declared as follows, viz. – 'It is a thing plainly repugnant to the Word of God, and the custom of the primitive Church, to have public prayer in the Church, or to minister the Sacrament, in a tongue not understood of the people.' That, Welsh being the language of the great majority of the population, and the dignified Clergy being, almost without an exception, Englishmen, and ignorant of the native idiom, the Ecclesiastical Ceremonies of confirming children, consecrating churches, and other important ministerial functions, are deprived of their solemnity, and their spiritual benefit, amongst the great majority of the people.

Though the Bath association was rather high church in complexion, its track record of support for the claims of the Welsh Church, especially during the attempt by the Ecclesiastical Commission to unite the two northern sees, was well known, and its example was warmly commended by the editor as an action that should be imitated by Welsh parishes.[36]

The message was clearly having an effect, as witness the long controversy that took place in the pages of the *Cardiff and Merthyr Guardian* during the early months of 1850 over the proposed Copleston Memorial. Sir Benjamin Hall made it quite clear that he regarded Anglo-Welsh bishops such as Copleston a disaster to the Welsh Church, and it appears, if the subsequent subscription list to the memorial is anything to go by, that many of the clergy agreed with him.[37]

In the previous year John Williams, the Liberal MP for Macclesfield, and a Welsh speaker, had begged an assurance that no clergyman would be appointed to a Welsh see without possessing a knowledge of the Welsh tongue. This was during the episcopal vacancy in Llandaff, and Williams pointed out that the numerous petitions he had presented already to the House of Commons 'unmistakably indicate the sense of the country'.[38] If Williams failed to receive an adequate answer, a clergyman, the rather eccentric R. W. Morgan of Tregynon in Montgomeryshire, managed to obtain one from Gladstone. He forced him to concede in 1856 that he would gladly see the day 'when all the occupants of the episcopal sees [in Wales] might be able to communicate with the people in their own cherished language, but, I must add, that I think it would be an error to recognise a knowledge of the Welsh tongue as dispensing with any other of the still more essential qualifications for the episcopal office'.[39] The answer may have satisfied Morgan, but its qualification caused immense difficulties to Gladstone when he was later called upon to advise the Crown regarding appointments to the Welsh sees.

The Result of the Pressure

The pressure, together with the justice of the case, for Welsh-speaking men to be appointed to Welsh dioceses, persuaded both

And your Memorialists would beg most respectively to put the case hypothetically with respect to England, and inquire how far would the English people approve of the adoption of a similar practice towards them? Would they silently submit to an attempt to fill all the English Bishoprics with men of another language, – men who did not understand and could not speak English, the language of the nation? Would they not condemn such a proceeding as unfair, impolitic, and unjust? And yet such has been the practice towards Wales, almost exclusively, for the last 130 years![51]

The long history of Christianity in Wales was also called as evidence to support this case for a native episcopate, even though its use was selective and arbitrary. The independence of the Welsh Church was asserted as from the earliest times, only having been lost in the days of Henry II. A Welsh episcopate had been restored by Elizabeth I, and her bishops were able to bring the light of the Reformation to Wales by the use of the Welsh language. This policy continued until the reign of Queen Anne, and produced the blessings of internal peace, such as loyalty to the monarch, obedience to the laws, harmony between landowner and tenant, and the continuance of religion and piety among all classes. Such matters had characterized Wales ever since, and presumably, if the argument was pressed, the appointment of Welsh-speaking bishops would further these apparently desirable attributes.

This argument was often coupled with a rather dubious theological one, but one which might have carried some weight in an age which held public fast days at times of national calamity:

That, as the blessing of Almighty God never rests upon any measure, civil or ecclesiastical, which is directly opposed to the spirit and letter of the New Testament, the practice of appointing *English* Bishops to *Welsh* Sees, being confessedly so opposed, has manifestly provoked the Divine displeasure, and spread a fearful blight over the entire of the Established Church in Wales [*sic*], which, if it be not arrested, must terminate in her utter ruin; for already four-fifths of the people have left her communion, and gone elsewhere to seek 'the bread of life'.[52]

These arguments gained a greater force when linked with the numerical argument, namely that as Welsh was the language of eight out of ten of the population in Wales, the bishops and clergy needed to speak it. In so doing they would follow the principles of the gospel, as well as the Articles of the Church, that the language of worship should be the common language of the people:

> as the Welsh is the prevailing language of the Principality, and the only language adequately understood by eight-tenths of the population, the native clergy, who have been trained up in the habitual use of that language, are the only persons competent to discharge the duties of the episcopal office in that country: consequently, the systematic appointment of Englishmen, utterly ignorant of the language, to fill that important office in Wales, is a ruthless violation of the first principles of common sense, of common justice, and of the Gospel of our Lord Jesus Christ – leading to the practical exhibition of that barbarous anomaly in the Welsh Church, which St Paul deprecated and put down in the church at Corinth, – that a minister should speak in the church in a language not understood of the people; and which anomaly it was the direct object of the 24th Article of the Church of England effectually to repress in all her ministrations.[53]

Though we might smile at the exegesis given above, it could be argued on historical grounds that because the Act of 1562 had required the Welsh bishops and the bishop of Hereford, or any three of them, to oversee the translation of the Welsh Book of Common Prayer, there is some apparent legislative force in the assertion that a bishop of a Welsh see needed to be a Welsh speaker.[54] But if these arguments cut no ice, there was one used by Daniel Jones in his prize essay that might have had some effect. Was it fair, he asked, that 500,000 unlettered people should learn a new language for the purpose of being taught, when all that was required was that a few men, who had spent their days in learning languages from their youth, should learn a language to fit them for being teachers? How different, he suggested, was the case with colonial bishops, who endeavoured to learn the language of their dioceses in order to speak to the native inhabitants.[55] But here again, many of his compatriots might have taken issue with him in so far as he was advocating that bishops of Welsh sees should be Welsh speakers, rather than *native* Welsh speakers.

The episcopal use of the English language in Welsh-speaking areas caused considerable annoyance, and gave added force to the numerical argument mentioned above. Joseph Hughes, a prominent member of the Association of Welsh Clergy, described the effect such English services had on Welsh communities when the bishop came to confirm or to consecrate a new church. He recalled the consecration of the new church at Rhosymedre in 1837 by Bishop Carey of St Asaph:

His lordship arrived at the hour fixed, accompanied by his officials. There were present several of the dignitaries of the church: the service was read in English, the sermon was English, and the consecration of the church and churchyard, English. The Welsh people gazed, they heard a sound, and wondered; doubting, whether it was the voice of the shepherd of a Christian Welsh flock . . . The language was unintelligible, but their persons and performances were seen, and became the subject of much conversation and astonishment. That the people of the village and neighbourhood might not spend the whole day in empty gazing, the good curate of the parish had provided a Welsh service in the afternoon. The new church was full, the service was read, and the native preacher delivered his discourse with a clear enunciation, and considerable power: it was no dry moral disquisition, but one containing the pure truths of the Gospel, plainly and yet forcibly set forth. The attention of the assembly was arrested, and their minds seemed solemnly impressed. But where was the bishop? Gone! His officials? Gone! The dignitaries of the church? Were they also gone? Gone! They had turned their back on the Welsh service; and the peasantry of Wales, the poor of the neighbourhood, had not a share in their sympathies; but what was perhaps better, they had, in their absence, the Gospel preached unto them. The following day, two elderly people, impressed with the Scripture truths so forcibly delivered in 'their own tongue, in which they were born,' said . . . 'If we had always such faithful Welsh Gospel preaching in the new church, it would be full every Sunday.'

In 1852 the new church of Llanfihangel-Ysgeifiog, in Anglesey, was consecrated. The whole service was in English, though the parish was thoroughly Welsh. After the service some of the 'respectable farmers' who attended it confessed they did not understand anything of the service whatsoever. Indeed there were only twenty people who spoke English in that congregation, and they were visitors. These farmers agreed that the service was 'very much like Popery'. Hughes added his own comment, however, that 'it was beyond Popery, for Roman Catholic priests do not *preach* to their flocks in the Latin tongue'.[56]

Of equal insult was the way in which the solemn rite of confirmation was administered by the Anglo-Welsh bishops. The same speaker quoted a letter from a Welsh cleric who wrote:

21

I was confirmed when I was about the age of thirteen by the late Bishop Jenkinson, previous to which I was once examined with several others in the church catechism, by the curate of the parish in which I then resided. The curate was an English settler, a sportsman and a fox-hunter, who had acquired a reading acquaintance with the Welsh tongue, peculiar to himself, in which it was most difficult to understand him. For I can truly say that, though I attended the church in which he officiated for many years, yet I never was able to make out two consecutive sentences of his Welsh sermons. I went to be confirmed in the parish church of a country town. The whole of the service usual on the occasion was performed in the English language, of which I was then, with the majority of those confirmed at the same time, entirely ignorant, except indeed that I had been taught to read in it fluently and correctly, without, however, comprehending the meaning of what I read. And when I reflected that a solemn rite of apostolic origin, and sanctioned by the New Testament scriptures, had been performed in an unknown tongue, and thereby converted into a meaningless ceremony, I felt truly disgusted that such a mockery of divine things should be perpetrated in the church which I most dearly loved.

In a service held in Aberystwyth during the time of Bishop Burgess, one Welsh-speaking candidate thought he understood one word of the English spoken during that service, 'more and more', and supposed it meant the sea (the Welsh word 'mor', pronounced as the English 'more', means 'sea'). Joseph Hughes asked whether such prayers and the exhortations of the service could be of any benefit to those who did not understand the language in which the service was conducted. He continued: 'surely no blessing can attend such solemn mockery, "For God is not the author of confusion". Neither can the Welsh people be expected to respect a rite or ordinance, that is continually presented before their notice in such an unscriptural light.'[57]

In a similar way David Griffith (1841–1910), who remained a curate throughout his ministerial life, argued that the Anglo-Welsh bishops missed a great opportunity at consecration services. People came to see rather than to hear the bishop, for he was little more than a 'foreign overseer'. Thus the bishops became objects of curiosity rather than of respect.[58]

Others asked how a non-Welsh-speaking bishop could make his own decisions about the qualifications of candidates for holy orders and applicants for his patronage.[59] Furthermore, a bishop, argued Daniel Jones, was still a presbyter, and he was thus required to teach and to catechize the people committed to his charge in the language that they understood.[60]

These bishops, it was argued, were at the mercy of their Welsh-speaking chaplains, for they alone could interpret to the bishop what was being said or preached by their clergy. As a result the bishops became the tools of these men, declared an editorial in the *Carnarvon and Denbigh Herald*. They could unduly influence promotion, create 'undue oppression', and while 'playing the part of an earwig', could also act 'as the pander, the detractor, the toad-eater, and the spy'.[61]

It was also alleged that these appointments of Englishmen to the Welsh sees were quite unfair to the native Welsh clergy. As the Association of Welsh Clergy in the West Riding noted in one of its petitions:

That the systematic exclusion of the Welsh clergy from the higher preferments of the church in their own country, and the equally systematic obtrusion of Englishmen, totally disqualified to discharge the duties required of them, into those preferments is, in the opinion of your petitioners, a species of abuse which could only be expected to prevail in the darkest ages of the church, and to proceed from the most despotic forms of civil government. It promotes to honour the *inefficient* Englishman, and suffers the *deserving* Welshman to go unrewarded. It makes the English clergy rich, and keeps the Welsh clergy poor. And it exhibits to the world this painful fact – that Englishmen in the ascendant care little how they deprive other nations of their rights and privileges so long as they are enabled thereby to advance their own interests, and make provision for their own kindred.[62]

A. J. Johnes asked a similar question as early as 1836. He answered himself by suggesting that the Welsh clergy, deemed to be unfit 'for the mitre', would never 'have swept the wealth of half a Diocese into the coffers of their families', or have alienated 'a whole people from the Establishment'.[63]

John Williams in a letter to David James wrote that the native clergy were 'crushed' by their exclusion from those cathedral appointments which should have been 'the reward of native learning and laborious exercise in the vineyard'. Instead these appointments went to 'the intrusive nominees of alien Bishops'.[64] John Griffith, then vicar of Aberdare, asked similar questions and made equally bitter assertions:

Why is it that the Welsh Clergy of the *present day* are looked upon as an uneducated, inferior, and degraded order of men? Why is it that they are said to be, as the burly Doctor of Leeds [Dr Hook] told the Bishop of St Davids they were, 'lax in principle and consequently lax in practice?' We have mixed much with our brethren in England. We have often heard the bitter taunt: we have often encountered the scoffing sneer hovering on their lips, whenever allusion was made to 'the Clergy of Wales'. Every one – every *brother* ready to declaim *against* us, but none ready to investigate the *cause* – none willing for a moment to suppose that it is THIS UNRIGHTEOUS SYSTEM EXERCISED BY THE GOVERNMENT, the Government of their own England, *that has forced this state of things upon us.* There was a time when the Welsh Clergy, as a body, were respected and honoured; and as noted for their *learning*, their *piety*, and their *integrity*, as their more favoured, their more wealthy, and their self-satisfied brethren of England. That time, however, is a long time ago. Another time succeeded it; a time which did not recognise either learning, or integrity, or moral worth, but nepotism, and favour, and *next of kin.*[65]

The nepotism of these bishops, well illustrated by Johnes, was summed up in a homely illustration by the same John Griffith. 'I remember very well', he wrote, 'when the present Bishop was translated to Bangor; an old North Wales Clergyman falling down on his knees and praying to God earnestly to grant that the new Bishop might have no children, no family, no friends, and no connections. At that time the prayer had a marked significance in the Diocese of Bangor . . .'[66]

Another result of this policy was that many good Welshmen were forced to seek preferment in England, as the Anglo-Welsh bishops gave preferment to their own kind rather than to native Welsh speakers. One speaker at the association's annual meeting of 1856 asked:

But why have I been placed for upwards of fifty years in Shropshire, Yorkshire, and Buckinghamshire, when I have a Welsh tongue in my mouth, and a Welsh heart in my body, seems a strange problem! Why English clergymen have driven me and many others from Wales into England, when, as far as we can see, we might be more useful at home, must remain a mystery! Such a fate is hard to be borne, and reflects no credit upon our Welsh ecclesiastical rulers. But so it is: the fact is certain.[67]

Lord John Russell and Lord Derby to appoint Welsh-speaking men to the Welsh episcopate. But unaware of the difference between a native speaker and one who had acquired the language as a foreign tongue, the appointments they made of Campbell and Ollivant to the sees of Bangor and Llandaff were regarded by the Welsh as simply half measures. This was a fact amply borne out by the way in which the new bishops spoke their acquired tongue. In addition, these Anglo-Welsh bishops had the cold and reserved manners of the English rather than the warmth of the Welsh character. It meant that, as Dean Perowne wrote to Randall Davidson, dean of Windsor and later archbishop of Canterbury, in 1890, their clergy knew little or nothing about them, specifically referring to Thirlwall (who had learnt Welsh after his appointment to St Davids) and Campbell.[40] Lady Hall was even more vehement regarding these bishops. The wife of Sir Benjamin Hall, MP, later Lord Llanover, she regarded herself as a leading Welsh patriot and an advocate of the Welsh language. In her private letters she described these men as 'bishops in disguise', 'shadows', 'puppets and counterfeits', while she was scathing of those Welsh people who were drawn into the 'episcophobia' plague which flattered the bishops on their use of Welsh. These 'poor miserable cowards and shufflers' had set back their cause by at least ten years through this 'humbug'. Those bishops who managed somehow to get through a Welsh sermon, translated for them, once or twice a year, were of no service to the Church in Wales. When would the Welsh stop their suicidal practice of lauding these Anglo-Welsh bishops as Welsh scholars?[41] Far better, she believed, to have a non-Welsh cleric than a 'quarter qualified' one, who if he could but say 'iawn da diolch i chwi' [*sic*] was regarded as an outstanding Welsh scholar by the Anglo-Welsh clergy.[42]

There had been one bright glimmer of expectation, which soon faded into darkness, although how widely this expectation was shared is not known. Lord Palmerston, when prime minister, had shown little interest in ecclesiastical affairs, and virtually permitted his stepdaughter's husband, Lord Shaftesbury, to attend to his Church appointments. Indeed the evangelical and reforming Shaftesbury suggested that his step father-in-law was unable to distinguish between Moses and Sydney Smith in so far as their respective theologies went, while a recent historian, D. W. R. Bahlman, has argued that Palmerston believed there were only two forms of churchmanship, namely high and low. As the high church was un-popular he believed it was advisable to appoint low churchmen, and thus he permitted Shaftesbury to advise him, knowing that he would not suggest any high church nominees. Shaftesbury, to the dismay of many, thus became virtually a bishop-maker, even though he stated that as he had to justify his suggested candidates, he some-times had to choose a good man rather than the best man, or advise a politically advantageous appointment. Shaftesbury's appointments were mainly of evangelical men, and failing that, as the number of acceptable evangelicals was limited, he chose men from the broad church party. Generally his appointments were of men who had served in the pastoral ministry, rather than the academics who had formerly gained episcopal preferment. But for the first time for a century an emphasis was placed on 'respectability' as a require-ment for office, while John Reynolds states that Shaftesbury was the first to break down the idea that episcopal patronage was to be used for political ends. Though he disliked Queen Victoria's eccle-siastical influence, it is said that Shaftesbury had the most import-ant say in the appointment of three archbishops, sixteen bishops and thirteen deans. None of his appointments were definitely bad, and most of those appointed did good work in their dioceses.[43]

Shaftesbury had spent some time in Wales studying the Welsh language, and had stayed in the homes of Welsh-speaking clergy, one of them being Thomas Richards, vicar of Llangynyw in Montgomeryshire. He was thus sympathetic to the demands being expressed for Welsh-speaking bishops. As a result, it was widely believed that had there been a vacancy in a Welsh see during the time of Palmerston's premiership, a Welsh-speaking man would have been appointed. It was equally thought that the man Shaftesbury had in mind was Thomas Thomas, the vicar of Caernarfon at that time. However, when the next Welsh vacancy arose in 1859 it was during the time of another administration, besides which Thomas was regarded as being too old to be considered.[44]

By the 1870s it is clear that it had been conceded that the Welsh language would continue to flourish and episcopal appointments to Welsh dioceses had to reflect this fact. This was the deciding factor in appointments to the Welsh sees and the reason why these appointments were different from and harder to fill than the English dioceses. Oliver Everett, the former librarian of Windsor Castle library, in a personal letter, states that the earliest letters relating to these appointments in the royal archives date to 1882, 'by which time it is clear that the appointment of Welsh-speaking men is a clearly established principle'. Archbishop Benson thus wrote to W. E. Gladstone, then prime minister, about 'a very oppressive conversation' he had had with the dean of Bangor, H. T. Edwards, in July 1883: 'it seems to me as if, for all practical purposes, Welsh must be regarded as a permanent language for not less than a century to come, and that, in the desire to hasten its departure, great mistakes are made which alienate the people from the clergy.'[45]

Gladstone was the first prime minister who accepted this argument and realized the distinction between a Welsh speaker who spoke the language 'from the hearth' and one who had acquired it as a foreign language. His appointment of Joshua Hughes to the see of St Asaph in 1870 was a recognition of this argument. Another factor in his nomination was the need for a Welsh preacher-bishop to outpreach Nonconformity. Gladstone was not alone in his belief that the strength and attraction of Nonconformity lay in its preaching ministry. Many, in particular Lord Aberdare, resisted this policy, especially as the number of eligible men who spoke Welsh was severely limited.

The Arguments for Welsh-speaking Bishops

The arguments used to obtain this admission about the need for Welsh-speaking bishops for Wales from the politicians and church leaders were many and profuse, but most could be summed up by the claim that the Anglo-Welsh bishops were 'incompetent through their total ignorance of the Welsh language'.[46] The rise of dissent was attributed to this incompetence, with the added hint that the selection of Welsh-speaking men as bishops would restore the multitudes to the Church, an argument fervently believed and acted upon by Gladstone. This argument became increasingly important to him as the threat of disestablishment became more pronounced. Gladstone clearly accepted what the memorial of 1835 had stated, namely that:

the policy pursued by the Government since the Accession of Queen Anne, of appointing to the Welsh Sees, Bishops totally unacquainted with the customs, manners, and language of the Natives, and consequently incompetent to judge of the qualifications requisite in Welsh

Ministers, or ascertain their suitableness to the particular spheres in which they were destined to labour, has tended most materially to alienate from it the affections of the people, to undermine its influence, and impair its efficiency.

The memorial also claimed that not only had this policy resulted in the increase of dissent and its bitterness towards the Church, it had diminished the value of the episcopal office by making it more a matter of 'Ministerial Patronage than of a Spiritual Office, essential to the constitution and prosperity of the Church of God'.[47]

David James felt that much blame attached to the Anglo-Welsh bishops themselves for accepting such office in the Welsh Church when 'they knew in their own consciences and before Almighty God, that they did not possess the requisite qualifications'. As the 'reckless abuse' [of nepotism] in the diocesan patronage of the bishops had been checked, so it was also time for the abuses in the prime ministers' episcopal patronage to be redressed. When this happened the same fortunate results seen in parishes where a Welshman had been instituted to the cure of souls would occur in the Welsh dioceses.[48]

There were many who asked how an English bishop could make the vows required of him at his consecration as a bishop knowing that he had been appointed to serve in a Welsh diocese:

In the service for consecrating bishops, the archbishop asks the bishop elect, 'Are you determined to *instruct the people* committed to your charge out of the Holy Scriptures?' The bishop elect replies, 'I am *so* determined by God's grace.' I do not see how a prelate can instruct a Welsh congregation while he is ignorant of the *Welsh* language, nor do I understand how he can conscientiously take such an oath, while he remains ignorant of the very first principles of the language of the people over whom he is to preside.[49]

Consequently it was maintained, on scriptural grounds, that a bishop of a Welsh diocese needed to be a Welshman. And this was an obvious reply to those who argued that the bishop was only concerned with the clergy of the diocese rather than its people.[50]

By contrast, it was frequently asked how would English people submit to a similar practice in England as Wales had been forced to undergo:

> And your Memorialists would beg most respectively to put the case hypothetically with respect to England, and inquire how far would the English people approve of the adoption of a similar practice towards them? Would they silently submit to an attempt to fill all the English Bishoprics with men of another language, – men who did not understand and could not speak English, the language of the nation? Would they not condemn such a proceeding as unfair, impolitic, and unjust? And yet such has been the practice towards Wales, almost exclusively, for the last 130 years![51]

The long history of Christianity in Wales was also called as evidence to support this case for a native episcopate, even though its use was selective and arbitrary. The independence of the Welsh Church was asserted as from the earliest times, only having been lost in the days of Henry II. A Welsh episcopate had been restored by Elizabeth I, and her bishops were able to bring the light of the Reformation to Wales by the use of the Welsh language. This policy continued until the reign of Queen Anne, and produced the blessings of internal peace, such as loyalty to the monarch, obedience to the laws, harmony between landowner and tenant, and the continuance of religion and piety among all classes. Such matters had characterized Wales ever since, and presumably, if the argument was pressed, the appointment of Welsh-speaking bishops would further these apparently desirable attributes.

This argument was often coupled with a rather dubious theological one, but one which might have carried some weight in an age which held public fast days at times of national calamity:

> That, as the blessing of Almighty God never rests upon any measure, civil or ecclesiastical, which is directly opposed to the spirit and letter of the New Testament, the practice of appointing *English* Bishops to *Welsh* Sees, being confessedly so opposed, has manifestly provoked the Divine displeasure, and spread a fearful blight over the entire of the Established Church in Wales [*sic*], which, if it be not arrested, must terminate in her utter ruin; for already four-fifths of the people have left her communion, and gone elsewhere to seek 'the bread of life'.[52]

These arguments gained a greater force when linked with the numerical argument, namely that as Welsh was the language of eight out of ten of the population in Wales, the bishops and clergy

needed to speak it. In so doing they would follow the principles of the gospel, as well as the Articles of the Church, that the language of worship should be the common language of the people:

> as the Welsh is the prevailing language of the Principality, and the only language adequately understood by eight-tenths of the population, the native clergy, who have been trained up in the habitual use of that language, are the only persons competent to discharge the duties of the episcopal office in that country: consequently, the systematic appointment of Englishmen, utterly ignorant of the language, to fill that important office in Wales, is a ruthless violation of the first principles of common sense, of common justice, and of the Gospel of our Lord Jesus Christ – leading to the practical exhibition of that barbarous anomaly in the Welsh Church, which St Paul deprecated and put down in the church at Corinth, – that a minister should speak in the church in a language not understood of the people; and which anomaly it was the direct object of the 24th Article of the Church of England effectually to repress in all her ministrations.[53]

Though we might smile at the exegesis given above, it could be argued on historical grounds that because the Act of 1562 had required the Welsh bishops and the bishop of Hereford, or any three of them, to oversee the translation of the Welsh Book of Common Prayer, there is some apparent legislative force in the assertion that a bishop of a Welsh see needed to be a Welsh speaker.[54] But if these arguments cut no ice, there was one used by Daniel Jones in his prize essay that might have had some effect. Was it fair, he asked, that 500,000 unlettered people should learn a new language for the purpose of being taught, when all that was required was that a few men, who had spent their days in learning languages from their youth, should learn a language to fit them for being teachers? How different, he suggested, was the case with colonial bishops, who endeavoured to learn the language of their dioceses in order to speak to the native inhabitants.[55] But here again, many of his compatriots might have taken issue with him in so far as he was advocating that bishops of Welsh sees should be Welsh speakers, rather than *native* Welsh speakers.

The episcopal use of the English language in Welsh-speaking areas caused considerable annoyance, and gave added force to the numerical argument mentioned above. Joseph Hughes, a prominent member of the Association of Welsh Clergy, described the effect

such English services had on Welsh communities when the bishop came to confirm or to consecrate a new church. He recalled the consecration of the new church at Rhosymedre in 1837 by Bishop Carey of St Asaph:

> His lordship arrived at the hour fixed, accompanied by his officials. There were present several of the dignitaries of the church: the service was read in English, the sermon was English, and the consecration of the church and churchyard, English. The Welsh people gazed, they heard a sound, and wondered; doubting, whether it was the voice of the shepherd of a Christian Welsh flock . . . The language was unintelligible, but their persons and performances were seen, and became the subject of much conversation and astonishment. That the people of the village and neighbourhood might not spend the whole day in empty gazing, the good curate of the parish had provided a Welsh service in the afternoon. The new church was full, the service was read, and the native preacher delivered his discourse with a clear enunciation, and considerable power: it was no dry moral disquisition, but one containing the pure truths of the Gospel, plainly and yet forcibly set forth. The attention of the assembly was arrested, and their minds seemed solemnly impressed. But where was the bishop? Gone! His officials? Gone! The dignitaries of the church? Were they also gone? Gone! They had turned their back on the Welsh service; and the peasantry of Wales, the poor of the neighbourhood, had not a share in their sympathies; but what was perhaps better, they had, in their absence, the Gospel preached unto them. The following day, two elderly people, impressed with the Scripture truths so forcibly delivered in 'their own tongue, in which they were born,' said . . . 'If we had always such faithful Welsh Gospel preaching in the new church, it would be full every Sunday.'

In 1852 the new church of Llanfihangel-Ysgeifiog, in Anglesey, was consecrated. The whole service was in English, though the parish was thoroughly Welsh. After the service some of the 'respectable farmers' who attended it confessed they did not understand anything of the service whatsoever. Indeed there were only twenty people who spoke English in that congregation, and they were visitors. These farmers agreed that the service was 'very much like Popery'. Hughes added his own comment, however, that 'it was beyond Popery, for Roman Catholic priests do not *preach* to their flocks in the Latin tongue'.[56]

Of equal insult was the way in which the solemn rite of confirmation was administered by the Anglo-Welsh bishops. The same speaker quoted a letter from a Welsh cleric who wrote:

I was confirmed when I was about the age of thirteen by the late Bishop Jenkinson, previous to which I was once examined with several others in the church catechism, by the curate of the parish in which I then resided. The curate was an English settler, a sportsman and a fox-hunter, who had acquired a reading acquaintance with the Welsh tongue, peculiar to himself, in which it was most difficult to understand him. For I can truly say that, though I attended the church in which he officiated for many years, yet I never was able to make out two consecutive sentences of his Welsh sermons. I went to be confirmed in the parish church of a country town. The whole of the service usual on the occasion was performed in the English language, of which I was then, with the majority of those confirmed at the same time, entirely ignorant, except indeed that I had been taught to read in it fluently and correctly, without, however, comprehending the meaning of what I read. And when I reflected that a solemn rite of apostolic origin, and sanctioned by the New Testament scriptures, had been performed in an unknown tongue, and thereby converted into a meaningless ceremony, I felt truly disgusted that such a mockery of divine things should be perpetrated in the church which I most dearly loved.

In a service held in Aberystwyth during the time of Bishop Burgess, one Welsh-speaking candidate thought he understood one word of the English spoken during that service, '*more* and *more*', and supposed it meant the sea (the Welsh word 'mor', pronounced as the English 'more', means 'sea'). Joseph Hughes asked whether such prayers and the exhortations of the service could be of any benefit to those who did not understand the language in which the service was conducted. He continued: 'surely no blessing can attend such solemn mockery, "For God is not the author of confusion". Neither can the Welsh people be expected to respect a rite or ordinance, that is continually presented before their notice in such an unscriptural light.'[57]

In a similar way David Griffith (1841–1910), who remained a curate throughout his ministerial life, argued that the Anglo-Welsh bishops missed a great opportunity at consecration services. People came to see rather than to hear the bishop, for he was little more than a 'foreign overseer'. Thus the bishops became objects of curiosity rather than of respect.[58]

Others asked how a non-Welsh-speaking bishop could make his own decisions about the qualifications of candidates for holy orders and applicants for his patronage.[59] Furthermore, a bishop,

argued Daniel Jones, was still a presbyter, and he was thus required to teach and to catechize the people committed to his charge in the language that they understood.[60]

These bishops, it was argued, were at the mercy of their Welsh-speaking chaplains, for they alone could interpret to the bishop what was being said or preached by their clergy. As a result the bishops became the tools of these men, declared an editorial in the *Carnarvon and Denbigh Herald*. They could unduly influence promotion, create 'undue oppression', and while 'playing the part of an earwig', could also act 'as the pander, the detractor, the toad-eater, and the spy'.[61]

It was also alleged that these appointments of Englishmen to the Welsh sees were quite unfair to the native Welsh clergy. As the Association of Welsh Clergy in the West Riding noted in one of its petitions:

> That the systematic exclusion of the Welsh clergy from the higher preferments of the church in their own country, and the equally systematic obtrusion of Englishmen, totally disqualified to discharge the duties required of them, into those preferments is, in the opinion of your petitioners, a species of abuse which could only be expected to prevail in the darkest ages of the church, and to proceed from the most despotic forms of civil government. It promotes to honour the *inefficient* Englishman, and suffers the *deserving* Welshman to go unrewarded. It makes the English clergy rich, and keeps the Welsh clergy poor. And it exhibits to the world this painful fact – that Englishmen in the ascendant care little how they deprive other nations of their rights and privileges so long as they are enabled thereby to advance their own interests, and make provision for their own kindred.[62]

A. J. Johnes asked a similar question as early as 1836. He answered himself by suggesting that the Welsh clergy, deemed to be unfit 'for the mitre', would never 'have swept the wealth of half a Diocese into the coffers of their families', or have alienated 'a whole people from the Establishment'.[63]

John Williams in a letter to David James wrote that the native clergy were 'crushed' by their exclusion from those cathedral appointments which should have been 'the reward of native learning and laborious exercise in the vineyard'. Instead these appointments went to 'the intrusive nominees of alien Bishops'.[64] John Griffith, then vicar of Aberdare, asked similar questions and made equally bitter assertions:

Why is it that the Welsh Clergy of the *present day* are looked upon as an uneducated, inferior, and degraded order of men? Why is it that they are said to be, as the burly Doctor of Leeds [Dr Hook] told the Bishop of St Davids they were, 'lax in principle and consequently lax in practice?' We have mixed much with our brethren in England. We have often heard the bitter taunt: we have often encountered the scoffing sneer hovering on their lips, whenever allusion was made to 'the Clergy of Wales'. Every one – every *brother* ready to declaim *against* us, but none ready to investigate the *cause* – none willing for a moment to suppose that it is THIS UNRIGHTEOUS SYSTEM EXERCISED BY THE GOVERNMENT, the Government of their own England, *that has forced this state of things upon us*. There was a time when the Welsh Clergy, as a body, were respected and honoured; and as noted for their *learning*, their *piety*, and their *integrity*, as their more favoured, their more wealthy, and their self-satisfied brethren of England. That time, however, is a long time ago. Another time succeeded it; a time which did not recognise either learning, or integrity, or moral worth, but nepotism, and favour, and *next of kin*.[65]

The nepotism of these bishops, well illustrated by Johnes, was summed up in a homely illustration by the same John Griffith. 'I remember very well', he wrote, 'when the present Bishop was translated to Bangor; an old North Wales Clergyman falling down on his knees and praying to God earnestly to grant that the new Bishop might have no children, no family, no friends, and no connections. At that time the prayer had a marked significance in the Diocese of Bangor . . .'[66]

Another result of this policy was that many good Welshmen were forced to seek preferment in England, as the Anglo-Welsh bishops gave preferment to their own kind rather than to native Welsh speakers. One speaker at the association's annual meeting of 1856 asked:

But why have I been placed for upwards of fifty years in Shropshire, Yorkshire, and Buckinghamshire, when I have a Welsh tongue in my mouth, and a Welsh heart in my body, seems a strange problem! Why English clergymen have driven me and many others from Wales into England, when, as far as we can see, we might be more useful at home, must remain a mystery! Such a fate is hard to be borne, and reflects no credit upon our Welsh ecclesiastical rulers. But so it is: the fact is certain.[67]

Many men were said to have been discouraged from entering the ministry of the Anglican Church for this reason.[68]

Consequently, those who advocated a native Welsh episcopate argued that scripture, tradition, common sense and ecclesiastical law were all on their side. If there was a law requiring prospective incumbents of Welsh parishes to be examined as to their linguistic ability before institution, at the bishop's discretion, then how much more should those appointed to the episcopal office in Welsh dioceses be fluent and native Welsh speakers? And equally, they hinted, a Welsh Church with native bishops would be a successful and a reforming Church, able to win back the nation to its historic loyalties.

Such men won their case. After 1870, with the possible exception of Basil Jones, all Welsh bishops were fluent Welsh speakers. Surprisingly, the first two appointments after disestablishment, made by the Church's own electoral college, almost reversed this policy. Dr Green's Welsh was more akin to the Welsh of Ollivant than that of Joshua Hughes – academic rather than domestic[69] – while Bishop Bevan of Swansea and Brecon spoke no Welsh at all, and his election aroused considerable speculation and anger on this score.[70]

The Defence of the Anglo-Welsh Bishops

It can hardly be expected that the Anglo-Welsh bishops accepted these criticisms about themselves without some defence of their position. Nevertheless, their defence was such as to suggest to their contemporaries that a raw nerve had been touched.

Christopher Bethell, bishop of Bangor from 1830 until his death in 1859, was clearly embarrassed by this outbreak of Welsh nationalism in his diocese and elsewhere. He, an Englishman and a monoglot English speaker, who had done well within the episcopal system (he had the distinction of being bishop successively of three sees in the same year) felt constrained to put his side of the case. He did so during the course of his reply to the clergy of the county of Anglesey. They had petitioned against the union of the two sees in north Wales and the transfer of the surplus funds to establish a new see at Manchester. This had been recommended by the Ecclesiastical Commission during 1836.

25

In his reply[71] Bethell immediately adopted a defensive position, informing his clergy that he regarded any assertion of nationalism in the matter of episcopal appointments as a criticism of his linguistic position and as an attack upon the royal prerogative by which he had been appointed.[72] A diocesan appointment was in a far different category to that of a parochial one, Bethell argued, for he accepted that it was wrong to appoint a man to a parochial living if he could not speak the language of his parishioners. But the bishop was primarily a pastor to his clergy, and all his clergy spoke English.[73]

If it was alleged that he had to confirm candidates in English, and this seemed contrary to article 24, Bethell pointed out that the act allowing the translation of the Bible and the Book of Common Prayer into Welsh did so in order to extend the knowledge of English through the medium of the Church's liturgy.[74] Every candidate, he avowed, had been instructed by his or her clergyman in the meaning of the ordinance and the words of the prayer used; his chaplain repeated the prayer in Welsh to every set of candidates as they appeared 'at the rails'; and after he had delivered the prayer in English, his chaplain repeated it in Welsh. While his predecessor and the bishop of St Asaph, Dr Carey, gave that former prayer themselves in Welsh, he felt 'a nervous apprehension that I might discompose the minds of our young people by some impropriety of pronunciation'. Consequently he did not adopt this practice.[75]

Denying that the Anglo-Welsh bishops had caused dissent, Bethell argued that an English bishop, being a stranger to Welsh alliances, connections and party feelings, could be more impartial in his patronage than a Welsh bishop and more diligent in seeing that Welsh speakers were appointed where needed. Far greater evils would be inflicted upon Wales if its dioceses were presided over by 'provincial' bishops. This was because a native bishop would find it impossible, because of his close ties with his clergy, to introduce into his diocese outside clergymen of 'zeal and talents and professional learning', who could help break up local associations and territorial feelings and infuse new life into the Church. Bethell conceded, however, 'This [the Anglo-Welsh episcopal system] I consider to be a disadvantage under which you labour, for which at present there is no remedy. But this disadvantage would, I am persuaded, be much aggravated, if the prerogative of the Crown, in the nomination of your Bishops, should be limited' as the Anglesey clergy had proposed, to those acquainted with the Welsh language.[76]

Though Bethell regretted the inconvenience of his not speaking Welsh, he nevertheless noted the tradition that when the last Welsh-speaking bishop had been translated to Ireland, the diocese had requested the appointment of an English successor rather than a Welsh one.[77] With his understanding that England formed 'one undivided and inseparable realm', Bethell told his readers: 'it is to be lamented . . . that a difference of language . . . should have hitherto prevented your countrymen from becoming thoroughly one with their English neighbours.' Nevertheless, the English language was gaining ground and thus Bethell called upon his diocesan clergy 'to take the lead in removing out of the way all needless causes of difference' (meaning, presumably, the Welsh language) 'and getting rid of all local and provincial jealousies and dislikes'. Instead he hoped they would manifest on all occasions 'a liberal . . . and a *British* spirit', and would consider Wales 'not as a civil and national, but as a geographical and territorial division'. Consequently he advised his clergy not to agitate for Welsh bishops but to leave the matter to the discretion of the Crown and 'the well-weighed decision of His Majesty's constitutional advisers'.[78] Bishop Bethell was obviously disconcerted by the power of the attack.

Bishop Copleston of Llandaff also attempted to defend the appointment of Anglo-Welsh bishops to Wales. In his charge of 1836 he argued that while it was his duty to ensure that Welsh parishes were staffed by Welsh speakers, it was not the Church's task to revive the language in areas where it was declining.[79] Then using much the same arguments as Bethell he endeavoured to justify his own appointment as a non-Welsh-speaking bishop of a Welsh diocese. A knowledge of the Welsh language was not essential to the episcopal office. His work as bishop was in the inspection and regulation of the clergy, the appointment of fit men to parishes, the settlement of disputes and differences and the correction of what was wrong. But as all the clergy used the English language as the sole medium of conversation amongst themselves (which may have been true of the clergy who surrounded him), there was clearly no need for him to speak Welsh. Copleston cleverly extended the argument by asserting that the inhabitants of Wales had perfect freedom to advance to the highest appointments in Church and state in England, without discrimination, so that it was only just that Englishmen could equally be permitted similar advantages in Wales.[80]

Though most Welshmen would have heartily disagreed with these attempts to justify these Anglo-Welsh episcopal appointments, there were some among the Welsh clergy who preferred them, being somewhat unhappy with the demand that Welshmen should be required for every Welsh see. One of them was David Evans, archdeacon of St Asaph in the 1900s, who argued that if people wanted learned or eloquent bishops in Wales it would be better to have Englishmen like Scott Holland, Archdeacon Sinclair or the bishop of Stepney (Lang), instead of men who only possessed a 'superficial varnish' as their passport to the episcopal bench.[81] This opinion was one also shared by many influential members of the laity, as will be seen especially during the controversy surrounding the appointment to St Asaph in 1870.

The Prime Minister's Difficulties

It is necessary to examine the various restraints and influences placed on the prime ministers of the day as they chose men to serve as bishops of the Welsh dioceses. In theory, of course, the appointment lay with the monarch, and the prime minister's task was to offer his advice; but in reality, although Queen Victoria somewhat modified the system, the prime minister's choice generally carried the day.

Although it was generally believed that a partisan bishop could immensely help a political party in his diocese, as will be noted later, the prime ministers generally found their task of submitting the names of men to the Crown for the vacant bishoprics extremely irksome. 'Damn it! another Bishop dead! . . . I believe they die to vex me,' cried Lord Melbourne, while Rosebery stated 'patronage is odious; ecclesiastical patronage distressing'.[82]

The care taken by the prime ministers in their choice of men varied widely. Disraeli could write to Queen Victoria advising a certain appointment to Ripon having consulted data 'that for amount and authenticity has rarely been in the possession of a minister', while on the same day that he had made his recommendation he could request his secretary to send down the clergy list as 'I don't know the names and descriptions of the persons I am recommending for deaneries and mitres!'[83] Disraeli left most of this work to his secretaries. Nevertheless, he was always careful to consider the prejudices of the laity and electorate in general, as C. K. F. Brown suggests.[84] Melbourne made quick and political decisions, as witness his appointment of Thirlwall in 1840. But Lord Derby was meticulous in his desire to find a Welsh-speaker for Bangor in 1859, though Salisbury, who had the majority of appointments to Welsh dioceses in the last years of the century, relied on others to offer him advice and information.

The one prime minister of the period who took time and enormous pains over his episcopal patronage was Gladstone. His Christian conscience would not allow him to leave one stone unturned to find the right man, irrespective of political or even ecclesiastical preferences, though he himself was a high churchman. His Church interests, which made Bahlman assume that he was not so dependent on advice concerning the qualifications of candidates as other prime ministers,[85] in fact worked the other way, for knowing the church leaders so well he relied much on their advice and went to endless pains to obtain it. Nevertheless, Bahlman is correct in asserting that Gladstone gave this time more willingly than most because he knew of the problems caused by the neglect of such care in the past. Indeed George Leverson-Gower noted that when an appointment had to be made 'the whole business of state seemed to be put aside whilst he poured forth a perfect avalanche of letters inquiring at great length and in minute detail as to the comparative merits and claims of various clergymen for preferment'.[86] At some stage Gladstone compiled a formidable list of the qualities he needed in a prospective bishop:

Piety. Learning (sacred). Eloquence. Administrative power. Faithful allegiance to the Church and to the church of England. Activity. Tact and courtesy in dealings with men; knowledge of the world. Accomplishments and literature. An equitable spirit. Faculty of working with brother bishops. Some legal habit of mind. Circumspection. Courage. Maturity of age and character. Corporal vigour. Liberal sentiments on public affairs. A representative character with reference to shades of opinion fairly allowable in the Church.[87]

Such a list of desiderata could not have made Gladstone's task any easier.

Until the 1870s and even beyond it was widely believed that bishops were appointed by the various prime ministers in order to assist their political masters in the House of Lords. Colin Lindsay, speaking at the first Church congress of 1861, not only hinted at this, but also felt that the prime ministers were unfit to be entrusted with this episcopal patronage. Not only were they so distracted by the affairs of state that they could not give sufficient attention to this work, they were also encumbered by the claims and demands of their political friends.[88] Melbourne's appointment of Thirlwall to St Davids was clearly activated by his need for episcopal support in the Lords, while the same premier was sufficiently concerned about 'his' bishops' role in the house that he is alleged to have told one of them to remember that he was his maker, not God. Bishop Longley, whom he appointed to Ripon in 1836, was thus reproved by Melbourne for voting against a government measure. This Melbourne regarded as a politically hostile, uncivil and inconsiderate course of action.[89] Palmerston felt the same way, even though he said he cared nothing for a man's political opinions. Nevertheless, he made it clear that he had no wish to see one of his nominees rise in the Lords 'and make strong motions against the Government'.[90]

Gladstone, with his strong Christian faith, his deep knowledge of the Church and wide theological reading (he appointed seventeen bishops and translated another four) was, says Bahlman, unique in putting political sentiments almost last on his list of considerations. Nevertheless, he was realistic in stating that many different factors had to be borne in mind in the appointment of bishops; the prime minister being only one of several interested parties, the others including the throne, the vacant diocese itself and the political party in office during that day.[91] In fact, Gladstone, during his first ministry, was not as true to his principles as perhaps he later became, feeling he had to promote men who would or who had come under 'the absolute inexorable ban' of the Tory party and as a result had been left out of previous preferment because of their political or religious beliefs.[92] By his second term of office political considerations played very little part in his choice, and by and large he refused to try to align the bench with his own political interests.[93] Yet Gladstone was still prepared to ask his episcopal appointees to support his measure for Irish disestablishment in 1869, the army bill of 1871, which abolished the purchase of commissions, and the franchise bill of 1884, and certainly enquired about the political views of his possible nominees. While he refused to make their political views a major consideration he still felt he could not leave it 'wholly out of view'.[94] In any case Gladstone regarded at least one of the Welsh bishoprics (Llandaff) as being so 'peculiar' a case that different factors came into play which totally excluded any political considerations.[95]

Both Palmerston and Disraeli believed that their appointments could win popular favour for their governments.[96] If Bishop Ellicott of Gloucester generally described Lord Salisbury as 'my political chief',[97] Bishop Sumner of Chester is said to have made Lancashire Conservative, a work which Canon McNeile continued at Liverpool.[98] They also naively accepted the opinion that church parties could be associated with political ideologies, so that the moderately high were linked with the Tories, and the broad church were mainly Liberals. Gladstone would have realized the absurdity of this, but Palmerston and Disraeli, with little interest in church affairs, were susceptible to such advice.[99]

Although *The Pall Mall Gazette* considered as late as 1869 that ecclesiastical appointments were received as 'the spoil of political partisans' and advised that sees should be kept vacant until 'the conflicting claims had been nicely adjusted',[100] this view was regarded as old-fashioned by the 1880s. However, the idea still lingered in popular ideology that bishops were obliged to support the party of the prime minister who had appointed them. Thus Bishop Hughes of St Asaph was reminded by Stuart Rendel, a Welsh Liberal MP, that he had been appointed by Gladstone and it was inconsistent on his part, especially as his diocese mainly consisted of Liberal Nonconformists, to justify Lord Salisbury and adopt his 'wild assertions'. This was as late as 1885, when Lord Salisbury had spoken against disestablishment at a meeting in Newport.[101]

These ideas partly collapsed because the episcopal bench had found a new concept of the office by which duty in the diocese was regarded as more important than participation in the House of Lords. Indeed they were often conspicuous in their absence there on even 'momentous occasions', to the disgust of several politicians, who as a result may well have supported a motion of 1884 recommending the removal of bishops from the House of Lords. It failed in the Commons by eleven votes.[102] One wonders how much this new concept of office was installed into the bench by the bishops appointed for pastoral reasons by Shaftesbury and Gladstone, although much was due to the influence of Bishop Wilberforce, whom Dean Burgon regarded as the remodeller of the Anglican episcopate.[103]

Another reason for the collapse of this political patronage and expectation was that politicians also became more realistic, accepting they could not limit episcopal appointment to their own supporters. They were aware of the uncomfortable truth that the use of such patronage not only created friends and assisted political manipulation, but also made enemies.[104] By and large they took Palmerston's advice, and chose the best man available unless he was so violently opposed to their policies that he might denounce them in the Lords. This appears to have become the deciding factor. One of the most interesting documents at Hatfield House, the home of the third marquess of Salisbury, a Tory prime minister, is his clerical appointments book for 1885 to 1887. This notes the names of those recommended to office, by whom they were recommended and the office suggested, but in some cases an entry is marked through in red ink with the comment 'radical' or 'extreme radical'. Such men were not appointed. But by 1906, a new prime minister, Campbell Bannerman, wrote that in these appointments he had to 'consider prejudice, circumstances, balances of opinion, fairness of distribution among parties, political interests and social'.[105] Political interests came low on this new list.

Another important factor in episcopal appointments during the nineteenth century was that of churchmanship. The nineteenth-century dislike of Puseyism prevented many high churchmen from obtaining episcopal appointments. This dislike was shared by the Queen (who had strong views about churchmanship), and she refused to have Canon Liddon of St Paul's elevated to the bench. She also disliked the evangelicals, although when a protest was made to Davidson at the lack of evangelical appointments to the bench he replied that it was difficult to find suitable men among their number.[106] In Wales, however, the prevailing mood was in favour of the low church party.

The Queen, as noted above, was yet another factor to be considered by the prime ministers in respect of these episcopal appointments. Queen Victoria took her responsibilities as head of the Church seriously, and though she disliked any extremes of churchmanship she insisted on interests being respected and her influence was another factor which helped end political appointments to the bench. Palmerston was chided for giving the impression that his patronage ran 'unduly toward party extremes', though he hit back at the Queen's use of non-constitutional advisors, seemingly unaware that he was doing the same in delegating his episcopal patronage to Shaftesbury.[107] Gladstone frequently came into collision with her in this area, the Queen suspecting his sympathy with the 'romanizing tendencies' in the Church.[108] Her basic principles may be illustrated by her letter to Archbishop Benson of 1890: 'the men to be chosen *must* not be taken with reference to satisfying one or the other *Party in the Church* or with reference to any political party, – but for their *real worth*',[109] while the Queen's ideal of a bishop was described as a '*really intellectual*, liberal-minded, courageous' man.[110]

From the time of Peel onwards the Queen endeavoured to have her own way in these episcopal appointments, even making her own list of nominees,[111] to the clear annoyance of Gladstone who tried to inform her that it was his constitutional position to advise her on these matters. On at least one occasion the Queen recommended a candidate to the prime minister, drawing Gladstone's attention to one of her chaplains, Llewelyn Davies, who might 'be thought of among others' for the Llandaff vacancy of 1882.[112] It is also quite clear that the Queen had a vast number of correspondents who could advise her about the qualifications of the men recommended to her, so that she was sometimes better informed about candidates than the prime minister himself. If there was a touch of scandal, however remote, or any extreme of churchmanship, the Queen generally knew, with the result that the correspondence she received about such men was so personal that until recently it was unavailable to researchers.

Her principal advisors were Lord Gerald Wellesley, dean of Windsor, and his eventual successor in that office, Randall Davidson. They generally acted as intermediaries between Windsor, Lambeth and Downing Street. Wellesley (a school contemporary of Gladstone) would not only inform the prime minister of the Queen's dislikes and likes, but would also at a later stage suggest to her the wisdom of the prime minister's choice. He also persuaded the Queen not to allow Dean Stanley, a close favourite, to act as her ecclesiastical advisor, as he had no formal constitutional relationship with her in such matters, though neither for that matter had Wellesley. Davidson even received a short cipher code in order to facilitate communication.[113] His strategic role in the appointment of Welsh bishops will be noted in later chapters.

On occasions the Queen queried or even vetoed appointments. This at least had the advantage of helping to end political appointments, and forced her prime ministers to justify their choices to her. It is well known, for example, that she refused to allow Disraeli's nomination of his partisan, Ellicott, to Canterbury, and Disraeli later claimed, in spite of his strong relationship with the Queen, that as a result of her interference many of his supporters felt they had been excluded from and unrewarded by his ecclesiastical patronage.[114] It may well be that it was the Queen who vetoed the appointment of Griffiths of Llandeilo to St Asaph in 1870, and Howell to the same diocese in 1889, though Davidson advised her that while the appointments of Lloyd to Bangor in 1890 and Owen to St Davids in 1898 might have been questionable, the objections were not sufficient for the Queen to exercise her right of veto. Bishop Edwards's indiscretion regarding the 1890 appointment of Lloyd to Bangor gave the prime minister, the archbishop and Davidson considerable anxiety as to how they should inform the Queen regarding this matter. As is noted elsewhere, Edwards had unsuccessfully endeavoured to so disgrace Lloyd after his appointment had been announced that he would be forced to withdraw. The Queen also strengthened Gladstone's hand in 1870 when he wished to appoint a native Welshman to the diocese of St Asaph: 'the Queen believes', she wrote, 'that a Welshman is almost necessary for a Welsh see on account of the language'.[115]

The Queen was thus one of a number of interested parties and factors any prime minister had to take into account in making his appointments. Some of these are specified by Gladstone in a letter to his daughter Mary:

> it is to be borne in mind that they [the bishops] are so preferred not by a single force but by many. If I am one of them, so the particular diocese is another, the Queen a third, the Liberal Party a fourth. It is the resultant of all these forces which determines the choice. Men of the highest stamp as a class should undoubtedly be chosen, but it cannot be the highest man in the class.[116]

Gladstone ignored a number of other restraints in the above quotation, such as the claims of families;[117] maintaining a balance between the ecclesiastical parties or between academic and pastoral appointments; the need to take care not to appoint men from too narrow a choice, such as schoolmasters and holders of chairs (the appointment of two schoolmaster bishops in Wales within a year of each other – Edwards and Lloyd – was particularly resented),[118] together with the assumption that the choice of bishops ought to be evenly divided between the two ancient universities.[119] But so far as the Church in Wales was concerned there was another restraint. This concerned the social background of the candidates, for it could not be forgotten that bishops were also peers of the realm and sat in the House of Lords. As Gladstone told R. W. Morgan, there were other equally important qualifications for the episcopal office in Wales other than the ability to speak Welsh.

Daniel Jones in his essay on *Welsh Bishops for Wales*[120] noted the absolute horror that seized an Englishman when he heard of the possibility of a Welshman being elevated to the episcopal bench. His assumption that this was an anti-national feeling was probably untrue. The real concern was about status: as to whether a Welshman could be found who was also a gentleman and a man of society, who could measure up to the stature of an English bishop and take his place in polite English society with ease and familiarity. For the bishop was expected not only to be the pastor of his clergy, but to also be the social equal of the leading men of his diocese. Mitre and coronet needed to be equal, as Bishop Wilberforce alleged.[121] Bishop Jayne of Chester, son of a truckshop manager in the Gwent valleys who had prospered, must have had his tongue in his cheek when he wrote to Lord Selbourne in 1899 regarding the vacant deanery of St Asaph. The appointment lay with the Crown in virtue of the fact that its previous dean had been appointed to the see of Bangor. Lord Mostyn had requested the deanery for his uncle, Hugh Mostyn, rector of Buckworth. Bishop Jayne accordingly wrote of this suggestion 'that there were well known reasons why the Welsh clergy needed to be strengthened on the social side', and argued that new blood could be brought in much more readily by the Crown than by a bishop.[122]

This was a problem that always remained. Over the centuries an enormous gulf had grown between the Welsh-speaking *gwerin* or native clergy, who cared for the mountain and industrial parishes and were ill-educated and often unused to the manners of polite society, and the sophisticated university men whose influential relatives obtained for them the wealthy English-speaking parishes of the vale of Glamorgan or the hinterland of St Asaph, for example.

One group was conversant in Welsh but lacked the social polish, the learning and the gentlemanly manner, that many believed were requirements for episcopal office and membership of the House of Lords. The other group had the background and the quality, we might say, but, alas, they did not have the Welsh language as part of their heritage. If that group could move with grace and discernment in high society, the other would feel as ill at ease within it as many of the *gwerin* ordinands did when they entered the portals of a bishop's palace.

The choice of good candidates was thus so limited that two prime ministers chose Englishmen for the vacancies of 1849 and 1859, whom they assumed had learnt to speak Welsh fluently. Gladstone, who realized there was a distinction between speaking Welsh as a native and having acquired the language as a second tongue, made 'the experiment' (as his detractors put it) of appointing a native Welshman to St Asaph in 1870. Although Bishop Hughes had married into gentry, his own social position was humble, and Gladstone was ill-advised to put his choice into the most aristocratic of the Welsh dioceses, whose leading clergy clearly resented their new bishop as a Welsh intruder. Disraeli, possibly in ignorance, reverted to the original policy and choose Basil Jones for St Davids in 1874. General Ponsonby, the Queen's secretary, noted that Jones was not only a Welshman by birth and was acquainted with the Welsh language, 'but is also a gentleman and a distinguished scholar', qualifications which he felt were generally lacking in 'the mere Welsh clergy, but which are requisite to maintain the authority and influence of a Bishop'.[123] Salisbury was lucky to find in Watkin Williams, whom he appointed to Bangor in 1898, both a Welsh speaker and the son of a baronet. But from the 1860s onwards a better class of Welsh cleric was emerging through the new opportunities presented by university education, and such men as Edwards, Pritchard Hughes, Lloyd and Owen came from this background. Yet as late as 1890 Dean Vaughan of Llandaff, writing to his protégé Randall Davidson, accepted that the necessity of Welsh-speaking bishops meant offering sees to men who were not really suitable for membership of the House of Lords, and who would not be on a level with English requirements 'in any shape'.[124]

The Development of Intrigue

A London correspondent, J. P. Owen, in attacking the 'Welshmen for Welsh sees' policy, argued that his reading of the old local papers had convinced him that there was a more free and independent expression of opinion practiced by the Welsh clergy before this policy had been adopted. Arguing that when a bishop was chosen because of his local knowledge and ties (he was writing regarding the election in the diocese of St Davids during 1897) he asserted it was almost impossible that the diocese could escape 'becoming a hot-bed of intrigue and heart-burning'.[125]

His criticisms were sound. Wales was a small country and most Welshmen were bound together by ties of language and culture. By the 1870s, when episcopal appointments were almost limited to Welsh-speaking men, there were many who believed that the situation could be manipulated in their own favour or to the advantage of their friends. There had always been the long tradition of newspaper controversy about these appointments. Editorial and letter columns were filled with speculation and suggestions. It is hardly surprising that some would-be candidates actually organized their own campaigns for promotion, as did Dr Griffiths of Llandeilo in 1870 and Lewis Lloyd in 1890. Petitions and letters to the prime minister and those in authority assisted this manipulation. A few were not above applying directly to the prime minister for their own appointment to a vacant see.[126] But by the 1880s a new element entered this scene. This was the formation of what Hartwell Jones described as a *clique* whose business was to ensure that a small group of Welshmen would obtain for themselves the leading clerical appointments in Wales. Though they declared themselves to be Church defenders, Jones argued that in fact these men ruthlessly opposed those who preferred the Church to defend itself against disestablishment by the quieter route of pastoral and spiritual care within the parishes and in the Church at large. Many of these men were linked with the educational establishments at Llandovery or Lampeter, and included Edwards, his brother-in-law Bishop Jayne of Chester, John Owen and others. Hartwell Jones continued:

anyone who stood in their way had to run the gauntlet and be exposed to the artillery of their malice, aided by a brood of sycophants from whose fangs no one's reputation was safe, employed to rake up incidents of the past which could be distorted to the detriment or disadvantage of victims . . . Trucklers, parasites and informers in two Welsh dioceses, to whom their ecclesiastical supporters lent a ready ear and eager encouragement, and who found delation a lucrative profession, may affect to question or attempt to disprove what has been said in the preceding pages; but the facts adduced are undeniable and the statements made irrefutable.[127]

A. G. Edwards was certainly the leader of this small group, which probably came into effect after his own appointment to the bench. The group was described by a friend of Edwards, Griffith Roberts, canon missioner of Llandaff diocese, as 'the St Asaph syndicate';[128] Herbert Ryle called it 'the Llandovery clique',[129] while Davidson, using local information, described it as 'the mutual admiration society'.[130] As bishop of Gladstone's home diocese, the confidential advisor on Welsh ecclesiastical affairs for Salisbury, and as one who had gained the respect of many politicians for his leadership and diplomacy during the tithe disputes of the 1890s, Edwards had an influential position. Many have argued that Hartwell Jones was simply expressing 'sour grapes' at not obtaining a bishopric for himself, but there is much evidence to suggest that there was a great deal of truth in what he said. David Howell lost the bishopric that would have been his when Edwards discovered an incident from the past in his life which reflected on his then moral conduct. Relayed to Queen Victoria it debarred him from appointment. Lloyd's appointment to Bangor was a bitter blow to this group, so much so that Edwards unsuccessfully endeavoured to deprive him of it by a mean and shabby course of action. As soon as he was aware of the serious nature of Bishop Basil Jones's illness, Edwards was campaigning for Owen as Jones's successor in the see of St David.

Others, with even more authentic voices than Hartwell Jones, echoed his sentiments. Archdeacon D. R. Thomas, a senior clergyman in Edwards's own diocese, protested strongly 'against the methods of a system which has been not ineptly described as a syndicate for working ecclesiastical promotion in Wales'. He believed this syndicate was doing great injury to the interests of the Church.[131] An unknown correspondent of 1904 described Edwards as 'a modern clerical Earl of Warwick, the king-maker of Wales in ecclesiastical circles'. He had made two Welsh bishops besides himself, and might just complete the 'quartette', he argued, while

he had also been influential in appointments to deaneries, arch-
deaconries, the principalship of Lampeter and the wardenship of
Llandovery.[132]

Alas, in their desire to serve the Church in Wales, these men
linked themselves to a policy that identified that Church with the
Church of England, and forced them to tear apart the long tradition of patriotism and nationalism that had given the Welsh
Church life and vitality over many years and enabled it to obtain
an ever-increasing influence in the affairs of the nation and in the
warmth of the people's hearts. They forced upon the Church a
long, bitter and controversial campaign against disestablishment,
using not the tactics of spiritual warfare but those of political
intrigue and verbal violence, cunning and ruthlessness. In stressing
the links between England and Wales they knew they would have
to adopt the views of some of their predecessors, thereby taking a
hostile attitude to the Welsh language and to Welsh culture.
Knowing they would meet the resistance of the older clergy
(Edwards had three great rows in St Asaph with his clergy during
the earlier days of his episcopate there) they promoted to high
office either younger men or men identified with their stated and
declared policy. By the pressure they were able to exert, and by
ruthlessly exploiting every opportunity to get their own men into
the Welsh sees, their policy became the general norm. Evangelicals
were identified as Nonconformists, their view of theology being
similar to those who would disestablish the Church. The result was
bitterness, within and without the Church. They won their way,
but the cost was a strong loss of identity within the Welsh Church
which began to believe it was both Tory and English, while Nonconformity was Liberal and Welsh. While one may clearly suggest
that Edwards formed his policy and continued with it ruthlessly
in the idea that this was the right way, his methods were open to
question. But he destroyed a long legacy which the Church in
Wales today has only just regained, but at a time when the very
existence of the language which upholds that nationality is at risk.

It is against this backcloth that we examine the individual
appointments made to the Welsh sees. Some of these appointments
were outstanding, others mediocre. If the period started out with
politicians using episcopal appointments for their own ends, it
ended with certain elements in the Welsh Church using the same
weapons and tactics to get their own nominees elected into office,

albeit in the belief that they were helping to defend it against disestablishment. The task of the prime minister was clearly not an enviable one: too many people endeavoured to influence his appointment, and one at least, the Queen, eventually had sufficient authority to veto his wishes. And until the final choice was made the newspapers had a field day. At least it shows that at that time the Church was at the centre of public interest, and the role of the bishop was regarded as a substantial one in the life of the nation.

~ 2 ~

The Last Political Appointment: The Appointment of Connop Thirlwall to St Davids, 1840

The last bishop of the *ancien régime* in St Davids, John Bankes Jenkinson, died at Great Malvern in July 1840 at the age of fifty-nine. Appointed in 1825, he owed his position to his cousin, Lord Liverpool, the then prime minister. Because of the poverty of the see, which made it impossible for its bishop 'to support the dignity of his station as a Peer of the realm', and as King George IV wished to show a mark of respect for Lord Liverpool, Jenkinson also received the deanery of Durham. It was valued at £9,000 per annum. He thus obtained an income from church preferments equalled only by the two archbishops.[1]

The new arrangements made by the Ecclesiastical Commission came into force at Jenkinson's death, life interests having been respected by the commissioners. The commission had been empowered to equalize the episcopal income of the Church in order to ensure a more just distribution of that income to the various sees. Jenkinson's death thus meant that for the first time for centuries the bishop of St Davids would receive an adequate income. Consequently the necessity of obtaining an additional dignity in order to augment that income was ended.

After many years of concern regarding the lack of Welsh-speaking bishops, it is hardly surprising that the papers that announced Jenkinson's death also declared the necessity of appointing a Welshman to the vacant see. The *Carmarthen Journal*, though it seemed to assume that the clergy's main task was preaching (an emphasis greatly disliked by the English episcopate), therefore considered that only a Welsh-speaking bishop was 'competent to form a correct opinion of pulpit talent'.[2]

Yr Haul produced sixteen reasons why a Welsh appointment was required, utilizing every historical, mythological, linguistic, judicial, ecclesiastical, national and pragmatic reason it could register for that purpose. It especially noted the harm done to the Welsh clergy by the appointment of English bishops, alleging that this policy killed their energy and frustrated their talents.[3]

The *Cardiff and Merthyr Guardian*, reporting a fear that the bishop of Norwich, Edward Stanley, might be translated, made the comment that this would be 'a jobbed elevation' of one who had neither the claims of superior learning nor of eminent service in the Church. Its editor, by contrast, stressed the need for a Welshman to be appointed with a nationality bred in him from the breast and a language rooted in him as a mother tongue.[4] A London press correspondent argued that the stigma and injustice of sacrificing the spiritual interests of Wales 'to political partizanship', by forcing upon the Welsh people 'an English supporter of the existing ministry', should be ended.[5]

An argument was soon heard that the bishops were pastors of their clergy, not of the people. It was only the 'inferior clergy' who needed to be acquainted with the Welsh tongue. Englishmen would do as well, or even better, than Welshmen as bishops in Wales. The *Carnarvon and Denbigh Herald* disputed this, and asserted that the bishop was concerned not only with his clergy, but with the whole Church in his diocese.[6]

Another argument was also being heard, a more subtle one, but more finely attuned to the needs of the government. An English partisan bishop would not do, but a Welsh-speaking partisan bishop was another matter, who might do much good for the Liberal party within Wales. Benjamin Hall, later Lord Llanover, who acted as the great parliamentary champion of the Welsh Church, exemplified this view, though he was later to deny it. In a letter that survives in the Melbourne archives at Windsor Castle, Hall expressed the hope to Lord Melbourne, who as Liberal prime minister would effectively make the appointment, that a Welsh speaker would be appointed to St Davids. As evidence of that hope he referred to the clause proposed, but eventually lost, in the Ecclesiastical Church Bill of 1836 that 'no clergyman should be appointed to any vacant see in Wales who was not fully conversant with the Language of the Country'. But Hall went on to argue that such a Welshman should be a Liberal in political sympathies:

> In Wales the clergy generally and especially in South Wales are very poor and are quite subservient in every respect to the bishop for the time being whoever he may be and it would materially strengthen the Liberal Interest if the clergymen in the Diocese of St David's had the countenance and support of a Bishop professing Liberal opinions.

Hall added that he well knew the difficulties in finding such a clergyman, 'but so great is the power of the Tory Aristocracy in South Wales that it is important this opportunity shall not be lost of strengthening the opposite interest'.[7] Hall clearly wanted to have his cake and eat it!

Hall was not alone in these sentiments. The *Carnarvon and Denbigh Herald*, in its issue of 25 July 1840, though it blamed the apathy of Wales for the appointment of an Englishman, considered that a contributory factor was the pronounced 'Toryism' of the Welsh clergy and their misplaced hostility to a Liberal administration. It conceded, however, as Hall did, that there were certain Welshmen who were 'worthy of the confidence' of a Liberal minister. Others by the same argument were not. Among their number was one of the most outstanding candidates for episcopal office that Wales has ever produced. This was Bruce Knight, chancellor of Llandaff and in effect the administrator of the diocese. But Knight, although Welsh speaking, was a Tory, and Glamorgan as a county had been hostile to the Whig party. Knight's appointment 'to an office of still higher influence in the Church', said the *Welshman*, 'could go to make the power of that political institution still more inimical to Her Majesty's government than it is already'.[8] Another candidate was Llewelyn Lewellin, principal of St David's College, Lampeter, whose claims to the office were urged on Melbourne by Lord Carrington. Melbourne, impressed by these claims, promised to put his name first on the list for recommendation, but then asked what his politics were. When he discovered Lewellin was a Tory 'of the good old sort', and that he was unlikely to change, Melbourne at once rescinded his promise, saying, 'I have plenty of Tories in the "House" already, and they are the plague of my life: I will not add to their number.'[9]

Welsh-speaking bishops were in order, it seemed, so long as they were prepared to propagate the political views of the Whig oligarchy. It was not a concept that enhanced the spiritual position of the episcopate. But, as we note later, Melbourne saw bishops more as political animals than as spiritual leaders. Bishops as political animals were high on his list. Welsh-speaking bishops hardly entered the arena of his thought. In any case, his acquaintance with the Welsh-speaking clergy was minimal.

Another allegation frequently made was that there were no Welsh-speaking clergy equal to the office of bishop. Melbourne may well have held this view himself. It is hardly surprising that this allegation was vigorously denied by the supporters of such an episcopate.[10] A list of names was offered by the *Sun* newspaper of Welshmen whom it thought could qualify for such office. Accepting that such appointments were often made on political grounds, it obligingly divided its recommendations into two groups according to known political persuasion. The names of the Whigs were Henry Parry, vicar of Llanasa, Archdeacon Newcombe of Ruthin, Walter Thomas, rector of Dinas, Pembrokeshire, John Hughes, vicar of Aberystwyth and Madock Williams, rector of Halkin. The conservative names were Archdeacon John Williams of Cardigan, Bruce Knight, chancellor of Llandaff, Dr Lewellin, principal of St David's College, Lampeter, and Walter Davies, rector of Llanrhaeadr. In addition the names of four clerics of unknown political views were offered: W. J. Rees of Casgob, William Jones, vicar of Llanfihangel Genau'r Glyn, David Parry of Llywel and Thomas Price, Crickhowell. All these men, the editor held, were qualified for episcopal office in terms of 'piety, learning and moral worth'.[11] Sir Benjamin Hall is also known to have furnished a list of men to the government, stressing that they should 'on no account appoint any *but a native* and *a really qualified native*'.[12]

Petitions for the appointment of a Welsh speaker to St Davids began to flow into Parliament from all directions. It was a spontaneous gesture, as the vacancy had released the pent-up feelings of the Welsh Church over the injustice done to the clergy and their own nation by the previous appointments. But the mood caught on, with the result that so many petitions were forwarded to Parliament that the editor of the *Cardiff and Merthyr Guardian* suggested in an editorial that

> never for centuries past has the principality of Wales been so strongly agitated on any subject as it is at this moment on the great question of appointing to the vacant bishopric of St Davids some one of the many

eminent Welsh scholars who adorn by their learning and their lives the pure and holy Church to which they belong.[13]

Petitions came from the Welsh societies in London and the Welsh inhabitants of Liverpool, as well as the inhabitants of Llandovery and other places, all 'numerously signed', urging the prime minister to appoint a Welsh speaker to the vacant bishopric.[14] The editor of the *Carnarvon and Denbigh Herald* regarded it as the duty and obligation of the Welsh public to memorialize the government 'making known their wishes and their wants, and reminding the Cabinet of its clear line of duty on the occasion'.[15]

One reason for these editorial remarks was that the Liverpool Welsh had formed a deputation to meet Lord Melbourne, in order to urge upon him the necessity of appointing a Welsh bishop to the vacant see, and so discontinue 'the injurious practice of sending English prelates to preside over the Church in Wales'. The editor added that the deputation needed as much backing as possible from Wales itself. Its members were Viscount Sandon, MP, Sir John Edwards, Bart, MP, Mr W. Bulkeley Hughes, MP, Mr D. Morris, MP, Dr Hughes, Mr J. Richards and the Revd David James, the latter three from Liverpool itself. They were joined by a number of other Welsh MPs in the eventual meeting with Lord Melbourne. A press report of this meeting stated that:

> Lord Melbourne listened with his usual urbanity to all the arguments brought forward by these gentlemen, and put to them several questions as they arose from the statements made, in reference to points on which his lordship seemed to desire information. One of these the deputation feel justified to state, in the hope that the Principality will give it, *practically*, the proper answer, 'If there be so strong a desire for Welsh Bishops, how comes it pass that there is no movement in the Principality, and among the Welsh Clergy, on the subject?' or words to that effect. Let the Welsh public and the Welsh press answer this question effectually. The probability is the appointment will be delayed for some time, and Lord Viscount Melbourne is fully prepared to entertain the request of the Welsh nation.[16]

The *Carmarthen Journal* made much of Melbourne's comment about the apparent apathy in Wales regarding a Welsh appointment:

The deputation could not *then* fall back on any manifestation of feeling, for it is only *since* the deputation waited on the Prime Minister that there has been any overt evidence of a strong interest in the nomination of a Welshman. By this direct appeal to popular apathy, the Premier cut off the ground from under the feet of the deputation, and in the absence of the evidence demanded by Lord Melbourne, they lost the vantage ground which they would occupy were the appeal to be made *now*, fortified as they would be by a strong and general expression of public feeling in the principality in favour of the object of their mission to Downing-street. The efforts that were made to impress on the government the justice and policy of appointing a Welsh Divine to the vacant Bishoprick, were desultory and disjointed, and failed for want of previous concert, and proper organization, and for want of mooting the subject some years ago, so that the national sentiment on this important subject should be brought out into prominent relief, and that the dormant dislike of filling Welsh Sees with Bishops ignorant of the vernacular language should be quickened into expressive activity. This blunder will not be repeated, for we learn that societies are in course of formation to consolidate the scattered energies of our countrymen, and to enable them not only to disarm the Premier of the foil with which he so dexterously parried the application . . .[17]

Nevertheless, Melbourne was not strictly truthful, for Hall and the Welsh newspapers had clearly expressed their mind. Melbourne, it was alleged, had stated some years earlier than he would appoint a Welsh-speaker at the next vacancy in a Welsh bishopric.[18] On the other hand the lack of any central Welsh ecclesiastical or political organization and the isolation of the country made it difficult to establish and mobilize an effective lobby for a Welsh-speaking bishop.

The Popular Candidates

The person who seemed to most people in Wales to be the most eligible candidate for the vacant bishopric was John Williams, archdeacon of Cardigan and rector of the Edinburgh Academy. He was, wrote an over-enthusiastic editor:

The '*facile princeps*' of Welsh scholars . . . We know that such an appointment would be highly satisfactory to the Clergy of the See, and if a brilliant academical career in which he bore away the first honours the University had to offer, and if a proud position in the republic of letters can recommend a talented man and a profound scholar, to the consideration of Her Majesty and her professional advisors, the name of the author of the Life of Alexander the Great, will come down endorsed on the *congè d'elire* [*sic*] to the Chapter of St Davids.[19]

Alas, it was generally thought that Archdeacon Williams had the wrong politics for a Whig administration,[20] a fact which, if the 'bias of political opinion' was to be the test of fitness for such promotion, also ruled out two other candidates mentioned by the same paper, namely Bruce Knight[21] and William Conybeare, who was later to succeed Knight as dean of Llandaff.

Archdeacon Williams, who was most anxious to be raised to the bench and certainly believed he had been given written promises that he would be chosen for a Welsh bishopric, obviously felt that he needed to reassure the prime minister about his political views.[22] Accordingly, his brother-in-law, D. Davies, wrote from 2 Berkeley Street to Lord Melbourne, enclosing testimonials regarding the archdeacon and his ability as a Welsh speaker, 'having heard from various quarters that it is the intention of Her Majesty to appoint a Welshman to the see of St David's now vacant'. More significantly he enclosed a note from the archdeacon about his 'political opinions'.[23] A rumour that Williams had been appointed was subsequently denied in the press.[24]

Other names were mentioned to the prime minister. Lord Lisburne, with the concurrence of Lord Albemarle, recommended one Mr Keppel (probably the deputy clerk of the closet to the Queen) 'a most respectable, as well as liberal clergyman', and offered to introduce him to the premier.[25] But at least one recommended himself. This was John Merewether, dean of Hereford since 1832, who brought before Melbourne 'the circumstances of my case'. It appears that one of his qualifications for the appointment to St Davids was his 'connection with Wales as an Incumbent of a living in Radnorshire [New Radnor] for some years past'. But there were other circumstances 'which I am inclined to think cannot but be esteemed of some weight with your Lordship, and as the course which I have taken in reference to the connection I have held with Her Majesty's Household and consequently with the Government has really placed me in a situation which strengthens the claims I might otherwise have pleaded for your Lordship's favour on this occasion, although I have been unsuccessful in others'.[26]

In spite of wearing the wrong political colours, Bruce Knight was highly recommended for the appointment by Archdeacon Richard Davies of Brecon, one of the three archdeacons of the vacant diocese, in a petition to the Queen. This petition was widely circulated and found considerable support. Pointing out the difficulties under which the diocese had laboured because of the previous appointment of non Welsh speakers to the see, Davies requested the appointment of a man qualified in the Welsh language. He then humbly reminded the Queen that 'there is amongst us a clergyman of unimpeached and unimpeachable private character, duly qualified, in every respect, for such a charge, who has for a very large portion of the last fifty years presided, in the absence of the Bishop, over a diocese in the Principality, with great credit to himself, and with incalculable advantage to the churches intrusted for so long a time to his direction'.[27] A petition in support of the archdeacon's plea was said to have been signed by 'thousands' of clergy and laity in the diocese of Llandaff.[28]

The Choice of Connop Thirlwall

As the newspapers reported the Liverpool deputation they also added a footnote about a rumour circulating that Connop Thirlwall had been appointed to the see.[29] In fact it was no rumour, for Melbourne in his reply to Merewether on 18 July noted that the appointment had been 'determined'.[30] This was a fact not divulged to that delegation when it met the premier two days earlier, although they appear to have conceded that Lord Melbourne had committed himself to an appointment. Sizing up the situation accurately, they thus addressed Melbourne personally, hoping that when another episcopal vacancy arose in England, the premier

will give that gentleman [that is, Thirlwall, though they were unaware of his name at that stage] a similar and better preferment *elsewhere*, and that your Lordship will still advise her Majesty to give us at this time a Welsh Bishop for St David's; and we beg to assure your Lordship, that it will prove the most popular boon that has been conferred on the principality since the time of the Reformation.

Melbourne promised to consider their suggestion.[31]

The offer had been made to Thirlwall on 15 July, though not accepted by him until six days later. Melbourne's comment about the lack of interest in Wales for a Welsh speaker was clearly a useful let-out clause for him at that time. Thus when the *Carmarthen Journal* of 24 July noted the appointment, it argued it was too much to ask Melbourne to reverse his decision. Nevertheless, it hoped that the deputation would have impressed future governments with the need to appoint Welsh speakers to Welsh bishoprics. Further reflection by the editor in his next issue of 31 July indicated that he felt Melbourne was justified in this appointment by the absence of any strong and national desire for a Welsh speaker. He wrote about the delegation:

> Lord Melbourne has told them in effect, 'Let me have some proof of the sincerity of your anxiety to see a Welshman made Bishop in a general expression of public opinion amongst your countrymen, and then I will consider your application; but *until* such a manifestation of public feeling – *until* you bestir yourselves, and shake off your lethargy, I will continue to tread in the same path as my Predecessors for the last 130 years, and make such appointments as may be congenial to my own feelings, and in accordance with a practice, which, whatever its effect on the interests of the Church in the Principality has the stream of precedent, and prescription in its favour.'

One assumes the editor soon realized his mistake as he became aware of the substantial but uncoordinated support for a Welsh speaker. Consequently in the next issue of 7 August the editor suggested that 'more systematic and energetic efforts' were needed to secure a Welsh bishop at the next vacancy. He likewise felt that Melbourne had committed himself to this policy, even though the premier might need to hear a great deal of persuasive Welsh oratory before he implemented it! Melbourne, he added, would be only too glad to escape 'the flood of consonants and gutturals with which he will be assailed in the sonorous outpouring of a stentorian Welsh orator'. And let this be in Welsh, he added, to show the difficulties an English bishop would encounter in replying in Welsh to such a speech.[32]

It is difficult to know when Melbourne decided to recommend Thirlwall as the new bishop of St Davids. The biographer of Bishop

Thirlwall, J. C. Thirlwall, Jr, suggests that Melbourne had kept Thirlwall's name before him for such promotion since his involvement in the dispute at Cambridge over the admission of Nonconformists to the university.[33] In 1834 Thirlwall had written 'in a liberal spirit' condemning the religious duties and teachings of the university. Christopher Wordsworth, master of Trinity College, of which Thirlwall was a fellow, demanded and obtained his resignation, whereupon Lord Brougham, the Whig Lord Chancellor, offered him the living of Kirby Underdale in Yorkshire, valued at nearly £1,000 per annum. Here Thirlwall wrote his celebrated history of Greece and a number of influential pamphlets on the Jewish and Irish questions. These opposed Peel's policy and probably endorsed Melbourne's good opinion of him. Nevertheless, there was a particular problem regarding Thirlwall's theological position. Some years earlier he had translated Schleiermacher's critical essay on the Gospel of Luke into English and seemingly endorsed some of its liberal theological views. Although Melbourne, to use Thirlwall's biographer's phrase, was 'not dismayed by quasi-heterodoxy', he demurred at appointing Thirlwall to the diocese of Norwich in 1837 as he felt unable to press the king's orthodox conscience any more, having already done so over Renn Dickson Hampden's appointment to the regius chair at Oxford in spite of the protests of high churchmen. Melbourne had sent Thirlwall's translation of Schleiermacher to the bishops of Ely and Chichester for their comments, and their expressions of unease at some of its contents probably confirmed him in his postponement of Thirlwall's elevation. Later, however, Melbourne was to use their opinion to justify Thirlwall's appointment as bishop of St Davids to the archbishop of Canterbury, William Howley.[34] But there was now a new monarch, Queen Victoria, on the throne, one much under Melbourne's tutelage, and the agnostic Melbourne had no qualms about Thirlwall's theological beliefs. It seems that Melbourne wanted Thirlwall, regarded by J. S. Mill as the best speaker he had ever heard,[35] in the House of Lords in order to meet the doughty Conservative champion, Dr Phillpotts, bishop of Exeter, who was regarded as the most powerful debater in the house.[36] It was immaterial that it was a Welsh diocese that was available: it was simply that Melbourne wanted Thirlwall's oratory in Parliament. Any see would have done.

Nevertheless, Melbourne did request the advice of a number of clerics and others, although it seems that he wanted confirmation of his choice rather than argument. The archbishop of Canterbury, William Howley, noted that he had no personal acquaintance with Thirlwall, and had always heard him spoken of 'as a very eminent classical scholar'. But he continued: 'I think it however my duty to state to your Lordship that considerable offence was given to many persons at Cambridge by a preface which he published a few years ago to a translation of Schleiermacher on the Gospel of St Luke.'[37]

But the archbishop had not read that preface. The prime minister in his reply to the archbishop of the following day made it clear that he was aware of the preface, but added that it had been published before Thirlwall was ordained. His knowledge of that publication, he continued, 'and the fear of the offence it might have given, has inclined me to defer for some time recommending Mr Thirlwall for that promotion in the church which I was told from all quarters that he deserved'. Although Melbourne confessed he had not read the book himself, as he lacked the necessary biblical training and time, he admitted that having '*curiously* looked at it I certainly think that it was not prudently selected for translation'. The two bishops who had examined the book had informed him that there were in the preface some passages respecting the inspiration of the New Testament which they considered objectionable, 'but at the same time they seemed to think that the errors considering the time and circumstances in which they were committed were not of such magnitude as to bar the promotion of a man of so much learning and ability'. He agreed, and while he felt himself 'bound to recommend for promotion clergymen whose general views upon Political Matters coincide with my own, I am most anxious not to advance any man, whose doctrines are not in union with those of the Established Church, or even whose promotion would be disagreeable to the great body of the Clergy . . .'[38] Clearly, Melbourne considered that Thirlwall did not come into this category.

Howley, we are told, shuddered at the multiplication of Whig bishops and detested liberalism in theology,[39] so that Melbourne's letter would have offered him little comfort. According to Jack Kemble, the archbishop 'hummed and hawed a great deal, but finding himself out-Bishopped, was fain to make the best face he could and gulped the pill'.[40] He might have been a little happier if he knew that Thirlwall was later to repudiate those sentiments, complaining that 'the tentative productions of a young lawyer ought not to be saddled on the bishop of St David's'.[41]

On the same day as his reply to the archbishop, Melbourne wrote to Thirlwall asking if he might put forward his name to the Queen for the see of St Davids. While he was unacquainted with him personally, he was aware of his writing and even more of his character and reputation.[42] It appears that the letter was misdirected to the wrong post town, and when it was delivered Thirlwall was away on a walking tour. Consequently, Thirlwall did not receive the letter for some days, and then after some deliberation travelled to London and sent his reply on 21 July from the Athenaeum. It was not without anxious consideration, he wrote, and 'I hope not with an altogether inadequate sense of the responsibility of the high station' that he accepted the offer. He continued,

> it would be impertinent to thank your Lordship, as for a personal favour, for the unsolicited preferment which you have given on no other than public grounds, to a stranger. I will only permit myself to say that my obligation to your Lordship will render me doubly anxious not to throw discredit – as far as depends on my own exertions – on your Lordship's recommendation.[43]

Melbourne would have been delighted with Thirlwall's sense of obligation, however expressed. Prime ministers have always liked that sentiment from their nominees.

It has been argued that Thirlwall at first wished to refuse the appointment, not so much to St Davids as to a bishopric, but his friends persuaded him that good bishops were needed. 'The Tractarians,' they argued, 'are bidding fair to disrupt the Church; the Evangelicals oppose all theological research. Can you stand selfishly aside?'[44] Thirlwall, Carlyle remarked to Froude, lay awake for three nights 'considering whether he was fit for such a place, or the place for him'.[45]

The Appointment Condemned

There was little approval of Melbourne's choice in Wales. Surprisingly enough, especially in view of his later disputes with Thirlwall, Sir Benjamin Hall wrote expressing his own great satisfaction and that of the Liberal Party for his appointment.[46] Clearly politics took precedence over national feelings for Hall on this occasion. At a later date his wife, Lady Llanover, expressed her 'indignation' that there were some who claimed that her husband had urged Thirlwall's appointment upon Melbourne 'in preference to any Welsh Man!!' She could hardly write with calmness and courtesy about 'these foul calumnies' against one

> to whom they owe everlasting gratitude for having stood by them *alone* thro' evil report, and good report – having urged – even *persecuted* the Ministry – with entreaties and with statements to force them to elect a *native* for every See as it became vacant – who never saw Dr Thirlwall in his life, or dreamed of his being a candidate for such an office, till he received a letter from Lord Lansdowne announcing the Appointment.

Furthermore, she pointed out (this was in 1851), he had continually reproached the government with Thirlwall's elevation. If her ladyship had been aware of the facts, she had conveniently forgotten them.[47] The *Welshman*, however, joined in with Hall's congratulations. Welcoming Thirlwall's appointment because of his Liberal sympathies and his known interest in civil and religious liberty, it felt his election would act as a 'curb' to the 'rampant Tory parsons who have hitherto taken such an active part at our elections, for we cannot believe that our new bishop will be pleased to witness one of his clergy performing the parts of drum majors in a political campaign, breaking up the forces, and marching by their side to the polling booth'.[48] But the *Welshman* was not entirely reflective of Welsh opinion.

The evangelical Lord Shaftesbury, who was later to exercise considerable influence over the episcopal appointments of his stepfather-in-law, Palmerston, regarded Thirlwall's appointment with abhorrence: 'amongst his bad acts,' he wrote of Melbourne, 'this is unusually bad, and in every point of view offensive'.[49] The high church party was equally scandalized. Melbourne had taken this into account in any case, but perhaps he had failed to realize the extent of the bitterness until the editor of the *Quarterly Review* described the new bishop as 'an infidel'.[50] Bishop Copleston of Llandaff used the same language and expressed his concern about Thirlwall's 'infidelity', although he hoped he had seen 'his error long ago'.[51] The Tractarians even endeavoured to prevent his election.

At first they tried on the grounds of intemperance, but this failed to hold water, and they then wondered if it was possible to devise some method of preventing the confirmation of his appointment by legal means.[52]

The main outcry came from the Welsh, as may have been expected. Their bitterness was all the more bitter because of their failure to coordinate their campaign for a Welsh appointment beforehand. Some of the clergy of the diocese of St Davids expressed their own regret that a non Welsh speaker had been appointed,[53] while the Welsh Church paper, *Yr Haul*, regarded Melbourne as a bitter enemy of the Welsh language and Thirlwall's appointment as a piece of 'political jobbery'. Those clergy who had welcomed the new appointment were reminded, rather bitterly, that there were 'some *priests* who can seek refuge under the mantle of an English bishop, who must stand or fall on their own merits under a Welshman'. Furthermore, it argued that no government would dare do such a thing in Ireland: rather Melbourne had taken advantage of their peaceful disposition and innocence. But now the prime minister had forfeited his right to have the support of the Welsh, and the Welsh people should now help to overthrow his ministry: 'the fire has been kindled. The Welsh blood has been heated.'[54]

The editor of the *Cardiff and Merthyr Guardian* was equally strong in his condemnation. Noting the details of the appointment, he rightly suggested there had been a measure 'of double dealing and meanness in the conduct of this affair', especially as Melbourne, while deluding the deputation with false hopes, knew an appointment had been made already, and had no intention of placing a mitre on any Welsh head. But although he had got rid of a deputation, he had now roused the spirit of the whole nation, 'a people who will not be put off like a deputation'. He would not regard Thirlwall as the bishop until he had seen the crozier in his hand, and by then the bishop would know that the Welsh regarded him as an intruder, 'forced upon them by an unjust but irresistible power'.[55]

The evangelical *Record* took the liberal *Morning Chronicle* to task for gilding the prospects of the diocese of St Davids under Thirlwall's administration. It approved the comment of *The Times* that had Thirlwall been appointed to a chair of Greek and Ancient History all would have applauded the appointment. But it had heard little of his work as a divine, save 'that he writes "Reverend" before his name'. It was unfortunate, it commented, that those liberal opinions in theology which had been the cause of his ejection from the university were now the reason for his elevation to the bench. Nevertheless, it trusted that the weight of his new responsibilities would lead him from such 'Neologian tendencies' to seek the 'only foundation of heavenly wisdom for guidance and instruction'.[56]

A stronger protest came from Joseph Hughes, *Carn Ingli*, a prominent clerical member of the Association of Welsh Clergy in the West Riding of Yorkshire. He was later to have a noted correspondence with Thirlwall about the subject of a bequest of £500 to the Welsh Sunday schools.[57] Writing to the *Record* he asked if the new bishop was acquainted with the Welsh language, 'the knowledge of which is indispensably necessary to the due and conscientious discharge of the Episcopal office in that part of the country'. He noted the various precedents for Welsh-speaking bishops, which included the Act of Uniformity. This act required the bishops of Hereford and the four Welsh sees, or any three of them, to examine and correct the then new Welsh Book of Common Prayer. This predisposed a knowledge of Welsh in Welsh bishops. 'Now suppose,' he asked, 'such a commission were issued in the present day, in what a dilemma would it place the Prelates of the Welsh Church.' At the time he wrote there was a controversy about the orthography of the Welsh Bible, but the bishops of the Welsh sees were 'incompetent to enter into the merits of the question owing to their want of knowledge of the Welsh language'. Hughes ended his protest with these words: 'I do say that such a state of things should continue no longer; it is a mere mockery of religion and an uncalled for outrage on the feelings of Churchmen in the Principality.'[58]

The *Liverpool Standard* believed that the failure to obtain a Welsh-speaking bishop after such a national demand could well lead to the cry 'No bishop wanted' and become an excuse for disestablishment. Nevertheless, it argued that the Welsh would have no objection to an Englishman or a Scotsman who had acquired the Welsh tongue – a prophetic statement if somewhat presumptuous at the time.[59]

It was quite clear to all interested parties that the agitation for a Welsh speaker to be appointed to a Welsh diocese had to continue. A skirmish had been lost, but many useful lessons had been learnt from it which would be important to remember in the subsequent campaign. Meanwhile, the Church had to cope with an English-speaking nominee to the bishopric. Could he be persuaded to decline the nomination? The thought was there, and two different courses of action were contemplated.

The first suggestion was made by the Liverpool committee. It suggested that the St Davids' chapter should 'postpone compliance with the Whig *conge d'elire*' requiring them to elect Thirlwall to the bishopric. But the elderly Archdeacon Davies of Brecon declined so to act, feeling he had no such discretionary power. His action brought him a public letter from David James, a member of that committee and the Welsh chaplain and vicar of Kirkdale in Liverpool:

> While we appreciate and respect the loyalty and submission to established authorities which pervade the letter of the Archdeacon, we cannot but say that this case affords another proof that the very virtues of our clergy are made a weapon against them in their transactions with the ministers of the Crown. A clergyman, in fact, should never have dealings with them without an attorney at his elbow . . .[60]

As a result of this refusal, David James took action himself, writing an open letter to Thirlwall, pointing out the implications of his office in a Welsh-speaking diocese. The letter was obviously written in a hope to dissuade Thirlwall from accepting that office, or if he had already done so, to accept translation to an English see at the first possible opportunity. The letter was widely publicized and applauded for its courage and statesmanship. It was sufficiently pointed to suggest to the editor of the *Liverpool Standard* that the new bishop should not accept office until he was able to reply in Welsh to James's letter.[61]

How could a bishop, who knew no Welsh, asked James, examine ordination candidates and prospective incumbents of Welsh-speaking parishes about their ability to minister and preach in Welsh? How could he confirm candidates in his diocese when nine-tenths of those confirmed knew no English?

The twenty-fourth article should have prevented this farce. Thirlwall, as a bishop, would have to subscribe to this article, which stated that the language used in worship should be one understood by the people: 'And you, if you accept the bishopric of St David, will, in celebrating the rite of confirmation deliberately contradict in practice your subscription to this Article, and do in the Church of God a thing plainly repugnant to the word of God. Sir, these things ought not to be.'

The Welsh nation, James claimed, was rising in revolt against the continuation of these practices:

> With a different appointment, due attention would be paid to the spiritual interests of the Welsh-speaking population; the machinery of the Welsh Church would be repaired; the working of it would be placed in skilful hands; and the country would hail these things as the dawn of a glorious reform.
>
> That you, Sir, who profess *reforming* principles, should by your acceptance of a Welsh bishopric, contribute to perpetuate one of the grossest and most deadly abuses that ever a country endured, is an event which requires explanation: for that explanation the Welsh people will continue to look, until, as it is to be hoped will be the case, you fling back with high and dignified disdain the poor bishopric of St David, and demand a better in England, where you may enjoy the emoluments of the See without inflicting present and eternal injury on the inhabitants.

'Consider well', said James's parting shot, 'whether you ought to allow yourself to be thrust into the vacant See amidst the execrations of a brave and loyal, but long-injured people. It will be the climax of inconsistency if you do. But I pray God to avert the evil from my country.'[62]

In some respects James was grossly unfair, especially in suggesting that Thirlwall, like some of his predecessors, had accepted the bishopric on mercenary grounds. It may have been true of a few, but not of all, and certainly not of Thirlwall, who generously used most of his episcopal income for projects within his diocese. James also exaggerated the extent of hostility in Wales to English-speaking bishops.

If James was unsuccessful in his main aim, his letter persuaded Thirlwall to learn the Welsh language. One of his teachers is said to have told him to put his tongue to the roof of his mouth and hiss like a goose. He even pronounced the benediction in Welsh on his first Sunday in Abergwili Church, the parish church near his palace, which 'produced a great and favourable sensation throughout the country'. The rumour, however, went round that he had actually preached in Welsh on that occasion, which possibly produced an even more favourable reaction. By September he was able to read 'any common Welsh book with tolerable ease'.[63] Speaking at the Abergavenny Cymregyddion Society in the presence of

Sir Benjamin and Lady Hall, Thirlwall stated that he had learnt the language as he felt it his duty to do so, though he still believed the English language was better suited to learning and education.[64] Even though it was alleged that the Welsh took pride in his mastery of the Welsh language, and perhaps flattered him 'for his *supposed* acquaintance', his was the language of the study and not of the hearth.[65] As such it was not readily understood. Archdeacon David Evans of St Asaph, brought up in Cardiganshire, recollected how Thirlwall had preached in Welsh at the consecration of a church. The local squire, ignorant of the language, asked one of his servants for his opinion, adding, 'pity it was in Welsh'. The reply came, 'Well, it wasn't Welsh where I was sitting.'[66] John Morgan noted that the bishop created 'consternation' at Nevern Church when he preached in Welsh. But his Welsh, he added, was more suited for the study than for everyday use, and never became his own.[67] Lady Hall said much the same. Though he was the only Welsh bishop who had avoided scandal by preaching a Welsh sermon, it was a pain to hear him, for 'he seemed afraid of every word lest he make a mistake'. His Welsh had been no use to his diocese, for when he and the other bishops who had learnt Welsh entered the pulpit, 'they are looked as like conjurors who are performing some wonderful tricks'.[68] Thirlwall would not have disagreed with her verdict. Writing at the same time (the 1870 St Asaph vacancy) he argued 'there is . . . an immense difference . . . between a native Welshman and one . . . who has only acquired the language as a foreigner. A little study and exercise will very soon bring the Welshman up to a mark which the Englishman will never reach as long as he lives.'[69]

Though Thirlwall had taken care to learn the language, he never understood the Welsh character. He was accused of hounding Welsh enthusiasm out of his diocese by his strictures against the preaching festivals and his failure to promote the senior Welsh clergy in his diocese to its major parishes and cathedral posts. On his resignation in 1874 the *Western Mail* commented that he was as unacquainted with the people at his retirement as he had been at his appointment. Though he had achieved distinction as a scholar, he was an indifferent bishop.[70] While his appointment had been justified by the claim that the bishop was more the superintendent of his clergy than a pastor to the laity, Thirlwall was said to have known less of his clergy than any other bishop on the bench.[71] On the other hand the work of church revival went on in his diocese, somewhat aided by him but never obstructed, and his influence, if dimmed in his own diocese (which never understood him), was substantial within the Church at large, where his real significance probably lay.

It is clear that Melbourne wanted Thirlwall as a Liberal spokesman in the House of Lords. It mattered little to Melbourne as to which diocese Thirlwall was offered. As such St Davids would do as well as any other diocese. The prime minister probably assumed that as Jenkinson had no Welsh, neither was it a necessary qualification for his successor. Although the premier was not as ignorant of the demands for a Welsh speaker as he made himself out to be, he both underestimated the strength of these demands, and also almost totally ignored those who made them, placing greater importance on the more immediate need of establishing Thirlwall's theological credentials. By the time an effective Welsh claim had been mounted by a Liverpool deputation, Thirlwall had been offered the bishopric and it was too late for a man of honour to withdraw that offer. On the other hand, it is not surprising that the Welsh claims took some time to formulate and were too late to be effective, for Jenkinson died on 7 July and the letter to Thirlwall was written a week later on 15 July. The Welsh had been trapped by Melbourne's almost indecent haste to obtain a new bishop.

If one result of the controversy that commenced after Thirlwall's appointment was that the new bishop learnt the Welsh tongue, another was that the Welsh became better organized in presenting their claims for a Welsh-speaking episcopate. Time was to show, however, that a distinction needed to be made between a man who had learnt Welsh as a second language and one who was a native speaker.

Melbourne's appointment of Thirlwall was the last manifestation of the eighteenth-century captivity of the Church to the state. His was a thoroughly political appointment, and was accepted as such on all sides. Melbourne may well have been influenced by Sir Benjamin Hall's statement that a political appointment was required. Although other later episcopal appointments to Welsh dioceses would assume the same nature, there were always other factors to redeem the situation, such as an ability to speak Welsh or an intimate relationship with Wales, and it was recognized that in some cases these appointments were made in order to retain a political balance on the bench itself.

The real tragedy of Thirlwall's elevation was not the fact of his appointment, but rather that the option presumably offered to Melbourne by the Liverpool deputation was never taken, namely to transfer the new bishop, if not Welsh speaking, to an English see when one became vacant.[72] Thirlwall remained at Abergwili for thirty-three years, an alien on an inhospitable shore.

~ 3 ~

The Alien Bishop in the North:
Bishop Short of St Asaph, 1846

William Carey,[1] bishop of St Asaph between 1830 and 1846, died in September 1846 during the long controversy about uniting the two sees of north Wales. The Ecclesiastical Commission, appointed to reform the Church's administrative and financial structures in 1835, had argued that although new sees were required in various populous areas, it was impossible to increase the number of bishops. At that time it was considered inadvisable for more bishops to sit in the House of Lords, and in spite of many precedents to the contrary the commissioners could not conceive of bishops who were not peers of the realm. The only way to create new sees, they maintained, was by abolishing existing ones. The sees of Gloucester and Bristol were united in order to form a new diocese to be based on Ripon. An order in council of December 1838, established by an act, 6 & 7 William IV, chap. 77, gave effect to another decision of the commissioners. During the first episcopal vacancy in the two sees of St Asaph and Bangor, the two dioceses were to be united and the surplus episcopal seat (and at one stage the surplus revenues) were to be transferred to a new see based on Manchester.

For many reasons no effective opposition was given to these proposals until 1842. But for the next four years a vigorous controversy took place, led by the second earl of Powis. He was assisted by a number of prominent Welsh and English clergy, notably Bishops Phillpotts of Exeter, Denison of Salisbury and Thirlwall of St Davids. Petitions were organized and memorials presented by counties, rural deaneries, parishes and universities. Lord Powis introduced three separate bills into the House of Lords to repeal the legislation uniting the two sees. One even reached its third reading before it had to be withdrawn. Gradually the ground shifted, and by 1846 Powis was proposing that the see of Manchester should be created without destroying either of the two north Wales dioceses, and that the junior bishop for the time being should not have a seat in the House of Lords.

Powis's third bill regarding this matter was introduced into the House of Lords in July 1846. The Whig government of Lord John Russell had replaced the Tory one led by Peel, in which the duke of Wellington was an influential figure. As both Peel and Wellington were adamantly opposed to any alteration of the original recommendations of the commission, and were petrified at the thought of an increase in the episcopate (remembering the anti-Church feelings at the time of the Reform Act), there were great hopes that a change of ministry would enable the two sees to be retained. But, alas, the Whigs were not as amenable to this hope as had been anticipated, though they were gracious enough to announce that they would offer no further resistance to the measure when it passed its second reading in the Lords with a majority of ten. While this seemed to offer a smooth passage for the bill's third reading in the upper house, the measure still had to pass the Commons. Pressed there on this matter, Lord John stated that he would have to oppose the bill if it came into the house at that time. However, he promised that if its promoters postponed the bill's progress, his government would examine the whole question 'in its widest extent', and introduce its own measure 'framed with a view to better episcopal superintendence in Wales' during the following year. The outcome seemed to be that Powis was either to risk losing his measure in the Commons, or allow the question of the two sees to be merged into the wider one of the increase of the episcopate.[2] It was at this rather crucial point in the debate that Bishop Carey died.

Carey's death was not unexpected. He had been in declining health for some years, and during the last two years of his life had been unable to visit his diocese, residing instead at his London home. During that time the bishop of Sodor and Man, Thomas Vowler Short, undertook the ordinations and confirmations within the see.[3] This was probably a private arrangement, for Short had been a protégé and lifelong friend of Carey, who had been his headmaster at Westminster School and had brought Short into his diocese at Exeter, before he (Carey) had been translated to St Asaph.[4] This episcopal arrangement was particularly welcome to Lord Powis and his colleagues, for they feared that if Bishop Bethell of Bangor had been asked to assist in St Asaph, their argument that a single diocese based on the union of the two sees would be too large a responsibility for one man to undertake, would have been easily challenged.

The commission, as well as the government, had too readily assumed that the surviving north Wales bishop would be willing to take over the additional see and work it with his own as a united diocese. So confident was the commission about this that it made no legal provision to ensure it would happen. The English press speculated that Bishop Bethell of Bangor would accept the vacant see as it would offer him an increased income of £5,800 as against his then stipend of £4,646. The *Carnarvon and Denbigh Herald*, however, argued that while a younger man might 'without being liable to the charge of avarice, fairly volunteer to discharge the double duty of the united see', the matter was different for an older man. This, of course, was at a time when bishops did not retire, (indeed, there was no provision made for their retirement) and Bethell was in his seventies. The editor continued by noting that Bishop Carey had not been in favour of the united see either, and quoted the editor of *The Globe* newspaper: 'Dr Bethell is rich, aged, a lover of ease, and opposed to the consolidation project.' But then, of course, the *Carnarvon and Denbigh Herald* was no lover of bishops, and soured its report by stating that 'a saint in crape is twice a saint in lawn [sleeves]'. It was hardly a complimentary remark.[5]

Noting these observations and being aware that Bethell had made it clear long before that he would not take charge of the two sees, the government consulted its law officers. They reported that the bishop of Bangor could not be obliged to take charge of the two sees if he was unwilling to do so. And this proved to be the case, though there are two different versions as to how this happened. In the first version Bethell claimed that Lord John Russell offered him the choice of taking over the two sees himself, or of having a new bishop appointed to St Asaph. Pleading his age, he chose the second alternative, but wrote to Lord Powis that his real reason was not to deprive his friends 'of the last hope of success'.[6] However, Lord John reported to the archbishop of Canterbury, William Howley, that after making his statement to the House about reintroducing the question of the two sees for further consideration, he could not with propriety or even in good faith request the bishop of Bangor to 'undertake the charge' of the vacant diocese.[7]

It therefore became his duty, declared Lord John, to recommend the Crown to fill the vacant bishopric. The legal officers, consulted again, found the right formula to allow the appointment: as the bishops of St Asaph and Bangor were included within the terms of the forty-first recommendation enacted in 6 & 7 William IV, chap. 77, the bishop of St Asaph could be considered as one of the other bishops under the forty-second recommendation![8] As a result of their recommendation the way was opened for a general extension of the episcopate within the Church of England.

Despite the rejoicing in north Wales a real fear was felt. Would the new bishop be required, as a condition of his appointment, to accept the see of Bangor in union with his own upon Bethell's death?[9] The suggestion was certainly made to Lord John Russell by Charles Wood, later Viscount Halifax, that the new bishop should be required to take any 'additional district' that 'might be thrown' into his diocese.[10] Consequently, Lord John suggested to Archbishop Howley that, if he approved, the appointment of the new bishop of St Asaph should 'be subject to any regulations affecting the foundations of his diocese, its revenues and its patronage, which Parliament and the Queen in Council should sanction'.[11]

Others feared the appointment of a bishop who would take over the episcopal functions in St Asaph in addition to his own see. The influential low-church *Record* recommended this, as it would allow the immediate creation of the new see at Manchester, which, it added, was the chief want. The question of the two sees in north Wales could then be discussed at leisure. The paper bitterly resented the Tractarian influence which sought to retain an ancient see instead of accepting a more utilitarian scheme based on population rather than sentiment. Its editor suggested a link with Sodor and Man, allowing for a reshuffle when Bangor became vacant, though a correspondent suggested a link with Chester.[12] This latter suggestion echoed another proposal of the government, namely that the eastern part of the diocese of Chester should be transferred to a new diocese of Manchester, and the rest linked to St Asaph.[13] The bishop of Durham, Edward Maltby, whose main aim seems to have been to promote his dean to the vacant bishopric as a reward for his Whig sympathies, nevertheless endorsed this scheme, suggesting that the bishop of Chester, John Bird Sumner, who also had a canonry at Durham, should be offered St Asaph. A better appointment could not be made, for Sumner had worked hard in his diocese, but was so 'uncomfortably lodged at Chester' in a 'dreary abode' that he might be 'easily induced to change', while the increased income of the new see would be an additional stimulus.[14] There exists a draft letter in which Sumner was offered the diocese of St Asaph. The letter insisted that the government retained the right to keep open the matter of the union of the two sees or to make other alternative arrangements. Sumner declined the see 'with grateful thanks to your Majesty'.[15] The government was clearly playing a rather cool game in arguing that if St Asaph survived, Chester could be forfeited for the new diocese of Manchester. Nevertheless, it clearly hoped that this plan, or various variations of it, would go far to satisfy all the parties 'who are disposed to be reasonable in any degree'. Though Lord John's ministers clearly preferred the original arrangements made by the commission, they had no wish to quarrel with the Church if that could be avoided.[16]

For one reason or another these plans fell to the ground. On 1 October the Tractarian *English Churchman*, quoting the *Chester Courant*, followed a little later by the evangelical *Record*, alleged that Bishop Short of Sodor and Man might continue to look after the diocese of St Asaph, albeit on a more official basis, presumably until Bethell's death permitted the union of the two sees.[17] Short's name had been mentioned in mid-September, but the bishop of Durham noted that he was an Oxford man, whereas the next turn required a Cambridge appointment.[18] Lord John was not concerned about niceties of university etiquette, and in early October offered Short the bishopric of St Asaph, having heard of his zeal in episcopal duties. But the offer came with another variant of the idea that if that bishopric was to be retained, another would be lost: 'You must be aware that under the Act of Parliament, if it is not altered, the Bishop of St Asaph may have to take charge of the Diocese of Bangor. If however St Asaph and Bangor are to be retained, it is my opinion that part of the diocese of Chester might be added to St Asaph and part of St Asaph to Bangor.' He also hinted that there might also be changes in the revenue and patronage of the bishopric.[19] The *English Churchman* was not too incorrect after all.

Short accepted the offer, not because he was unhappy in Sodor and Man – he was to look back on it as the happiest period of his life – but because his wife needed medical attention which was not available on the island. Sadly she died after a year spent in their new Welsh home.[20]

Thomas Vowler Short and his Appointment

Thomas Vowler Short (1790–1872) was the son of an archdeacon of Cornwall who was also chaplain to Princess Charlotte, and a nephew by marriage of Dr Ireland, dean of Westminster. He was educated at Westminster and Christ Church, Oxford, where he took a double first in 1812, and had held various livings while residing at Oxford where he tutored both Gladstone and Pusey, examined Newman for his degree, and became a close friend of Keble. In 1834 he became rector of St George's, Bloomsbury. His book *Parochialia* described the pastoral work in that parish which made him a model town incumbent, though his use of district visitors to search out the deserving poor meant they were popularly regarded as agents and spies of the state Church. In 1841 he became bishop of Sodor and Man. Short reckoned its income of £2,000 was worth at least half more through the cheapness of living on that island. His palace was no more than a 'good English parsonage', and he had his own home farm.[21] These things were neatly described in letter after letter to his close friend, Bishop Longley of Ripon, later archbishop of Canterbury.[22] The task of bishop was well suited to him he wrote to Longley, and would do him good.[23] But if that sounded presumptuous, he nevertheless achieved much in that diocese, improving the tone of the clergy and in providing educational facilities for the islanders as well as for his future clergy. Short thus achieved considerably popularity.[24]

The new bishop was not unknown to his new diocese, which he served from 1846 until he retired in 1870. In 1823 the SPCK published a sermon of his translated into Welsh, and he had acted for Carey for the last two years of his episcopate. Perhaps he had expressed himself a little too forcibly regarding his dislike of the Welsh language during that period (he certainly did so afterwards), but for one reason or another it was not a popular appointment. It may well be that the action of Lord Powis in preventing an effective lobby for a Welsh-speaking bishop caused a backlash against the English bishop who was eventually appointed. But it may also have been that because he was a Whig appointment it was assumed he shared that political viewpoint.

It is not surprising, therefore, that there were many who felt extremely suspicious about Short's appointment. They believed it was not only a short-term measure on the part of the Whig government, but also that Short had consented to various agreements in order to be appointed to a more lucrative see. In essence, they grasped after a half truth, but their bitterness about the whole question became a matter of political personal animosity against Short. One of the more telling of these critics, R. W. Morgan (who shared to the full the Tory instincts of the Welsh clergy), wrote:

Sodor and Man is a Spouse with but £2000 per annum dowry, little patronage, and no Coronet on her brow. Why did Dr. Vowler Short, at the summons of the great Church Reformer, Lord John Russell, desert her, whose language he knew, whose dominions were in proportion to his power of embrace, whose favours could scarcely be abused, for a spiritual spouse to whose language he was a barbarian, whose just demands and exactions of obedience he could only ignominiously deprecate and whose family, knowing his antecedents and disqualifications, regarded him with well-founded antipathy and disgust? Because St Asaph is a Peeress; because St Asaph sits in the House of Lords; because St Asaph has a hundred and twenty Benefices at her disposal. St Asaph was therefore prostituted by the Whig Political Pandar to the Whig Manx Bishop for two considerations:
1. Dr. Vowler Short engaged himself to do all in his power to Whiggify the Church, by means of
2. Changing every Clergyman into a State-Schoolmaster, and degrading the Church itself, the Ministry of Souls, into a Commercial Academy.

Morgan went on to point out that Bethell was as little qualified as Short 'for the right discharge of his Episcopal Functions towards the Welsh People', but unlike Short he was nevertheless 'a Christian Gentleman entertaining a certain sense of honour towards his own Church'. The evidence for this was Bethell's refusal to accept the joint see when offered to him. However:

On that refusal the Whig ministry came to an understanding with Dr. Vowler Short, then Bishop of Sodor and Man, that if he were appointed to St. Asaph, he would, on Dr. Bethell's demise accept both Bishoprics, abandoning the revenues of Bangor to Manchester, but retaining the united Patronage in his own hands. And that Patronage was to be 'worked' to make the whole Church Establishment in North Wales a Whig Borough. I speak from both interior knowledge and exterior evidence. Dr. Vowler Short not only assented to, but grasped at the compact. He engaged, not being able to discharge the simplest Ministerial Duty towards one soul in the Principality, and being fully cognizant of the fact and grounds of Dr. Bethell's refusal, to take *two Bishoprics* with all their responsibilities into his own single hand. Bangor or St. Asaph was to be abolished, and Dr. Vowler Short was, in his own person, to be the sole Bishop of North Wales. Those were evil days.[25]

Exaggeration there undoubtedly was, and also a touch of paranoia and deep resentment, but Morgan was simply reiterating what many believed to be true. At a time when bishops were political appointees such statements would be readily believed. Morgan's comments, and those of his uncle, Archdeacon Williams of Cardigan (a disappointed candidate in the 1840 election), were probably as much influenced by political considerations as by linguistic and nationalistic concerns. These reflections may not have been shared by many, but what is clear is that there was a ground-swell of feeling against the appointment of a non-Welsh bishop. This manifested itself long before it was known that Short had been nominated to the see. In view of the deep concern expressed over Thirlwall's appointment, and the claim by Lord Melbourne that he had been unaware of the feelings of the Welsh Church, it is not surprising that a lobby for a Welsh bishop had been formed. This lobby was effectively silenced by Lord Powis, who ensured that as little publicity as possible was given to these concerns. This was because Lord Powis had a deeper concern, namely the retention of the see, which he thought this particular lobby would disturb if it pressed its case too far. He was probably mistaken in his opinion that Lord John would have backed down from his promise to appoint a new bishop of St Asaph because of the clamour that its bishop needed to be Welsh speaking, but, mistaken or not, Lord Powis's opinion was influential and respected.

Lord Powis thus endeavoured to counteract this local feeling, which was being displayed in the public press and by projected petitions and memorials. His point of view was that even if the new bishop was being groomed to be the bishop of a united see for north Wales, it was nevertheless a temporary remission. He was sufficiently concerned to ensure that this temporary remission took place that he persuaded his son, Lord Clive, to request the more vociferous of the Welsh clergy, such as W. H. Owen of Tremeirchion, to hold their peace about the need for a Welsh-speaking bishop. Although Clive accepted that the question of Welsh-speaking bishops had been first 'mooted' in Parliament in 1832–33, he argued now that the question had to be suspended until 'the more pressing question' of the see of St Asaph had been settled.[26]

Clive and his father were only partly successful but the restraint they imposed upon the clergy of north Wales, who honoured Powis for his long fight to retain the two sees, probably enabled a non-Welsh appointment to be made. For the government at one point were clearly investigating the possibility of a Welsh appointment, even though this option was being considered alongside the claims of Short. Lord Richard Grosvenor, an influential advisor of Lord John, had sounded out various Welsh correspondents and reported back to his master. The dean of Windsor, George Neville Grenville, whom Grosvenor noted had held a large living in the vacant diocese for many years (he was rector of Hawarden between 1814 and 1834), and Lloyd Mostyn, 'the great seigneur of that county', both advised the appointment of a Welsh speaker. This, said the dean, would be the greatest blessing that could be conferred upon that country, and Grosvenor reported that Mostyn had offered his thanks to him 'for endeavouring to demonstrate to Lord John the necessity of appointing' a Welshman. There was also the desire that the new bishop should be distinguished for piety and in the successful management of a large and populous parish, rather than as the head of a college. What was required, added Mostyn, was a man whose pastoral concern would win the hearts of the people. He added that a clergyman who had not passed through the 'ordeal' of parochial life was unqualified, in his opinion, for 'the sacred office'. One name had even been suggested to Grosvenor which he had followed up with various enquiries. This was Joseph Baylee, vicar of Birkenhead and founder and principal of what later became St Aidan's theological college. Lord Denbigh noted that as he had a considerable number of Welsh people in his parish, he had learnt Welsh and preached to them regularly. Furthermore, he was in the prime of life and he possessed great physical and mental energy.[27]

A promise had also been made by Lord John, then leader of the House of Commons, when the clause requiring Welsh-speaking bishops had been struck out of the Established Church Bill of 1836, that he would regard its principle as binding upon himself and his party.[28] It was certainly believed that a more powerful advocacy of these Welsh claims, and this promise in particular, might have swayed Lord John to favour such an appointment. Certainly some pressure in favour of a Welsh appointment was exerted, but it was not sufficient to attract government notice. For example, some agitation was made by the same lobby which had protested against Thirlwall's appointment to St Davids in 1840 and whose pressure had encouraged him to learn the language sufficiently well to enable him to preach in it – to the admiration if not the edification of his hearers!

W. H. Owen has already been noted as one of the leaders of the pro-Welsh bishop lobby. His own position was summed up by his comment that while he did not attribute the extensive and alarming prevalence of dissent in Wales to the episcopal ignorance of the Welsh language, he yet believed there was little or no hope of reforming and reviving the Church until it had active Welsh-speaking bishops. In his three letters to Clive he noted that his clerical brethren in St Asaph felt that an effort ought to be made to obtain a Welsh bishop, adding by way of clarification, 'I mean acquaintance with the Welsh language'. Another letter stated that the feeling was more widespread than even he had originally thought. At a Church Missionary Society meeting at Mold the clergy had 'expressed themselves warmly on this subject', and as a result Archdeacon Clough had consented to call a meeting of the clergy in order to petition the Queen for the appointment of a clergyman acquainted with the Welsh language to the see. He asked if Clive believed that Lord John Russell would delay any appointment until this memorial had been presented.[29] At the same time a connection was drawn between the need for a Welsh speaker and the exercise of the considerable patronage in the gift of the bishop of St Asaph, which a number of writers believed Bishop Carey had used in an unjust way.[30]

The newspapers too added their comments. *The Carnarvon and Denbigh Herald* not only promoted the appointment of a Welsh-speaking candidate, it also attacked those who argued otherwise. It even suggested that pressure was being exerted for the appointment of the Tory and English-speaking dean of Bangor, J. H. Cotton. Nevertheless, the paper rather spoilt itself by suggesting that the new bishop should be pledged to accept the see of Bangor when that became vacant, and so open the way for the new see of Manchester.[31]

The restraint commanded by Lord Powis was lifted when Short's appointment was announced. One of many protests may be noted. This was in the form of an open letter to Lord John Russell. Signed by 'Snowdonensis', it appeared in the *Carnarvon and Denbigh Herald* of 7 November 1846. The writer argued that the appointment of Dr Short as bishop of a Welsh see in so far as he was not Welsh speaking 'is wholly unjustifiable on any principle of reason, justice, common sense, or sound policy; as no Bishop, under such circumstances, can efficiently discharge the important duties of his office'. One might imagine a case in which an English bishop was appointed to New Zealand, or some such 'uncivilised country', and one would expect him to learn the local language, but this was an area where it would not be expected that native speakers were suitable for episcopal office. But surely, the writer continued, this was not the case in Wales? Was the prime minister declaring that Wales had no persons qualified for the office of bishop? If Lord John claimed to be a great reformer, and one opposed to all abuses, why should he allow this particular abuse to continue? There could be but one answer. In his appointment of bishops he is accountable to no one, and he 'therefore appoints a political or private friend'. But, pondered 'Snowdonensis', 'is the *temporal good of one individual* to be considered paramount to the spiritual and eternal good of thousands?' He trusted that this 'appointment of a Bishop ignorant of the Welsh language will be the last instance of such long, shameful and crying injustice to this country; to which is principally attributable the present state of dissent and disorder in the Church'.[32]

It may be that Lord John Russell or his advisors took note of this and other remarks, for his next appointment to a Welsh see, that of Alfred Ollivant to Llandaff in 1849, was governed by his desire to find a 'divine who, with eminent learning, and those other qualifications which are generally sought for in a person filling the office of bishop, combined a knowledge of the Welsh language'.[33]

Short's Episcopate

There was thus a muted opposition to Short's appointment to St Asaph on linguistic grounds, linked with a clearly articulated fear that a bishop having so much patronage at his disposal would possess a substantial power over his clergy. Bishop Bethell of Bangor and several of the other Anglo-Welsh bishops frequently ridiculed these assertions. They argued that because most of their diocesan work lay in supervising and advising their clergy, all of whom spoke English, their infrequent excursions into their dioceses to confirm or to consecrate new churches did not matter that much. Did not the local clergy carefully prepare the confirmees about the meaning of the English rite they would undergo, and did not the bishop's chaplain translate into Welsh the bishop's English words? Yet however right such sentiments may have been in theory, it was surely not the way to endorse the Church's ministry to Welsh speakers, and clearly the Welsh clergy never felt at ease with such English bishops as Thirlwall and Short. The position was not made any easier by Short's insistence that Wales was but a part of England,[34] or by his obvious disparagement of the Welsh tongue, possibly reflecting his own sense of linguistic inferiority. David Howell, then vicar of Wrexham and later dean of St Davids, speaking to the Manchester Church Congress of 1888, gave an illustration of this disparagement. After administering confirmation in English in an exclusively Welsh parish in the 1860's, Short publicly thanked God, at the luncheon which followed, that he did not understand Welsh.[35] 'Cymro', writing in a local paper, suggested that Short was 'labouring under the most intense prejudice against every thing belonging to Wales, sorely to the detriment of good feeling in the diocese'.[36] Those who had opposed his appointment on linguistic grounds had clearly left their mark.

Two of Short's clergy came into violent confrontation with him, and the record they themselves wrote of these episodes, however biased they may have been, illustrates further the difficulties foreseen at the time of Short's appointment.

Robert Roberts, 'Y Sgolor Mawr', (1834–85) was one of the two. Ordained by Short he served various curacies in the diocese, until Short virtually expelled him from the ministry of the Church for having been seen inebriated, assuming his guilt before he had heard Roberts's defence. Roberts complained of Short's 'hard, callous, treatment',[37] and discovered that his bishop had so much patronage in his diocese that he could make life impossible for a curate who fell out with him. Indeed, he could ruin his chances elsewhere by writing to an episcopal colleague to blacken his character should he dare seek clerical employment in another diocese. Roberts later emigrated to Australia where he wrote his now celebrated auto-biography. He noted Short's love of flattery, and humourously commented on the senior clerics who offered it to him![38]

Roberts's strictures were mild compared to those of Richard Williams Morgan. Morgan was perpetual curate of Tregynon between 1842 and 1862; an eisteddfod figure, prolific writer, and later in his life an *episcopi vagantes*. A grandson of John Williams, the cele-brated headmaster of Ystrad Meurig grammar school – a notable seminary for Welsh clergy – and thus a nephew of John Williams, archdeacon of Cardigan and an eminent educationalist, Morgan believed he had incurred the enmity of Short because he had opposed his appointment to St Asaph; an appointment he claimed had been in 'defiance of the personal expostulation' of the Queen.[39] Morgan was no diplomat, and in a series of pamphlets denounced Short over and over again. In his *Scheme for the Reconstruction of the Church Episcopate and its Patronage in Wales*[40] Morgan pro-posed a plan to take most of the episcopal patronage out of the bishops' hands, citing as evidence one of Short's appointments, that of the bishop's brother-in-law, Robert Wickham, to the archdeaconry of St Asaph. Wickham knew no Welsh but was yet required to visit Welsh parishes, charge Welsh churchwardens, and examine Welsh candidates for Holy Orders.[41] After suggesting that Short and Bethell would never have accepted their bishoprics had their value been £200 per annum, but would have declined them because of their linguistic incapacity, to the admiration of all, he continued:

> Every Clergyman in North Wales has his ministry at this moment para-lyzed by the men he is compelled to acknowledge as his Bishops. These two words, 'Your Bishops,' shut him up . . . Thus, one of the worst effects we owe to the Anglo-Welsh Bishops is the annihilation of the Faith of the People in the moral sincerity of the Established Clergy. The People see that those men who ought to be the first to vindicate the Principles of the Prayer Book and of the Church in which they hold their livings . . . fear to breathe a whisper against a Bishop who can nei-ther administer the Sacraments nor preach the Gospel – who is himself the incarnation in its most lucrative form of a depravation infinitely more destructive to all true Religion, and more condemned by the Church, than the milder schism and aberrations of Dissent, against which both High-Church and Low-Church pour a constant roll of ful-minations from their Pulpits. The explanation lies on the surface. The

Clergy are at the mercy of their Bishops. They dare not, for the sake of their families, their livings, and their prospects, utter a syllable against the chief Dissenter of all – *because that Dissenter has the Patronage of the whole Diocese in his hands* . . . The Clergy of Wales, so long as they choose for such dangerous reasons to submit to Anglo-Welsh Bishops, are disqualified from objecting to Dissent. The great Dissent in Wales is not that which itinerates the country, preaching in Welsh to the Welsh Yeomanry and Peasantry on moss and moor and wild, for its bare travelling expenses, but that which sits clothed in fine linen in Palaces, and draws its quarterly cheques in thousands for not preaching to the Welsh People at all.[42]

In his *The Church and its Episcopal Corruptions in Wales*,[43] Morgan even accused Short of being a Whig commissioner in Wales rather than a bishop of the Church. He alleged that ' "I" was a letter more in favour with Dr Short than all the rest of the Alphabet'.[44] It was not to be wondered at that Short, in all his dealings in his diocese, had shown his bigoted hatred of all things Welsh; calling Welsh speakers, from peers to peasants, barbarians, and describing Wales as a barbarian country so long as it was inhabited by the Welsh.[45] With such beliefs claimed Morgan, it was not surprising that Short marked out 'as the special objects of his vindictiveness, any clergyman whose opinions were known to be adverse' to his episcopal appointment and to his incapacity in the Welsh language.[46] Here Morgan was perceptive, for this was a trait well known in Short's life ever since his Oxford days as a tutor, 'where he made every matter of insubordination a personal quarrel, not a simple question of right and wrong'.[47] This trait may well have increased after the death of Mrs Short.

Morgan's own case illustrated this episcopal vindictiveness. On the testimony of an unreliable Roman Catholic in Lancashire, the vicar of whose parish had warned Short of his character, Morgan was accused by the bishop of having fathered an illegitimate child with his former maid. Even though Short had admitted at one stage that he had no evidence to support his allegations, he allowed Morgan no redress whatsoever. He had refused to countersign testimonials in Morgan's favour, even though they were signed by prominent and respected clergymen in his diocese, and supported in one case by three episcopal signatures. The result was that Morgan was unable to obtain any alternative clerical employment. Equally unable on the grounds of cost to take the matter to the ecclesiastical courts, Morgan had to suffer what he believed was a case of monstrous injustice. No wonder he was bitter, especially when Short sequestrated his parish. In published correspondence between himself and the archbishop of Canterbury, Morgan argued that Short was a usurper, pretender and intruder in describing himself as a bishop of a Welsh see when he could not minister in a language understood by the people, contrary to the twenty-fourth article and the coronation oath of the Queen.[48] Morgan may well have been consumed by anger and was almost paranoid about Short, but his basic contention about the damage done to a Welsh diocese by an English bishop holding such vast patronage was shared by many. Not all were in a position to speak up and others lacked the courage to do so, but one group and one individual made their own feelings quite plain.

The group was the Association of Welsh Clergy in the West Riding of Yorkshire. In 1852 the Revd Thomas James (Llallawg), speaking at the annual meeting of that year, complained at the way in which English bishops in Wales were introducing English-speaking clergymen into Welsh-speaking parishes. While legislation existed to prevent this happening in private patronage, it did not apply to those livings in episcopal hands, and in this instance Dr Short of St Asaph was a prime offender. Indeed he accused Short of establishing a policy 'to effect an intermixture of races', hinting that it was in order to hasten the demise of the Welsh language:

> They might certainly laugh at the sheer absurdity of Dr Short's novel scheme; but the bishop appeared to be quite sanguine of ultimate success. His lordship's plan of introducing aliens into the diocese would operate most unjustly upon the native clergy, who ought to be appointed to those benefices, to which persons unacquainted with the vernacular can have no qualification, nor particle of claim.

These livings to which Short was introducing his friends and relatives were not the poorer livings, 'he never heard of Englishmen being introduced into Wales in order to take charge of small incumbencies', rather they were the most valuable livings in the diocese. Was this to be tolerated? 'Were the Welsh clergy to be treated, as they had been stigmatized, as a set of "cart horses" to do the work, whilst aliens received their revenues, and did nothing?' He hoped his fellow countrymen 'would defend their ancient rights and privileges, against the aggression of aliens'.[49]

The individual who testified to these allegations against Short is an impressive witness: John Williams (1792–1858), archdeacon of Cardigan, who has been mentioned already. Celebrated as a classical scholar and an educationalist (he was the first rector of the Edinburgh Academy) he retained a passionate concern for his country and native Church, and was bitterly disappointed that he had not been elected to the bishopric of St Davids in 1840. In his pamphlet, *On the Inexpediency, Folly and Sin of a 'Barbarian Episcopate' in a Christian Principality* published in the year of his death, he made a bitter attack on Short as a 'mute bishop'. As Short had acted previously for Carey he could not plead ignorance that a Welsh-speaking people formed a major part of his diocese. Equally, Short was aware that his duties involved confirming candidates in these Welsh parishes, and must have realized that when the candidate could not understand the bishop's charge or his words of blessing then 'the whole character of the ceremony is changed from its original intention, and degenerates into a childish farce'. Yet he was still prepared to thrust himself into that office for which he must have known himself to be unfit.

Williams's logic was overwhelming: clearly Short knew of the necessity of a Welsh-speaking bishop for St Asaph, and that any bishop appointed who lacked these qualifications would be unable to perform its essential duties. Short had therefore compromised both the dignity and utility of his office, and

> must have entered upon it without a particle of that 'spirit of wisdom and understanding, of counsel and ghostly strength, of knowledge, true godliness, and holy fear of God' . . . The man who most needs to be prayed for is the wretched official who unable to earn them by the performance of his duties, blushes not to accept the wages of unrighteousness, and to occupy a seat which he most unworthily fills.

In drawing up the form of the ordaining of a bishop the Church had

> never contemplated the possibility of the consecration of a person who, like Dr Short, was unable to perform the duties of the office. It charitably presumed that no candidate for the episcopate would be so utterly lost to all sense of shame as to affirm the truth of his call, while in reality his condition was such as to render the remainder of the service a delusion, a snare, and a mockery.

Gaining office by such deceptions looked rather like 'a sin against the Holy Ghost'.[50] But Williams, of course, had been a candidate himself for Welsh episcopal honours. He also wrote in defence of his nephew.[51]

It is difficult to know how far these sentiments were held, albeit privately, by the clergy of Short's diocese. In 1857 an attempt was made to present an address to the Queen in order to remove Short from the diocese. It appears that the petition originated with a group of people in Mold, who persuaded their member of Parliament, Colonel Mostyn, to present it to Parliament. It may not have been unconnected with the bishops' resignation bill then going through Parliament. The *Carnarvon and Denbigh Herald* commented that both the north Wales bishops should take advantage of this bill if it passed, for 'their room would be far more valuable than their company'.

An undated counter-petition, signed by nearly 200 clergymen in the diocese (probably little short of the total number), noted the high estimation in which the bishop was held in the diocese and offered him their sympathy and support. It went on to mention how in the first three years of his episcopate the bishop had visited every parish in 'the wild and mountainous district' of his diocese, had encouraged his clergy to hold 'free communication' with him regarding their parishes and had been ready to advise and assist them in every difficulty. Furthermore, due to the bishop's energy and perseverance, as well as the large sums he had contributed, there had been 'a rapid increase' in the number of new churches and schools. It ended by trusting that the bishop would long remain over them 'in a situation where his labours had been blessed with so great and beneficial results'.[52]

However much one suspects that this petition was signed by many as an expedient rather than a honest statement,[53] it is only fair to point out that its eulogy of Short was not unjust as far as it went. While Short himself wrote to Longley on his appointment to Sodor and Man requesting his prayers that he would not domineer,[54] it is clear he shared the episcopal temper of the time which did domineer, but it was the kind of dominance that meant he was deeply hurt by the considerable criticism he received.[55] Nevertheless, he gave a leadership to his diocese it had not enjoyed for a considerable period beforehand. He kept his clergy in touch with the great Church societies of the day through his own involvement in them, and he actively promoted clerical education and encouraged his clergy to use the catechetical system of teaching. During his episcopate churches were restored or rebuilt at a rate of five each year and national or church schools provided on such a scale that Forster (the originator of the 1870 Education Act which introduced board schools) argued that his office as President of the Board of Education would have been scarcely necessary had all the dioceses of England been so well provided with schools as was St Asaph.[56] Longley appears to have used Short's own description of the work of a rural dean, based on his Dorset experience, in his terms of reference to his rural deans at Ripon, and these were frequently cited by other bishops as well.[57] In his visitation charges Short constantly urged the clergy to pursue a pastoral ministry, declaring in his 1853 charge that the improvement in his diocese would come not through episcopal regulations but through the improvement of their parochial ministry. He urged clergy to stress the need of family prayer, and in that charge included an appendix devoted to this subject. Furthermore, he had substantial private means so that half his official income could be given to the diocese.[58] In his reminiscences, Archdeacon David Evans, who had served as a young man under Short, was impressed by Short's encouragement of the clergy in their pastoral ministry and his desire that they should meet together in deaneries for 'clerical meetings'. He was a true Israelite, he concluded, an evangelical preacher, and one whose sermons would not go over the heads of his listeners.[59]

These, of course, were the qualities of a good bishop, but for a Welsh diocese there was still one thing missing. However inflated the claims and denunciations of Morgan, Williams and their friends (the allegations of his mercenary interest in being appointed bishop of St Asaph must have been particularly wounding to Short[60]) it must be conceded that there is no doubt that Short abhorred the Welsh language and felt much more at home in the polite English society that the Anglicized areas of his diocese afforded. He was prejudiced, it was said, against all things Welsh.[61] He was never a true bishop to the Welsh people of his diocese, nor, for that matter, of his Welsh clergy. Many were acutely suspicious that he was leading a movement to supplant Welsh in his diocese, at a time when the Welsh language was becoming a matter of high sensitivity. It was the result of their pressure, along with the actual example of Short, that probably persuaded all subsequent governments to appoint men to Welsh sees whom they had reason to believe were Welsh speakers. Ollivant of Llandaff and Campbell of Bangor owed their elections to this pressure, which culminated in Joshua Hughes's appointment as Short's successor, for Gladstone realized, as no one else in government circles had realized before, that an Englishman who had learnt Welsh was a quite different animal from a native Welsh speaker.

If the Welsh were grateful that a bishop had been appointed to St Asaph in 1846, they yet held it against Short that he, a non Welsh speaker who knew the diocese was Welsh, had accepted it, and possibly under circumstances which would have forced him to become the bishop of a united see in north Wales. It was not an auspicious start: neither, so far as the Welsh were concerned, was it improved upon. If Short made a reasonable job of his episcopate, it was at the expense of other factors, and clearly he would have done far better in an English see.

~ 4 ~

The Deceit of Lord John:
The Appointment of Alfred Ollivant
to Llandaff, 1849

Edward Copleston (1776–1849) was the last bishop of the old regime in Llandaff. Of a line of Devonshire parsons, he had been appointed provost of Oriel College, Oxford, having brought that college to pre-eminence as a tutor, and having defended the classical education of the university (which he had helped reform) against the calumnies of the *Edinburgh Review*. As a Tory he had been appointed to the bishopric of Llandaff by Lord Liverpool, to which was attached, *in commendam*, the deanery of St Paul's, this being the only possible way by which the new bishop could be given an income equal to his episcopal expenses. The income from the diocese was £700 per year. It was later said that Copleston gave away more than he received from that source. Although he supported the measure to remove Roman Catholic disabilities, he opposed the Reform Bill, though it seems this was more for reasons of procedure than from any disagreement about the need for reform.

According to the standards of his own day Copleston was a conscientious bishop. He spent most of the year in London on his parliamentary duties and in literary circles, the summer at his Devonshire home, and the autumn months in his diocese. Bruce Knight acted as his deputy in the diocese for most of the year. During his episcopate there was a small though notable development in the extension of the Church into the industrial areas of the diocese, and a number of churches and schools were built. But Copleston was more remembered for the unusual care he took over his patronage. Parishes were bestowed on merit. He never listened, it was said, to the solicitations of the great nor to the dictates of private or personal regard. None of his family received promotion in his diocese. Furthermore, Copleston took care that Welsh-speaking parishes received Welsh-speaking incumbents. He made his displeasure felt at the common practice of a non-Welsh-speaking incumbent in such a parish employing a Welsh curate to do his work for him. He came into conflict with patrons on a number of occasions through his concern in this matter, even with Lord Chancellor Cottenham. It was also held to his credit that he never sought translation to a more lucrative diocese, resolving to remain in the diocese until his days closed. The poor curates of his diocese 'felt they had lost a father and friend', said Thomas Dale at his memorial service at St Paul's. But on the other hand it was agreed that he was more an academic than a bishop, and had been appointed more for the service he could render to the then government in the House of Lords than for any assumed ability as a diocesan bishop. When he left Oriel, suggested the evangelical *Record* (quoting contemporary papers), 'the eventful portion of his life in a great degree terminated'. Nevertheless, the paper regarded the late bishop as an evangelical man who had 'firm confidence in the redemption of Christ'. In fact, Copleston adhered to the old-fashioned high church party.[1]

With Copleston's death the new arrangements made by the Ecclesiastical Commissioners for the diocese were effected. By these arrangements the new bishop would receive an income of £4,200 from the episcopal fund. The commissioners also purchased Llandaff House as a palace for the bishop. Copleston had purchased Hardwick House near Chepstow for that purpose, probably convenient for his journeyings to and from London, but, situated at the edge of the diocese, it did not facilitate easy communication with it.[2] The new bishop of Llandaff would be able to devote more time to his see and live near his cathedral church.

Promises and Expectations

As the bishop lay dying (he died on 14 October), Archdeacon John Williams of Cardigan, who was also warden of Llandovery College and, as mentioned before, a former head of the Edinburgh Academy, wrote to David James, vicar of Kirkdale in Liverpool, a prominent Welsh figure and a leading advocate for Welsh-speaking bishops, whose letter to Thirlwall had prompted him to learn Welsh. In this letter of 27 September Williams wrote about his suspicion that the bishop was dying, and added 'if we are to make a rally *now* is the time. Lord John Russel's [sic] promise that the resolution of the

House of Commons would be regarded by him and his party as binding upon them ought to be made public.'[3]

This was a promise repeatedly asserted, but which even Williams found difficult to verify. In a further letter to David James of 18 October, John Williams made it clear it was given after the defeat in the House of Lords of the 1836 resolution that Welsh bishops needed to be proficient in the Welsh language. Lord John Russell, Williams noted, had said that he would regard the resolution of the Commons as 'sacred as if it was law'. Let this promise be made as public as possible, urged Williams of his friends, for while it might not make him a bishop, yet it might make another Welshman so 'if well managed'.[4]

As we have noted, Russell's declaration not only failed to influence Melbourne in his appointment of Thirlwall to St Davids in 1840, but it does not even appear to have been mentioned or remembered at that time. But Melbourne's half-justified assertion that the Welsh had made no effective case to him about the appointment of a Welsh speaker on that occasion was remembered in Wales. As a result many resolved that at the next vacancy great pressure would be exerted on the government of the day to appoint a native Welshman. However, during the next vacancy, that of St Asaph in 1846, Lord Powis requested the Welsh lobby to remain quiet, for there was considerable uncertainty as to whether Lord John Russell would appoint to the vacant see or follow the designated plan of the Ecclesiastical Commissioners by which that see would be united with Bangor.

On Copleston's death, therefore, the Welsh floodgates opened, the need for Welsh-speaking bishops was circulated to the press, and it was once more asserted that the moribund state of the Welsh Church was due to its long domination by the Anglo-Welsh bishops. But not all accepted this argument. The low state of the Welsh Church in the diocese of St Asaph, wrote one newspaper writer who signed himself 'Presbyter', was due more to the failure of the Welsh clergy than to the appointment of foreign bishops. The clergy were intemperate, cold in their preaching and lacked pastoral concern. Although there had been some improvement in the 'tone' of the clergy, this improvement could not be attributed to the appointment of Welsh bishops, as some claimed, for there had been no Welsh-speaking bishops in that diocese for at least a century.[5] Whilst many accepted his historical picture, most preferred to believe such statements as those later articulated by the Association of Welsh Clergy in the West Riding of Yorkshire. It proclaimed that 'it would be impossible for Welsh bishops, whatever their character might be, whether high or low, learned or ignorant, to reduce the church to a lower position than it occupies in the present day'.[6]

An important distinction was made by a number of people on this occasion, although it apparently did not reach or influence the premier. This was the difference between a man possessing that 'classic knowledge of Welsh which an English scholar may acquire by study, and that colloquial familiarity with the vernacular idiom of the Principality, which can scarcely ever be acquired by an adult, however diligently he may strive to attain it'. This statement by John Williams, MP for Macclesfield, was amplified by the editor of the *Carnarvon and Denbigh Herald*, who managed to reduce its effect by admitting 'that the almost complete impossibility of an English adult acquiring a colloquial familiarity of the Welsh, and the fullness of its idiomatic phraseology, is not so important in the case of a Bishop, as in that of a School Inspector'. It was admitted too that even Bishop Thirlwall, who after the protests made against his appointment on linguistic grounds had learnt Welsh, and was able to preach 'effectually in Welsh', was yet unable to 'converse familiarly with the common people'.[7] As a speaker put it at a London meeting, if such an outstanding linguist as the bishop had failed in this respect there could be little hope of less accomplished people obtaining the desired proficiency.[8] However, not all were convinced that there was a need for the Welsh language, let alone for bishops able to speak it. 'Trefaldwyn', writing in the same paper, regarded the Welsh language as a curse to Wales, limiting its progress and its people's advancement.[9] By the end of the century many would agree with him.

Another anonymous correspondent, 'Asaphensis', writing to his fellow countrymen, argued that there were Welshmen in every post of dignity in the country, but 'in *Divinity* alone is the crop short, and the soil barren. We are of the house of Levi, we are, – hewers of wood, and drawers of water, – we have no claim to the house of Aeron; the jewelled mitre would lose its lustre were it set on a Welsh brow.' The Welsh soil was impoverished by plants of another clime, and the result was that the Church had fallen into ruin, a people had been alienated, and a hierarchy despised. But all this could be changed, he argued, if only the clergy and laity would rouse themselves to get 'an *independent, energetic, active, unbiased* HEAD. This is your work now,' he continued, 'obtain this and the rest will follow. But if you fail in getting a Bishop conversant with yourselves, and with your language, there is but one doom for you, the old system over again, and which must end finally in your utter ruin . . .' 'Be firm', he exhorted, 'be united, and the government are sure to heed you.'[10]

Following this effusion of newspaper controversy and debate, as well as Archdeacon Williams's advice, a number of memorials were addressed to the prime minister, Lord John Russell, about the need for a Welsh-speaking appointment, and probably reminding him of his earlier promise. One, organized by the third earl of Powis, endeavoured 'to gain a hearing for the earnest prayer of Wales, that she might have bishops who understood and could preach in the language of the people'.[11] Powis's concern may have been the greater since his late father had persuaded the Welsh lobby to desist from promoting this cause in the previous St Asaph vacancy.

The inhabitants of Anglesey also presented their petition, of which the *Carnarvon and Denbigh Herald* stated: 'we have never seen the great question more tersely and emphatically put . . . there must be a moral blindness in those who cannot see the sole inference capable of being deducted from such unquestionable facts.' The arguments, which have been stated elsewhere, commenced by stating that the great bulk of the inhabitants of north Wales worshipped God in their native language. Claiming that the linguistic inability of the bishops of the Welsh Church had alienated the people from that Church, the petition concluded with these words:

> Your petitioners, therefore, humbly pray that your honourable House will be pleased to pass such legal enactments as shall prevent any person from being hereafter appointed to the Office of Bishop or other dignity in the Welsh Church, who is not, by his thorough knowledge of the language, fully competent to the discharge of the various high and responsible duties thereunto appertaining.[12]

An influential group of London Welshmen called a public meeting at the Freemasons' Tavern in Great Queen Street. This was to arrange a petition in favour of a Welsh speaking bishop for the vacant diocese. It received the support of the earl of Powis, Viscount Fielding, Sir Benjamin Hall and various other Welsh members of Parliament. During this meeting speeches were heard declaiming against the evils of English bishops in Wales, and a resolution was made to memorialize the prime minister requesting that he recommend a Welshman to the vacant see. Unfortunately, Robert Jones of Rotherhithe's insistence that the memorial should spell out the necessity of appointing a native Welsh speaker was overruled. Instead it was resolved that while the meeting believed it to be 'most essential that the bishops appointed to the sees in Wales should be conversant with the Welsh language . . . they should be Welshmen by birth or lineage as often as practicable'. It was a fine but dangerous distinction.

John Williams, member for Macclesfield, seems to have been the principal speaker at a subsequent meeting to the above. He might well have been the instigator of these meetings, for the comment was later made that a member of Parliament sitting for an English constituency who had come from *gwerin* stock had raised the question, rather than a member representing a Welsh constituency, most of whom had been born with silver spoons in their mouths and had lost the language of their people. His words were widely quoted by the press. Many of the gentry and aristocracy of Wales, he alleged, because they were not Welsh speaking, 'were accustomed to ask where a Welshman was to be found who was fitted to fill a vacancy of a high character'. 'Why,' he replied, 'there were scores of persons in his country who would shed lustre on almost any office which could be conferred upon them.' Noting occasions when he had been present at the consecration of churches, when hardly twenty people out of many hundreds had understood the English service used, or the bishop or dean present could not understand the Welsh sermon preached, he asked how long should this state of affairs continue. It was a matter of right:

> that those who were thenceforth appointed to watch over the souls of the people should be, at least, acquainted with their language . . . Had Wales depended solely on the established church she might be in a state of heathenism at that moment; but, in the absence of bishops and deans who knew the language, God had raised up men in the humbler ranks to keep alive the religious feelings of the people.

Williams also noted his correspondence with Lord John, in which he had pointed out the results of these English appointments to Welsh sees. Noting the numerous petitions he had introduced into the house which 'indicated the sense of the country', he asked:

> Surely, then, my lord, some weight, some consideration ought in justice to be manifested for the welfare of those for whom I am pleading. I do not press upon your lordship the appointment of any particular individual. I have no private interests to gratify. I merely claim as a member of the House of Commons, connected with Wales, the same privileges for my fellow-countrymen which are unhesitatingly accorded to the New Zealander and to the Hindoo. The colonial bishops (as I am informed) are peremptorily required to possess a competent knowledge of the language of the distant people among whom they are appointed to minister. And yet this inestimable boon has for years been withheld from the peaceful, religious, and loyal people of the Principality of Wales.

It was a dangerous argument in one sense, for it would suggest to the premier that a man who had learnt Welsh, as a colonial bishop would learn the language of his diocese, would suffice, whereas the Welsh were arguing for a native Welshman. Lord John acknowledged his letter on 18 October, in which stated that he would 'give due consideration to the remarks contained in it'. It was hardly an auspicious answer.[13]

The member for Cardigan, Pryse Loveden, not to be outdone by an English member, also wrote a letter to Lord John. His argument was a little different and more to the point about the need for a native bishop. 'The system hitherto acted on of appointing Englishmen, appears to me a great slight to the clergy of Wales. Is it not practically telling them that there are none among them of sufficient piety, talent, and education, to hold the high and important office of bishop?'[14]

David James of Kirkdale, whose correspondence with Archdeacon John Williams has already been noted, also sent a memorial to Lord John Russell regarding this appointment. Having noted the usual arguments, James requested that a return should be made 'to the policy uniformly pursued by Queen Elizabeth of blessed memory, by appointing some good and patriotic Welsh clergyman to the ancient See of Llandaff, now vacant by the demise of Dr Copleston'. James continued:

If you should desire a man of deep piety and parochial experience, there are a few rectors, vicars, and curates in Wales, that answer to that description, upon any one of whom a mitre would look well.

If you should require a man of sound learning and fervid eloquence, the Principality of Wales abounds with such men.

But if, in addition to these qualifications, you should insist on having a man of unfettered mind – of catholic spirit, and generally concurring in the measure of her Majesty's present government – then let me point to the Venerable Archdeacon Williams, of Llandovery, late rector of the Edinburgh Academy – a Welshman by birth – a patriot in heart and practice – a giant in intellect – the greatest Greek, Latin and Celtic scholar of the age – a good orator – a writer of established reputation – and the author of the cleverest Treatise on 'GOD'S LAWS versus CORN LAWS' that ever was penned. I send your lordship a copy of it. *Nevertheless we beg to leave your lordship entirely free to make your own choice of the future Welsh Bishop of Llandaff.*[15]

James's petition was flawed. James had not only offered a name that was unlikely to go down well with Lord John Russell, but he had also compromised himself by partly justifying Williams's appointment on political grounds.

The Association of Welsh Clergy in the West Riding of Yorkshire also sent its own petition to Lord John, asking for a Welsh appointment as a matter of justice to the people of Wales. It claimed that it was expressing the feelings 'of the vast majority of the Clergy in Wales, who dare not make their sentiments known publicly for fear of offending their Diocesans, and thereby of prejudicing their prospects of advancement in the Church'. A number of its members, if not the association, supported the candidature of Archdeacon John Williams.[16]

The *Liverpool Standard* and the Bath Lay Association, and even *The Times*, agreed with the need; *The Times* stating that 'a considerable feeling was shown in favour of conferring the mitre on a Welshman'. Its editor concluded that while it was legally impossible to appoint a non-Welsh-speaking cleric to a Welsh parish, it was surely unwise to appoint a non-Welsh-speaking bishop to a Welsh diocese, although he added, 'the same objection does not apply so strongly to a bishop as a preacher'.[17] This was strong testimony, even if it was poisoned in part by the final clause. Hopes were certainly high that Lord John would yield to the pressure for a Welsh-speaking bishop.

And yet it must be said that the voice of the vacant diocese, Llandaff, seems to have been strangely and disturbingly quiet about its alleged need for a Welsh-speaking bishop. One of its major news-papers, the *Monmouthshire Merlin*, in announcing Copleston's death, readily suggested that if a native Welsh speaker was not available, a cleric who had some acquaintance with the language and habits of the inhabitants would be acceptable. Much of the battle appears to have been conducted in north Wales or among the exiled Welsh in Liverpool, London and Yorkshire. Some claimed that the reason for this inactivity in the diocese was that the Welsh language had been neglected within it, though both Evan Jenkins, rector of Dowlais, and J. C. Campbell, then rector of Merthyr and later bishop of Bangor, protested that this was certainly not true of their parishes.[18] 'Laicus', a noted writer to the Cardiff papers, replying to a criticism made of the subsequent appointment that Ollivant was not sufficiently competent in Welsh, argued that many of the leading men in the diocese

> do not trouble themselves to ascertain whether he knows the language or not, so little importance do they think the acquirement to be in the man who is set over their Church as chief pastor, whose duties lie not so much in the routine of parochial pastoral labour, as in the superinten-dence and oversight of those whose work lies among the community.[19]

This may well have been the reason for the lack of interest in this question within the diocese, and it is perhaps significant that one of the few Llandaff clergy known to have been involved was that fire-brand, John Griffith, vicar of Aberdare. But his actual involvement in the agitation is not recorded save that 'Cymro' said of him that he fought the battle 'strenuously', while he claimed himself to have raised such a storm that the premier did not dare to appoint any-one to the see of Llandaff who was unacquainted with the Welsh language.[20] The diocese does not appear to have been that con-cerned, and this lack of interest in the diocese for the need of a Welsh-speaking bishop became a matter of some embarrassment to the Welsh lobby.

The Candidates

Although it is said that the names of many candidates were passed on to the prime minister for his consideration, the names of only five Welsh candidates have been recorded.

It is possible that many thought that Archdeacon John Williams was such a natural choice for the vacant diocese it was hardly worth mentioning the name of anyone else. It was widely believed that in the 1840 vacancy he had had some claim to the favour of the then government, which they had unfortunately ignored or forgotten. As noted above, Williams was clearly the choice of David James but his paean of praise was so overdone it was more likely to damn him than commend him. Williams managed to obtain the support of many of the Welsh clergy in Yorkshire, including Lewis Jones and Thomas Hughes, and a number of influential Scottish peers, as well as some of the leading Welsh evangelical clergy including David Parry, vicar of Llywel and one of the major pulpit orators of his day, Timothy Davies of Defynnog and John Griffiths of Cwm Afan, many of whom had written to Lord John supporting his candidature. The Church would never thrive, wrote Parry to David James (who seems to have acted as Williams's campaign manager), until a man acquainted with the language, habits and peculiar habits of the people was appointed bishop.

Williams was so desperate to be appointed that he requested his friends to remind Lord John Russell of his solemn pledge, emphasizing at the same time his current political partisanship with the Liberals, though in 1840 he was noted as belonging to the Conservative interest. David Parry wrote expressly to his evangelical colleagues explaining that the archdeacon was, unlike his bishop, a supporter of the clerical preaching meetings they had established. Williams was well aware of the opposition to his candidature. Although the clergy were said to be well-affected towards him, they knew that the Anglo-Welsh bishops were against a Welsh appointment. So strong was their opposition that W. H. Owen maintained that the clergy feared openly to support a campaign for Welsh bishops, believing that if they did so they would lose any hope of advancement. Williams also alleged that the aristocracy were also against him for he would not allow their abuses of patronage to continue, while they knew he would be their 'inflexible opponent'. And, alas, he wrote, the 'popular' or Welsh clergy did not know a friend.[21]

Although Benjamin Hall, according to his wife, 'echoed and re-echoed his entreaties for a *native* Bishop', pointing to Thirlwall's episcopate 'as a sad proof of what he had always said would be the result . . . of all the most learned Englishman *could*, or *would* ever perform',[22] John Richards had a different story. He wrote that Hall, having been given a list of nine eligible Welsh candidates (having said he knew of none), and then discovering Williams's name on the list, said he preferred the present abuses to be perpetuated rather than appoint such a Tory as a Welsh bishop.[23] Obviously, Williams was now doing his best to become a wolf in sheep's clothing, but he did not succeed. Like Giraldus Cambrensis (Gerald of Wales), no mitre came his way.

Another archdeacon was mentioned for the appointment. This was Thomas Williams, archdeacon of Llandaff. One correspondent of the *Cardiff and Merthyr Guardian* wrote that various qualifications for a bishop had been suggested, namely that he be publicly known, pastorally concerned for his diocese and clergy, given to hospitality and eloquent in the pulpit. If such a man could be found, the paper added, his abilities would enable his diocese to be regenerated and he might kindle a flame of life that would spread far and wide. All who knew the archdeacon, suggested this correspondent, would recognize that he possessed all these qualifications. This was so. Thomas Williams was placed by Archbishop Sumner alongside Ollivant in his list of eligible candidates.[24]

Yet a third archdeacon was favourably mentioned. This was Charles Butler Clough of St Asaph, and even the archbishop of Canterbury suggested that his appointment would be much approved of as he was a north Walian.[25] By contrast, another candidate recommended himself. This was Sir Erasmus Williams, a clerical baronet, rector of St Peter's, Marlborough, who wrote to Lord Lansdowne noting the need for a Welsh speaker, and virtually offering himself for the vacancy. He was a Liberal supporter as his family had been for 160 years, and asserted that no other clergyman had claims equal to his own.[26]

Sir Benjamin Hall was said to have urged Lord John Russell to appoint his favoured candidate. In all probability this was Hugh Williams, chancellor of the diocese of Llandaff, and Hall's cousin. Archbishop Sumner, probably consulted, advised the premier not to be confused between the two Llandaff Williams's, and enclosing a note from his brother (then bishop of Winchester and formerly of

Llandaff, who was most interested in the appointment), which suggested that both were safe men.[27]

The Choice of Ollivant

In spite of all this canvassing, Lord John had picked his man, and that man was not one of these Welsh dignitaries, although it does appear that Archdeacon Williams of Llandaff had been a close runner. Rather his choice fell on Alfred Ollivant, then regius professor of divinity at Cambridge and the first vice-principal of St David's College, Lampeter. It appears that Archbishop Sumner had suggested his name to Russell, describing him as highly popular, a good Welsh scholar, and an excellent man. His letter almost suggested he had been the head of St David's College rather than his deputy.[28] Born in Manchester, Ollivant had had a fine scholastic career at Cambridge, and it was Charles Simeon, the evangelical leader of his day, who pointed him out to Bishop Burgess when he was searching for a vice-principal for his new college at Lampeter. If Burgess wanted a man of deep piety and extensive learning, wrote Simeon, Ollivant could be safely recommended.[29] Ollivant had gained the respect of all at the university, wrote one reporter, and in spite of his Cambridge chair he was regarded as being more distinguished as a godly man than as a scholar. In politics he was believed to be of a more 'conservative cast'.[30]

Ollivant's appointment had been rumoured by the *Carnarvon and Denbigh Herald* in its issue of 3 November, with the comment, 'but as the fact is not gazetted we are still in hope'.[31] Ollivant, however, had been offered the see during the last week of October,[32] though it was widely believed with some reason that his nomination had been a 'change of mind' on the part of Lord John Russell. The *Cardiff and Merthyr Guardian* in its issue of 10 November, quoting the *Cambridge Chronicle*, thus suggested that 'to whatever cause we owe the Premier's change of mind', the Church should be thankful for his appointment.[33] Archdeacon John Williams in his letter to David James of 18 October believed that if Lord John's projected appointment could be stopped for eight days then the chances of a Welshman being appointed would be much increased.[34] Although we do not know the circumstances, it seems this is what happened, and Russell's first choice, rumoured to be Lord Auckland, was deemed to be an inappropriate appointment for a Welsh diocese. Lord Auckland, bishop of Sodor and Man, had given meritorious service as a pastor in Battersea, and had ten children to support, but if he had no tractarian sympathies neither had he any command of the Welsh language.[35] His appointment was even announced in the *Monmouthshire Merlin* of 27 October 1849, accompanied by strictures on the Church's enforced connection with the state in general, and more particularly on Lord John Russell's choice of bishops and especially for his elevation of this Englishman.[36] On the other hand, Lord Aberdare, quoted in the *Western Mail's* obituary to Ollivant many years later, claimed that he happened 'to know that the selection of Dr. Ollivant for this diocese was made with peculiar care by the Prime Minister of that day, with reference to the wants and circumstances of the district, because I had it from the lips of the Prime Minister himself, the late Lord Russell'.[37] It seems possible, therefore, that Russell's choice was altered because of the pressure placed on him by the Welsh lobby for a Welsh speaker to be appointed.

A Half and Half Choice

No man, suggested the *Record*, pleased about the choice of an evangelical man and follower of Simeon, 'is more popular in the Principality . . . and we think no appointment could have been better, as none will be more generally acceptable'.[38] Sound though the *Record's* sentiments may have been, they were a little too optimistic. To those in Wales who wanted a native bishop Ollivant was an Englishman who appeared to have acquired a smattering of Welsh during his years at Lampeter. *Yr Haul* suggested that Lord John Russell had dishonoured the Welsh nation, trodden its privileges to the dust, and humbled its people. Like the Israelites in their Babylonian captivity Welsh clerics had to face the taunt, 'there is no Taff who is fit for the Mitre'.[39] The *Weekly News* suggested it was another example of the kind of appointment Englishmen preferred to see in Wales rather than a question of what the Welsh thought of the matter.[40] The appointment was in defiance of the cries of the Welsh, argued the Welsh clergy in the West Riding. Ollivant, one of its reports stated, owed his elevation 'to the agitation in which their society had been engaged', but his nomination had clearly failed to meet their expectations.[41] Archdeacon John Williams was downcast, both for the sake of his country and for his own rejection. Writing to David James he blamed his rejection and Ollivant's nomination on 'the Lampeter men and those of your party [evangelical] in the Church, Hughes of Cardiganshire heading them there'. Yet he added, 'it is not a bad nomination if you overlook the hypocrisy which requires us to accept him as a real Welshman'.[42] And in this choice phrase Williams summed up the dilemma of all those who had asked for a Welsh speaker. Lord John Russell could reply that he had complied with their wishes, but his choice was not a native of Wales and there was doubt about the extent of his knowledge of the language.

Though this criticism of Lord John's appointment died out when it was accepted he had acted in good faith, doubt about Ollivant's linguistic qualifications continued to be a subject of debate for many years. There were some who believed that Ollivant had practiced some deceit in order to obtain the bishopric, for it was believed that 'the Premier required the strongest assurances of his being thoroughly acquainted with the Welsh language, before he consented to his appointment'.[43] But this was to put more faith in the assumed actions of politicians than reliance upon the integrity of Ollivant. Benjamin Hall, the self-elevated champion of the established Church, was more charitable, and in a letter to S. R. Bosanquet hoped that the new bishop would avoid his predecessor's errors and minister to the spiritual needs of the Welsh inhabitants. His wife was far less charitable, and wrote to David James that she believed that as Thirlwall had been 'caressed and flattered by the Welsh clergy for his supposed acquaintance with the [Welsh] language, that when Llandaff was vacant the Ministry had discovered they could try another humbug with impunity'.[44] She argued in another letter that the appointment was designed 'to make an appearance of a concession' to Welsh feelings.[45] But Lady Hall's Welsh was equally questionable.

The question seemed to resolve itself into a test case. Did Ollivant speak Welsh at Lampeter and in those Welsh-speaking parishes that he served as sinecure rector during that period? Some believed that in these parishes he had acquired a competent and a complete knowledge of the Welsh language. The *Principality* claimed that few, if any, of the native clergy were esteemed superior to him as Welsh preachers.[46] A Welsh cleric, brought up at Llangeler, where Ollivant was sinecure rector from 1832 to 1835, and where he spent his vacations, claimed that not only would Ollivant have heard daily prayers in Welsh at the college, he had also held sermon classes where he had discussed the Welsh sermons preached at the clerical meetings held in the parish church. Furthermore, at Llangeler Ollivant had conducted a class himself in the Sunday School and held a weekly meeting during the winter where he taught 'the peasantry' to read their Bibles in the Welsh language.[47] But perhaps this was to lose the distinction between the ability to read written Welsh in the pulpit and lecture room and to converse in conversational Welsh. It was reported too that Ollivant had preached with 'ease and vigour' at the Welsh Church in Ely Place, London, the year after his appointment,[48] while he had preached with general acceptance at the opening of the new buildings at Gelligaer School in that same year. On this occasion a parliamentary row had broken out when it was alleged that Ollivant was unable to reply in Welsh to an extempore speech in Welsh made at the ensuing celebrations. Mr Horsman, MP, the scourge of the Ecclesiastical Commission, argued that the premier had been deceived by someone about the appointment, and endeavoured to suggest that the deceiver was, in fact, the new bishop.[49]

Writing after Ollivant's death, a *Western Mail* correspondent, under the rather trying name of 'Noncon Quill', argued that while the bishop had 'fairly succeeded' in qualifying himself to minister at Llangeler and his other Welsh appointments during his Lampeter years, he had failed to 'speak with any pleasure to himself or edification to his congregation. I heard it said that they understood him tolerably well when he spoke to them in English, but they understood not a syllable when he addressed them in Welsh.' This 'book-knowledge' Welsh was 'all Greek to his country hearers'. Ollivant, he claimed, was 'a stranger with a foreign accent . . .' whose 'cold piercing eye', and 'his unemotional nature chilled the enthusiasm of every young Welshman who entered his presence'. But this was not his fault so much as that of 'the mischievous system' which had thrust him into office.[50]

One voice at least was heard calling for a commission into the state of the Welsh Church in the same way as William Williams had obtained the 1846–47 commission into the state of education in Wales. This person hoped that the archdeacon of Cardigan would be able to give it the whole truth, though 'he has told me over and over again, that he does not wish to be a martyr'.[51] Others had called for the cancellation of Ollivant's appointment as his knowledge of Welsh was not sufficient for his position. But 'Laicus' in reply argued that there were many whose names had been suggested to the prime minister who had nothing to recommend them '*but* a knowledge of Welsh, and whose appointment would have inflicted on the Church in Wales a far heavier blow, and greater discouragement, than it has received from the long succession – so much complained of – of English bishops'.[52] A north Wales curate endeavoured to redeem the situation. He felt there ought to be thankfulness that the premier had been compelled to 'yield to the voice of the nation to a certain extent. A precedent has been established, which can never again be disregarded, and a door has been opened which can never be closed.'[53]

Ollivant died in December 1883 after an episcopate of thirty-three years. He had certainly started with one advantage, namely that he had trained many of his clergy at Lampeter; indeed, some of his rural deans were his former students. He retained his evangelical sympathy to the end; his voice, argued the *Record* with approval, was raised on the right side when the pressure of supposed public opinion or the usual episcopal terror of 'committing oneself' kept others silent.[54] His main concerns during that long episcopate were to equip the Church to face the growing demands of an industrialized society and to ensure that his clergy were reasonably learned and morally, spiritually and pastorally fit for their charges. Though there were many difficulties he probably accomplished more than most men might have done under the same circumstances. Unlike his predecessors he rarely strayed from his diocese, only attending London when church matters in the House of Lords or Convocation justified his attendance. His courtesy was proverbial, and though in his later years he grew a little testy with regard to the various tractarian controversies in his diocese (which often aroused evangelical fury), it was recognized that he had given outstanding leadership that had seen not simply the cathedral building restored, but a new spiritual energy and life imparted throughout the diocese.

The Welsh agitation for a Welsh speaker as a bishop had certainly been heard. The archbishop even congratulated Russell on 'consulting the feelings of the Welsh' in this appointment.[55] The agitation was seemingly sufficiently strong and influential to make

Lord John Russell change his choice from Lord Auckland to Alfred Ollivant, even though there was little agitation for a Welsh appointment from the vacant diocese. Archdeacon Williams of Llandaff was hardly known in London circles, while his colleague and namesake of Cardigan was sufficiently well known to be regarded as far too independent in character. The prime minister probably ignored the claim for a native Welshman to be appointed, assuming of course he understood the distinction between a *native* Welsh-speaker and a person who was familiar with the language. Even those who wished for the former expressed themselves with some ambiguity about this distinction. Consequently Lord John Russell was not given a clear message, while he noted all too well the Welsh gratification at Thirlwall's apparent success in learning the language, and the parliamentarian John Williams's argument that colonial bishops were required to learn the language of their adopted country. This permitted him to ignore those arguments that made a distinction between an academic knowledge of the Welsh tongue and a conversational ability in it. It was the latter the Welsh really required, yet it was hardly unnatural for the prime minister to see Ollivant, a man known in both Welsh and English church circles as a good, learned and spiritual man, one who was believed to possess an adequate knowledge of the Welsh language, as the most suitable man for the diocese. The Welsh flattery of Thirlwall may have had much to answer for, but it is undisputed that Ollivant was the best man for the job and that he became one of the great bishops of his diocese.[56] And yet it is equally true that the Welsh felt deceived by his appointment.

~ 5 ~

The Scotch Bishop:
James Colquhoun Campbell and
the Appointment to Bangor, 1859

Christopher Bethell (1773–1859) was the oldest prelate on the episcopal bench when he died on 19 April 1859. He had held three episcopal charges: Gloucester 1824–30, Exeter for some months in 1830, and Bangor from 1830 until his death. Each appointment was more lucrative than the previous, and he owed these favours to his support of the Tory party, being as 'high' in politics as he was in an old-fashioned style of churchmanship. He constantly defended his high church views in pulpit, charges and pamphlets, attacking Welsh Nonconformity for its rivalry and 'sermon-tasting', and the evangelical party and its leader, Charles Simeon, for looking back in their delusion to a mere 300 years of history![1] But Bethell's enthusiasm for the early Church and its tradition still permitted him to accept the erastian nature of his episcopal appointments, and to remain as bishop of the most Welsh-speaking diocese in Wales even though he could not speak the language himself. He must have been aware that this limitation severely curtailed the effectiveness of his ministry. On his death the universal opinion was that he had left the diocese demoralized and dispirited, and his linguistic inability had made him 'a bad, because an utterly useless Bishop – a Bishop lingually unfit to exercise the functions of his office'. His death, it was said, offered the premier, Lord Derby, the change to rectify the damage Bethell had done to the Welsh Church, and it would also benefit the 'Protestant interest of the Country'.[2] This appointment would be Derby's first episcopal nomination, and many in Wales regarded it as a test case of his government's commitment to the Welsh Church.

Immediately following the announcement of Bethell's death the Welsh lobby swung into action. Believing themselves to have lost St Davids in 1840 because of their delay in presenting their case,

St Asaph in 1846 because of other political pressures, and Llandaff in 1849 as Lord John Russell was unable to distinguish between a native Welsh speaker and one who had acquired a knowledge of the language, this lobby was now determined that its old and twin grievances of not having indigenous and Welsh-speaking bishops should be remedied. The *Record*, whose local Welsh correspondents ensured the paper maintained an impressive pro-Welsh stance, argued that the prime minister needed to be reminded that it did not follow that if a person held preferment in Wales he was a competent Welsh speaker. It warned in early May before any appointment had been announced that both Archdeacon Campbell of Llandaff and Canon Maurice Bonnor, vicar of Ruabon, were good men and might seem to be attractive appointments, but they were not native Welsh speakers.[3] A number, however, queried this need for a Welsh-speaking bishop. Sir Thomas Phillips, the celebrated mayor of Newport and now a lawyer in London, was one of them. He argued that as Welshmen were eligible for all public and ecclesiastical offices in England, it was unfair they should claim a monopoly of these offices in Wales. Although a knowledge of the language might be essential for some appointments, Phillips did not believe that it was always essential for a *native* Welsh speaker to be appointed.[4]

That Phillips was speaking for an influential group is made clear by the vehemence of an attack made on him by an anonymous correspondent in the *Carnarvon and Denbigh Herald*. Writing under the pseudonym 'A Welsh Layman' he suggested that the appointment of a non Welsh-speaking Welshman would be worse than that of an Englishman, as he would be 'a wolf in sheep's clothing', having despised the language of his country. Arguing that successive governments had tried to eradicate the Welsh language, and that the appointment of English bishops was one of the means to this end, he alleged that 'having failed to make the Welsh abandon their language and worship in English, the experiment was next tried of having Englishmen who were to learn Welsh after they were bishops of Wales'. But neither Thirlwall nor Ollivant could do more than read through a Welsh sermon 'with evident and painful care and labour', and if an incumbent insisted on a Welsh confirmation that service would 'also be laboured through by them with painful trepidation'. The Welsh people wanted something better, namely:

a good tried Welsh clergyman of many years standing in country parochial experience . . . a man who has habitually preached for years in Welsh, who has a well organised Welsh parish, a Welsh congregation, and many communicants, who has the art of governing with kindness and gentleness, who is everywhere a Christian, firm and dignified, yet meek and unassuming. It is not necessary for a Welsh bishop to be a first-class man at Oxford, or first wrangler at Cambridge – or any wrangler at all. Oxford and Cambridge may be very well in their way, but they never yet have produced a Welsh qualified or efficient Welsh bishop, and never will unless there is such a phenomenon as a Welshman accustomed from early youth and mature life to Welsh parochial work – who has flown through one of those universities without forgetting his mother tongue, and what is quite as bad, losing his feeling for his countrymen!

These Anglo-Welsh bishops, even if they had acquired 'a trifling knowledge' of the Welsh language, knew little 'of the daily duties and difficulties of a Welsh parish'. They could not understand the use of 'methodist' practices such as cottage meetings and extempore prayer, and censured the clergy who followed these practices as 'low Dissenter[s]' who lacked 'church discipline'. This 'Welsh Layman' summed up his feelings in this way:

The distance and difference between the bishop and the inferior clergy is generally so great, that few of the latter are able, after a long life of successful labour, to arrive at the point when they can confer with their diocesan with any comfort or confidence. The former knows nothing of Welsh character or Welsh parochial work. He never has been accustomed to do Welsh duty as a native to natives, and he only submits to be spoken to as a penance, with the preconceived notion that a Welsh incumbent can inform him of nothing. He takes all his counsel from Anglo-Welsh clergy, who say only what will please and suit an unqualified Anglo-Welsh bishop.[5]

It was an eloquent appeal, and although there was some exaggeration and inaccuracy about detail, it witnesses to what many were feeling and saying in that day.

R. W. Morgan was one of the few correspondents to the public press willing to write under his own name. His letter to Lord Derby, requesting a native appointment, argued that there had been little dissent in Wales when there were native Welsh bishops.

But now, as in Bangor diocese, after a century of English bishops, there were only 5,000 church people in a population of 300,000. Although the Welsh people were paying £200,000 for the 'episcopal establishment' they did not have a bishop who could pray the Lord's prayer by the side of a dying Welshman. The appointment of such men, unable to speak the language of their people, was contrary to the very ethos of a Protestant Church, to the law of the land and the principles of the Reformation, which the Crown itself was 'sworn to uphold and observe'. But Morgan appeared to hold a trump card, which he now played. On a previous occasion, when Derby was not in office, and probably at the time of Ollivant's appointment, he had replied to Morgan that 'justice would in this matter . . . be done to Wales' if he ever 'assumed the reins of government'. Because of this pledge, claimed Morgan, 'we desisted from agitating the principality upon it'. Although Derby would receive many recommendations from high and influential quarters, Morgan believed the premier would disregard them in favour of his earlier declaration. This, he concluded, would bring in 'a new era in the annals of an unfortunate and abused church'.[6]

In spite of these assurances by Morgan the Welsh lobby left nothing to chance. The third earl of Powis, who as Lord Clive had helped preserve intact the two northern sees, and Lord Mostyn, organized a memorial to the prime minister, praying for the appointment of a Welsh speaker to the vacant see. Once again, in response to the argument that bishops did not need to speak Welsh because they were primarily pastors of the clergy, all of whom spoke English, it was stated: 'we consider . . . it is essential that he should take an active part in preaching and teaching among his people.' The petition concluded:

> The strong feelings of Nationality entertained by the Welsh, cause many, who are well versed in English, still to resort to Welsh Congregations and Services; and we feel assured that the extension to North Wales of the precedents followed in the last appointments to the Sees of St Davids and Llandaff, will be conducive to the efficiency and popularity of the church.

The full force of the last sentence was not to be noted until the appointment had been made, and bitter were the lamentations about it.[7]

The London Welsh, who had actively campaigned for Welsh appointments in 1840 and 1849, held yet another meeting at the Freemason's Tavern. The chairman of that meeting, William Jones, 'Gwrgant', supported by Robert Jones, rector of Rotherhithe, suggested that they could approach the question of Welsh bishops

> untrammelled by influences which bore upon those who lived in Wales. They had no favour to curry, no fear to apprehend, and no revenge to gratify. They could deal with great principles without entering into personalities: personal attacks had been too prominent in the discussions of this question in many instances.

It was high-minded stuff, which the meeting applauded, though in truth they possessed no higher moral ground than anyone else in the business of obtaining Welsh bishops. The meeting adopted a memorial requesting the earl of Derby 'to recommend to her most gracious Majesty the Queen, some native Welshman, acquainted with the language of the country, to fill up the vacant see of Bangor.'[8]

The evangelical *Record* also added its weight to this campaign, although it added a new argument to the campaign for a Welsh-speaking bishop. The Church in Wales, it argued, was not 'destitute of ministers of superior abilities and attainments' who could fill the episcopal office. Its editorial pointed out that a Welsh bishop, if he was to compete with the leaders of dissent, would need to be a Welsh preacher. His sermons needed to be extempore, delivered from the heart, and none but natives, whose native tongue was Welsh, were capable of this. Although Englishmen might acquire the language so as to read a Welsh sermon, they could never 'charm a Welsh audience like a native'. Besides this, a Welsh-speaking native bishop could do mighty things for the Welsh Church, bringing alive the Church on his confirmation visits and re-establishing the Welsh church press.[9]

John Griffith, then vicar of Aberdare, during the St Asaph vacancy of 1870, claimed he had 'raised such a feeling' in Wales for a Welsh appointment both in 1849 and on this occasion, that the prime minister had not dared appoint anyone who was not acquainted with the Welsh language.[10] This was probably typical Griffith bravado, but as he gained by Campbell's elevation, by being appointed by the Crown in his place at Merthyr Tydfil, his assertions may have brought his claims forward for this piece of minor though lucrative patronage.

And thus the arguments were made. But would they influence Derby? The Welsh lobby hoped they would, but no one really knew.

Recommended Names

As was general on the occasion of these episcopal appointments, numerous names for consideration were presented to Lord Derby by his political colleagues or by friends of interested clerics. On the very day that Bethell died Derby wrote to say that he had received a number of such applications; though it appears he was then unaware of his death.[11] Colonel Pennant and the earl of Powis were among those who enclosed lists of names for his consideration.[12]

The correspondent of the *Record* favoured the appointment of Archdeacon Hughes of Aberystwyth; he would fill the office 'with the greatest efficiency and zeal'.[13] Thomas Thomas, vicar of Caernarfon, who it was thought would have been selected for a Welsh bishopric had Palmerston remained in office long enough,[14] and Hugh Jones, vicar of Holywell, were equally recommended by that paper.[15] Viscount Newport was asked for his opinion of William Rowland, vicar of Bishops Castle in Shropshire, who had been highly recommended to Derby. He was ominously asked in particular about his familiarity with the Welsh language.[16]

A number of clergy in the diocese of Llandaff were also recommended and commented upon by Derby. Among their number was Hugh Williams, rector of both Radyr and Bassaleg, and chancellor of the diocese; D. H. Griffith, vicar of Cadoxton ('of whose exertions in the service of the Church I have received very favourable accounts'); Archdeacon Campbell of Merthyr ('favourably mentioned to me in another quarter') and Dean Thomas Williams. Derby regarded the dean as too old at seventy for the job, though he admitted he may have confused another Thomas Williams with him, accounts of whom were in any case rather contradictory.[17]

A real fear manifested itself that Maurice Bonnor of Ruabon, a man of English parentage but of Welsh descent through his mother, would be offered the see, possibly because of his friendship with Bishop Short, who appointed him dean of St Asaph in the same year. His linguistic fitness and patriotism were questionable, argued a correspondent in the *Carnarvon and Denbigh Herald*, for he had left the Welsh preaching in his extensive Welsh parish to a curate, 'and was a bitter enemy of Wales and everything Welsh', being a 'subservient tool of the Anti-Welsh Party' of Bishop Short. His appointment, he added, would imply even more hostility to the Welsh Church and language.[18] Bonnor's name was certainly mentioned to Derby, for he wrote to Lady Williams-Wynn, who lived in his parish, asking for her advice, though noting that she was unlikely to recommend a man whom she had complained about because of his frequent absences from the parish due to ill health.[19] R. W. Morgan averred that Bonnor had been recommended to the Queen for election to the diocese. He felt that Lord Derby should know, however, that Bonnor had no ability in Welsh, alleging that 'he cannot write, nor without difficulty, maintain a conversation in it [Welsh], nor has he preached in Welsh a dozen times in so many years'. Morgan also mentioned that Bonnor had to employ a Welsh curate for these duties in his parish. However, there was an even more serious disqualification: he was husband of three wives. Morgan took literally the scriptural requirement that a bishop should be the husband of only one wife. It was not that Morgan was accusing Bonnor of being a bigamist, but rather that he had married three times, two of his wives having died young. This, of course, was the time of the controversy about marrying a deceased wife's sister although this was not true in Bonnor's case.[20] But consciences were tender within the high church party on these and related matters. It was also alleged that the Powis and Wynne interests were campaigning for the appointment of Archdeacon Clive of Montgomery, who was a relative of Lord Powis.[21]

Derby's Search for a Welsh Bishop

R. W. Morgan suggested in late April that Lord Derby was allegedly taking his time in making the appointment to the vacant see because he could not find a man who combined both the necessary learning and experience needed in a bishop with a knowledge of the Welsh tongue.[22] Morgan was anxious to deny that this was the case, but in fact Derby had other considerations on his mind. Writing to Viscount Newport regarding a possible candidate, Derby noted the qualifications he expected: a man 'tolerably familiar with the Welsh language and able to converse and preach in it', one who was not a high churchman, and one who would not 'be a rabid political opponent, though I do not want a man who would be a government hack, like some I could name on the other side'.[23] He put these thoughts in a more delicate way to the bishop of Llandaff. After noting that tractarian opinions or high church views would be an absolute disqualification for the see of Bangor (even though the previous bishop belonged to the latter camp), he added that he did 'not wish to appoint a political Partisan nor an active Politician of any colour,' but, he added, 'your Lordship will not consider it unnatural that, *ceteris paribus*, I should be disposed to give a preference to one who, if in the House of Lords, would give a general support to a Government professing the Conservative opinions which I myself entertain.'[24]

One fact was absolutely clear: Derby wished to appoint a Welsh speaker to the diocese of Bangor. Replying to Sir Hugh Cairns who had recommended Dr Hugh McNeile of Liverpool, he wrote that if he was appointed he 'would have all Wales up in arms against me, for if there is one subject on which Welshmen appear to be all but unanimous, and I cannot blame them, it is that a Welsh Bishop ought to be familiar with the Welsh language'.[25] If this was a negative attitude, he wrote more positively to Bishop Ollivant, that while the primary duty of a bishop may be to be 'Pastor Pastorum' to his clergy, 'yet an obstacle which prevents him from freely communicating with his flock at large, and ministering to them the rites of Religion in their own language, cannot but be a serious drawback to his practical usefulness.'[26] He accepted the arguments of Lord Powis that the man appointed must be able to preach in Welsh and use the language colloquially, which he considered 'of the highest importance'.[27] Equally Derby diplomatically replied to J. W. Patten who had recommended Horatio Powys, bishop of Sodor and Man, that speaking Welsh was not among his merits,[28] while he wrote to Sir Benjamin Hall that the knowledge of the Welsh language and character 'is a very important qualification for the office of a Welsh bishop'.[29] Writing to Sir William Jolliffe, he made clear that he wished to meet the wishes of the Welsh people and fully shared the feeling expressed by the great majority of those who had written to him stating that it was most desirable that a Welsh-speaking bishop should be appointed. Only Sir Watkin and Lady Wynne had argued that the advantages of this might be neutralized by other objections.[30] Though there were many who did not consider this Welsh qualification an important point, 'I confess

I am of a different opinion', wrote Derby to J. P. Williams.[31] In another letter to this correspondent he stated 'that a knowledge of the language and the People is, if not indispensable, at all events, a very desirable qualification'. Although Derby added that this concern narrowed his field of selection, there appears to be a hint that he was significantly qualifying his initial desire to appoint a man who could speak Welsh colloquially.[32]

It is clear that Derby committed himself to obtain a Welsh-speaking bishop for Bangor as soon as he realized that Bethell was on his death bed, while the same realization had caused others to write to him recommending various candidates as Bethell's successor in the diocese.[33] Indeed, Derby was to wish that Bethell had chosen a more convenient time for dying (it was in the midst of a general election) though he added that 'as he had no option, I ought not to blame him'.[34] Nevertheless, Derby realized that to recommend a new bishop for Bangor, with all the complications this involved, would 'add considerably to my occupations at this moment'.[35]

The Right Man?

In spite of warnings that Campbell's Welsh was nondescript, Derby, writing to J. W. Patten on 28 April, wrote that he believed he had found the right man for the diocese, though it had not been 'a very easy task, and it has taken up a good deal of my time when I have not had a great deal to spare'.[36] Some days later Derby wrote to Lord Dungannon stating he had not yet 'absolutely selected a Successor to the late Bishop'. Nevertheless, he had rejected the claims of his nominee, Canon Trevor, the chancellor of the diocese of Bangor, as 'my enquiries have led me to the conclusion that the Diocese would not be the worse for the infusion of a little fresh blood'.[37] But on that same day, 2 May, Derby wrote to Archdeacon Campbell in these words: 'I am very anxious to have an opportunity of conversing with you on a subject of great interest to the Welsh Church; and though I am very unwilling to give you the trouble of so long a journey the matter is one which can be so much better treated vivâ voce than by letter . . .'[38] On 4 May, Derby submitted Campbell's name to the Queen for her approval with 'great confidence' in his choice. In this letter he quoted Bishop Ollivant's recommendation: 'he has been for several years (15) Rector of the populous and important Town of Merthyr Tydfil where he has won universal respect by his high principle, his laborious exertions, his gentlemanly bearing and his firm but conciliatory disposition and conduct.' Lord Tredegar had spoken of him in terms of equal commendation. Campbell had never meddled with politics, though his opinions were Conservative, and 'in religious questions his leaning is toward the low Church, which Lord Derby considers a recommendation in a Diocese where Dissenters and especially Wesleyans, are very numerous. Though not a Welshman by birth, he has made himself perfectly master of the language, and has been in the habit of preaching in it.'[39]

Writing to Campbell to confirm the Queen's approval Derby noted that it was understood he would resign the parish of Merthyr Tydfil. He continued: 'I have every hope that you will find your new duties agreeable, and that your promotion may give general Satisfaction to all who desire the welfare and advancement of the Church of England in the Principality.'[40] Derby also wrote on the same day to inform Lord Powis of his choice, mentioning Campbell's fluency in the Welsh language and his knowledge of Welsh habits and feelings, and pointing out that there were some excellent names on Powis's list of possible candidates besides that of Campbell.[41]

Campbell was born in Argyleshire in 1813 but had come to Wales (it was often said) because of his connection with the Bute family of whom he was a distant relation.[42] He had married a sister of H. A. Bruce, later the first Lord Aberdare, a prominent Liberal politician. He had been appointed rector of Merthyr Tydfil in 1844 by the marquess of Bute and archdeacon of Llandaff in 1857 by Bishop Ollivant. His reputation in Merthyr was high, and his 'exemplary piety, forbearance, and unwearied zeal as a Minister of the Gospel and Pastor of the Church', as well as his devotion to the poor during the recent cholera epidemic, had won him much good will. When he entered upon his duties in that parish he was the only clergyman there and had only one church to serve. When he left the parish there were five churches and eight clergymen on its staff, and Cyfartha had become a separate district.[43]

The *Record* welcomed his appointment as he was a warm supporter of evangelical societies such as the Bible Society, the Jews' Society, the Church Missionary Society and the Church Pastoral-Aid Society. Although it would have preferred a Welshman who could preach extempore in Welsh, rather than a Scotsman, its editor wished him well, noting that the diocese of Bangor was like a 'desolate wilderness' whose 'bright spots' were few and far between.[44] The same paper claimed at a later date that Campbell's appointment was 'a first installment, and an earnest of a fuller recognition' of the Welsh claims for a Welsh-speaking bishop.[45] The *Cardiff and Merthyr Guardian* maintained that Campbell's appointment had been received in south Wales with 'unmingled satisfaction', for he was, after all, an adopted son of their county, having given it the best years of his life. He had rebuilt his parish, giving it much of his private means, and had cared deeply for its poor. The appointment showed that the prime minister had combined 'as far as possible, the advantages of a University education and training with a knowledge of the Welsh language and of the Welsh people'. Yet this paper too (though it supported the Tories) had to concede that the advocates of native Welsh-speaking bishops had only been 'met half way' by the appointment of a man with Celtic blood who had acquired the ability to speak the Welsh language.[46]

Although Campbell maintained that he had met nothing but 'generous kindness and the most friendly feeling and greeting' in his new diocese, and there was nothing to indicate that they regarded him as a stranger,[47] the same friendliness could not be said to have greeted the news of his appointment. The voices of the *Record* and the *Cardiff and Merthyr Guardian* were muted, but even they had expressed some reservations. Other papers were far less friendly to the new bishop, who rapidly became known as 'the Scotch Bishop'.

The *Carnarvon and Denbigh Herald* argued that as Campbell was a Scotsman he was not qualified to be a Welsh bishop, but, being a favourite of the 'English Bishop of Llandaff', he had been exalted over the heads of the native clergy. It added that he was known as 'Doleful Jim' because of his 'remarkably lugubrious countenance'. Indeed, the editor added, all the chief places in Llandaff during the previous nine years had gone to Englishmen and Merthyr Tydfil, about to be vacated by the new bishop, would probably go in the same direction (it did not). Another matter allowed further vilification of the new bishop by this anti-Tory paper: Campbell was a lackey of the Bute family and had come into the diocese of Llandaff on the strength of this connection, having learnt a little of the Welsh language in order to qualify himself for that family's patronage. But his knowledge of Welsh was so slight that all the Welsh work in Merthyr had to be carried out by his 'deputy curate'. It noted too that his brother-in-law, H. A. Bruce, had opposed the appointment of Welsh-speaking chaplains in Welsh prisons. The editor continued:

> If the Scotch Bishop elect is not a Tory, he must be the most ungrateful of the favourites of ecclesiastical and political patronage, as he has been carried on Tory wings up to the See of Bangor, flying from Rectory to Canonry and Archdeaconry, and before there has been time to congratulate him on the last advance, he is again on a higher Welsh bough!
> So much for *justice to Wales*, and the favours shown by the Derby Government. The Anglo-Bishop of Llandaff might have been satisfied with *his own* Bishopric, and not have imposed his Scotch Archdeacon on Bangor. One person, however, will be pleased in North Wales, and that is the Bishop of Llandaff's friend, Dr. Short, who, if he did fail to place *the Brother* in a fat Welsh Living, will now see the sister's husband Bishop of Bangor – and thereby (if the Bishop of Llandaff dares do it), make room for the Rev. W. Bruce, in Merthyr – or some equally unqualified favourite.[48]

There were some who believed that Bishop Short himself had influenced Derby's choice of Campbell in order better to 'fortify himself against the barbarous Welsh'. Even the late bishop of Bangor kept himself aloof from that unpopular bishop, stated 'Cambrian' in the *Carnarvon and Denbigh Herald*. He continued in terms of heavy sarcasm by hoping that the diocese of Bangor would find in Dr Campbell 'a pious, laborious, chief pastor who will use the *pastoral crook*, and not run about the diocese with a *birch rod* in one hand, and *vulgar fractions* . . . in the other'. (Bishop Short had written a school-text on mathematics.) At least Campbell, unlike Short, had the northern ability of thinking twice before speaking once.[49]

There were others who placed the blame for Campbell's elevation upon the shoulders of Bishop Ollivant. One of those who did so was John Richards of Bron Menai, Caernarfon, who had previously written to Lord Derby in favour of a Welsh appointment and been heartened by his assurances. He now wrote to Derby, and published his letter in the press, to state that Campbell's appointment had not given satisfaction to Wales. Had Lord Derby made sufficient inquiry he would have discovered that 'Archdeacon

Campbell' 'was not the man for the See of Bangor, in consequence of his stiff, awkward, and imperfect practice of the Welsh tongue'. He understood that Derby had consulted Ollivant 'as to the competency of Mr. Campbell to officiate in the vernacular language of Wales. How came your lordship for a moment to suppose that Dr. Ollivant was himself competent to give an opinion on the subject?' Although Ollivant had learnt the language as a scholar, he had never achieved sufficient proficiency in Welsh because:

> to use it freely and idiomatically in conversation, public speaking, and preaching, like a native is quite another thing. His performances in that language have been characterised, by the most venerable of his own clergy, as resembling 'the first attempts of a school boy to read Greek'.

Richards continued:

> No doubt, Dr Campbell, from his long experience in a populous Welsh parish, will make a much better bishop in Bangor than the late Dr. Christopher Bethel [*sic*] did. Nevertheless, we can never regard him in other light than as a good man in the *wrong* place. The clergy and laity, who have heard him officiate, testify that he is but a very indifferent preacher, even in the English tongue – and no platform speaker at all. How then can such a man be expected to excel in a language in which he was neither brought up as a child, nor has been accustomed to officiate as a clergyman? . . .
>
> Now, my Lord, when is this infamous monopoly of the Welsh Bishoprics to cease? Why are Welshmen studiously excluded from the highest and most important office in the Church in their own country? What answer can you and your predecessors in office give to the Great Head of the Church, at the last day, for this impious abuse of patronage?[50]

Letters published by the *Carnarvon and Denbigh Herald* spoke the same language. 'Arvonius' felt that the Papists had obtained more satisfaction from Derby's ministry than the Welsh, who had been betrayed and given over to the spoilers. Better to continue 'the old disgraceful system of appointing only Englishmen', he bitterly argued, than to resort to such tricks and evasions by which 'the honest fulfillment of promises made and hopes excited' had been evaded. Another writer drew attention to Powis's memorial which had prayed 'for the extension to North Wales of the benefits of such appointments as those of Llandaff and of St Davids'. Lord Derby had acceded to their aristocratic wishes, for the signatories of this memorial were those who:

> are themselves English in feelings, tongue and interests; they bring up their children to dislike and despise the language they are never taught to understand (unlike all other countries); they endeavour to extinguish the tongue which stands between the total appropriation of all the preferment in Wales. They are not satisfied with having all the bishoprics, all the deaneries, most of the chancellorships and archdeaconries, but they must have all, and still they wage their war against the language of the Cymry. And who are the leaders in the movement? Why, the peers who have Welsh possessions, and the M.P.s who are sent to advocate Welsh claims![51]

R. W. Morgan, however, never ceased to surprise. He now welcomed the appointment of Campbell, although in so doing he earned the reproof of both editor and correspondents of the *Carnarvon and Denbigh Herald*. His claim to have been the originator of the campaign for Welsh episcopal appointments was passed over with some contempt, and the editor castigated Morgan for ignoring the insult shown to the Welsh clergy by the appointment of a Scottish bishop. The paper's correspondents were even more bitter, stating that it was inconsistent for Morgan to demand a Welsh episcopate and then to express satisfaction at the appointment of a stranger imperfectly acquainted with the Welsh language.[52] Morgan however made some points that were not easily refuted. He wrote:

> In making it [this appointment], Lord Derby has, I consider, kept faith and honour with us, accepted the principle we have maintained, and restored to the right basis of the scriptures and the reformation the future appointments to Welsh sees. Being a liberal, I am the more bound to do justice in this important matter to Lord Derby, and no one will, I think, charge me with fearing or flattering bishops. Personally, I know nothing of Dr Campbell, nor of his friends, relatives, and connections. It is on broad public grounds I express the above opinion.

Starting from the premise that England and Wales were a united nation, Morgan argued that Englishmen were as welcome as Welshmen to fill the nation's pulpits 'provided they are equal to the duties of their position. The question is not between this and that race, but between competency and incompetency, ability and disability.' In his letter to Lord Derby, Morgan had argued:

> We care not whether the bishop to be appointed to Bangor be English, Scotch, Welsh, or Irish by birth or blood, provided he has long ministered in the Welsh tongue in the Welsh Church itself among our own people. From this principle I have never swerved, knowing it to be the true one, the only one in unison with the inexclusive brotherhood of the Christian Church, the only one that could never fail us, and that would ultimately be sure to crown our efforts and sacrifices with success.

As all the evidence from south Wales affirmed that Campbell spoke, ministered in and preached in Welsh, Morgan believed that Lord Derby had given the Welsh Church the justice for which it prayed. Furthermore, he added, 'no previous bishop has laboured parochially in a Welsh parish, or devoted his days to Welsh work, or earned promotion by services in the midst of the Welsh people.' Campbell had spent fifteen years in 'the largest, the most exhausting, and the least attractive town in the Principality'. They had asked Lord Derby to give them a bishop 'who had long ministered in the Welsh tongue in the church itself, among our own people'. Lord Derby had done so. Not only did this appointment 'establish the principle of Welsh-speaking prelates, but practically it lays down that henceforth important Welsh parishes in Wales, will be the nurseries and stepping stones to our Welsh sees'. But what could be more unjust than that a Scotsman, 'who ministers in Welsh as effectively as nineteen Welsh clergymen out of twenty, who has by long and arduous labours identified himself with the Welsh people, should be excluded from our bishoprics not because he is disqualified, but because he is not a Welshman born'. Welshmen would soon complain, Morgan hinted, if they were excluded from appointments in England on the grounds that they were Welsh.

Morgan took heart from this appointment, and that of John Griffith who succeeded Campbell at Merthyr. This appointment was also made by the Crown which claimed the right of appointing the successor of any man nominated to a bishopric. He advised the diocese of Bangor to 'let the Scot have fair play, and if you find him such as he is represented, rally round him . . . Welcome him heartily, and strengthen him with both hands.' But 'let him at the same time clearly understand we expect him to prove the Welshman he is assumed to be . . .'[53]

The Alleged Deception

Was Morgan mistaken? Clearly he relied on the reports that the new bishop spoke Welsh fluently. Opinions varied considerably. If one said that Campbell had had sermons translated for him into Welsh but even then had to struggle hard to get the right pronunciation, another wrote that 'it was out of the question' that he could examine ordination candidates in Welsh. Some suggested that to test his ability he should be given plenty of Welsh addresses which would require an extempore reply, and that every Welshman should converse with him in Welsh![54]

The new bishop's farewell sermons at Merthyr were in both languages, the morning one being in English. In the evening he preached a Welsh translation of the morning's English sermon at the old church. It was said that many attended this service in order to hear how the bishop 'would overcome the difficulties of the Kymric tongue'. But in doing so, wrote the local reporter of the *Cardiff and Merthyr Guardian*:

> he furnished abundant evidence of his having overcome the principal difficulties of the Welsh language, and what is still more important than mere elocutionary proficiency, the study he must have devoted to the subject, shows his strong sympathy with the Welsh people, and his deep sense of the importance of being able to commune with the humbler portions of them in their own language. It would be folly to expect any man to speak well and fluently in a language which he did not habitually use; and it would be an injustice to the Bishop of Bangor, who has not naturally a good voice, to expect him to preach with the silvery clearness of a native Welshman. Suffice that he preached as well as could reasonably have been expected; that we were perfectly well able to follow him through the whole of his discourse; that beyond the occasional shortening of a few long vowels, his delivery presented but few faults; and that any occasional indistinctness was attributable to the quality of his voice than to any other cause. On the whole, we believe that the congregation generally came away with a persuasion that the diocese of Bangor will be fortunate in having his lordship for its spiritual guardian . . .[55]

The *North Wales Chronicle* thus argued that the bishop possessed 'the correct pronunciation of the ancient British tongue . . .
We can unhesitatingly state, for the benefit of those who have not yet
heard him, that the right rev. prelate has acquired a command over
the idiomatic expression of the Welsh language quite equal, if not
superior, to many native clergymen.'[56]

But how could there be such variation in these statements about
Campbell's ability in Welsh? The editor of the *Carnarvon and
Denbigh Herald* had no doubts why this was so. Those who disputed
Campbell's

> lingual fitness to preach in the native tongue of Wales, and to discourse
> colloquially in the vernacular and idiomatic Welsh, are themselves ster-
> ling Welsh patriots, of pure Welsh extraction, imbued thoroughly with
> Welsh feelings, aspirations, tastes, and sympathies; and thoroughly able
> to appreciate the differences that must obtain between a mere cold, for-
> mal, grammatical study of Welsh, as a dead or classic language, and
> that practical, off-hand, free use of its colloquy and peculiar idiom . . .

Those who endorsed Campbell's claims to linguistic fitness were
generally not distinguished for their use of Welsh, but 'are known
to be very little in the habit of using it themselves beyond the
precincts of the butlery, the larder, the stable, and the mart'.[57]

This was undoubtedly true. 'Deiniol Wyn', writing in *Yr Haul*
after Campbell's death, notes that his first Welsh sermon in Bangor
cathedral was 'an awful disappointment'. Many of those present
were Nonconformists who had come to see the novelty of a bishop
preaching in Welsh. Although Campbell had learnt the language as
well as any Englishman [*sic*] could, his effort was a failure, de-
claimed this writer, adding that Thirlwall had admitted the same
about himself.[58]

Why then did Derby make such a mistake when he was so insis-
tent that he would appoint a Welsh speaker to the see of Bangor?
One may note how Derby, facing the difficulties of finding a fluent
Welsh-speaker who could sit with ease in the House of Lords, fit in
with his own requirements of being a 'low churchman', and in a
general way support his political principles, began to regard this
additional Welsh qualification as a desirable extra rather than an
essential qualification.

But there was also another issue. Derby was simply badly

advised. It was natural he would accept the advice offered by his fellow peers and the Welsh members of Parliament whom he assumed understood the position in Wales. It was an erroneous assumption, for Derby never realized, as Gladstone did, the enormous gulf between the gentry and peasantry of Wales. It was a gulf that transcended every aspect of life: social, political, linguistic and religious. It was Powis's petition that suggested to him that the appointments of Thirlwall and Ollivant were satisfactory to the Welsh, that is, of Englishmen who had learnt the language and occasionally used it. He leaned heavily on the advice of Bishop Ollivant, unaware that he was not regarded as a good guide to 'things Welsh' by Welsh-speaking Welshmen. Yet, it must also be said, the Welsh too had a part to play in all this drama. Flattered that a bishop had bothered to learn their language, they pretended that the bishop had spoken their language with an elegance, style and grace that marked him as a perfect Welshman, whereas they probably had hardly understood what he was saying. Such flattery, which Ollivant clearly received, probably made him believe he was a reasonable, if not good, speaker of idiomatic Welsh, and if that was the case with him, then clearly Campbell came into the same category.

Thus the appointment was made of Campbell to the diocese of Bangor by a prime minister who clearly believed he was appointing a good Welsh speaker. The Welsh, after their initial annoyance, put on a brave face, and held that it was at least an interim measure and that it meant that their case for a Welsh-speaking Welshman to be appointed had been conceded. This proved to be the case at the next vacancy, of St Asaph, in 1870. The appointment then of Joshua Hughes also justified R. W. Morgan's comments about the wisdom of appointing Welsh parochial clergy to the Welsh sees. This policy was to be honoured in five out of the eight subsequent elections until the time of disestablishment.

It was generally agreed that Campbell's episcopate was not a notable one. The *Church Times* criticized him as early as 1869 for giving a bad example of duty to his clergy by holding only one confirmation tour every three years.[59] On his retirement after an episcopate of thirty-one years, the *Western Mail* argued that it had not been marked by any personal achievement of real importance. The new zeal and energy now displayed by the Diocese of Bangor, as in the rest of the Church, it continued, could hardly be said to have received its initiative from him. Though good to his clergy Bishop Campbell's quiet personality was not suited for the headship of that diocese, whose real leader over many years had been the late Dean Edwards.[60]

~ 6 ~

'Wales for the Welsh':
The Appointment of Joshua Hughes
to St Asaph, 1870

'What an interesting contribution to a future History of the Church in Wales it would make!' was H. A. Bruce's comment to Gladstone on reading some of the correspondence relating to this appointment.[1] It is hardly surprising that this election of 1870 has fascinated historians and given rise to much scholarly attention.[2]

The Vacancy in St Asaph

Thomas Vowler Short, bishop of St Asaph since 1846, announced in January 1870 that he would take advantage of the act passed in the previous year which permitted bishops to resign their sees.[3] It took time for people to realize that under the terms of that act he was entitled to claim £2,000 of the income of the see, thus depriving his successor of that income during his, that is Short's, own lifetime, and also claim the use of the episcopal palace.[4]

Although a conscientious bishop, much given to exhorting his clergy about their pastoral and spiritual responsibilities, Short's main interest had been in the field of church education. Unfortunately, Short suffered from a common affliction in bishops; like royalty, to use Disraeli's phrase, he needed flattery to be laid on with a trowel. Possibly because of this Short never realized the low morale that existed in his diocese or the wide gulf that separated the aristocratic Anglicized clergy of the wealthier livings from the generally ill-educated and ill-mannered Welsh-speaking and *gwerin* clergy who, nevertheless, served their poorer parishes with much devotion and spiritual care. Regretfully these men faced the scorn of their bishop who felt that they regarded preaching as the most important part of their ministry. It was these men, too, who saw their prospects of promotion diminish under a bishop who never understood them, and who surrounded himself with men of a different background who equally despised them. Furthermore, they felt that his policy of educational reform was undermining the Welsh language. Short's visitation charges, which frequently suggested that Wales was coterminous with England, only added to this suspicion. Short, of course, was not a Welsh speaker, but not only did he provide the diocese with a strong administrative system, he was also extremely generous to it.[5]

The news of Short's impending resignation re-established the Welsh patriotic lobby's demand for a native Welsh-speaking bishop. It is hardly surprising that it felt that the previous two appointments, of Ollivant to Llandaff and Campbell to Bangor, were merely 'half-measures', for both bishops had only a theoretical rather than a conversational knowledge of the Welsh tongue.

It was assumed that Gladstone, now prime minister, would be more sympathetic to this demand for a native Welsh-speaking bishop for the vacant see. There were a number of reasons for this assumption that was not unjustified. Although Gladstone was an Englishman by birth and breeding he had married into a border family, the Glynne's of Hawarden, Flintshire. Gladstone had made his home there, which was on the fringe of the vacant diocese, and thus knew from first-hand experience its needs, and above all, the inroads made upon it by dissent, especially by Welsh Methodism. It was these dissenters who were Gladstone's political allies in Wales, especially Thomas Gee of Denbigh. Thus Gladstone was well aware of the arguments used by both churchmen and Nonconformists, namely that Nonconformity had settled and grown in Wales because of the Church's neglect of its duties and mission; a neglect occasioned by the practice of appointing English bishops to Welsh dioceses, with the resultant loss of Welsh identity within the Church itself. The argument was widely believed, although it was not completely true. Gladstone accepted that the efforts of the Anglo-Welsh bishops in learning Welsh in order to meet this need was not sufficient. Writing of their use of Welsh, great as its 'utility' had been, he argued that it had 'not answered the great and *paramount* purpose, that of placing the Welsh Episcopate . . . in a direct pastoral and spiritual relation with the mind and what is still more important with the heart of an estranged but affectionate people'.[6]

Not only was Gladstone familiar with Wales, he was almost unique among prime ministers in being a conscientious churchman, and a high churchman at that! Not only did he regard his political life as a sacred duty, he also accepted that his task in advising the Queen about her episcopal appointments was one of his most weighty responsibilities. His concern for the Church outweighed his political sympathies, and in this respect again he was far different from his predecessors. There was thus the feeling that Gladstone would consider the needs of the Church above all else, and that he was aware, as a resident of the diocese itself, of the Welsh Church's need for Welsh-speaking bishops. In fact Gladstone was convinced of the justice of this case, and so indeed was the Queen.[7] Furthermore, he accepted the urgency of the situation. The disestablishment campaign had just commenced, and as a result it seems clear that Gladstone saw his task not as simply appointing another bishop but rather of regenerating the Church in Wales so that it could become an effective part of the Established Church.

It has been alleged that two essays greatly influenced Gladstone in his belief that he ought to appoint a native Welshman to a Welsh see, if such an opportunity presented itself. The first was Henry Richard's letters regarding Wales which appeared in the *Morning Post* during 1866. These were later published in book form during that same year as *Letters on the Social and Political Condition of the Principality of Wales*. Matthew Cragoe rightly points out that in this essay Richard was endeavouring to offset the criticisms of the 1847 Blue Books Report which had identified Nonconformity with the Welsh language, ignorance, and immorality. Significantly, he comments that Richard was using the report's negativism as a means of providing a positive image of the Welsh people.[8] Richard, born at Tregaron of a noted Welsh Methodist family, was a Liberal MP who had received international recognition for his work with the Peace Society, though he was also a leading figure in the Liberation Society, which sought to disestablish the Church for its own good.

Richard's principal thesis was the time honoured one that Wales was a nation of Nonconformists because of the Church's linguistic and spiritual failure. Significantly, he attributed the success of Nonconformity to the 'surpassing power of the Welsh pulpit'. It was this preaching, which he described as 'intense earnestness', that had 'roused Wales from its spiritual torpor'. Compared to

Nonconformity, the Church was a 'hostile garrison' which had lost the confidence of the Welsh people and whose clergy were respected more as benevolent laymen than as pastors and preachers.[9]

It is quite clear that Richard's letters had a profound effect on Gladstone. Speaking at the Mold eisteddfod in 1873 Gladstone confessed that he knew little of Wales and of Welsh life until he had read these articles.[10] But this may have been padding for a Nonconformist audience to whom Richard was a hero.

The second essay was another letter, *The Church of the Cymry. A Letter to the Rt. Hon. W. E. Gladstone, M.P.*, written by Henry T. Edwards, the recently appointed vicar of Caernarfon, and published on 22 January 1870, with the clear view of encouraging Gladstone to choose a native Welsh speaker for the vacant see.[11]

The influence of Edwards's letter is less certain, though much has been claimed for it, even to the extent that it was this letter that persuaded Gladstone to appoint a Welshman to the see. But Gladstone was already convinced of this need, although Edwards's letter may have reinforced his previous conclusions. In fact Edwards admitted that his letter was a rehash of all the arguments used in previous campaigns to obtain a native Welsh bishop, so that Gladstone would have been reasonably familiar with his arguments.

Edwards reiterated Richard's arguments about the failure of the Welsh Church. The Anglo-Welsh episcopate, whom he blamed for the growth of Nonconformity, had been unable to contain the eighteenth-century revival within the life of the Church. They had also made the native clergy into 'a feeble imitation of an Englishman'. The real bishop in Wales, alleged Edwards, was no 'episcopal creature of the State', but a Nonconformist divine, Henry Rees, who had recently died. Though 'he wore no mitre and enjoyed no revenue' he was, in his day, 'the successor of St. David in his authority over the religious mind of his country'.

In the light of past appointments and in a desire to avoid another half-measure, Edwards knew that it was important to make a distinction between a native Welsh speaker and one who had acquired a knowledge of Welsh as a second language. Although two 'living prelates' had endeavoured to qualify themselves for their office as bishops in Welsh dioceses, they lacked the fluency and authority of a native speaker. Their sermons and addresses:

however grammatically composed, which are read falteringly, with a most unmistakable foreign accent, and an utter want of native force and fire, are peculiarly ineffective, fall on the ear without reaching the heart, and have a tendency to alienate the people from a Church which unnecessarily subjects them to the necessity of hearing her most authoritative utterances in foreign forms of thought, feeling, and diction.

The Welsh, Edwards concluded, while proud of their English connection, nevertheless demanded justice and consideration for their language and nationality. Furthermore, the fear of disestablishment, argued Edwards, was far less real than the need for justice to be shown to the Church in Wales, and he therefore appealed that Gladstone's 'ears will not be deaf to demands the justice of which cannot be denied'.[12]

Gladstone's Policy

Gladstone, however, had already accepted the justice of this case. Indeed, he was endeavouring to find the kind of bishop that Henry Edwards claimed was needed. Stephen Gladstone, vicar of Hawarden and the premier's clerical son, said his father had been determined to discontinue the old policy of appointing Englishmen to Welsh sees, which he strongly believed was wrong in itself, as well as causing the decline of the Church from its popularity during the previous century.[13]

It might be argued that this was no sudden conversion on the part of Gladstone as a result of these letters, for he had expressed his convictions as early as 1856. In that year he replied to a letter sent to him on this subject by a man we have already met, Richard Williams Morgan, perpetual curate of Tregynon in Montgomeryshire. In his reply Gladstone pointed out that while at that time he had nothing to do with patronage, he yet accepted Morgan's concern that episcopal appointments should not be used for the purposes of political patronage, and like him he lamented the estrangement of many Welsh people from the Church. He continued:

I should very gladly see the day when all the occupants of the episcopal sees [in Wales] might be able to communicate with the people in their own cherished language; but, I must add, that I think it would be an error to recognise a knowledge of the Welsh tongue as dispensing with any other of the still more essential qualifications for the episcopal office.[14]

Nevertheless, these two letters may have convinced Gladstone of two further matters which he had to take into consideration if his planned appointment was to be beneficial to the Welsh Church.

First, while these letters clearly confirmed Gladstone in his accept-ance of the great Nonconformist myth about the Church under the previous Anglo-Welsh prelates, they also made him conclude that the strength of Nonconformity lay in its preaching ministry. Gladstone thus concluded that the Church needed bishops who could out-preach the Nonconformist pulpit giants. Only thus, Gladstone believed, could dissent be brought back into the fold of *Yr Hen Fam*, the old Mother Church.[15]

By January 1870, Gladstone had clearly formulated this policy of finding a native and Welsh-preaching bishop for St Asaph. This emerges in letters he wrote early that month to the two archbishops, in which he noted Short's anticipated resignation and Archbishop Tait's recommendation of Archdeacon Basil Jones to fill the vacant see, and to H. A. Bruce. But, wrote Gladstone to the archbishops, 'for more than a century and a half, the Welsh episcopate has been, as a spiritual power exercising direct influence, unknown to the Welsh people'. This had been the principal cause of dissent in Wales, which had been built up 'into a system of extra-ordinary strength and compactness by the use of an instrument, which the Church, or the powers that be, by their influence on the Church, had cast away. I mean the instrument of preaching.' While several bishops, much to their credit, had made themselves Welsh scholars, and so obliterated the scandal of confirming candidates in a foreign tongue, much more was required. Although he requested their advice as to how the Welsh Church might be strengthened, Gladstone had already determined his course of action. This was, as he wrote to Bruce, to obtain a native Welsh bishop who could preach in the Welsh language in as powerful a way as the dissenting ministers of Wales, provided he possessed the other requisite qualifications for the episcopate 'in a sufficient degree'. This alone could strengthen the Church, while it would also let the Welsh clergy know that the way to the episcopate was not barred against them.[16] Gladstone consequently wrote to Dean Wellesley, dean of Windsor and the

Queen's confident in matters ecclesiastical, that he hoped, by his nomination, to redress the 'immense injury' the Welsh Church had received from the Anglo-Welsh establishment over past years.[17] Gladstone undoubtedly hoped that his appointment to St Asaph would act as a catalyst for the restoration and renewal of Church life in Wales.

Thus Gladstone's policy for this appointment of 1870, however much it might have been reinforced and modified by Richard's and Edwards's letters, was of an earlier date, possibly prior to 1856. This policy might be summed up by his letter to Bishop Thirlwall of St Davids, requesting his assistance in finding the right man:

> My own impression is that it is most important to find if possible some one who has the gift of preaching together with the free & popular use of the Welsh tongue, provided that besides being a man of zeal & piety & loyalty to the Church, he has the qualities necessary to make a just governor, & attentive administrator.[18]

The second consideration arose as a result of Gladstone's desire to appoint to the vacant see a bishop who would be capable of out-preaching the Welsh Nonconformists themselves. It meant that he needed to find a 'native Welchman . . .' who was 'a practical efficient and compulsive preacher in the Welch tongue' and yet a man who possessed all the other qualifications traditionally required for episcopal office.[19]

These traditional qualifications were social rather than ecclesiastical, English rather than Welsh. For a bishop was also a peer of the realm with a seat in the House of Lords. It was therefore expected that any person nominated for episcopal office would be not simply a scholar and a gentleman, but also one able to take his place with ease in this polite society. Alas, the forces of history were against Gladstone in this respect. The scholars and gentlemen among the Welsh diocesan clergy were, by their upbringing, education and backgrounds, thoroughly Anglicized. The Welsh language was not their linguistic habitat. But, on the other hand, the Welsh-speaking clergy, mainly because of their lacklustre upbringing, had neither funds at their disposal to enable them to receive anything more than a rudimentary education, nor were they gentlemen by birth.[20] There were a few exceptions, but these were mainly men who spoke an imperfect Welsh or who had served most of their ministry outside Wales. Basil Jones, appointed by Disraeli to the see of St Davids in 1874, was of this class.

An editorial in the *Saturday Review* summed up extremely well Gladstone's essential dilemma. After suggesting that the real need was for a native Welshman, the editor continued:

> In the present distress of the Welsh Church, it would be a great gain to find a man who has enough of the Welshman about him to bring his influence to bear on the alienated masses of the Welsh people; but it would never do to put a man on an episcopal throne who might indeed be a fluent haranguer in Welsh, but whose promotion would make the Church ridiculous in the eyes either of Englishmen or of educated Welshmen . . . It would be a mistake to choose a man, however eloquent in Welsh, who could not on occasion address the House of Lords in intelligible English . . . We grant that the choice is difficult, because the qualified persons are few. To find a man who is at once a Welshman, gentleman, and scholar, who is known both in Wales and out of Wales, whose appointment would be at once acceptable to local feeling and conducive to the good of the Church at large, is certainly not impossible. The breed is rare, but it is not non-existent . . . As long as Welsh is spoken, Welsh sees must be held by Welsh Bishops; but it would not be to the honour of Wales to be represented in parliament or convocation by bishops who could not hold their place on a perfect equality with their brethren from all parts of the kingdom.[21]

John Griffith, the fiery and provocative rector of Merthyr, disagreed with this summary and wrote in defence of the Welsh preacher-type clergy. The Welsh, he wrote, still had little hostility to the Church or to episcopacy. They would travel far to catch a sight of a bishop, and did not worry if a man could preach with acceptance whether he was church or chapel.

The Welsh Church, Griffith continued in another letter to the *Guardian*, was served by men from Cardiganshire and Carmarthenshire. These men might be of a low social position, rough, coarse, uneducated and rude in manner. But they could keep congregations, unlike those who are 'everything that gentlemen and scholars and parish priests ought to be. They [the Anglo-Welsh clergy] are laborious in their calling, anxious to do their duty, painstaking, and would be all that one can desire, were it not that they *lack one thing, and that is everything, a knowledge of the language of the people among whom they labour . . .*' and of which they had gained only a sufficient knowledge as to obtain a parish for themselves. It was from these rough home-spun men whom Griffith championed that Gladstone would have to make his choice if he persisted in his desire for a native Welsh-preaching bishop for the vacant see of St Asaph.[22]

Gladstone's vision of a Welsh-preaching bishop possessing all the qualifications of the English episcopate rapidly faded as he faced the reality of the situation depicted by John Griffith and the *Saturday Review*. Consequently, Gladstone was forced to change his mind about those 'other . . . qualifications' he had mentioned in his reply to R. W. Morgan in 1856. No doubt he regretted having to do so, but the urgency of the task set before him of regenerating a small but significant part of the Church of England, at a time when disestablishment was becoming a political issue, demanded that Gladstone ask the basic but generally neglected question, 'What is a bishop?' And if he answered his question by stating that a bishop was more a pastor of his flock than a figure in the House of Lords it might well be said that he got it right, even though it was a radical departure from the customary perception of a Church of England bishop of the day. It might be argued that by putting his answer into practice Gladstone helped further that pastoral conception of episcopacy allegedly introduced by Bishop Wilberforce of Oxford some years earlier. But Gladstone also had to recognize that to obtain such a man as he desired for St Asaph would be a laborious and time-consuming task for himself, and would cause much heart searching amongst his supporters. Not only did it prove to be one of the most difficult tasks he had to undertake in his premiership, but the advice given to him was not only contradictory but often challenged his basic assumptions.

Gladstone's Dilemma

Short's resignation was one of many vacancies at that time. These vacancies caused Gladstone endless trouble. 'Bishops seem to have a special spite against Mr Gladstone,' suggested the *Church Times*, 'for during his premiership we have been constantly hearing of either resignations or deaths.'[23] The St Asaph vacancy was the eighth since Gladstone began his premiership, and was the most difficult of them all for, as he wrote to Tait, 'the duty of recommending for this vacancy is most grave'.[24] This was in spite of the fact that Temple's appointment to Exeter had caused a wave of protest throughout the Church. The *Western Mail* even suggested that Temple was 'a heretical bishop forced by a despotic and self-willed Prime Minister on a tolerant and peculiarly orthodox diocese'.[25] Thus the prime minister had an existing bad press for his episcopal nominations, while he was also handicapped by the subsequent illness of Tait which made Gladstone unwilling to trouble him unnecessarily in his 'greatest ecclesiastical difficulty'.[26]

Nevertheless, in spite of these remarks, Gladstone took great delight in these vacancies, as his staff sometimes noted with wry amusement. Edward Hamilton considered that a vacant see excited Gladstone more than a political crisis. In 1882 he wrote of his chief: 'I doubt if a Prime Minister ever was so conscientious on this matter before or took so much pains or had so much personal knowledge of individual clerics.' George Leveson-Gower wrote in a similar fashion, and described some of Gladstone's methods in filling a vacant see:

> Whenever a Church dignitary happened to die – and we used to say that we thought that they did so on purpose to spite Mr G. – the whole business of State seemed to be put aside while he poured forth a perfect avalanche of letters inquiring at great length and in minute detail as to the comparative merits and claims of various clergymen for preferment. In fact he seemed hardly able to give his full mind to any other matter, however weighty or urgent, until this Bishopric, Deanery, or even Canonry were filled.[27]

Short's impending resignation was generally known by the autumn of 1869, with the result that letters offering advice, admonition or warning poured into 10 Downing Street from all over Wales. A meeting was held at Caernarfon in November in order to prepare a memorial requesting the prime minister to appoint a Welshman to the diocese of St Asaph.[28] Rumour after rumour swept through clerical circles in Wales, gaining added force from the apparent length of the vacancy. Indeed, on one occasion, the *Chester Guardian* was said to have been authorized to state that no appointment had been made as the bishop had yet to resign. This was in early February.[29]

Gladstone asked for advice from all those who were qualified to give it, and conferred with a considerable number of leading

Churchmen both by correspondence or by personal interview, as may be seen from the columns of Matthew's edition of Gladstone's *Diary*.[30] It is fairly clear that those who tendered such advice were aware of his desire for a Welsh preacher to be appointed to the see.

One of his more frequent, though possibly not so welcome, correspondents was that Welsh patriot, Lady Llanover, who clearly availed herself of his request for advice in letter after letter. Her letters contained intimate and often biased details of those 'candidates' she supported, and perhaps more to the point, of those she did not favour, an even more numerous group. If Gladstone seemed to flag in zeal for a Welsh appointment, she made it clear it was necessary for the sake of the Church, while she warned him against any other advisor who might be recommending the names of men she disliked.[31] Thirlwall, who was recommending Basil Jones, was a bad judge of character and utterly unfit to be a Welsh bishop,[32] and Ollivant, so far as being a Welsh bishop was concerned, might as well be in New Zealand.[33]

The prime minister made it clear to Lady Llanover that he much valued 'any assistance' given him 'in this most important duty' by her or by the Welsh bishops whom she was so willing to denigrate.[34] Thirlwall was not that helpful, however, often stating, when asked for a detailed report on a particular candidate, that he could offer little assistance. Furthermore, Thirlwall disliked Gladstone's request for details of a man's political opinions, for as he put it, he never made such enquiry about the political opinions of his clergy, assuming that with few exceptions, 'every Welsh clergyman is a rank Tory'.[35] Thankfully Alfred Ollivant, the bishop of Llandaff, was more helpful and Gladstone leaned much on Ollivant's advice.

Although Gladstone could report to Dean Wellesley in early February, perhaps too optimistically, that those correspondents who understood the position of the Welsh Church and its history were in favour of a Welsh appointment,[36] the actual task of finding a man to fit such an appointment was extraordinarily difficult and time consuming. 'I feel with you', wrote Tait, 'that it is very difficult to find a man who can speak good Welsh' and possessing 'all that [is] required for a bishop.'[37] In a letter to his intimate friend, Bishop Jacobson of Chester, Gladstone confided that finding a bishop of this class, that is a Welsh bishop, 'occupies much of my thought and no small portion of my time'.[38] Writing to Bishop Ollivant of Llandaff on the same day he added that he felt oppressed by this 'duty',[39] while he wrote to Bruce: 'I feel this to be very much the weightiest episcopal problem which has yet come to me.'[40] These were written in mid-January. A month later he was 'still anxiously engaged in considering the various claims to the Bishopric of St Asaph',[41] and at the time when the 'claims' of Dr Griffiths of Llandeilo were being challenged, Gladstone wrote a note of agony to Bruce: 'if you read in the papers some morning that I have been carried to Bedlam and that a straight waistcoat is considered necessary, please to remember it will be entirely owing to the vacancy in the See of St Asaph.'[42] The situation was so difficult that by the end of that month Gladstone had modified his opinion as to the kind of man who should be appointed. Replying to the bishop of Ely, E. H. Browne, himself a former vice-principal of Lampeter, he stated his modified requirement: a Welshman 'not greatly deficient in any other requisites of a Bishop'.[43] Such an admission must have caused him even more anxiety. Gladstone's great love of ecclesiastical appointments had turned terribly sour.

These remarks about the necessity of appointing a Welsh-preaching bishop to the vacant see, even if his abilities were inferior to those expected of an English bishop, might well have been written by Gladstone in defiance of those who tried to dissuade him from what his detractors later described as his 'experiment'. The most influential critic of his policy was H. A. Bruce, his home secretary, later Lord Aberdare. Lady Llanover's fear of Bruce's influence was considerable. It is clear, she wrote, that the home secretary is not one who has the slightest feeling for Wales and its people. She reminded Gladstone that his colleague had been thrown out at Merthyr Tydfil at the 1868 election 'against a real Welshman who never paid a penny for his election'.[44] But in this respect her fears were unjustified. Gladstone remained unimpressed by Bruce's advice.

Bruce commenced his rearguard action against Gladstone's preference for a Welsh appointment in early January. He then wrote to Gladstone that while he was aware of the strong feeling in Wales for a Welsh-speaking bishop, 'I have often inquired whether there was known to exist any Welsh clergyman adequately furnished with ability, learning and character to justify his appointment, even after making a large deduction from the average English standard of eminence, and I have utterly failed to discover what I sought.' While Dean Williams of Llandaff had been spoken of as a possibility he lacked the language, while he was a Tory of the Tories. That diocese contained no other men of the requisite qualification: 'our best men are either English or of English families settled in Wales and hardly regarded as Welsh by the natives.' Ollivant had had to replace his (Bruce's) brother, who had resigned a canonry, with an English import, Perowne of Lampeter, as he could not find a fit man among his own clergy. St Davids had no outstanding Welsh clerics, while Bishop Campbell of Bangor, his brother-in-law, had bewailed to him that he had to confer his best posts on men of inferior ability. The Welsh clergy who were regarded as leaders in the Church were those, like James of Panteg, who had obtained a certain celebrity through their eisteddfod interests and their eloquence, though he himself had found such men 'to be shallow, pretentious, and wanting in honesty and dignity of character'. The choice of three Welsh-speaking Englishmen, Thirlwall, Ollivant and Campbell, had been 'forced upon your reluctant predecessors by the absolute blank among the native clergy'.

Bruce now made clear his basic argument: 'I am sure you will find that a superior Englishman is better suited to the work of a "Pastor Pastorum" in Wales than a too inferior Welshman.' He dismissed out of hand the argument of Johnes and others that English bishops and clergymen had caused the spread of dissent in Wales. The weakness, ignorance and often intemperance of the clergy, together with the driving out of the Church of the few earnest men, generally the Methodist clergy, had caused dissent to grow, rather than the appointment of English clergymen to parishes or dioceses in Wales. Furthermore, Bruce refused to accept the argument that a knowledge of Welsh was an absolute necessity for a bishop of one of the four Welsh dioceses, and even suggested that such a knowledge would not 'increase his influence and usefulness'.[45]

As Gladstone continued to press forward his desire for the appointment of a Welsh preacher, Bruce emphasized his case even more strongly. Gladstone would never obtain a Welsh Wilberforce or Temple. He had heard most of the popular preachers of the Church and all they possessed was 'nothing besides the gift of a popular eloquence suited to an uneducated people'. But there was a far greater need within the Church than that of conciliating 'a people fond of lively sermons and impassioned oratory'. That need was the gradual improvement of the Welsh clergy. The Anglo-Welsh bishops had done much good here, but 'under bishops of the "popular preacher" type there would be a great danger of retrogression in this respect'.[46]

The Anglo-Welsh bishops shared Bruce's opinion, not surprisingly, as Gladstone's comments could be taken as a reflection upon their episcopal ministry. Thirlwall, while accepting that a mastery of the Welsh language 'as an incident of Welsh birth should be a sine qua non', nevertheless warned that 'a mere popular preacher, suited to their Welsh taste, would lower the Episcopate, without any compensatory benefit to the Church'.[47] He certainly had no suitable men in his own diocese who would fit Gladstone's description of his ideal candidate. The prime minister might have 'to pay rather dear' for his desire, he concluded, and he hoped the appointment would not 'come down to a mere popular Welsh preacher'.[48] Campbell of Bangor obviously thought alike with his brother-in-law, H. A. Bruce, and believed that the cry for Welsh bishops was hardly an honest one. At least one clergyman, he believed, who made use of it, did so for a purely selfish purpose, and in particular in order to 'veil his ignorance of the language'. One wonders if he had in mind his successor in his former parish, Griffith of Merthyr? The Welsh, he believed, would be as happy with a native of the country as with one who spoke their language. While the latter qualification was of great importance, the real grievance, he believed, was a sentimental one, namely that no Welshman had been appointed to a Welsh see since the Hanoverian succession.[49]

Gladstone's brother-in-law, Sir Stephen Glynne, shared these doubts. He wondered if a 'Taffy could be found who in addition to some powers of Welch preaching was possessed of tact and activity and will be able to govern the clergy and influence the laity'. Nor was he 'very sanguine' about Gladstone's hope of reclaiming Welsh dissent to the Church, whose 'system is now deep rooted and political rather more than religious'. He would hope for the best, however, for Gladstone deserved 'to be rewarded by its proving successful'.[50]

Gladstone himself was almost taken in by these arguments. Writing to the archbishop of York regarding his recommendation of his archdeacon, Basil Jones, he wrote that his desire to find a native Welsh bishop would mean he would 'not be able to find among thorough Welsh preachers a man in all other respects equal to your good archdeacon'.[51] On the following day the prime minister wrote to Lord Cawdor, a prominent landowner in west Wales:

'If I am driven to the conclusion that no such man is to be found, I shall arrive at it with keen regret.'[52] And so it proved to be.

Applications and Advice

Gladstone was besieged with applications for the vacant see. Archdeacon David Archard Williams of Carmarthen,[53] Dean Thomas Williams of Llandaff,[54] P. Constable Ellis of Llanfairfechan,[55] William Bruce, rector of St Nicholas and a brother-in-law of Bishop Campbell,[56] Archdeacon Ffoulkes of Montgomery,[57] Canon Hugh Jones of Holywell,[58] Dr Charles Williams of Jesus College, Oxford (who was a little given to alcohol),[59] Dr James of Panteg, a former and rather inadequate warden of Llandovery College, who had campaigned much for the case of Welsh bishops,[60] and Herbert Williams, rector of Penobyr, were all recommended to the premier by various people. Lord Cawdor wrote in protest about the inclusion of the last name. He was shocked that his brother-in-law, 'C. R.', had recommended him. Although he was a friend of his, an agreeable companion who came over to him for the shooting, and held three of his livings, he was quite careless as a clergyman.[61]

Lady Llanover commented on many of these names. J. Powell Jones, vicar of Llantrisant and a prime mover against Rowland Williams (the arch-heretic of his day) in the diocese of Llandaff, was described as a good and pious man, but one totally unacquainted with the ways of human nature. But he still did good work in his parish and should remain there, for, her ladyship added, 'he is not a vine to bear much transplanting'. She also condemned Canon Thomas, formerly of Caernarfon and the man whom Shaftesbury wished to see appointed to a Welsh bishopric, for passing Richard Lewis as competent in Welsh in order to qualify himself for the incumbency of Lampeter Velfry. Lewis was later to become bishop of Llandaff.[62] Her real venom, however, was reserved for John Griffith, rector of Merthyr. Griffith, she wrote, was an alien in feeling, and only his recent conviction that the prime minister wanted a Welshman for St Asaph had induced him 'to press his Patriotism by publishing some truths against the Bishop of Llandaff. Heaven defend Wales from the Griffith of the "Blue Books" notoriety.'[63]

Gladstone's First List

These men, however, were those whose claims to episcopal office were not particularly great, and if their claims were noted by Gladstone and his advisors they were soon rejected. But there were other men whose candidature was taken more seriously, and it was these men whose names were probably placed on Gladstone's first list of possibilities. Many of them later achieved high office in the Church. Basil Jones became bishop of St Davids, Edwards and Pryce deans of Bangor, and Phillips and Howell deans of St Davids. This list was then sent to his advisors for their comments, in the course of which Gladstone hoped one name would emerge as the person he should nominate to the Queen for the vacant diocese. As this list was being formulated Gladstone wondered if Bishop Campbell of Bangor, Bruce's brother-in-law, might accept a translation to St Asaph. Gladstone clearly believed it would be easier to appoint a native Welsh speaker to Bangor, a thoroughly Welsh diocese, than to the mixed and rather aristocratic diocese of St Asaph. Campbell, while willing to make any sacrifice 'considered best for the Church', felt unequal to this new challenge and accordingly declined Gladstone's suggestion.[64]

Bishop Jacobson of Chester, a contemporary and friend of Gladstone at Oxford, was requested by him to give his opinion of Henry Thomas Edwards, whom he had appointed as vicar of Caernarfon, which was in his patronage as bishop of Chester. Edwards was, of course, the author of the *Church of the Cymry*. In particular Gladstone wanted to know about Edwards's age and his power as a Welsh preacher. The reply came back that Edwards was educated at Westminster School, had been selected by the Bute trustees from forty-three candidates for the parish of Aberdare, and Jacobson had decided in his favour for the parish of Caernarfon 'amidst a bewildering large number of applications for the living'. High testimony in his favour had come on that occasion from the bishops of Bangor and Llandaff and from H. A. Bruce. Nevertheless, Jacobson commended Basil Jones and Lewis Gilbertson, at that time vice-principal of Jesus College. Ollivant wrote that he had a high opinion of Edwards and of his Welshness and intellectual power, and regretted that the bishop of Chester had taken him to Caernarfon 'away from us'. But he subsequently wrote, and presumably Gladstone agreed with his verdict, that he was young and comparatively untried.[65]

Evan Owen Phillips of Aberystwyth was regarded by Dean Wellesley of Windsor as out of the question, having had some experience of his preaching as a holidaymaker at that seaside resort. But he was favoured by Lady Llanover. He was a good scholar who preaches well in both languages, she wrote, though not one of the 'great fuses', in the prime of life and accustomed to moving amongst the higher classes, having a private income of between £1,500 and £2,000 per annum through his wife. A former warden of Llandovery he had been sent to Aberystwyth by the bishop, the parish being in such a dreadful state. He now kept a large Welsh congregation together in spite of the chapels and their large English congregations. Such a man, she concluded, was more fit to be a Welsh bishop than any of those at present wearing the Welsh mitre. On the other hand, his own bishop, Thirlwall, had a different picture to paint. While he considered Phillips a worthy and amiable man he was not singularly gifted, not even as a popular preacher, and utterly deficient in 'the intellectual stuff required for such a position', although this was written in comparison with Basil Jones rather than with Dr Griffiths. Gladstone, strangely puzzled by such different facts given about a single individual, referred the bishop to Lady Llanover's comments. He replied that while he had never heard Phillips preach in Welsh, her ladyship had probably never heard him preach in English. If she had her way she would not allow an English sermon to be preached in Wales. Phillips's sermons lacked preparation and relied too much on his power of extempore preaching. When he last heard him preach Dr Hook of Leeds was in the same pew and 'in the consciousness of his presence I hid my face'.[66]

The sister of Rowland Williams, one Mrs Williams, had written to a Mr Chance asking that he might lay the claims of her brother-in-law, John Pryce, vicar of Bangor, before the prime minister. Gladstone took these claims seriously, especially as they were later endorsed by Archdeacon John Evans of Merioneth. He was a good hardworking man, reported his bishop, Campbell, who added that 'in many respects I do not know a better man in the Diocese'. Unfortunately, he was a man of humble origin, and his manners were hardly those of polite society. 'But as I have said,' he added, 'if you want a Welshman pure and simple, you must make a sacrifice.' His chief drawbacks, according to Campbell in a later reply, were a third-class degree, that he was not a popular preacher, and that he was afflicted with 'a thickness of utterance, as if his tongue

132

was too large for his mouth, which interferes with his elocution'. He also suffered from 'a want of dignity of manner'. His book for Welsh schoolmasters was admired by Bruce, and indicated 'reading and cultivation' far beyond the measure of the ordinary Welsh clergyman. However, Bruce added a qualifying comment; 'if honestly done and not compiled'. Stephen Glynne considered Pryce to be an excellent man with an outstanding record for zeal and activity. Although he noted his connection with the 'notorious' Dr Rowland Williams, he concluded he was too young to be placed at the head of a diocese, while 'his low connections and deficiency of good manners are certainly a disadvantage'.[67]

John Griffiths, rector of Neath, and a prominent figure in the cultural and patriotic movements of Wales, was not one of Lady Llanover's favourites. She commented that he was an ambitious 'scatter brained' Welshman with restless activity and without any system of steady perseverance. He hardly ever used Welsh, and his ambition was to be an English platform orator. Ollivant thought Howell better than him, though Osborne Morgan, a Liberal MP and son of a vicar of Conwy, suggested that his appointment would give the greatest satisfaction not only to the diocese but to the whole of Wales. Henry Richard had been informed that he was better qualified than any other Welsh clergyman for a bishopric. He was a broad-minded evangelical and, above all, a thorough Liberal. But Richard contradicted his fellow MP, arguing that his appointment might be distasteful because of the liberality of his politics and religion, and unpopular with his fellow clergy because of his general sympathy and activity among Welsh people and causes. But although any appointment might cause 'a nice day's row', Griffiths was yet 'the man for a respectable, discreet, active and popular bishop'. Beware of him, warned Bruce, there was no 'real stuff' about him. He was not even to be compared with Howell or Pryce. 'A glib speaker at eisteddfods, a tolerable preacher, but a very indifferent clergyman', was his summing up of Griffith. Even though his appointment might be popular, Bruce was horrified that his name was even being considered by Gladstone.[68]

By early November, as soon as he was aware of Short's projected resignation, the archbishop of York was recommending his senior archdeacon, Basil Jones, to Gladstone. By early January Archbishop Tait was also writing in Jones's support. Although he argued that he was one of the few Welsh scholars known to him who also enjoyed a high university reputation, Archbishop Thomson was unable to state how far Jones was acquainted with the Welsh language, or whether as a Welsh preacher he could 'stir the hearts of the Welsh people' as Gladstone desired. His manner of preaching was not one that would satisfy a Welsh dissenting congregation used to a passionate and emotional style, but on the other hand he would 'plainly and earnestly put before his people the things of God'. While Jones was worthy of a bishopric, Archbishop Tait recognized that he might not be the man Gladstone needed at St Asaph if he still required 'an energetic and eloquent Welsh preacher' who would be able to recover the ground hitherto lost to the Church in Wales.[69]

If Lady Llanover warned the premier that Jones was totally unqualified on the grounds of his lack of Welsh and his sympathy for ritualism,[70] Thirlwall was more optimistic about Jones's linguistic ability. Although Jones was worthy of the bench he understood he was only familiar with spoken but not literary Welsh. He then added the rider already quoted that there was 'an immense difference . . . between a native Welshman and one . . . who has only acquired the language as a foreigner'.[71] Although Bruce disliked Gladstone's policy of making a Welsh appointment, he supported Jones as the best candidate, 'the *facile princeps*', even though he was deficient in the Welsh qualifications demanded.[72]

The *Wrexham Advertiser*, hearing a rumour of Jones's appointment, regarded him as liberal in politics and as such acceptable to many, but the *Record*, an evangelical paper, reacted in a different way. Believing that Jones was a moderate high churchman, it noted Gladstone's aversion to evangelicals, and warned that those papers that described him as belonging to the evangelical section of the Church were guilty of deceiving the public.[73] This included the *Spectator* which had said that the premier had made a 'lucky hit': he had found a clergyman who was 'a Welsh scholar, a commentator on Sophocles, and an evangelical of the moderate but decided school', and had made him bishop of St Asaph. As the *Welshman*, quoting this remark, commented: 'to please the Church, the *Record*, Wales, and the *Spectator*, all together, – what a hit!'[74] But two days later when this appointment was denied, the *Record* suggested that this was because Gladstone's friends, angered at 'his prejudicial aversion' to evangelical clergy, had persuaded him to change his mind and not mock his expressed desire to give the

Welsh an evangelical bishop.[75] Meanwhile Osborne Morgan wrote to say that the news of Jones's appointment had given the greatest satisfaction to his constituents.[76] Even Thirlwall, hearing the reputed news, wrote that he considered it an excellent appointment.[77]

David Howell, vicar of Cardiff, was regarded by Gladstone as one of the more eligible candidates, and he went to considerable trouble to obtain details about his life and work. Howell may well have been handicapped in so far as he was one of Lady Llanover's 'pets', having taken a prominent part for many years in the Abergavenny eisteddfodau of which she was the patron. Howell, she argued, was one of the finest preachers in Wales with 'marvellous eloquence', and he could compete with any English popular preacher. The Welsh would go miles to hear him. Howell, her ladyship continued, was one of the most laborious and hardworking of parish priests, and he possessed great intelligence. Although he had no university antecedents he could fill churches and put his whole heart into the work. He had built a church for the Welsh in Cardiff, while he had an overflowing Welsh congregation at the parish church. Both he and his wife had the most simple habits but were of pleasing manners. Howell possessed much tact, and in a most difficult situation in Cardiff had managed not to quarrel with any of the contending parties.[78]

Although Arthur Kinnaird (later Lord Kinnaird), preferring Canon Hugh Jones, suggested that Howell's lack of a university education might make him 'timid, feeling . . . he was at a disadvantage, and so be a bar to [his] usefulness',[79] there must have been others, besides Lady Llanover, who recommended him to Gladstone. For on 12 January Gladstone wrote to both Bruce and Ollivant stating that of the Welsh preacher candidates Mr Howell was 'the likeliest looking', and that he was 'the one among them to whom thus far the testimony has been highest'.[80]

Ollivant, replying to Gladstone's request for information, stated that Howell was a truly religious man, deeply concerned with promoting the spiritual welfare of his parishes. Through his deputation work for the evangelical Church Pastoral-Aid Society he had become a fluent and sensible speaker in English at public meetings. While he had the reputation of being a good Welsh preacher his work in Cardiff was in English and Ollivant had had no opportunity to hear him in Welsh. He had thought at first that his appointment to St John's Cardiff was the wrong step because he was throwing away his Welsh tongue, which the Church in Wales might have profited by, and I thought that his social position and that of Mrs Howell would prevent him from getting that influence over the educated portion of his parishioners, which a graduate of an English university might be expected to acquire. But I am bound to say that he has so conducted himself as to secure . . . universal respect.

There were 'so many matters coming under a Bishop's consideration which required not only good common sense, but also the help which sound learning can alone supply', argued Ollivant, adding that, much as he respected Howell, he lacked the latter. While he was 'by no means ill-mannered or unfit to associate with the Gentry of a Diocese . . . his wife has not had even the advantages which he has enjoyed, and I fear that, as a bishop's wife, she would hardly be able to take and retain her proper place'. But he had heard nothing to her discredit.

Howell, concluded Ollivant, would make a better bishop and the Church would be better served by his elevation than by Griffith of Merthyr, Griffiths of Neath or Jones of Panteg.[81] On another occasion Gladstone asked Ollivant to judge between Howell and Dr Griffiths of Llandeilo. Griffiths, Ollivant replied, had stronger claims through his age, pulpit experience and a doctorate, and was more disposed to mix freely with good men of all parties than Howell, though he believed in Howell's case that the pressures of parochial life had forced him to avoid his brother clergy or to exchange opinions with them. Howell, he repeated again, was a man of real piety, good sense, independence of character and diligent in his parochial work.[82]

A correspondent of Henry Richard confessed he hardly knew Howell but felt he would not be acceptable in Church circles though he was 'a churchman enough'. But he then added the rather damning statement that he 'did all he could to oppose us at our last recently contested election'.[83]

Bruce wrote two lengthy letters to Gladstone regarding Howell, indicating how favourably inclined the prime minister was to his appointment. Both letters, though fair, made it quite clear that he considered Howell unsuitable. He had only met him once at Llanover, where Howell had made 'a very absurd, but rather eloquent speech, in favour of the Welsh three-stringed Harp, and flattered Lady Llanover's mania to the top of her bent'. A clerical correspondent whose judgement was sound had written to him to say that Howell had

> just the qualities which, resembling as they do those of the better class of Dissenting Ministers, make a clergyman popular in Wales. In learning, professional and social position, weight of character, and capacity to deal with the Clergy, and administer the affairs of a Diocese, I should judge him to be deficient.

'The Welsh curate,' Bruce noted, probably referring to Howell, rarely had in him that 'dignity of character which compensates for want of tact and refinement, and which are not infrequently found in men of the same class in Northern England or those whom you have hitherto mentioned'. He quoted from his correspondent: 'I believe the Revd D. Howell of Cardiff to be a very good and pious man – sincerely desirous of promoting the spiritual welfare of his Parishioners. He is certainly a man of ability and a good extempore speaker, though somewhat after the Celtic type.' But, he added, he had little learning; his father, still alive, drove his own farm cart, and because of his social position and that of his wife Bishop Ollivant protested to the dean and chapter of Gloucester when he heard of their intention to appoint him to Cardiff. However, Lady Llanover 'carried the day'.

Bruce's comment was that while Howell was better and more sincere than Griffiths of Neath, he was still not the man to administer the affairs of a diocese.[84] At the end of the month Bruce wrote that he preferred him to Pryce of Bangor if Gladstone wanted one of 'the preacher class'. He thought that both Howell and Pryce would excel themselves in promoting hard, useful work among their clergy, which was doubly important as they would be unable to secure intellectual eminence among them.[85] But as Gladstone appears to have agreed with Kinnaird's later suggestion regarding Howell, 'being young can *wait*',[86] he looked elsewhere.

By this time, late January, Gladstone was clearly looking in the direction of Dr Griffiths of Llandeilo as his favoured candidate for St Asaph. Writing to Wellesley on 2 February he remarked: 'Dr Griffiths . . . *looks* to me like the most suitable man among the pure Welsh.'[87] There were strong rumours that Gladstone was about to offer the bishopric to Dr Griffiths.

Griffiths was born in the parish of Llandyfriog, Cardiganshire, in 1806, and though his was a Church family it was a locality much influenced by the revivalist Daniel Rowland. Educated at Lampeter, from which college he obtained a BD in 1854, he was an assistant master at Llangeler and Cardigan grammar schools before Ollivant, as sinecure rector, offered him the vicarage of Llangeler. Here there was a noted ministry during which he rebuilt the Church life of the parish and attracted crowds to hear him preach. After twenty years there, and an appointment as rural dean, he moved to Llandeilo (almost an English parish at that time) and later on, in 1877, Lord Dynevor appointed him to Llandyfeisant, a neighbouring parish. He died in the following year.[88]

Gladstone, however, was mortified that Griffiths might be the person he would have to recommend to the Crown for the appointment. This was because Griffiths had masterminded his own campaign for the bishopric, and had openly canvassed all those whom he thought might have some influence with the prime minister. 'I own it does not much please me (nor probably you) when a Clergyman puts himself forward for that office,' Gladstone wrote to Cawdor, though he had to accept that some of the testimonials in his favour were weighty; while he wrote to Ollivant of his 'impression that Dr Griffith himself has moved too much in this matter'. Griffiths was not alone in these activities. Lord Arthur Hervey, appointed to Bath and Wells in 1869, had been 'a great solicitor of a Bishopric', wrote Gladstone, 'which I do not like at all'.[89]

In a letter to Lady Llanover, Griffiths wrote that it was widely known that the prime minister intended to appoint a Welshman to St Asaph. He had received letter after letter urging him to present his claims to the prime minister. Accordingly he asked for her 'Testimonial' which would be 'the utmost and the most valuable importance to my success'. He even told her that he had the support of the lord lieutenant [Cawdor], members of the Quarter Sessions, three of the Welsh bishops, and, he hinted, the support of the archbishop of Canterbury! (This may have been an allusion to Tait having conferred on him a Lambeth DD.) Her ladyship refused, unimpressed by his apparent degree of support, and instead wrote to Gladstone stating that he was utterly unfit to be a bishop.[90] The message was repeated in letter after letter.[91] However, when she believed that Basil Jones might be appointed, her ladyship slightly changed her tune. Even Griffiths was worth a dozen of such men as Basil Jones: his preaching powers would give him an influence, and while he might be a 'one eyed . . . one legged . . . one kneed king' he would not destroy the Church in Wales, which the others might do through their ignorance of the language.[92] It was the one instance when it might have been of profit for Gladstone to have taken her initial advice.

Similar letters were written by Griffiths to others requesting their assistance in his projected elevation. Each letter claimed that in this endeavour he had the support of a host of dignitaries. One wonders if Griffiths ever realized that bishops sometimes exchanged notes with one another! Or did he naively assume that polite letters of dismissal were in fact letters of support? He claimed in a letter, seeking Bishop Campbell's support, that the archbishop had befriended him and had written to the prime minister on his behalf, as had the lord lieutenant and the bishops of Llandaff and St Davids. Furthermore, he claimed that Gladstone had in 'a favourable letter' urged him to 'present my claims and qualifications [to him] before he finally disposed of the vacancy'. Under ordinary circumstances he would not have made such an application to the bishop, but 'as the Premier is so disposed, I was prevailed upon to do so'. If Campbell could perhaps use his influence with the archbishop, Bruce or Gladstone, he believed it 'would prevail at head quarters'.[93] It must have been one of the most astonishing letters Campbell ever received.

Lord Cawdor received a similar letter from Griffiths, but unlike the others, Cawdor at least wrote a kind of testimonial for him. Griffiths, he wrote to Gladstone, clearly believed that the archbishop would recommend him for the bishopric. He was a man of good character, he wrote, whom he believed was a good preacher in Welsh; he was certainly not a high churchman, nor did he profess to be low church, for, as he added, 'the pure Welsh clergy jog on without troubling themselves on such details. He is a very fair specimen, above the average, of the clergy in South Wales, and if you wish to go on with the cry of Wales for the Welsh, he might do as well as another.' It was not perhaps the reference Griffiths wanted, especially as Cawdor added a postscript: 'I don't think I should appoint a Welshman, unless obviously fit in other respects.'[94] Cawdor, in another response, agreed that Griffiths had given him an unfavourable impression by asking him to press his claims and requesting Lady Cawdor to use her influence with the Queen. He simply lacked the character a bishop needed and would be 'a cipher and harmless', unless he followed the custom of Welshmen and 'took to jobbing and making bad use of his patronage'.[95]

While there were some like Wellesley who told Gladstone that he was making the gift of Welsh preaching too important a qualification and sacrificing other and perhaps more essential requirements for it,[96] most of Gladstone's correspondents simply replied giving the details about Griffiths he requested, but obviously hoping that the premier would read between the lines and sense their unease.

Ollivant, whom Gladstone told Mrs Tait thought favourably of Griffiths,[97] replied that he was a blameless young man in his youth and had kept that reputation, was probably the most eloquent preacher in Welsh of his day, and he believed that his award of a DD could be a deciding factor in his candidature. He was popular with his fellow clergy, and by no means a vulgar and obtrusive man, but in manner he believed David Howell was superior to him. A later letter made it clear that Ollivant had somewhat changed his opinion after Griffiths had asked him to submit his name to the prime minister as a candidate, 'saying he had himself addressed you on the subject'. Nevertheless, Ollivant was charitable. Allowances had to be made: 'it is just one of those things that mark the difference between the Welsh clergyman of *this* class, the popular Welsh minister, without a thoroughly good education, and not having had the advantage of having mixed from boyhood with good Society . . .'[98]

His own bishop, Thirlwall, refused to pronounce on Griffiths's 'fitness for the mitre', but noted, in a rather derogatory manner, that 'if you are looking out for a popular Welsh preacher, and as to other qualifications would be content with some thing rather below the average, I think you would be safe in the choice of Dr Griffiths . . .'. But, he warned, 'what passes for eloquence in a Welsh preacher is by no means always that which would be thought by educated men to deserve that name in an English one.'[99]

Bruce thought his name should be excluded from any list of candidates as he lacked learning, dignity of character and the merits of a good parish priest.[100]

Yet, in spite of all these warnings, Gladstone obstinately kept Griffiths's name at the head of his list, making all possible allowances for his conduct. Ollivant, who was now suggesting the name of Joshua Hughes to the prime minister, declined to interview

Griffiths, though requested by Gladstone to do so, stating that he could see little advantage in it. He possibly thought Griffiths might make too much of it having already seen him some days earlier, although by now Ollivant was aware that Griffiths was the premier's first choice. Accordingly he wrote that while Griffiths was certainly not what they would wish a bishop should be, he was a hardworking clergyman of good character. The reasons that could be given 'which would induce the clergy of Wales to acquiesce in [his] selection' could not be urged in favour of others, by which Ollivant probably meant Griffiths's honorary doctorate.[101] It seemed reasonably clear that Gladstone would nominate him to the Queen for the vacant bishopric, even though he was horrified that he was selecting one who had applied for the appointment, a matter he had hoped would never have occurred.[102]

But then came a bombshell. The archbishop's secretary forwarded a letter to Downing Street from Rees Goring Thomas of Llanelli, a local landowner and an influential lay churchman. The archbishop's covering letter suggested that this letter seemed to imply some personal disagreement between Thomas and Griffiths.[103] Thomas, said Bruce, who had also received a similar letter from him, was a gentleman of education and high character who lived near Llandeilo, and thus knew Griffiths intimately.[104] In all probability Thomas wrote a sufficiently disturbing letter in order to force Gladstone or one of his secretaries to interview him personally, upon which even more disturbing matters came to light.[105]

Thomas's subsequent and various letters to Bruce, Gladstone, and Sir Stephen Glynne alleged that Griffiths's canvassing was well known and had been greeted with dismay. People were shocked that such an unfit man might be appointed. The diocese of St Asaph was in equal dismay. Griffiths was a man of no learning, no education, imperfectly acquainted with the English language, devoid of courage and firmness, a poor parish priest, deficit in organization and much advanced in years. He left his parish work to his curates, and though he was a popular preacher among the uneducated this was more due to his ringing voice and pleasing manner than the matter of his discourses. There was a lack of firmness in him, and he could not speak in English! He was dilatory, and had been unable to make up his mind whether to go to Llandeilo or not; applying, turning it down and re-applying. Such a man could have no influence over his clergy or laity, the latter finding it hard enough to have so large a proportion of their parish clergy coming from the lowest of the people in any case. To appoint this man to St Asaph would be a dire calamity to the Welsh Church.[106] Furthermore, he did not deserve promotion at the hands of the Liberals, for he was anti-Gladstone during the time of Irish disestablishment.[107]

But there was another matter that was not raised in correspondence, but was probably brought out in that personal interview. The evidence of immorality, for such was the accusation, appears to have been substantiated in letters from a Mr Walters (a man of some ability, said Bruce, but troublesome and litigious, a good preacher but not a good pastor), and a former dissenting minister, Thomas Nicholas, a promoter of the Welsh university and an author.[108]

Thirlwall, written to urgently, had not heard any adverse report of Griffiths's personal character, and wondered whether the rumours were 'a float' designed to prevent his candidature. However, he could state that Griffiths's deceased wife was of such character that had she still been living it would have been impossible to raise him to the bench,[109] a statement that Bruce elaborated. His wife had been a dressmaker but had been a confirmed drunkard for many years. But Griffiths was not to blame for anything in connection with that misfortune.[110]

Ollivant was surprised to hear these charges 'of gross immoralities' against Dr Griffiths. He believed him to be a blameless person, and wondered if he had been confused with one of his own clergy, Evans of Rhymney, who had been born at Llangeler, who also had a wife who had disgraced herself as an alcoholic and had been falsely accused of immorality by one Prothero who was later tried for his life for murder. As to politics, he believed Griffiths was a Conservative.[111]

But was this simply malicious scandal designed to prevent Griffiths's candidature, as Kinnaird assumed?[112] Henry Venn, a noted evangelical leader and an old friend of Griffiths through their links with the Bible Society, seems to have been used as an intermediary, and he received several letters from the Llandeilo parishioners expressing their concern that an attempt had been made to damage Griffiths's reputation.[113]

By 15 February, Thirlwall's secretary wrote that their enquiries had brought to light 'something . . . about a woman'. This he charitably suggested concerned his late wife, whose reputation was obviously known to them.[114] But a week later a letter from Thirlwall's nephew was passed on to Gladstone. It seemed to substantiate the allegations. Griffiths, the writer alleged, had had a child by a woman when incumbent of his previous parish, and he had continued his adulterous connection with her since he had been in Llandeilo. The letter alleged that this was known to many.[115] William Morris, a former Liberal MP, now added further if easier complications. Griffiths's appointment would not give satisfaction to the Liberal party in Wales, as he was a political opponent, while north Wales did not want a south Walian as bishop.[116]

The conflict of evidence was bewildering, but at the end of February Gladstone confided to Wellesley: 'I am utterly thrown out and have to begin again about St Asaph.' At the same time he wrote to Ollivant: 'The case of Dr Griffiths has, I am sorry to say, after all broken down.'[117] It was back to the drawing board for Gladstone.

Was it politics or morality that lost Griffiths the bishopric? It was well known that he had been considered for the bishopric by Gladstone (and Griffiths made certain people knew this too),[118] but the *Western Mail* of June 1874 carried a letter defending Thirlwall, who had just resigned, from the charge that he had ignored the Welshmen in his diocese. It provides a clue to the dilemma, for the letter added that 'the same influences which influenced Mr Gladstone to pass over Dr Griffiths here, it may be, induced the Bishop of St Davids to pass him over in the distribution of further rewards.'[119] Alas, it does appear that it was a question of morality.

The Second Round

Gladstone was now forced to enter a second round of bishop-choosing. It seems that his advisors, knowing that he would not be deflated from his desire to appoint a Welsh-preaching bishop, now looked around for other names to offer him, aware that most of his 'first round' candidates had been eliminated. In fact the process had started almost before the difficulties were becoming apparent with Griffiths, for Joshua Hughes's name had been offered to Gladstone early in February. One suspects that many of Gladstone's advisors felt that if such a man as Griffiths was being considered, then there were better men available whom no one had bothered to mention beforehand as it was assumed that their claims for consideration were too insignificant. By the end of February Gladstone had drawn up a new short list on which the names of Hughes and the two Williams from Llanelli (causing some confusion) were prominent.

David Williams, vicar of Llanelli, may have been suggested to Gladstone by the bishop of Winchester, E. H. Browne, who had been vice-principal at Lampeter during Williams's student days at the college. The son of a small farmer in Breconshire, Browne wrote, his work at the college would have done credit to an honours candidate at one of the ancient universities. Browne had dissuaded him from proceeding to one of the universities, not because of any incapacity on his part, but because the Church in Wales needed all that could be done for it by 'its ablest and most faithful sons'. Alas, too many of those who entered Oxford or Cambridge never returned to Wales. After his final examination Williams was made an assistant tutor of the college and later held the chair of Welsh. He had married well, was now a good parish priest and a good preacher, but after a gap of twenty years Browne could not say whether 'the homeliness of his manners (they never were vulgar) has worn off'. While he would never be considered for an English bishopric, the choice of fit Welshmen was so restricted that Browne believed Williams was one of the few native Welsh speakers who could be considered for a Welsh bishopric. A disqualification might be the great simplicity of thought and knowledge in persons brought up in a Welsh farmhouse, a Welsh school and a Welsh college, but having married an English lady, a Miss Nevill, sister to the vicar of Great Yarmouth, Williams had travelled extensively and mixed in society, and thus had gained a deeper experience of men and society than would otherwise have been the case.[120]

Rees Goring Thomas, now placed in a position of some eminence, it seems, by his exposure of Griffiths, was also asked for his opinion of Williams. It caused him some embarrassment, for Williams was his brother-in-law, and there could be the suggestion that he had knocked down one man in order to forward a relative. The late vicar of Llanelli, he wrote, had died three years ago, and the Church there 'was in poor shape'. This vicar was Ebenezer Morris, a pugnacious and difficult character. They had left no stone unturned to find the best man, and he had persuaded his brother-in-law to give up his Lampeter post with its lucrative sinecure rectory in order to take over this parish with its small pay and much hard work. Williams had been very successful, but he had never thought of him in terms of a bishopric.[121] On the other hand he and others had never thought of Griffiths as episcopal material either and he had nearly made it!

Thirlwall was more encouraging. He had not mentioned his name because he believed that Gladstone wished to obtain a Welsh preacher for the vacant see. Although Williams was no preacher, even if he 'took pains in the pulpit', he was an earnest and conscientious man.[122] William Nicholl, who identified himself as another brother-in-law of Williams, wrote that while he regarded him as having worked energetically and successfully in a most neglected parish, he was a little inclined to the high church, though he charitably considered him to be sensible and good tempered about it. But his manners were somewhat constricted, and he was not sufficiently at his ease, or firm enough in his position, to be a leader of men. In his opinion he was not fit for episcopal office at the present time, and he hoped Gladstone would not sacrifice too much to the popular cry for a Welsh bishop.[123]

In commending David Williams of Llanelli, Thirlwall noted he had to be distinguished from another D. E. Williams who was vicar of St Paul's, Llanelli. His cause was being promoted by a Llewelyn Bevan, a Welsh dissenting minister, who had canvassed Bishop Browne for his support.[124] Bevan, who came from the Llanelli area, was then pastor of Whitefield's Tabernacle in London. This D. E. Williams had written a work entitled, *The Church of the Future: being an expansion of a paper read before the clergy of the Rural Deanery of Kidwelly, 1855*, but not published until 1869. In this paper he emphasized the importance of the voluntary principle, commended the weekly offertory to avoid living on past generosity, argued that the liberation of the Church from state control would lead to the revitilization of Christianity and remove one of the main stumbling blocks to unity, and wished the laity to have a greater share in the counsels of the Church.

Rees Goring Thomas described him as man who never lost an opportunity of asking for preferment; Nicholl considered him unfit, ill-tempered, quarrelsome, doing nothing in his parish on grounds of ill health, and not a gentleman; while Thirlwall described him as a good preacher but a former Wesleyan who had been recommended to him by Bishop Blomfield. A local Llanelli person, Colonel Stepney, was also said to have recommended him.[125]

As Gladstone was becoming increasingly disillusioned with his choice of Dr Griffiths, the name of Joshua Hughes of Llandovery was brought to his attention. He may perhaps have realized that George Borrow had written about him and spoken highly of his earnestness and excellence as a preacher.[126] Ollivant wrote to Gladstone in early February decrying Griffiths but suggesting that there was a better man, 'a good man, a pupil of mine, with whom I have entertained very friendly relations ever since my early connection. I have not mentioned him before, as he is not in my diocese.'

Interested in this new arrival, Gladstone soon discovered from Ollivant that Hughes was a popular preacher in both tongues, and a proctor in Convocation where he had spoken with sense and ability. He was not a scholar or a university graduate but a well-read and thoughtful man. A gentleman, his disposition was amiable and conciliatory, and his wife was a baronet's daughter and a lady in manner though nervous and timid. Asked to evaluate this new candidate Ollivant summed Hughes up by suggesting that he surpassed Howell in age, authority as a proctor and in family circumstances, and though Griffiths was a better preacher, the only distinction Griffiths had over him was that doctorate which seemed to dazzle Gladstone.

As the case for Griffiths collapsed, Ollivant was obviously asked to supply even more information about Hughes to the premier. At the end of February Ollivant enclosed a copy of a pamphlet Hughes had written on the Welsh Church. This Ollivant suggested showed his character and his qualifications for a higher position than he then occupied. As March began Gladstone received a bundle of letters that Hughes had sent to Ollivant over the years. These, Ollivant claimed, would give the measure of the man, as would his Convocation speeches, whose references he provided. He added that Hughes was a man of gentlemanly feeling, and though not of high extraction, could bear himself well in any society in which he might be placed. Furthermore, he preached from the heart. He was also a BD of Lampeter so that he was not without a degree; an important observation in view of later controversy.[127]

Thirlwall believed there were two drawbacks to Hughes's appointment. First, Hughes was 'an out and out Evangelical', though he conceded that not only would this be for many a strong recommendation, but also that Hughes was 'as candid and tolerant as is consistent with an earnest holding of very decided opinions'. Secondly, however, he spoke with a Welsh accent that was not quite agreeable to English ears. But he was a man of agreeable presence and of good social standing through his marriage and had inherited an estate on lake Como which permitted him the use of some title, a baronetcy, he thought, which he had not chosen to take up.[128]

Henry Richard regarded him as a respectable parish priest but little known in Wales.[129] Recourse was also made to Lady Llanover's comments about Hughes of the previous November. Although he was a good-working Welsh clergyman, she wrote, he was very inferior to the good Welsh dissenting ministers; a very insecure character who would be quite unfit for a bishopric 'though superficially agreeable'.[130] Bruce made the comment, however, that Hughes had fallen out with her over some matter regarding Llandovery College, of which they were both trustees, and she had not forgiven him.[131]

Archbishop Tait had made his feelings plain much earlier on. Writing of Griffiths he had remarked that 'perhaps Hughes is the more important of the two'.[132] By the beginning of March Gladstone was accepting that this was so, especially in view of Wellesley's comment that 'on good authority' he had heard Hughes was the only man in south Wales whose appointment would be in the smallest degree satisfactory. He was only outclassed in his preaching by Griffiths, but was a man of catholic spirit. In his reply Gladstone agreed this was the case, and there was 'a greater likelihood of finding him the best man,' though he added characteristically, he was still pursuing other enquiries. Writing to Sir Stephen Glynne, Gladstone thought that Hughes would be 'found at least fairly equal to all the duties of a Bishop'. In compensation for this inadequacy, he expressed his hope that Hughes's appointment would help redress 'the previous fatal policy' which had estranged the Welsh from the Church.[133] On 8 March, Gladstone wrote to the Queen recommending Hughes for the bishopric. In his letter he mentioned his 'very long search' for a clergyman who could freely use his 'native tongue in pastoral ministration, with all the aid he could procure from Episcopal and other quarters'.[134]

On 11 March, Gladstone wrote the following letter to the Revd Joshua Hughes:

I have to propose to you, with the sanction of Her Majesty, that you should be nominated by the Dean & Chapter of St Asaph as the successor to Bishop Short.

The selection of your name has been the result of a long and very laborious though interesting search in which I have been engaged for some two months past. You owe my recommendation of you simply to the belief I entertain respecting the true necessities of the Church in Wales, and your capacity to meet them. I have been fully informed as to your sentiments on matters which divide the Church: but I have also been assured that you are a person likely to govern a diocese in a spirit liberal and kindly towards those who differ from you. I venture to mention this circumstance because the Clergy, and I believe the Laity, or the leading laity of St Asaph though I think very free from extremes, would not be found to lean quite in the same direction, for the most part with yourself.

I hope it may be agreeable to you to accept the proposal I now make and I sincerely trust that if you do your accession to the Episcopal Bench may be followed by all the religious advantages which I am led to anticipate from that event.[135]

Hughes replied on the following day begging time to consider Gladstone's 'so important and unexpected a communication'. Two days later he ventured to accept the offer, feeling much the responsibility 'but in humble dependence upon that help, which is never refused to an earnest seeker'.[136] Some days later he wrote to Archbishop Tait, stating that he was much indebted to the archbishop for his encouragement, and prayed that if he himself might be of the slightest service in promoting the increased efficiency of the Church in Wales, then 'to Him be all the praise'.[137] Clearly the archbishop had helped Hughes make up his mind to accept the nomination, but the expectations of his appointment were dangerously high.

The new bishop was born near Nevern, Pembrokeshire, in 1807, and came under the influence of David Griffiths, its celebrated evangelical vicar whose ministry survived the Methodist secession of 1811 and brought new life into the Church in those parts. Two of Hughes's brothers were also ordained and all served under Archdeacon John Hughes at Aberystwyth, he being another noted evangelical preacher and leader in the Church of his day. Trained at Ystrad Meurig, then a licensed divinity school, he had become one of the first students at Lampeter when it opened in 1827, and though thoroughly Welsh, the system decreed he had to be ordained in Bristol by *letters dimissory*. A first incumbency at St David's, Carmarthen led to promotion to Abergwili, in which parish the bishop's palace lay, and here he gained the friendship of Thirlwall to whom he taught Welsh. In 1845 Thirlwall presented him to the more important living of Llandovery. By 1870, when he was 63 years of age, he was rural dean and a proctor in convocation for the diocese, was regarded as Liberal in politics, and had achieved a reputation of being a godly man who had a high view of the pastoral ministry, a Welsh patriot and an outstanding Welsh preacher. In 1832 he married Margaret, the daughter of Sir Thomas Mckenny, an Irish baronet, and the widow of Captain Gun, but it is not known how they met one another. Hughes died at Crieff, Scotland, after a long and lingering illness in January 1889.[138]

There was one slight difficulty about Hughes's appointment, which received much comment in selected circles both then and thereafter. It concerned Hughes's entry in Crockford's *Clerical Directory* which stated that he was a BA of Cambridge University. In noting his appointment the *Record* stated he was a Cambridge man, educated at Queen's College.[139] Gladstone however, had been clearly informed by Ollivant that Hughes's BD was from Lampeter. Gladstone, it is said, placed too much reliance on Crockford and understood Hughes to be a Cambridge graduate. He even informed the Queen that Hughes had received his 'early education' at Cambridge.[140] He was thus horrified to discover this was not so, probably having been informed of his mistake by the Revd Sir Erasmus Williams.[141]

Gladstone wrote to Hughes:

you are entered in Crockford's Clerical Directory as BA Queen's College, Cambridge, 1842. Will you kindly inform me whether this is incorrect. I ought to add that this description did not vitally affect my recommendation of your name, but though not as regarding yourself it influenced my conduct in another matter.

What this matter was he did not indicate, unless it referred to the distribution of episcopal patronage between the two universities. But Gladstone sweetened the difficulty for Hughes by adding that he wished him well for the future 'which will find me personally as I trust in your diocese'.[142] 'I am very sorry for the mistake to which you call my attention', wrote Hughes in reply, 'and I extremely regret if it has caused you any inconvenience. The moment I saw it in "The Times" I wrote to the editor begging him to insert my correction of it.' He was not aware of Crockford's mistake as he had always contented himself with the cheaper *Clergy List*.[143] The allegation that Hughes had supplied false information in order to impress others was undoubtedly without foundation.

Others made more of this mistake by the editor of Crockford than did Gladstone. Hartwell Jones relays a nasty bit of hearsay which is entirely contradicted by the tone of Gladstone's query to Hughes and by the general thoroughness of his investigations. It is probably something invented by the aristocratic clergy of St Asaph who disliked Hughes's appointment intensely. 'Gladstone', wrote Hartwell Jones, 'repented of the appointment almost as soon as he had made it. "I have just committed a blunder"; he said to a Welsh magnate, whom he met at a garden party. "I have nominated a Welsh vicar to St Asaph under the impression that he was a university man." '[144] But this was generally believed. A correspondent writing in the *Western Mail* made this comment during the 1882 vacancy in Llandaff: 'Mr Gladstone has said he will never appoint again a non-university man, and I have no doubt he will keep his word. He will not on this occasion be misled by Crockford's or any other clerical directory.'[145]

Rejoicing and Dismay

The whole of Wales was said to have rejoiced at Hughes's appointment. At last, said the *Carmarthen Journal*, the Church in Wales had a shepherd who was able to appeal to the hearts of its people in the fight against disestablishment.[146] The rights of the Church had been acknowledged, argued the *Cardiff and Merthyr Guardian*, adding that a continuation of the old policy would have endangered the Church.[147] The *Wrexham Advertiser* regarded Hughes as properly qualified to become the 'overseer' of the Church in that diocese which had been, on account of bad management, an object of pity from the friends of the Church and of frequent attacks in the public press.[148] The Carmarthen based *Welshman* compared his appointment to Thirlwall's, to that bishop's great disadvantage.[149]

Sir Stephen Glynne, who shared his home with the Gladstone family, considered Hughes 'to be a superior man, not of narrow views and clearly much in advance of the ordinary Welsh clergy'. He expressed concern as to how Hughes would fit into a predominately English and somewhat high-church diocese, for if he took 'a decidedly low Church line' he would do 'much mischief'. A subsequent letter noted that the St Asaph clergy were decidedly superior to those of the other Welsh dioceses, and some of them were 'quite English'. It was a clear hint. There were men far superior to Hughes who would have to serve under him as bishop. Among their number Glynne specifically referred to Walsham How, rector of Whittington, who later became the first bishop of Wakefield.[150]

Gladstone did not only receive bouquets regarding his appointments but brickbats as well. It was hardly to be expected that Lady Llanover would refrain from comment in view of her previous remarks about Hughes. In fact she was absolutely horrified on hearing the first report: 'if I had *seen myself announced as the Bishop of St Asaph* I could not have been more astonished!' Was this rumour of his appointment true or false? Gladstone admitted it was true, but made it clear it was the best choice available to him under the circumstances: 'if I have erred in this recommendation it has not been from grudging the expenditure of time and labour, or from failing to gather out of every quarter both information, and authority.' Hoping to take the wind out of her sails he added that one of the men she had apparently recommended, possibly David Howell or E. O. Phillips, 'whose claims may one day deserve an absolute preference', had written to him to say that it would not have been possible to have made a better appointment. But her ladyship was to have the last word. She sarcastically replied that if she had not known Hughes as well as she did she would have thought it a good appointment, but his heart was on the wrong side of him and he could not even write his own language. But at least she thanked Gladstone for 'the pains' he had taken over this appointment and for his choice of a Welshman.[151] He must have been gratified for at least one complimentary remark from her ladyship.

The English press, reported *Y Faner*, was equally critical. The *Spectator* described Hughes's appointment as 'very worthy, but uninteresting', and the *Cambria Daily Leader* said that Wales ought to be grateful for small mercies, though 'it would be difficult to get one smaller than is now given by Mr Gladstone'.[152] Some clergymen, wrote the *Western Mail*, had openly expressed their disappointment, not so much that Hughes had been elected, but rather because they had not been preferred themselves. Some had believed a little too readily that the principal requirement for office was taking a prominent part in various eisteddfodau. The editor reported that some of these men, who had been too open about their disappointment, had become the victims of a practical joke. They received through the post a pocket handkerchief with a deep mourning border, but on each corner was embroidered a bishop's mitre reversed, together with a card on which was engraved the motto, 'Paradise Lost'.[153]

A subsequent bishop of St Asaph, William Havard, believed that Hughes's episcopate had been a great success. His love of Wales and its people won the respect of all.[154] Hughes's obituaries spoke of his friendship with his clergy, his endeavour to placate Nonconformist consciences by his support of the burial bill, and his dislike of the militant view of church defence which was so fully expounded by his successor, A. G. Edwards. It was wrong, he wrote, to have one hand at work and the other holding a weapon. The *Record* suggested that his clergy found him more like a loving father or an affectionate elder brother than a high dignitary of the Church. This may have been so for the younger and evangelical clergy of the diocese, but their senior felt rather differently, as we note later.[155]

There were many, however, who regarded Hughes's appointment as a 'doubtful experiment' both at the time and thereafter.[156] 'Laicus', writing in the *Western Mail* about the 1874 election to St Davids, dismissed Archdeacon Ffoulkes as a candidate, but noted that 'he is far in advance of, and far superior to his own diocesan', Bishop Hughes. The appointment of the latter was an experiment in response to the cry, 'Wales! and a Welsh Bishop!' and a pretty mess has been made, 'for a more violent partizan never caused more heart-burnings in a diocese than he'.[157] The diocese, in Gladstone's estimate, was 'moderately High Church' though it had no clergy with ritualistic tendencies.[158] But, on the other hand, there were few evangelical clergy either. Ollivant had informed Walsham How, then an incumbent in the St Asaph diocese, that Hughes was 'a great friend of mine . . . he told me we should like him very much, for, though a decided Evangelical, he is by no means a party man'.[159] But even with that recommendation, Hughes was not really welcomed.

Hughes may never have realized the hostility he aroused in some of the more senior of his diocesan clergy. Many, on the grounds of learning or social position, must have considered themselves more eligible for episcopal office than he, especially as they knew that his Welsh background was the decisive factor in his election. For many of those clergy that Welsh background was a decidedly inferior affair and they felt that Hughes could not stand up to them on their own level, educationally or socially. Such a background of discontent should have persuaded Hughes that he needed to proceed with much caution. He seems not to have done so, and consequently he failed to win the respect of many of his leading clergy. In particular he overemphasized his evangelical convictions in a diocese which was more latitudinarian in its theology than anything else and whose opinion of evangelicals was therefore not particularly high.[160]

Hughes's concern for the use of Welsh at parish level meant that some of the English-speaking clergymen of the diocese found themselves unable to obtain preferment on account of their unfamiliarity with the Welsh tongue, while those already in Welsh-speaking parishes were required to employ Welsh-speaking curates for the Welsh services Hughes demanded they should provide for their parishioners. Many who anticipated preferment to a family living or to a local parish discovered that their bishop required them to qualify themselves linguistically before they could be instituted. Furthermore, there was a shortage of experienced Welsh-speaking clergy in the diocese, and Hughes was not above importing them into his diocese from elsewhere. There was much criticism of the number of men he imported who shared his evangelical position or who came from St David's College. Specific criticism was levelled at him for his appointment of David Howell to Wrexham, which many thought should have gone to a diocesan clergyman. But as Hughes possessed considerable patronage within his diocese he was able to place his own men without much difficulty. Consequently, his policy was resented, especially by those who regarded evangelicals as a lower breed of churchmen and the Welsh language as crude and unworthy of notice. Even Howell considered that, for all his real merits, Hughes was not as broad in his sympathies as a churchman as the existing circumstances of the Church required.[161] With this policy and his lack of educational and personal social qualifications it is not surprising that Hughes should fall foul of what was the most aristocratic diocese of the Welsh Church. Both its clerical and lay leaders regarded his episcopate as a disaster and they and their friends in other dioceses were not backward in requesting prime ministers during other episcopal vacancies to take note of this disastrous 'St Asaph experiment'.

Hartwell Jones may well have been expressing a considerable part of the truth when he wrote of Hughes:

> In an absolutely just world, that fact would and should not (I suppose) have operated to his detriment; but it is a fact that Bishop Hughes failed to evoke enthusiasm in the diocese and that clergymen nursing imaginary grievances flouted his authority, and a few raised the standard of rebellion. The moral of the story seems to be that alumni of Oxford and Cambridge are in Wales, as elsewhere, more at their ease than alumni of Lampeter and better able to command obedience in exalted spiritual spheres.[162]

Hughes may well have been the right man for the episcopate under these circumstances, but he was placed in the one diocese in Wales that would have resented this experiment. His chance of success was reduced accordingly. If he failed – if fail he did – it was because there were those in the diocese to which he was appointed who were determined he would not succeed, and that Gladstone's policy should be effectively ended. If such men won in the short run, they failed in their greater concern. For Gladstone had so paved the way, that (apart from the appointment of Basil Jones to St Davids by an ignorant and complacent Disraeli) the policy established in 1870 continued until the day of disestablishment. Every bishop was required not simply to have an understanding of the Welsh tongue, but to be able to speak it as a born and bred native. The appointment must also have gratified the Welsh clergy, who felt their own claims had, at last, been recognized. As such, Hughes's appointment was an important factor in the development of the Welsh identity in the late nineteenth century, and it helped to end the belief that the Church was an alien element in Welsh culture. But, it must be said, the appointment was made at a time when the Welsh language was giving way to English pressure.

In a wider field, however, far too much had been expected of this Welsh appointment. In one sense, Gladstone had appointed a bishop for Wales rather than to a particular diocese. The expectations were national, therefore, not simply diocesan. It was totally unrealistic to expect the new bishop so to outpreach the Nonconformists that their adherents would come flocking back to the Church. Though this appointment gratified these people, in so far as Welsh claims were now respected, they had no intention of leaving their Ebenezers and Salems for the Anglican Church. In this respect Gladstone was far too optimistic and totally unrealistic. If there was a failure in this appointment it was because Gladstone had allowed others to set the sights too high and it is hardly surprising that the expected results did not materialize. Yet if Gladstone had not appointed Hughes then the way to the episcopate might well have been debarred to John Owen, later bishop of St Davids. But perhaps too there were some who saw in Gladstone's appointment of Hughes a parable of the gospel enacted. A despised Welshman had been appointed, in preference to the gentlemen suggested by Bruce, the episcopate and the establishment. The hero of Liberal Wales had turned the tables yet again.

~ 7 ~

Mr Disraeli's Choice:
The Appointment of Basil Jones
to St Davids, 1874

Connop Thirlwall, appointed to St Davids as one of the last of the Whig bishops in 1840, resigned his see during the May of 1874 and retired to Bath, where he died a year later.[1] Some of his clergy saw this resignation as a crisis in the life of the diocese; Thirlwall was the only bishop most of them had ever known.[2] Although his resignation was expected, and the press and politicians had had time to consider and speculate as to who might be appointed in his place, Disraeli, then prime minister in the Conservative interest, procrastinated, with the result that the Tory MP for Radnor, Arthur Walsh, wrote to Disraeli's secretary, Montagu Corry, that he had been inundated with letters from his constituents. 'It will save me', he commented, 'and other Welsh members something in postage stamps when Mr Disraeli fills up the vacant Bishoprick. At present every parson and squire in my County thinks that the making of the Bishop entirely depends on me . . .'[3]

It is not difficult to suggest the reason for Disraeli's delay. Unlike Gladstone he was not particularly interested in ecclesiastical appointments and appointments to Welsh dioceses were becoming especially difficult because of the demand for native Welsh speakers. Gladstone had given in to this demand in 1870 when he recommended Joshua Hughes to St Asaph. But it seems clear that Hughes's appointment had intensified the debate about the wisdom of this policy. If the Welsh were now demanding that this policy be repeated, those who opposed it pointed out rather forcibly that it meant the appointment of mediocre men who were unable to take their place in the House of Lords with any degree of credit.

As Disraeli (or rather his secretaries, for he could not be said to have taken a prominent part in this appointment) took his or their time to find a suitable candidate, the Welsh papers not only continued the arguments for and against a Welsh appointment, but their letter columns discussed with great acrimony the claims of various would-be or projected candidates. Those who were in favour of a Welsh speaker found it necessary to distinguish between a native-born speaker, and one who had acquired an ability to speak Welsh as a second language, as had Bishops Ollivant and Campbell. This was emphasized in a memorial signed by the principal and some of the professors of St David's College, Lampeter.[4] It was a distinction which those brought up in the classical tradition of the public schools and universities found hard to accept, for they had mastered the Latin or Greek tongue as part of their education, and surely, went the argument, one could as equally well master the Welsh tongue? This was a difficult argument to refute without entering into strong criticism of those bishops who were continually put forward as successful examples of this policy.

There were others who presented compromise solutions. It was now argued that an English bishop could be appointed who could work the diocese with a Welsh suffragan. This, suggested the clerical-peer, Lord Dynevor, would be the greatest insult that could be offered to the Welsh.[5] Nevertheless, a few days earlier Dynevor had almost suggested his own name for that office, using the very arrangement he was now condemning.[6] Many had suggested that the great diocese of St Davids should be divided. A new diocese could be centred on Brecon. An English speaker would be sufficient for the new diocese, and thus appointments could be made that would satisfy both parties.[7]

The need for a Welsh-speaking bishop was generally supported by the Welsh press, though the *Western Mail* rather compromised its position by hinting that one who possessed 'a considerable personal knowledge' of Wales would be as acceptable as a Welsh speaker.[8] That paper, however, was conducted in the Tory interest. Surprisingly the evangelical *Record*, published from London, supported this demand, arguing that it would 'be suicidal to the best interests of the Church' not to appoint a Welsh speaker, even though it recognized the growing use of the English tongue among the Welsh people. It seemed to be quite proud of its unproven claim that it was the first London paper publicly to draw attention to this particular need in Wales at the time of the appointment to Bangor in 1859.[9] There were others, however, who hinted that a Welsh appointment was necessary not only for the well-being of Wales, but also for the safety of the government. A north Wales MP, W. W. E. Wynne, thus noted that a clerical meeting at Dolgellau had exhibited 'a strong feeling of intended hostility to the government . . . in the event of a *Saxon* being appointed to St David's!!'[10]

Lord Dynevor, who wanted a Welsh speaker appointed to the vacant see, felt constrained to write to Lord Barrington, one of Disraeli's political aides, protesting about the 'nasty insinuations' which had been made to the prime minister and in the press regarding Bishop Hughes's episcopate. 'Laicus', for example, had cruelly suggested that those who favoured a Welsh appointment would do well to study the situation in the diocese of St Asaph before crying out for any more 'Welsh literate or illiterate bishops'.[11] Dynevor was confident that Hughes's episcopate had been no failure. He recognized, however, that the bishop's aim of promoting Welsh preaching among the clergy in the Welsh-speaking areas of the diocese, together with his own strong Welsh accent, 'has not been quite acceptable to the English gentry', even though it had conciliated the feelings of the Welsh towards the Church. Hughes had told him that when he had entered the diocese he had found a state of things almost like Scotland; the gentry were Church and the masses dissenters. He had also said that bishops were needed who could outdo the dissenting ministers in extempore preaching, many of whom were men of great power. The opportunities were there, added Dynevor, for at confirmations and church openings the churches were crowded with dissenters and church people who had been drawn there by a good Welsh preacher. 'Your Lordship has no idea how many sermons a Welshman can take in a day,' he added, 'I preached one of six sermons at a church opening and that is no uncommon thing.'[12]

The demand for the appointment of a Welsh speaker was once again regarded with horror by an influential cross section of Welsh society. It was not simply a question of language, it was argued; there was also the fact that the bishop would be a member of the House of Lords. As 'Young Wales' reminded the readers of the *Western Mail*, many of the parochial men who were regarded as episcopal candidates by the Welsh lobby might be large fish in a river but would be small fish in the sea – his pun was clearly intentional. In England the choice was on the scale of one in 10,000, but in Wales, if a Welsh speaker was required, a much lower ratio prevailed, of about one in 1,000. He concluded with an order of episcopacy: there were English bishops, colonial bishops, missionary bishops and then, finally, Welsh bishops.[13]

If 'Young Wales' and 'Laicus' were cruel to say such things publicly, Lord Cawdor, possibly the leading Tory peer residing in the diocese of St Davids, said much the same privately. In a letter to Montagu Corry written within days of the announcement of Thirlwall's resignation, Cawdor claimed there were many influential leaders in Welsh society who preferred not to have a Welsh bishop. He continued:

> My object is to get someone to urge Mr D. *not* to appoint an average Welsh Parson – as Gladstone did to St Asaph, by way of pandering to the cry of Wales for the Welsh – a most suicidal one for Wales if carried out. What we want is a real good 1st Rate man and his knowledge of Welsh is quite a secondary consideration . . . So far from the appointment of Dr Hughes to St Asaph being popular among the Clergy – they all thought they were quite as fit as him. Somebody above them in position as well as intellect is wanted to raise the tone, and stir up and direct the dormant energies of the Diocese.

Cawdor believed his sentiments were widely held within the diocese, and asserted that there was much feeling against the appointment of a popular Welsh preacher to the bishopric.[14] The same views were expressed by 'Laicus' in another letter to the *Western Mail*. Noting the candidates put forward by various correspondents in the local press he enquired: 'Is the mightiest intellect in Europe to be succeeded by such men as those brought forward by partisans who lack more discretion than zeal in urging the claims of their would-be patrons . . . Or is it supposed that the mantle of Bishop Thirlwall will descend with a double portion of his spirit upon his successor?'[15]

There was widespread agreement too with another of 'Laicus's' letters to the *Western Mail*. In this letter he argued that many of those whose names were being suggested in the press as possible candidates would continue their episcopate in the same spirit in which they had entered this 'controversy'. Intolerance, jealously and partisanship would be the guiding factors of their rule, he claimed, and their patronage would be dispensed with 'one-handed favouritism'. Better perhaps for men like John Griffiths of Neath or John Griffith of Merthyr Tydfil to have a reward fairly earned than to see such honours 'thrown away upon men who have done nothing for the Church'. If one of the more popular candidates were appointed (he mentioned Perowne in this instance) Lampeter graduates would hail the appointment with glee, high churchmen would sigh with relief, and dissenters would smile, for the Church would continue to slumber a little longer. But he added, put a Frazer, Selwyn, Magee or Wordsworth on the Welsh Bench, and 'what a change would soon be affected throughout Wales'.[16] Inglis-Jones of Deri Ormond near Lampeter, another Welsh Tory, was even more dogmatic when he wrote to Corry regarding the 'nonsense about Welsh bishops and their cursed language . . .' A gentleman was required, a thorough man of the world, and 'this I defy you to find among the native Welsh Clergy; some drink a trifle less brandy than others; but one and all at heart are a low sneaking narrow minded, impossible divisive, [sic] jealous of each other, and without any respect for each other.'[17]

Dean E. Owen Phillips, writing an obituary tribute to Basil Jones in 1897, cast his mind back to these days. In so doing he revealed the dilemma faced by the government in this and other Welsh appointments. There was a great anxiety, he wrote, that a bishop was not appointed to St Davids who would be of inferior status and qualifications to the average English bishop, 'as the inference would invariably [have] been drawn that a lower standard of bishops would satisfy the requirements of the Church in Wales, as formerly the old judges and barristers who went on circuit in the Principality, with their woollen wigs and inferior standing, were thought good enough for the Welsh . . .'[18] In spite of Lord Dynevor's defence, Phillips clearly felt that Gladstone's appointment of Hughes was not a good precedent to follow. Others too, like 'Laicus', felt that it was an experiment that had failed and should not be repeated.

Controversy and Claims

It has been noted already that there was a vigorous and sometimes bitter controversy in the letter columns of the newspapers about this appointment. There were many who protested about the personal attacks made on some individuals whose names had been mentioned in connection with it. It seemed that no major ecclesiastical appointment in Wales could pass without bringing out the worst in people, suggested one writer, annoyed that the editor of the *Western Mail* was prepared to print the more extreme letters. Another asked if it was fair to 'traduce the reputation of gentlemen whose lives have been irreproachable' or 'to throw suspicion upon the characters of men of unsullied honour and integrity'.[19] John Jones in the same paper noted the jealously aroused when the name of any particular person was mentioned in connection with the vacancy. Only name a Welshman, he commented, and immediately there is such a 'hue and cry' raised against him that his moral character is dissected, his motives are travestied and his talents ridiculed. And this would be done by anonymous correspondents in the hope of bringing him down. Such men do not mind a stranger getting the appointment, he added, but they could not bear one obtaining it whom they already knew. Yet suggest the name of a man with the highest qualifications and the answer is immediate, 'Oh, he would never do!'[20] Archdeacon Blosse, speaking at a Lampeter degree ceremony, felt that silence was the most appropriate comment he could make regarding the vacancy. He continued:

> every man's name, whether he had any kind of pretensions or not . . . has been brought before the public and paraded there; and the worse of the case was this, that as soon as a man's name was mentioned in any public way, that same moment somebody else started up to pull him down, and say something unkind about him.[21]

But another anonymous writer, 'Spectator', argued differently. If the friends of these would-be candidates were so eager to set the mitre of St Davids on their heads so as to parade their claims before the public, they ought not to get angry when those claims were called into question.[22]

It is hardly surprising that a number of newspaper correspondents suspected that several of these candidates were getting 'their friends to write them up'. One correspondent, 'Clericus em Dee', was so angry at this practice that he wrote a letter entitled 'How to make a Welsh Bishop'. In it he stated:

> Get a friend or friends to write to the *Western Mail* to say what a wonderful clever man you are; how the Principality would rejoice to see the mantle of the great Thirlwall fall on your shoulders; how gracefully it would sit there; and that your great pulpit and platform talents have

always marked you out for some high position in the Church. If you have never been at an university, and so have never had a chance of competing with the choice spirits there, get your friends to detail the number of half-crown prizes you took at the theological college you were brought up in; and record what great things the examiner, who is now himself a bishop, thought of you; that it was no fault of yours you did not go to Oxford or Cambridge.

Then, he added, with one letter published, other writers, 'expectant of livings, would endorse your claims'.[23] There is a suspicion that some of this backlash was directed against the claims of Latimer Jones, the ambitious vicar of Carmarthen, whose friends were certainly puffing him up in the way indicated above. But one wonders if all this was not simply a paper exercise? What influence had the *Western Mail* in Disraeli's choice? The probability is that he never read it.

The Public's Suggestions

A vast number of names were mentioned in connection with this vacancy at St Davids. 'Laicus', writing in the *Western Mail*, after noting most of the candidates described below, argued that the list clearly showed the weakness of the Church in Wales, 'for in the parishes of every one of these here commented upon Churchmanship, Church principles, Church doctrines, are almost unknown'.[24] Those whose names appear to have been seriously considered in government circles will be mentioned later. But first we note some of the names mentioned in the public papers or in private letters to Disraeli's advisors.

Archdeacon Ffoulkes, rector of Llandyssil, Montgomeryshire, and archdeacon of Montgomery, was frequently mentioned as an eligible candidate, although his main qualification appears to have been that he was 'far superior to his own diocesan' (Hughes of St Asaph). He was more than slightly damned by being described as a 'very worthy efficient clergyman who has the best interests of the Church at heart', though his fourth-class Oxford degree, even if from Balliol, his only partial knowledge of the Welsh language, and his inability to 'grasp the difficult and vital questions of Church polity which seem to be shaking the Establishment to its very centre', were regarded as substantial disqualifications for an episcopal appointment.[25]

Another archdeacon mentioned was John Griffiths, archdeacon of Llandaff and rector of Neath. No man was better known in the Principality, suggested the *Western Mail*, and 'the episcopal mantle would fall gracefully' upon his shoulders. Lord Dynevor recommended him too. Griffiths, he wrote, was a good scholar even though he was not a university man, a fine preacher in both languages, a good presence, and, in spite of being conciliatory to Nonconformity, a good churchman. 'Laicus' was more reserved. If ' "claims" could be measured by the amount of good done in past years', he argued, 'instead of private influence, electioneering stumping, and toadying', then perhaps, he would stand higher than many others in these episcopal stakes. But 'in all the higher qualifications for episcopal office he is deficient', for he was 'intolerant and hasty', he failed to manage 'his own or parochial affairs', and though disappointed in 1870 he was still unsuitable for a second chance.[26]

Yet another archdeacon mentioned was Archard Williams of Carmarthen. Son of a cleric and orphaned at an early age, he had been brought up for the Church. In his favour it was said that many of his former pupils at Carmarthen Grammar School, of which he had been headmaster, had been ordained. John Jones, a former Conservative MP, regarded him as the ablest man in the three countries of west Wales, adding that his judgements as chancellor of the diocese showed he possessed a well balanced mind. Another writer described him as being more than 'qualified for the post' for he was a gentleman and a scholar as well as a 'divine'. All interested parties in the episcopal vacancy, including the local members, were urged to come together in order to ensure his appointment, but though it was said he was a stranger to fatigue others considered him to be too old at seventy.[27]

John Griffiths's famous contemporary in his diocese, John Griffith, rector of Merthyr, was a much more controversial character, as was noted during the 1870 election by Lady Llanover. 'Churchman' argued that if the Church wanted to stem the disestablishment campaign, then looming large, it needed to enlist his services rather than provoke him by ill-treatment and force him to use his energies instead in exposing the Church's defects and corruptions. This was a negative recommendation to say the least, as was that of 'Laicus'. He felt, alluding to Griffith's habit of taking the summer off to sail around the coast in his yacht, that he would find the pond at Abergwili Palace too small for his interests and insufficient for his wanderings. He also hinted rather unkindly at some deficiencies in Griffith's lifestyle which would make his conformity to the injunctions regarding a bishop's character in 1 Timothy 3, verses 1–6, somewhat incomplete. Still, he added, he is young and so had time to sober down and may 'be more like a bishop *in futuro* than at present'.[28]

J. Powell Jones, vicar of Llantrisant in Glamorgan, was also mentioned in the press as being a suitable candidate for the vacant see. His qualifications for episcopal office were said to be a commentary on the book of Leviticus which had been serialized in some Welsh periodical, his defence of orthodoxy against Rowland Williams and Bishop Colenso, and his educational and pastoral work.[29] William Thomas, vicar of Aberafan, Port Talbot, was also suggested by a friend who called him 'that luminary of our Church', having had a brilliant 'academical' and university career.[30] Dr Thomas Walters, vicar of Llansamlet and a noted controversialist and pamphleteer, was recommended for the vacant see by Godfrey Morgan of Tredegar. Lord Dynevor, possibly consulted about his claims by Barrington, felt he was not a man of repute. He had given the bishop of Llandaff a great deal of trouble, having attacked him in the press about his appointments to Welsh parishes.[31] Dean Bonnor wrote that he was an extreme anti-ritualist. As evidence for this he cited Walters's protest at the singing of a processional hymn at a church opening in south Wales by remaining in the vestry, and his finding fault with clergy for bowing to the east in the creed. He would, he concluded, simply be 'an Evangelical Pope who would tend to create party feelings on both sides', when a wiser treatment 'of earnest minded enthusiasm' might have kept such excesses within bounds and be more in accordance with the tolerant comprehensiveness of the Church of England'.[32]

The name of Canon David Williams, rector of Castle Caereinion in Montgomeryshire and a proctor in Convocation, also appears to have been mentioned to Disraeli as a possible candidate, probably by his relations as he was a son-in-law of Sir Edward Vaughan Colt, Bart. Lord Dynevor claimed that Williams was not popular and he was very angry when Bishop Hughes refused him a living in the vale of Clwyd. The bishop did not tell him, however, that the whole parish had petitioned against his appointment.[33] Hugh

Jones, rector of Llanrwst, in that same diocese of St Asaph, received a more favourable recommendation. Dynevor, having spoken to Bishop Hughes, commented that he was a man of good presence, fit for any society, and would be able to 'hold his own among the English bishops', while Dean Bonnor of St Asaph, in a letter forwarded to Corry, noted that while he was a party man, his Christian spirit and sincere piety would 'fit him I think to be a fair and moderate Ruler in the Church'. He added for good measure that Jones ruled well in his own house, commenting, 'I don't know a family better brought up.'[34]

The name of Dr John Griffiths, vicar of Llandeilo, was frequently mentioned but as frequently glossed over. If one writer could assert that he had the highest claim upon the see and that the appointment of this 'irreproachable and most successful' clergyman would be a blessing to the diocese and give the greatest satisfaction to the clergy, another could hint at some dark secret which barred any consideration of his claims.[35]

Henry T. Edwards, then vicar of Caernarfon and later dean of Bangor and probably the most controversial figure in the Welsh Church of his day, had his claims for the vacant diocese presented to Disraeli by his own brother, Ebenezer Wood Edwards, vicar of Ruabon. Ebenezer wrote to Lord John Manners that his brother had written a celebrated letter to Gladstone in 1870 which he believed (wrongly in fact) had influenced Gladstone to appoint a Welsh speaker to the see of St Asaph. It was only just that he should be given some recognition for this achievement, which his brother hinted would not come his way from a Liberal administration because of his strong Conservative views. And what better recognition could there be than a Welsh bishopric? Henry had come in at the head of the poll for proctor in Convocation for the diocese of Bangor even though he had been but a short time in the diocese. He was thus clearly popular with the clergy – perhaps, we might add, a rather dubious recommendation for a bishop. His own bishop had pressed him, in spite of his vast parochial duties, to act as editor of a monthly church periodical produced by the Diocesan Church Extension Society. Henry only consented to do so when the society offered to provide at its own cost a curate who would relieve him of some of his parochial responsibilities. A leading Nonconformist had told a friend of his (the writer) that since reading this paper he had had no idea there was so much that could be said on behalf of the Church. If ill health had prevented him taking the university honours that should have been his, Henry had had vast parochial experience, zeal and energy, fluency in both languages, and an interest in Welsh matters. But, in addition to these qualifications there was an even greater one. Henry, according to his brother, was 'a thorough Conservative', so much so that during 'the last contested election for Carnarvonshire he considered it his duty as a Churchman to take an active part [in it], and Lord Penrhyn's son wrote to him after the election attributing his success in a great measure to the efforts he had made in his behalf'. Of course, Ebenezer added, he could not be impartial about the claims of his own brother, but he had no hesitation in saying that the great majority of the Welsh clergy would agree with him. It would be difficult to appoint, he concluded, 'a Welsh-preaching Clergyman better qualified for the work of a Welsh Bishop or who would be likely to do more for the prosperity of the Church and the extension of its influence' than his brother.[36] Such blatant political campaigning was probably the reason why Henry Edwards's candidature got no further. The Tories did things much more subtly than that! However, Edwards's name was seriously considered during the next vacancy.

The name of Latimer Maurice Jones, vicar of Carmarthen, has already been noted in connection with various scurrilous attacks on would-be candidates, and it has been hinted that his candidature may have been promoted by his friends. It is difficult to know how far his claims were seriously considered. The son of a Carmarthenshire cleric, Thomas Jones of Llanybri, he had won, so it was said, every prize open to him at Lampeter, and his examiners there, Dean Mansel of St Paul's Cathedral and Canon Perowne, had urged him to proceed to read for a degree at Oxford or Cambridge. Bracketed first out of twenty-eight in his deacon's examination, even over university men, he had become curate of St Peter's, Carmarthen, under Archdeacon Bevan, and had followed him into that living. Elected proctor for the clergy of the diocese (a clear sign of clerical favour, said his friends) he had made a notable speech in Convocation on the Public Worship Bill. It was furthermore claimed for him that he was a man of great energy, force of character and perseverance, who not only possessed great administrative ability but also had a remarkable power of influencing men's minds. The apostolic requirement for bishops was also brought into play on behalf of Latimer, for it was claimed that he was much given to providing hospitality for his fellow clergy when they visited Carmarthen on business. And in addition it was claimed that he was a notable Welsh preacher. Both the *Western Mail* and the *Wrexham Guardian* noted a further qualification, namely that Jones had 'certain claims upon the notice of the Crown'. Regretfully neither paper explained what lay behind this interesting statement. But Lord Dynevor regarded Latimer Jones as conceited and given to strong language, while 'Laicus', in the public press, derided his claims unmercifully. His hospitality to his supporters during the election for the proctorship would have unseated a member of the civil parliament, and his pretence to learning was a sham and a delusion. 'May that day never arrive when a mitre is set upon his head,' he exclaimed. Only his friends, 'that particular clique who minister to his vanity and his eccentricities', would acclaim his appointment to the vacant see, having already secured his election as proctor. If he was appointed no living would be vacant in St Davids 'but what the walls of Abergwili Palace would resound to their cries "O Baal, hear us?"' 'If ability to learn sermons and speeches, and to deliver them with studied effect, if eccentricity are the sole qualifications for a bishop,' then Latimer was the man to be appointed. 'But if sound scholarly attainments, if judgment and discriminating impartiality, if being "above suspicion", are a few of the requisites for the episcopal office,' added 'Laicus' with lethal penmanship, then those who knew him better 'than his present admirers would sigh with unfeigned sorrow and regret as having to bow to such a superior . . .' were his ambitions to be realized.[37]

Gilbert Harries received many an honourable mention as a possible successor to Thirlwall. Rector of Gelligaer in the Glamorgan coalfield and a member of a distinguished Pembrokeshire family (his father and brother were both sheriffs), Harries was also prominent in the affairs of the diocese of Llandaff, being secretary of the Llandaff Home Mission Society and its Education Board. Widely regarded as one of the most efficient parochial clergymen in Wales, and deeply concerned with the Church's educational work, it was claimed by some that he lacked scholarly attainments, judgement or discrimination. Lord Dynevor relayed his bishop's opinions of him to Barrington. He seemed to agree with these negative sentiments, although he added that Harries was a competent Welsh speaker but not a great preacher. He had one thing against him, however, namely that he was infected by ritualism. This he illustrated by an incident which had occurred at the funeral of the late vicar of All Saints, Cardiff, two years previously. Harries turned his back on the people at the prayer of consecration. This caused great offence and Ollivant had received a number of complaints about it. This, for Ollivant, was a deciding factor against Harries's candidature.[38]

A Possible Shortlist

It is not known whether Latimer Jones and Gilbert Harries were serious 'candidates' for the vacant see in the sense that their names were considered for the appointment by the prime minister or his advisers. From what others wrote of them it seems clear that some people believed this to be the case. But the names of six men appear to have been shortlisted so far as one can tell from the letters of recommendation or advice still contained in the Disraeli archives. We note them in the reverse order of selection.

David Howell's claims were regarded as substantial. His pulpit abilities were so great that his 'father in the ministry', Archdeacon Griffiths of Neath, described him as 'his father in eloquence'. He may not have been a man of learning, but, as a correspondent of the *Western Mail* wrote, had Thirlwall spent more time in the diocese and less in his library he would have made a better bishop. Ollivant regarded him as good in both languages and a first-class man, but rather damned him by stating he was '*not* a university man'. Nevertheless, Ollivant was quoted by Barrington, one of Disraeli's aides, as saying that for Howell's knowledge of Welsh, personal piety and good sense, 'there is no-one in his diocese he should prefer', presumably as bishop of St Davids. Lord Dynevor favoured him, claiming personal knowledge of Howell, but concluded, in a later letter, that although Howell was a wonderful man, of great tact, and decidedly acceptable to the clergy, like Bishop Hughes, his want of scholarship 'would be a bar lest he should be despised by the upper classes'. And thus Dynevor changed his allegiance to Evan Owen Phillips who had this advantage, although he regarded him as unequal to Howell in ability and natural genius.[39]

Bishop Ollivant also preferred Phillips, who was then vicar of Aberystwyth, and whose name had been briefly considered during the 1870 vacancy by Gladstone. There was no doubt, said the bishop, about his ability in the Welsh language. Lord Dynevor wrote that Bishop Hughes thought well of Phillips and had told him he had a good knowledge of human nature and was able to manage men wonderfully well.[40]

Henry Spence, a former professor at St David's College, Lampeter and now rector of St Mary-le-Crypt, Gloucester, was, said Inglis-Jones, more vigorous than Perowne (another candidate), clever and connected through both his own and his wife's family with some of the more influential families in Wales. Spence's politics were Conservative. This was an important consideration for Inglis-Jones, for he threatened to withdraw his family's support for that party if a candidate of opposite views was appointed, pointing out that members of his family had represented Carmarthenshire in Parliament for the previous twenty-two years. Ollivant, however, warned the prime minister's advisors against Spence. A Welsh archdeacon had told him he would be a failure if appointed, and Ollivant disclosed that both his father and mother had committed suicide. Another letter expressing strong reservations came from John Talbot, who passed on to Disraeli a letter of a Carmarthenshire cousin, Edward Tilly, of Ael-y-bryn, Llanelli, whose family had worked hard for the Conservative cause in that county. Although the county members for Gloucestershire and the bishop of Gloucester supported his candidature, Tilly argued that Spence was utterly unfit and unworthy of the office and his appointment to it would be a real calamity. But no one, it appears, bothered to state whether Spence was a Welsh speaker or not.[41]

Lewis Gilbertson, then rector of Braunston near Rugby, but a former rector of Llangorwen in Cardiganshire and vice-principal of Jesus College from 1855 to 1872, was also believed to be front-runner for the appointment. This would certainly account for the numerous remarks made against him by Lord Dynevor in his several letters to Barrington. Such a man, he argued, having the charge of a small country parish, would hardly do for a great diocese. Though he was a man of unimpeachable moral character, and had the ability to speak Welsh, he was not a superior man in talent or attainments. But the real objection against him was his ritualistic tendencies. These had given much offence to his Welsh parishioners. The Llandovery trustees had told him in 1854 that because of his views they would not consider him for the wardenship, and thus he had withdrawn from that contest. He had signed Dr Pusey's declaration for auricular confession in the previous year, and both Ollivant and Lord Cawdor, the leading Tory in the vacant diocese, had expressed strong views against Gilbertson's form of ritualism. Indeed Cawdor had been so incensed by the ritualism practiced at Tenby that he had refused to give flowers from his hothouse to decorate its church. Furthermore, Gilbertson's lectures at Jesus College were said to be of a very poor quality. He would not be respected, there-fore, on the grounds of intellectual superiority, and the press would make much of his appointment to the injury of the Church.[42]

It is quite certain that serious consideration was given to J. J. S. Perowne, canon of Llandaff, chaplain to the Queen and Hulsean professor at Cambridge. He was a former vice-principal at Lampeter, where it was thought he had acquired some knowledge of the Welsh language. But if the government proceeded on this assump-tion, there were many prepared to suggest otherwise. 'Is he Welsh? Is a scholar needed? Did he have any spiritual sympathy with the Welsh people when he was at Lampeter?' asked the *Western Mail*. It clearly anticipated the answer 'no' to every question. J. L. D. Wain of Llanybydder noted that when he was at Lampeter Perowne and his wife were always expressing great contempt for Wales. Ollivant felt that because of his 'studious habit' he would be unable to carry on 'so large a correspondence as the see must entail upon him'. Besides he was English and his appointment would create an uproar. He would however be well suited, he argued, for a diocese such as Chichester, but he warned Disraeli that if Perowne or an Englishman was appointed there would be 'a just outcry' from Wales. Popular opinion suspected that most of the Welsh bishops supported Perowne, so that Ollivant's remarks were not represen-tative of the Welsh bench nor possibly of the Anglo-Welsh clergy. One of them, for example, signing himself as 'a graduate', wrote to the *Western Mail* claiming that there could be no worthier succes-sor to Thirlwall than Canon Perowne.

Others were more critical if not derogatory of Perowne's charac-ter. Edward Woolcombe of Balliol, writing to Archbishop Tait, feared that Perowne had been 'pointed out to our new premier by his *Hebrew* knowledge'. However, he added, whether we have Hebrew or Welsh to give it, 'poor Wales will believe but in dissent'. Some sympathy with Perowne was expressed by those who knew of his frustrated desire for a bishopric. Bishop Hughes in a letter to Perowne noted he would be the most qualified man for the post if the Welsh language was not regarded by the government as a *sine qua non*. Latimer Jones, another candidate, told him with what must have been a certain degree of hypocrisy that while the clergy of several of the rural deaneries in the vacant diocese had memorialized the prime minister for a Welsh appointment, he had refused to do so, for that would 'keep from the bishopric, for example, a man like Canon Perowne'. 'May heaven send you back to the diocese a Bishop,' he concluded. J. Rowson Lumby, a Lampeter examiner, assuming that 'heaven' had performed Latimer's good if sycophantic desire and Perowne had been appointed, wondered how the news would be received at Lampeter: 'I expect the Dean will have a fit and die at once, and the rest of the Board will grow black in the face with rage and vexation.'

Apart from this linguistic objection, two other objections were made to Perowne's appointment. His opinions were too unorthodox, some felt, for he shared the same liberal theological views as Dean Stanley and Bishop Temple. As 'Laicus' wrote, 'if the Church is to maintain her ground and combat Romanism on the one hand and infidelity and indifferentations [*sic*] on the other, its Bishop should be a champion of its creeds, a defender of its formularies, and not one to sneer at the apostolical succession it claims for its ministers and the baptismal regeneration for its members.' The other reason was expressed by Inglis-Jones of Deri Ormond, who knew both Perowne and Spence intimately as former neighbours. A delicate man, unfitted for hard work, he wrote disparagingly of Perowne, who came down to Lampeter in order to avoid work. His wife was vulgar, but in politics he was a radical as compared to Spence who was Conservative. This, in fact, was his real argument against Perowne's appointment, for he advised that 'we cannot afford to lose a vote in Carmarthenshire and Cardiganshire, and if Perowne is appointed you will lose them by the hundred'.[43] This fear alone was probably sufficient to cause Perowne's name to be dropped, although, as already noted, many believed he should have been appointed and rumours to that effect abounded.[44]

It may well be that many of these names were brought forward by Disraeli's advisors in order to test the claims of Basil Jones for the vacant see of St David. Jones was archdeacon of York (to his friend and schoolfellow, Archbishop Thomson) and scion of an old Welsh house. His father was a former sheriff of Cardiganshire. The heir of the Gwynfryn estate in that county, Jones had had a distinguished university career culminating in a fellowship and an appointment as public examiner. His edition of Sophocles' *Oedipus Tyrannus* was well known, as was his work, with Freeman, on the architecture of St Davids Cathedral. Others saw him as a protégé of the archbishop of York (who had pressed his claims in 1870), and regarded his popularity with the clergy of Yorkshire as an earnest of the success he might achieve 'in a higher sphere of labour'. He was on the Queen's list of suitable names for appointment, which had been drawn up by Dean Stanley, the Queen rightly fearing the mediocre choices Disraeli had made when left to his own devices.[45] There was no doubt in most minds that he was the leading candidate. The only matter that stood against his appointment was his lack of colloquial Welsh. It was known too that Gladstone had seriously considered Jones's claims for the bishopric of St Asaph in 1870, and had only come down against him because of his assumed inability to speak Welsh. But in spite of this apparent disqualification in the eyes of some, Basil Jones was a scholar, an ecclesiastical dignitary and a gentleman of Welsh descent. No other candidate could offer such strong claims.

Although it was generally accepted that Jones had studied the Welsh language grammatically, there were considerable doubts as to his ability in spoken Welsh. Some argued that he spoke the language well and had used it in Welsh services in his native parish of Llangynfelyn. William Wynne thought his Welsh was acceptable. But the newspaper writer, 'Laicus', regarded him as Welsh in name only. Gee, the editor of *Baner*, expressed his doubts, but suggested that he should give proof of his ability by preaching in Welsh in all the churches of the diocese if he were appointed. Lord Dynevor too felt he would have no power as a Welsh preacher, and as such was not fit for a bishopric in Wales. Dynevor, however, had another objection which would have weighed less with Disraeli. He believed that Basil Jones had 'ritualistic tendencies' which would make him an unsuitable choice for a strongly evangelical diocese. The *Church Times*, in its obituary of Jones, when it was perhaps better informed, pointed out that while Jones had been a supporter of the tractarians in his Oxford days, he had ceased his connection after Newman's secession and had become a moderate evangelical.

One of the strongest supporters of Basil Jones was Llewelyn Lewellin, dean of St Davids, principal of St David's College, Lampeter, and self-confessed trainer of three-quarters of the clergy of the diocese, whose memorial for the appointment of a Welsh speaker to the diocese has already been mentioned. Lewellin probably felt that Basil Jones came into this linguistic category. There was, however, a further consideration to be borne in mind. Basil Jones was a member of the Conservative party, the party then in power. Writing to Arthur Walsh, member for Radnorshire, who forwarded the letter to Corry, Lewellin pointed out that he had a vote in every county in south Wales and Monmouth, and 'had never failed to support our cause with energy'. Under Thirlwall's regime, he wrote, 'Conservatives have felt they have been more or less under a cloud'. Lewellin made clear that a man was required who would not only be a sound churchman, a scholar and a gentleman, but also one who had the additional qualification of being a Conservative in politics. Lewellin, like the prime minister, obviously considered that bishops were political animals as well as spiritual leaders. Basil Jones, he believed, fitted all these qualifications. He therefore asked Walsh to use his influence with the government for Jones's appointment, pointing out that the bishop of St Davids has 'great patronage in your county'.[46]

Public Comment

As expected, Basil Jones was appointed to what the *Pall Mall Gazette* described as the most difficult diocese in the Church of England, and as the successor to one who had the 'greatest personal eminence among living English bishops'.[47] Disraeli wrote to the Queen with his recommendation of Basil Jones on 1 July, emphasizing that not only was he a Welshman by birth and acquainted with the Welsh language, but he was 'a gentleman and distinguished scholar; qualifications which are wanting in the mere [*sic*] Welch clergy, but which are requisite to maintain the authority and influence of a Bishop'.[48] Was Disraeli responding to criticisms about the last Welsh appointment? The new bishop accepted the offer on 4 July 'with gratitude, but not without serious misgiving, as I already know something of the peculiar difficulties of the Diocese. If I am called to undertake this work . . . I pray that God may give me strength for it.'[49]

A polite correspondence passed between Archbishop Tait and Thirlwall. Tait wrote that he would be thinking of Thirlwall as he consecrated Jones to the episcopate. 'I hope,' he added, 'you like what you hear of your successor.' He had known him for a number of years and was aware of the high opinion the archbishop of York held of him. 'We are all glad that a man of some eminence as a scholar and divine should sit in the chair, and he is, I hear, a man of sound judgement.' Thirlwall replied that he believed Jones would justify the archbishop of York's high opinion of him and it gave him pleasure to know that he had offered the new bishop a canonry at St Davids, which he had been unable to accept as he had not been in orders long enough.[50]

Others echoed the same sentiments more publicly, if less discreetly. Disraeli was congratulated for not falling back into 'the old way of neglecting all local needs and putting a Welsh district under the care of a mere Englishman', but neither had he 'yielded to the most modern cry of all' and appointed someone of whom there would be nothing to be said 'except that he is a mere Welshman'. And while the new bishop was Welsh, he was also free from 'absurd local prejudices'.[51]

The *Record* also applauded Disraeli's choice, though no doubt he gave the Queen the credit for it. The editor was all for filling the Welsh bishoprics from the ranks of Welshmen who could speak the language and sympathize with the feelings of 'their ancient nation', besides which an eminent evangelical was noted as saying that the new bishop had a good record for answering letters, was able to master details of diocesan business, and had a voice which filled York Minster.[52]

Although others were to accuse him of hypocrisy, it was an appointment commended by John Griffith of Merthyr, who has already been mentioned as a would-be candidate. He had long advocated the need for native Welsh-speaking bishops, and he had conducted a 'bilingual crusade in Wales' for over twenty years. The new bishop, he alleged, had a better knowledge of the Welsh tongue than many believed. Disraeli was to be congratulated for refusing to listen to the Anglo-Welsh prelates who had their own chosen man whom they had 'highly recommended', and for giving Wales a Welsh-speaking bishop who was not only equal to but in point of rank superior to the favoured candidate (could this be Perowne?). Griffith could not lose the opportunity for moralizing on the issue, alleging that too many Welsh dignitaries had hoped that the new bishop would not be a Welshman. 'Dignitaries of the

Welsh Church', he wrote, 'have been saying these last four years, "Wales will never have another Welsh bishop." Old ladies and old maids re-echoed the cry, "Oh, do let us hope, whoever he may be, that he will not be a Welshman." And even now they say, as though it really were a qualification for the bishopric, "Ah, yes, he was born in Wales, but he cannot speak Welsh." ' But, Griffith continued, these people were like 'Dick Shôn Davydd' who had concealed his Welsh background believing that all that was Welsh was vulgar 'and whatever is not Welsh is genteel'. Such people believed that those who spoke Welsh must have been 'born at the cow's tail', and to own oneself as Welsh was to make oneself 'a vulgar ass'. Disraeli's appointment of a Welshman over against an Englishman would cost such men's 'gentility a deal of soreness'.[53]

Basil Jones's episcopate may be said to have lived up to these expectations, although his knowledge of Welsh was not great and it sometimes betrayed him 'into mistakes which sometimes amused or embarrassed his hearers'. The work of the diocese flourished under his administrative ability; a diocesan conference was established, new diocesan organizations and parochial improvements became the order of the day, and he was much concerned about the spiritual life of his clergy. But on the other hand it might be argued that his diocese was simply continuing the work of church expansion then going on within the Church at large. Though Jones was an evangelical who had never adopted the eastward position, the *Church Times* considered that he liked to have 'a few ritualists to give colour' to his diocese. While he could be stiff and reserved he was yet generous to his clergy and during the tithe disputes gave £500 to one of his archdeacons to relieve clerical suffering. A reconciler, rather than a fighting bishop, was how one person described his life, although even this was a veiled criticism of his then colleague at St Asaph. He died in January 1897 aged seventy-four.[54]

What were the determining factors that led Disraeli to recommend Basil Jones to the Crown for the bishopric of St Davids? It is very hard to know to what extent Disraeli was involved in any case. All the correspondence in this instance was directed either to his secretary, Montagu Corry, or to his political aide, Lord Barrington. It is hard to know whether Lord Dynevor acted as an official intermediary between the Welsh bishops (he was a close friend of Ollivant) and peers or was simply an interfering busybody. When

Ollivant requested a meeting with Dynevor it was in the clear knowledge that a memorandum would be drawn up regarding the claims of various candidates and passed to the prime minister's office.[55] But on the other hand Barrington sent one of Dynevor's letters to Corry with the comment that it should be 'put into the bag with the other memoranda on the subject'.[56]

Apart from the growing influence of Queen Victoria over ecclesiastical appointments, there were two factors which influenced prime ministers in every vacancy, and a third which related specifically to Welsh episcopal appointments. The first two concerned ecclesiastical party and politics, the third language. A note found in the Disraeli papers entitled 'Lord Beaconsfield's Appointments since 1874' considered that three of his episcopal appointments were of high church men, Benson, Lightfoot and Maclagan. Three were low, Thorold, Rowley Hill and the bishop in Jerusalem, and one was broad, Basil Jones.[57] Clearly then, the appointment to St Davids had to fit in with the general distribution of patronage between the various church parties, although it would be hard to believe that Disraeli had much interest in these matters. All he wanted was an even distribution of this patronage.

The colour of a man's politics mattered a great deal to Disraeli, and one wonders if Lewellin's demand for a political appointment finally secured the bishopric for Basil Jones rather than for his nearest rival, Perowne, who was described as a Liberal in politics. Inglis-Jones was one of many who believed that this appointment would be affected by political considerations. He wrote to Corry stating that it hardly mattered to him if the devil was appointed, but he would not like to see the Conservatives discredited by the appointment of such a radical as Perowne.[58] Lord Dynevor also gave advice that was loaded with political references.

The last factor, though about language, also referred to social status. There were few Welshmen qualified both socially and culturally for episcopal distinction, and the critics of Gladstone's precedent of 1870 were quite right to feel, if one accepted the initial premise that a bishop was also a spiritual peer, that further appointments of that kind would suggest that the bishops of the Welsh dioceses were of a lower and lesser status than their English counterparts. To make such a distinction at a time when disestablishment was being pressed by Nonconformity and the Welsh Church was stressing its links with England would have been a tragic mistake. Gladstone had realized that there was a distinction between a native Welsh speaker and one who had acquired that language in later life. Although this distinction was pointed out to Disraeli, he probably never understood it. And even if he had realized it, this cynical Christian convert would undoubtedly have considered that other factors, such as political issues, overruled this argument.

Disraeli's choice of Jones was almost inevitable under these circumstances. He was Welsh – even if his knowledge of the language was not particularly good – a scholar, a gentleman, one who could take his place in the House of Lords with ease and nobility, and he was a Conservative whose appointment would please Disraeli's local supporters. The only wonder is that Disraeli took so long to make up his mind, although this may simply be a sign of his indifference. And yet having said this, one must add that while Gladstone agonized over the appointment to St Asaph, and eventually appointed one whose episcopate was not particularly successful, Disraeli hardly bothered and yet picked a winner.

~ 8 ~

Unexpected and Unknown:
Gladstone's Choice for Llandaff, 1883

Alfred Ollivant, bishop of Llandaff since 1849, died in office in December 1882 at the then great age of eighty-four. His death was unexpected and much mourned: his portrait had only been presented to him some weeks earlier. He was then the senior bishop of the Church of England by date of consecration, but his death was somewhat overshadowed by the death of Archbishop Tait of Canterbury. Indeed, Gladstone's task as premier in filling the vacancy was rendered much more difficult by the archbishop's death. Ollivant, a man of uncomplicated evangelical faith, was the first resident bishop for many generations in his diocese. It was a time when the industrialization of south Wales meant that the population of the diocese was increasing rapidly, and the Church faced enormous difficulties in meeting the missionary situation this created. Although in his later years Ollivant became increasingly autocratic, he was nevertheless one of the great bishops of that see, and under his leadership the Church tackled vigorously the social and ecclesiastical problems of the day. Lord Aberdare, however, surprisingly thought that Ollivant's predecessor, Bishop Copleston, was the more popular bishop, as he possessed greater social qualities.[1]

The appointment was in the hands of the then Liberal prime minister, William Ewart Gladstone. As we have seen, his appointment of the Welsh-speaking Joshua Hughes to the see of St Asaph in 1870 marked a significant change in the history of the Church in Wales. Disraeli, in his appointment of Basil Jones to the bishopric of St Davids in 1874, had reverted to an earlier policy, by choosing a man familiar with Welsh but not necessarily conversationally fluent in that language. Disraeli and his advisors, bearing in mind social and political factors, probably thought this a sufficient gesture to meet the demand for a Welsh-speaking bishop. Gladstone, however, as in 1870, still wished to choose native Welsh-speaking bishops for the Welsh dioceses, not only because of this demand, but also in order to strengthen the Church by providing a preaching episcopate able to outpreach Nonconformity at a time when the disestablishment campaign was becoming a major issue.

Gladstone strove hard to find the right man. He followed the same pattern as before, namely of requesting assistance from his political colleagues and the senior ecclesiastics of the Church, and compiling a number of shortlists of possible candidates. Randall Davidson considered him 'the most painstaking [premier] in regard to appointments' he had known, and this vacancy was one of his most difficult appointments.[2] Writing to Bishop Lightfoot of Durham, Gladstone revealed a little of what Davidson meant:

> A vacancy in a Welch see costs me more trouble than six English vacancies. I feel it my duty to ascertain if possible by a process of exhaustion whether there is any completely fit person to be had among men of Welsh mother tongue. In the main it is a business of constantly examining likely or plausible cases and finding they break down. The Welsh are to be got at through the pulpit; and yet here is a special danger, for among the more striking Welsh clergy there is as much wordy and windy preaching as among the Irish.[3]

It was no easy task. The expectations of the public were alarmingly high, as indeed were Gladstone's own. Every move on his part would be subjected to critical scrutiny, while the number who believed they had the right to offer the prime minister advice and comment was substantial.

Rumours and Requests

Almost as soon as Ollivant had died, and certainly before his funeral at Llandaff Cathedral, letters and requests poured into 10 Downing Street. As K. O. Morgan writes, a 'flood of exhortation and acrimony engulfed the unfortunate Prime Minister'.[4] G. Hartwell Jones, himself a disappointed Welsh episcopal candidate, recalled:

The first episcopal election of which I have any, and that only a faint, recollection was that of a successor to Bishop Ollivant of Llandaff. A Welsh peer with whom I was familiar, received from Gladstone a dispatch-box full of letters setting forth the claims and antecedents of the various candidates; he told me in after years that the correspondence left an unpleasant impression on his mind.[5]

Many of these letters have been destroyed. What remains in the Gladstone papers at the British Library is obviously a representative selection, though even then their number is substantial. Some of these letters were from clergy who pressed their own claims. Among them was Aeron Roberts, vicar of Newchurch in Carmarthen and chaplain to the county prison, who duly applied for 'promotion' to the see of Llandaff. To enhance his claim he enclosed a number of printed testimonials which concerned his unsuccessful candidature for various tutorial posts and the parish of Coety, in Glamorgan, twenty years previously.[6] There were also letters from various pressure groups who endeavoured to get their own man in, whether organized by that man himself or by others with or without his consent. Significantly, it was Henry Thomas Edwards, dean of Bangor, who wrote, albeit critically, of this practice, for it was his brother, Alfred George Edwards, later elected as the first archbishop of Wales, who became the leading practitioner of this art. Writing to the poet Lewis Morris, a prominent member of the Liberal party and a friend and confidant of Gladstone, Edwards indicated his dislike of this practice:

> I consider it indecent for a man to press his friends to recommend him for high promotion. I have asked no one to do so, not either my *Bishop* and noble friends at the Castle [Penrhyn] connected as they are with Hawarden by marriage. Some of my friends have written to express their anxiety on my behalf and I have been gratified by their high opinion of me . . . I should be very sorry that anyone should write on my behalf, from personal kindness, while not convinced of my fitness.

But as Morris was obviously convinced of his claims he could go ahead and petition for Edwards's appointment! The dean continued,

> I am relieved by your note to find I have seen in your mind. I ask no one to do anything. I do not ask you. But if your own judgement tells you

that I could serve my country and the Church at Llandaff, you must be well aware that the expression of that opinion to the Premier and Lord Aberdare by so eminent a Welsh layman as yourself would have much weight.[7]

Clearly Edwards was canvassing for the appointment, though in such a delicate way that even Gladstone did not hold it against him. Edwards might have been gratified to know that Gladstone had been shown this letter by Morris.

Edwards's activities would hardly have pleased John Griffith of Merthyr. He complained about the tremendous 'wire pulling' that was going on everywhere from Bangor to Llandaff in order to secure the appointment of a candidate who would repay these wire-pullers, if chosen, with livings and dignitaries, just as the American president did to those who had helped him to the White House. 'It is a scandal to any country, much more to Wales, to witness any-thing so unseemingly,' he wrote, mentioning in the same breath the 'simony' of the press which exceeded 'anything that Simon Magnus ever dreamt of'. It was alleged that Griffith had the dean of Bangor in mind when he wrote these words.[8]

Randall Davidson, chaplain to the former archbishop and about to become dean of Windsor and the Queen's ecclesiastical con-fident, faced the same onslaught. 'As to the Welsh see,' he wrote, 'I have had such a *"to do"*. All the *ladies* have been writing to me and saying there was nobody suitable except their pet man.' Lady Llanover and Lady Londonderry were both named by him in this context.[9]

This episcopal 'contest' produced the same human reactions as other elections recorded in this book, save that on this occasion they were even more openly expressed. It was asserted, for example, that envy, hatred, malice and uncharitableness ruled the day. The reputations of the clergymen whose names had been mentioned in the public press as possible candidates were treated with 'the malice of the most savage stamp' by newspaper correspondents.[10] To quote an example taken from these letter columns: 'one points to the great evangelical candidate who could slide softly into the easy seat and dream away life's dream. Another to the militant ecclesiastic who would keep his diocese in a flame. There is still another who confounds the duties of a bishop with those of the president of an eisteddfod.'[11] He was probably mentioning in turn

David Howell, Dean Edwards and John Griffiths of Neath. It was also widely regretted that the public debate about a successor should start while Bishop Ollivant was 'hardly dead'. Dean Vaughan said in his sermon about the deceased bishop the Sunday after his death: 'already, yes, even before he was in his grave, a perfect hurricane of unseemly wrangling, of impertinent altercation has arisen over the question of his successor . . .' And he asked where 'admidst all this indecent scuffling and scrambling' and 'strife of tongues' had been the 'prayer to the Lord of the Harvest?'[12] The papers saw no need to censure themselves. The *Western Mail*, for example, censured Vaughan for his statements, while its editor felt perfectly at ease in feeding his readers with rumour after rumour about Gladstone's choice. Before the bishop's funeral he reported that Dean Edwards would be appointed to the see,[13] but after the funeral he suggested that David Howell was likely to be offered it instead.[14] At the end of December, Rowland Ellis was to be appointed. A fortnight later Dean Edwards was to be offered the see, and David Howell of Wrexham would succeed Edwards in the deanery of Bangor. The following day the paper reported the rumour that Canon Williams of Llanelli had been appointed. None of these assertions was true, though the latter rumour must have come from a well-informed source.[15] If the prime minister anticipated a quiet search for the right man, he was rudely awakened to a public and acrimonious debate in the press.

The English/Welsh Debate

The names of possible candidates submitted to Gladstone for his consideration generally fell into one of four distinct categories, namely, those of political, ecclesiastical, English or Welsh recommendations. While Gladstone was advised in these matters by Lord Richard Grosvenor, a Liberal whip and his political manager, there is nothing to suggest that he was unduly influenced by political considerations. Indeed, he was more influenced by Grosvenor's advice that there was a 'universal howl' against the appointment of the dean of Bangor, Henry Thomas Edwards, high churchman and Liberal though he was.[16] Gladstone was equally prepared to ignore Thomas Gee's recommendation of Archdeacon Griffiths, even though Gee was probably the most influential Liberal supporter and Nonconformist within Welsh-speaking Wales.[17] Gladstone also ignored Queen Victoria's suggestion that Llewellyn Davies, rector of Marylebone and one of her honorary chaplains, should be 'thought of among others'. She understood he spoke Welsh, which 'is desirable in this see'.[18]

Lewis Gilbertson, a former vicar of a Welsh parish and vice-principal of Jesus College, and a leading tractarian, wrote from his Midlands rectory that 'Church principles' were needed in Wales. 'The genius of the people', he added, 'naturally adapts to Catholic ways' when they were fairly set before them. Believing that Gladstone shared his enthusiasm for such matters, he pointed out that such religious truths could only be taught through the medium of Welsh. Having pointed out this requirement Gilbertson went on to produce his man, Dean Edwards.[19] The press feared the appointment of a high churchman. The *Western Mail*, quoting the *Echo*, argued that a ritualistic bishop would rouse the militant spirit of the nation.[20] Other 'advisors' emphasized that their man was high or low, ritualistic or evangelical. Gladstone paid little attention. He wanted the best man, regardless of churchmanship.

The Welsh lobby was the loudest and most persistent of them all. Lady Llanover was of this school, and seems to have believed that she had been given a divine mission to advise the various prime ministers whenever there was a Welsh vacancy. She was one of the few, however, who commenced her letters with the hope that God would guide the prime minister in his choice, although one has the distinct impression that her ladyship was strongly of the belief that He was Welsh speaking as well.[21] It is hard to know whether Lady Llanover's forceful intervention did more disservice to those she warned against with her strong vehemence, or praised with loud enthusiasm. In all probability the prime ministers never read her long and near illegible letters. Generally they were summarized by a secretary with a terse endorsement, 'from Lady Llanover (apparently), long rigmarole on rumoured appointment to see of Llandaff . . . Nil.'[22] On the occasion of this election she wrote a number of letters to Gladstone, each one reiterating her ceaseless demand for indigenous bishops in Wales. It was a disgrace, she lectured, that there was not one dignitary in Llandaff who could speak or write Welsh. She had known five bishops of Llandaff and the Welsh clergy were unable to consult or confide in any one of them.[23] Her wants were clear: David Howell was the man 'beyond all doubt';

although William Evans of Rhymney and Chancellor Phillips of Aberystwyth might have been gratified to learn they had gained her approval for high office. Her dislikes were equally plain. For the time being they were centred on Archdeacon Griffiths of Neath.[24]

Bishop Hughes of St Asaph, Gladstone's nominee of 1870, also wrote, and did so immediately after he had attended Ollivant's funeral. There seems to have been some talk among the dignitaries present after the funeral as to the kind of man Gladstone might appoint to Llandaff. As a result Hughes clearly thought the prime minister needed to be strengthened in his resolve to appoint a native Welshman to the see. Though many might favour an Englishman for Llandaff, 'I thank God you that know better,' he wrote, but he went on at such length to establish this point that it seems clear he was not too sure whether the prime minister did actually 'know better'. It was now a great opportunity for strengthening the 'stables of our Zion' as the pulpit was still the great power in Wales. His recommendation was for Archdeacon Griffiths of Neath.[25] The Welsh press too joined in the same clamour. A man was needed who was thoroughly identified with the wants, the prejudices and the aspirations of the Welsh people, suggested the *Morning Post*.[26] The Welsh Church, said a correspondent of the *Western Mail*, 'has not many prizes to give away; but the few it has ought on every principle of justice to be given to those who have served her faithfully and long, and not to gentlemen, however scholarly and estimable they may be, who have spent their strength and best days in other fields'.[27]

The English lobby may not have been as large as the Welsh one, but its influence was substantial and extended into both governmental and episcopal circles. Lord Aberdare was probably its more prominent exponent. Aberdare, who as H. A. Bruce had served in Gladstone's cabinet as home secretary between 1869 and 1873, continued to act as the prime minister's confident in most Welsh matters. He was a brother-in-law of Bishop Campbell of Bangor, an intimate friend of the late Bishop of Llandaff, and in many respects the leading layman of the vacant diocese. He advised that Llandaff was less Welsh in character than St Asaph or Bangor[28] and argued (as he had done in 1870) that other qualifications were needed in a Welsh bishop than simply an ability to preach in the vernacular.[29] Apart from a few noisy clergymen who had pretensions, he claimed that the general body of the clergy had no wish 'to see fitness for the great office of Bishop sacrificed to a knowledge of Welsh'.[30]

As a result of the discussions which took place after Ollivant's funeral Aberdare claimed there was no Welsh-speaking clergyman equal to the task of keeping up Ollivant's work of maintaining the standards of clerical duty, who would also command respect for his character, attributes and theological attainments.[31] Pointing out the good work done by those he described as 'such half and half men' as Ollivant and Campbell, and those, such as Jayne, Vaughan and Perowne, who continued their good work,[32] he went to the touchstone of his argument (as expressed in an earlier letter), 'I sum up, All parties I think gave you credit for your desperate efforts to find a true Welshman for St Asaph. Few, very few, would desire to see the experiment renewed.'[33] His brother-in-law, Bishop Campbell, was one of many who noted Aberdare's pessimism. Misreading a telegram from Gladstone as asking for his opinion about Aberdare's integrity, he was able to testify to it but added significantly, 'possibly Lord Aberdare despairs of bringing back the Welsh masses to the Church by the eloquence of a Bishop in their own language. Others may be more hopeful.'[34]

There were many others who agreed with Aberdare. Rees Goring Thomas of Llanelli summed up their viewpoint by stating that while it was desirable to have a Welsh-speaking bishop, the ability to speak fluent Welsh should not be seen as an absolute necessity in the absence of more important qualifications.[35] C. R. Knight, vicar of Merthyr Mawr and a proctor in Convocation, asserted that the Llandaff clergy had no wish for a Welsh-speaking bishop and particularly not for the dean of Bangor. Should Wales 'be debarred from the best man the Church can supply by a mere sentiment?' he asked, in order to accommodate the 'narrow and unpatriotic principle of "Welshmen for Wales" '.[36] Knight's assertions came close to showing the painful linguistic divide in the Welsh Church and it is hardly surprising he was answered back in no uncertain terms. The struggle for Welsh bishops had been won in two of the four Welsh sees and would be waged strenuously in the other two. The Welsh would win there also.[37]

The *Western Mail* itself had little time for those who favoured the appointment of a Welsh-speaking bishop. Welsh was becoming the *sine qua non* of the appointment, even above the other necessary qualifications for the office, wrote its editor. But why was

Welsh needed? To help restore dissent to the Church? If the appointment of a Welsh bishop, like the foundation of the Church Army, was for no better reason than to fill the Church with the 'sweepings' of society, the process could only be accomplished 'at the expense of the splendid influence and prestige she at present enjoys'.[38]

The English episcopate also tendered their advice. Lightfoot of Durham wrote that he regarded Llandaff as a missionary bishopric. Few English sees could be considered as so important. No doubt a Welshman was preferable, but an Englishman might be better than a Welshman of inferior qualifications. He too had his man if that was the case: G. H. Wilkinson, a London incumbent.[39] Gladstone noted his advice, and indeed appointed Wilkinson to a Celtic bishopric, but in this case Truro, vacated by Benson's elevation to Canterbury. On the other hand the case for a Welsh bishop could be put another way. One writer argued that the Welsh did not want fewer but more qualifications for their bishops than those required for an Anglo-Welsh appointment.[40]

Many regarded John Griffith of Merthyr's letter, advocating the appointment of Dean Vaughan of Llandaff, as a betrayal of the cause of the Welsh movement in the Church which he had long championed. His letter had shaken the confidence of Welshmen in the sincerity of his motives, wrote one. It was one of his worst mistakes.[41] Griffith was publicly accused of disliking any Welsh appointment which overlooked himself. He would swallow 'all the teaching of his life' in order to keep out John Griffiths of Neath.[42] Griffith, who had over the years pontificated against the injuries inflicted upon the Church by its English bishops, now suggested that Vaughan's skill and tact, his large heart, and his sweetness of temper were needed in order to reconcile the differences of party into which the diocese was now divided, even though the dean was not Welsh speaking. Though people might snipe against him on the grounds he had sacrificed his principles in advocating the dean's appointment, Griffith defended himself by arguing that the diocese of Llandaff was different from the other Welsh dioceses as the number of monoglot Welsh speakers within it was extremely low. Referring to the 1870 appointment Griffith wrote: 'There should be no fiasco this time. Mr Gladstone thoroughly understands what I mean. And, though he was compelled by circumstances when he tried his hand before, Mr Gladstone will, all Welshmen trust, take time now and do nothing in a hurry.' A 'mere knowledge of Welsh and the capacity of sprouting out bottled eloquence at an eisteddfod' was not needed, instead a university man, a scholar and a gentlemen was required.[43]

Whether he nominated an Englishman or a Welsh speaker to the see of Llandaff, Gladstone was going to alienate at least one section of the ecclesiastical community.

The Suggested Candidates

A considerable number of names were offered to Gladstone for his consideration. Dr Percival of Clifton College;[44] the archdeacon of Norfolk, Henry Ralph Nevill, who had been born and bred in south Wales;[45] and Dr Vaughan, master of the Temple and dean of Llandaff, were among the 'English' candidates. Vaughan, though the general favourite of the Llandaff clergy and regarded as a Liberal in politics, did not speak Welsh and had already declined two sees,[46] and so his name was not seriously considered by Gladstone. D. R. Thomas of Meifod was suggested by Lord Richard Grosvenor as one well spoken of for learning, moderation, tact and ability, but Lord Richard knew nothing personally about him. Thomas was later archdeacon of Montgomery and the noted historian of his diocese.[47] Grosvenor, whose family home was at Eaton Hall near Chester, recommended another cleric from that diocese of St Asaph, Rowland Ellis the vicar of Mold. While he was a good man, he did not consider him intellectually strong. A correspondent in the *Western Mail*, hearing a rumour that Ellis had been nominated for the bishopric, asked who he was. How could Gladstone overlook the labours and merits of well-known Welshman in favour of 'an obscure neighbour'? If he was appointed, what would be the incentive to labour and usefulness on the part of the Welsh clergy? Bishop Hughes, Ellis's diocesan, felt he was more adapted to parochial life than diocesan, more English than Welsh, and doubted if he had sufficient influence with the clergy to infuse new life into the Church. A noted tractarian, Ellis later became bishop of Aberdeen in the Episcopal Church of Scotland. Although a frequent visitor to Hawarden, Gladstone's home, there is no evidence that Gladstone seriously contemplated his appointment.[48]

Chancellor Owen Phillips, vicar of St Michael's, Aberystwyth, was recommended by Lady Llanover as well as by others. It was noted that Phillips had an ample private income and a presentable wife, which were remarked upon as important considerations, although others claimed he had never identified himself with any national movement. Another consideration was that he lived outside the vacant diocese.[49]

Evan Lewis, then vicar of Dolgellau and later dean of Bangor, a noted tractarian leader, was also recommended to Gladstone as a suitable candidate. Lord Aberdare commented, however, that having known him as vicar of Aberdare, he would say that while devoted to his work Lewis lacked the intellectual power and learning required for a bishopric. He was no more than a moderately good preacher. Others thought him far too young or pointed out that he was not a fluent Welsh speaker, although one writer believed he stood 'head and shoulders' above Dean Edwards.[50] Arthur Jones, vicar of St Mary's, Cardiff, was also recommended to Gladstone, although he was more of a ritualist than a tractarian. Bishop Hughes replied to Gladstone's query that he had often heard Bishop Ollivant lament his 'proclivities to extreme ritualism', his utter want of judgement and his refusal to consider the feelings of his parishioners. His appointment would be a heavy blow to the Church in Wales.[51]

Dr Jayne, principal of St David's College, Lampeter, who had 'pulled up' that college (to use Lord Aberdare's expression), a Welsh speaker and the son of 'a respectable tradesman in the Monmouthshire hills', was noted as a possible candidate by Hussey Vivian, the Liberal MP for Swansea. Lord Aberdare wrote that Dean Vaughan supported the submission of his name 'for consideration'. The Nonconformist and Liberal MP, Henry Richard, in a letter forwarded to Gladstone, regarded Jayne as the ablest man who had given evidence before the Welsh education committee. His principalship of St David's College was one of 'conspicuous success'. But, he added, 'he does not speak the Welsh language'. However, William Sinclair, later archdeacon of London, a relation of Bishop Campbell, thought him rather insignificant. He might be eligible for a Welsh diocese in ten or fifteen years' time, he suggested of Jayne, who seven years later was enthroned as bishop of Chester.[52]

David Howell, formerly vicar of Cardiff and since 1875 vicar of Wrexham, was regarded by many as one of the more eligible candidates for episcopal office. It was widely and correctly believed that Gladstone had seriously considered him for the diocese of St Asaph in 1870. *The North Wales Guardian* wrote of the golden opinions Howell had won for his zeal and energy in church work, and its editor suggested that the duke of Westminster was going to use his great influence with Mr Gladstone on his behalf.[53] But Howell was Lady Llanover's pet, and her over-enthusiastic recommendation on his behalf probably did him no good. He was of the right age, she wrote, was one of the finest preachers in Wales, and had done marvellous work at Wrexham. Gladstone gave a guarded reply. Although Howell was well known to him by repute, there were other qualifications needed for episcopal office besides an ability to preach. It was met by a broadside from her ladyship. Yes, Howell's preaching powers were paramount, but they were more than equalled by his pastoral ministry, especially to the poor, the sick and the dying. Her ladyship alleged that some of the most senior clergy in the Church in Wales wished to see him become bishop of Llandaff. But what, said Gladstone in his reply, has Howell done to deserve a bishopric? He is Welsh, she replied, knew both the north and the south, is an excellent trainer of curates, and had attracted large Welsh congregations in all his parishes.[54] The *Western Mail* also favoured his candidature, and pointed out the universal regard in which he was held when he was vicar of Cardiff, his moderate views and ecclesiastical practices, his earnest Christian life and broad practical Christianity. Clearly Howell was a Welsh version of muscular Christianity. Letters in its correspondence columns asserted that Howell was more acceptable in Welsh national assemblies than Archdeacon Griffiths, his assumed rival, and alleged he was one of the most successful parochial clergymen of modern times, though at least one writer argued that Howell was not much of a churchman.[55] To what extent Gladstone considered Howell's suitability for episcopal office is not known, though Grosvenor, sounding out people on Gladstone's behalf, thought Gladstone knew more about Howell than he did.[56] Nevertheless, it seems probable that royal circles considered Howell to be a close runner, for a note headed 'Facts: The Revd. David Howell' of December 1882 is in the royal archives. It noted his fluency in both languages, his unequalled ministerial experience in Wales and his conciliatory disposition. His appointment would be welcomed by Nonconformists as well as by some of the leading clergymen in Wales.[57]

A Shortlist of Three

By 25 December 1882, obviously a working day for the prime minister, Gladstone had established a shortlist of three candidates. He felt this was a little insufficient, and so he wrote to Bishop Campbell asking his opinion about four other Welshmen: Williams of Llanelli, Evans of Rhymney, Ellis of Mold, and Arthur Jones of St Mary's, Cardiff.[58] The last two have been noted, the first is discussed below. But who made up the actual shortlist? The following names may be suggested: Archdeacon Griffiths of Neath, Archdeacon Watkins of Durham, Dean Perowne of Peterborough and Dean Edwards of Bangor. The first and the last names were of men well identified with Welsh interests and culture. The other two, although both were considered as having an interest in things Welsh, were mainly regarded as being more English than Welsh.

John Griffiths, archdeacon of Llandaff and rector of Neath, was generally regarded as the *eminence grise* of the diocese of Llandaff during Ollivant's closing years.[59] Henry Richard, who reminded Gladstone of this, also testified to Griffiths's irreproachable character. In addition, he was the most effective preacher of the Church. Besides this qualification Richard suggested that Griffith was 'a man of very liberal sentiments' who had done much for such national movements as the eisteddfod and the Welsh university. Although not a favourite with the upper classes Griffiths was held in high honour by the Nonconformists, who would vote for him if the appointment was made by popular election. Thomas Gee, in recommending him, noted his evangelical churchmanship and support of the eisteddfod movement. Griffiths, he added, was respected even by those who differed from him, and his appointment to Llandaff would be well received by all parties within the Church. Bishop Hughes of St Asaph wrote of his involvement in national movements, his friendship with Nonconformists, which would enable him to heal rather than widen the breach between them and the Church, and pointed out that as archdeacon Griffiths had brought new life to many parishes in the vacant diocese, of which he had an intimate knowledge. His appointment, he added in a later letter, would strengthen and extend the influence of the Church, and though (like the writer) he had no university qualifications, he had something that no university could confer: an especial qualification for the work of the ministry.[60] Even the *Western*

190

Mail suggested he would be the best appointment. It was only fitting that 'a life so useful to the nation and so devoted to the Church should be crowned with a bishop's mitre'.[61]

But it was not to be. Lady Llanover had quarrelled with him in the past over the matter of Llandovery College, of which they were both trustees, and she had no wish to see the archdeacon raised to the episcopate. Although he could preach in Welsh, he declined to do so, she wrote, contradicting herself by alleging that his Welsh was no better than if he was ignorant of the language. If Gladstone was looking for a preacher he was not the man, for his Welsh never attracted the crowds. The rumour that he had been appointed reached her in mid-January. With villainous pen she expressed her horror to Gladstone. His sister had been her dairymaid and her husband her bailiff, but when dismissed he took a public house with a rather low clientele in the Cardiff area. In old age the archdeacon had married a young wife at St George's, Hanover Square. Her main interest was in fashion, and her bad taste was not forgotten by those who knew his first wife and her antecedents. While he could talk patriotism loudly with patriots, the archdeacon had not preached in Welsh for years as he could not compete with others, and the only Welsh service at Neath was a monthly communion.[62] Lord Aberdare regarded Griffiths as just 'another platform speaker', less able than the dean of Bangor but 'of that line and less educated'. He carried no moral weight with the clergy and laity of the diocese, although a 'certain fluent facility of speech' made him popular with the multitude. However much the appointment of such a pulpit orator could conciliate Welsh opinion towards the Church, it would be received with dismay.[63] Gladstone must have been amazed with these differing accounts about Griffiths's linguistic and preaching ability, and thus it is not too surprising to note that by the end of December Bishop Hughes, probably at Gladstone's request, was enquiring about another candidate if Archdeacon Griffiths would 'not do'.[64]

Another archdeacon on Gladstone's list of possibilities was Henry William Watkins, archdeacon of Auckland and professor of Hebrew in the university of Durham. Brought up as a Wesleyan in south Wales his father had become churchwarden at Abergavenny, but Watkins had left for England at an early age. Originally intended for the Wesleyan ministry, he had trained at King's College, London, and studied at Balliol College, Oxford. His rise in the

Church was rapid, and after some years as warden of St Augustine's College at Canterbury he had become an archdeacon in his mid-thirties. A good administrator, the life and soul of all he undertook, and a man of eloquent fire, Watkins was Archdeacon Sinclair of Westminster's nomination for the bishopric, even though he wrote that the loss to the bishop of Durham would be great indeed. When consulted Bishop Hughes was rather negative about Watkins. No amount of scholarship could compensate for his inadequate knowledge of Welsh. Despairing of finding a Welshman for Llandaff, Gladstone wrote to Bishop Lightfoot of Durham asking for his opinion. The reply was conclusive. Watkins, replied Lightfoot, was only half a Welshman. He had an idea that his name was being mentioned for Llandaff and asked his bishop 'to stop it'. It was inadvisable for him to go there because of the problems of his father's second marriage, which was too local for him not to be involved in if he was appointed. This, said Lightfoot, was no reflection on the archdeacon, and with some 'longer discipline' to mature him he would be well qualified for the bishopric that should be his. This advice, wrote the prime minister to Bishop Campbell, had eliminated Watkins's name from his list of candidates for Llandaff.[65]

If Gladstone wanted an Englishman, argued Bishop Campbell, the best man was Dean Perowne of Peterborough. Others thought differently. He had received his deanery as a reward for his 'Jingo speeches' and his Tory instincts, declared the London *Echo*.[66] As a former vice-principal of St David's College, Lampeter, and canon of Llandaff, Perowne had acquired some smattering of Welsh which was subsequently regarded by Lord Salisbury as sufficient for him to be offered the diocese of Bangor in 1890, which he was persuaded to decline. Sinclair regarded Perowne as dry and chilling, lacking in energy, and added that he had quarrelled with the Welshmen whilst he was at Lampeter. Lord Aberdare, who had known him at Llandaff, felt he had no knowledge of Welsh though he had a high reputation in the south Wales dioceses, and as a writer on theology had done more than Jayne. But Lewis Gilbertson had heard that he was not orthodox. In his Lampeter lectures and Peterborough preachings Perowne had argued that the apostolic succession was not necessary to the constitution of the Church. How could one be loyal to the Prayer Book with such a belief? argued Gilbertson, apparently unaware that the vast majority of Welsh clergy would fall into this category. Gilbertson concluded that in the present circumstances his appointment would be 'disastrous'.[67]

Most observers believed, whether they were for him or against his appointment, that Henry Thomas Edwards, dean of Bangor, was the favoured candidate. Gladstone writing to Aberdare said that if a Welshman was to be appointed his 'claims' were very prominent. His own bishop felt that if Gladstone wanted a Welshman then the dean was probably the best candidate, though he pointed out that the Llandaff clergy were much against his appointment. Gladstone, in his reply, argued that if he could believe that he, the bishop of Bangor, could have a steadying influence on him, 'it would incline me much towards naming him'. In fact so close was Edwards to being nominated to the Queen for the vacant see that T. W. Vaughan, vicar of Gwyddelwern in Merionethshire, congratulated the prime minister upon his elevation of Edwards as 'an Act of Justice to the Principality', and both Dean Vaughan and Lord Aberdare were quoted by Bishop Campbell as having begged Gladstone to reconsider his assumed decision in his favour.[68] 'Half the letters I receive are about him,' wrote Gladstone, 'all vehement, whether aye or no', while Grosvenor told his chief that all his contacts had sounded 'a universal howl' against him on the grounds of his affront to Nonconformists. Welsh Calvinists '*never* forget or forgive', he added.[69]

The dean's case for episcopal promotion was pressed by Lewis Morris. He wrote to Grosvenor on Edwards's behalf, suggesting him for the vacant bishopric, and enclosing a letter of the dean, which has already been quoted. Grosvenor, who thought it 'a very sensible and proper letter', sent it on to Gladstone. Morris, knowing the weak chink in the dean's armour, argued that despite his attacks on the Nonconformists he was by no means unpopular with them because he was an ardent Welshman. 'If he held his hand', he almost wrote in despair, 'as age and office would certainly make him do, he would be the most popular cleric in Wales.' Edwards was also aware that Lord Aberdare, once his best friend, now judged him less favourably since the Harper affair (the attempt by the principal of Jesus College to de-nationalize that college). He needed to regain that favour if he was to be endorsed as an episcopal candidate. Considering that honesty was the best policy, Edwards now admitted in that same letter to Morris that in this controversy his pen and ingenuity had run away with him. But he would not be the turbulent or fighting bishop Aberdare thought he would be, for then he would be the judge, not the advocate. Responsibility would tone him down, and his short experience in Canada and the States had convinced him that not only should the Church 'live side by side with the sects amicably' but had also greatly modified his horror of disestablishment. If he had no wish to push for office, Edwards clearly was glad someone was pushing him, and he was quite prepared to help from the sidelines.[70]

Bishop Jacobson of Chester, one of Gladstone's oldest contemporaries, had appointed Edwards to the parish of Caernarfon. He spoke well of Edwards, but rather spoilt the effect by adding that he had heard him spoken of as impetuous and better qualified for north than for south Wales. Nevertheless, he enclosed a letter from Canon Robert Williams, rector of Llanfaelog in Anglesey, and a well-known evangelical leader in the north. Williams argued for a 'Welsh' bishop, as the Welsh were leaving the Church because of an alien episcopate. He feared lest the prime minister, acting on limited knowledge, might appoint a Welsh speaker who lacked the necessary higher qualifications of a spiritual life. He believed the dean ought to be appointed.[71] Thomas Biscoe, vicar of Holyhead, also recommended Edwards as one respected by Nonconformists,[72] a point also taken up in a letter by 'Ex Monte' to the *Western Mail*. Edwards, he pointed out, was the only clergyman who would defend the Church from Nonconformist attacks in the press. He had chased away those 'hirelings' of the Liberation Society who had done so much to set Nonconformity against the Church. Furthermore, Edwards was admired by the Nonconformists for his pluck, honesty and integrity.[73] 'Churchman', writing in the *North Wales Guardian*, wrote of the dean's scholarship, his successful administration, tried experience and untiring energy, but he knew there were objections which had to be faced. Was he too young? Certainly not, was the reply. Rather it was an injustice to crown the declining years of a man with a bishopric when he had to see through the eyes of other men and lean upon their judgement. If Edwards was too controversial in his defence of the Church, then the bench was no place for rambling and backboneless men.[74] A fellow scholar with Edwards at Jesus College, Owen Roberts, who identified himself as a Liberal and a churchman, likewise defended him on this score. The dean had married into two strong Welsh

Nonconformist families, had cooperated with the Nonconformists in the temperance and Sunday closing movements, and was well spoken of by them.[75] Hartwell Jones mentions in his autobiography that an objection was made to Edwards's promotion because of his attacks on Nonconformity. Grosvenor replied that the writer was mistaken. The dean had 'recently changed his opinions on the drawbacks of Dissent'.[76] One wonders if this was part of an organized attempt by Edwards to obtain a bishopric.

Edwards had many supporters, but an equal if not a greater number of people had no wish to see Edwards mitred. Henry Richard felt that Edwards had created such a bitter feeling in Wales that he feared for the peace of a diocese under his rule. He was a man of 'an ambitious and imperious temper'. His recent article in the *Quarterly Review* endeavoured to blacken the character of the Welsh people in order to discredit dissent. It had caused a bitter feeling.[77]

Hussey Vivian wrote that people dreaded Edwards's high church 'proclivities' and feared that the harmony of the diocese would be upset if he was appointed. G. G. Talbot, writing from Falconhurst, Kent, argued that his tone and temper debarred him from office. David Howell, writing to Gladstone as a result of an intermediary's request, considered the dean superior in mental energy to any other Welsh clergyman, in force of character, and equal to any in moral courage and zeal, but he felt he would be lacking in frankness if he concealed his apprehension that his uncertain temper, his attitude towards Nonconformity and his love of controversy would disturb the peace of his diocese. A letter of J. W. Wynne-Jones, vicar of Aberdare, to his father-in-law, Lord Aberdare, shown to Gladstone, notes the respect Jones felt for him as his curate at Caernarfon. But he also mentioned the great faults of character Edwards had struggled against and from which he would never be safe. His temper too was uncertain, while his ability as an orator all too often encouraged him to overstretch his arguments with antitheses and dichotomies that had no basis in fact.[78] The *Western Mail* was of the same opinion, declaring Edwards to be the knight errant of the church militant. It accused him of having used his abilities to outrage the religious sensibilities of Nonconformity. The diocese of Llandaff did not need a fighting and attacking sort of bishop, but one who without sacrificing any principles was fair and sympathetic to all people irrespective of denomination. This the dean was not, and his appointment would signal the renewal of hostilities.[79] 'Cyw Bawddwr', writing in the same paper, suggested that the dean's supporters formed a mutual 'audition' society 'to gratify their decided *penchant* for what the Welsh call *Pwffyddiaeth*'.[80]

As Gladstone began to regard Edwards as the favoured candidate, Lord Aberdare became correspondingly more decisive in his advice. His letters now revealed his strong antipathy towards the dean. Aberdare had known Edwards especially well during his tenure of the parish of Aberdare. His two years there had been disastrous. Arriving in the parish during the midst of a cholera epidemic, during which the previous vicar, Evan Lewis, had acted with courage and devotion, Edwards was seized 'with such an extreme terror that he took to his bed without any ailment and finally fled . . .' For six months of his two-year tenure he was absent from the parish due to a nervous breakdown caused by the 'rupture of a matrimonial engagement with one of the Fothergill daughters'. He was not absolutely insane, but incapacitated from business. The consequence was a great restlessness, a want of discretion, and a need for excitement. He had acquiesced in Edwards's appointment to the deanery (a major factor in his favour for episcopal office) as he thought it would help his balance of mind, although he had obtained it mainly because of the scarcity of eligible men in that diocese. Aberdare thought the dean was 'singularly unfit' for such office. He was not a good-working clergyman; rather he was an ineffective preacher, 'a poor presence, feeble physique, and a dull style of utterance'; his character could be summed up by the epithets 'loud, sweeping, inaccurate and impulsive'. His attitude to the question of Jesus College changed as public opinion moved, and he had given great annoyance to and aroused the disgust of Dean Vaughan for his recent speech to the Llandaff Church Extension Society, which was in startling contrast to the speech of David Howell. He may undoubtedly be popular, Aberdare concluded, but the *vox populi* was a very unsafe guide when it came to the selection of bishops. If he was to be appointed, he would come 'with a flourish of trumpets from the Welsh press, and a chorus of congratulations from the Nonconformists', who did not understand what sober churchmen required in their bishops.[81]

With such divergent views expressed about Edwards, Gladstone appealed to the bishops for their assistance. Hughes of St Asaph replied that while the dean was honest in his convictions, and was so good natured that few could be angry with him for long, his commentary on St Matthew's gospel had described the Nonconformist ministers as workers of iniquity and as having separated themselves from the true apostolic ministry of the Church. Dr Lewis Edwards of Bala, Welsh Nonconformity's premier theologian, had been strong in his criticism of these statements. The Welsh clergy were more of the school of Hooker, Hughes thought, and Edwards's churchmanship would not be congenial to them. The hint was thus made that those Nonconformists who were still friendly to the Church believed Edwards's appointment would injure that relationship which Hughes had no wish to see checked or destroyed. There were better men, he advised, such as Archdeacon Griffiths, who could be chosen instead of Edwards.[82]

The dean's own bishop, Dr Campbell, who had appointed him to the deanery, felt at first that if Gladstone wanted a Welshman then the best choice was Edwards. Though the dean was impulsive and self-willed he was yet amenable to advice. Furthermore, he was well educated ('rather rare among the pure Welsh'), and well liked by the Nonconformists as a temperance leader. In later letters he argued that while no one had done more for the Church in Wales through the medium of Welsh than the dean, he was excitable and impulsive and his besetting sin was vanity. Impatient of contradiction, Edwards had had sharp confrontations with the local clergy, while he could be overbearing to those under him. Nevertheless, Edwards had worked cordially with him and he was indebted to him for much assistance. Time and experience would 'ripen' him and make him a valuable addition to the bench.[83]

As a result of these letters Gladstone concluded that Edwards needed more experience before he could be placed on the episcopal bench. Writing a little later (for Gladstone seems to have temporarily placed the dean's name onto his second shortlist of candidates) Gladstone told Campbell that it was with 'pain and reluctance' he had taken his name off that list. He wanted 'more ripening', Gladstone stated, but he also argued that the 'entourage' at Llandaff, 'which cannot be put wholly out of view, would tend greatly to aggravate the disadvantages and neutralise the merits of such a choice'. Whether he was wise to speak about his correspondent's family in this way is open to doubt (Aberdare was Campbell's brother-in-law), but at least he wished Edwards well, and hoped he would find his way to the bench. Campbell, in his reply, expressed a similar hope, but accepted that as there were so many influential people against Edwards's appointment in the diocese of Llandaff, it would be a 'dangerous experiment to alienate the tried friends of the Church [in order] to conciliate those whose feelings are more nationalistic than religious'.[84] But time did not allow. Always of a nervous disposition, Edwards took his own life a year later. The mitre was eventually picked up by his younger brother, Alfred George, who gained it by combining the militancy of his brother with a taste for statistics and intrigue. What had damned his elder brother six years earlier became the means of his promotion. Quite simply, the dean lived under the wrong government.

The Final Choice

His original list of candidates discredited, Gladstone was left in a difficult position. His shortlist had been completely trumped. Llandaff was not the easiest of dioceses to fill, and it might be easier to find a bishop from another see. Perhaps if he were to arrange a translation to, rather than a new appointment for, Llandaff, his difficulties would be over. Aberdare had made this suggestion to him some time earlier, and as his shortlist was falling to pieces Gladstone now acted on his advice. Aberdare had further suggested that his brother-in-law of Bangor might be willing to move to Llandaff, where he had many friends, and had served for many years. If this were so, argued Gladstone, the dean of Bangor would be far better received at Bangor as bishop than at Llandaff. The evangelical *Record* recorded this development by early January, though its supposed candidate for Bangor was Dr Vaughan.

Campbell was rather surprised at Gladstone's suggestion. He felt that Bangor of all dioceses needed a Welshman who was 'one of themselves in nationality and language' (he had got the message twenty-three years too late), and he felt somewhat attracted to Llandaff. Gladstone replied a little too eagerly: his respect for the bishop's character and his confidence in his judgement would make him willing to submit his name to the Queen if Campbell thought a translation desirable. The bishop thought it over but replied by the next post. At the age of sixty-two it was no time to be seeking a new and larger post of duty.[85] A correspondent in the *Western*

Mail was scathing in his condemnation of this suggestion. Campbell, a Scotsman, he wrote, had acquired only a superficial knowledge of the Welsh language and people, and was now advanced in years. Bangor was a kind of 'sleepy hollow' which was never disturbed save for 'the occasional war-whoops of its doughty dean'. But whoever hears of its bishop? he asked. It was simply a case of the old game of making diocesan sees a reward for personal friendship. To offer such an old man these 'tremendous responsibilities' was almost an act of cruelty.[86] Overtures were also made to Basil Jones, bishop of St Davids. He could 'be called upon to untie the knot', suggested Aberdare, and Evan Lewis could take his place, or alternatively Campbell be translated there. The idea was explored but soon rejected.[87]

Gladstone was clearly perplexed. His candidates for office were all 'breaking down'. Writing to Campbell on New Year's day he sighed, 'the wood seems to get more tangled as I penetrate further into it'.[88] At this point he seems to have noted a letter he had received a few days before which had recommended yet another candidate. This was the recommendation of Richard Lewis, archdeacon of St Davids, by Lewis Morris and the bishop of St Davids. Lord Aberdare had passed on the bishop's letter to Gladstone, stating that Lord Cawdor had also suggested Lewis, and then adding the significant remark that it was satisfactory to know that there was more than one Welsh-speaking cleric who was qualified for episcopal office.[89] His lordship must have changed his mind, for in an earlier letter he had queried Lewis Morris's assertion that Lewis had the necessary qualification for a Welsh bishopric.[90] Nevertheless, the bishop of St Davids wrote directly to Gladstone as soon as Christmas was over. He knew it was essential for a Welsh bishop to speak Welsh, especially for his confirmation work, for many people were ignorant of English in these dioceses. Basil Jones also recognized Gladstone's difficulty of finding a Welsh-speaking man who was qualified for episcopal office. It was a difficulty which could only grow as the Welsh language 'goes downward'. Having consulted with two other men of influence in his diocese he felt it right to bring his archdeacon's name to the notice of the premier. Lewis was an excellent man of business, a good and popular archdeacon, rector of a bilingual parish, and a gentleman of a good social position. No other Welshman could stand alongside him even though he might be called a high, though not an extreme, clergyman.[91]

It was clearly what Gladstone wanted to hear. Here, perhaps, was his man.

Richard Lewis was the son of a gentry family long domiciled at Henllan, Pembrokeshire, to which estate he eventually succeeded. For the previous thirty years he had been rector of Lampeter Velfrey, with a population of just over 1,000, and since 1874 he had been archdeacon of St Davids, to which he had been nominated by Disraeli during the vacancy in the see. It was said that he only accepted it when he learnt that the new bishop, Basil Jones, had suggested the appointment to the premier. Lewis had been instituted to Lampeter Velfrey after a celebrated ecclesiastical battle. Thirlwall, then bishop of St Davids, was not convinced that Lewis's Welsh was good enough for a bilingual parish. Under the terms of 1 and 2 Victoria, chap. 106, the bishop appointed three examiners to test Lewis's competence: one of them was Joshua Hughes, later bishop of St Asaph. They failed him, stating that while his reading was tolerable his composition would excite ridicule and expose him to contempt. Lewis appealed to the archbishop of Canterbury, claiming in his defence that the bishop's examiners had examined him not so much in 'ordinary' Welsh as for an honours degree in the subject. Furthermore, he was ill at the time and not properly prepared. The archbishop appointed his own examiner under the terms of the above act, Thomas Thomas, vicar of Caernarfon. Before he underwent the second examination Lewis spent much time preparing for it by assisting various clergymen in their bilingual parishes, taking Welsh services and preaching in Welsh. The result was that he obtained a considerable number of testimonials as to his linguistic competence in the Welsh tongue, and after a successful examination Thomas Thomas expressed himself satisfied that Lewis was qualified in spirit and letter for the requirements of that act. He was thus instituted to the living by Thirlwall.[92] As an 'esteemed' correspondent of the *Western Mail* put it at a later date, 'this plucky little man was not to be ousted from such a prize too readily'.[93] Lewis had done much good work at Lampeter Velfrey. His communicants had increased from fifteen to 130, and although he had had problems regarding the tithes, he had done good work as an educationist.[94] The archdeacon was also regarded as a mild tractarian, having signed the dean of St Paul's memorial in favour of toleration in matters of ritual. His activities as SPG organizing secretary in his diocese seemed to confirm this viewpoint, as did his introduction of a 'moderate ritualism' into his church services with intoned responses and surplices for the choir. In politics he was regarded as a Conservative.[95] Lewis was also a Freemason who later compromised his Christian convictions by serving as grand chaplain of the order.[96]

An incident of some years earlier was probably remembered in his diocese, and would undoubtedly have been mentioned had it been thought he was a serious candidate for the episcopate. This had occurred during the 1874 election for proctors to represent the clergy of the diocese of St Davids in the lower house of Convocation. These were open elections, normally conducted in Carmarthen, with election speeches and printed election addresses. The election was normally held after an open debate, during which the candidates and their sponsors spoke. The speeches on these occasions were widely reported in the local press. They frequently made unseemly reading, and even more so when the candidates, their supporters and their opponents subsequently attacked one another in the letter columns of the local newspapers. On this occasion Lewis was elected but his chief rival, the Welsh champion Dr Thomas Walters of Llansamlet, was not. Walters accused Lewis, after the event, of ignoring and ridiculing the interests of the Welsh-speaking members of the Church in Wales in his election speech, and of doing so in a sarcastic and insulting manner. Lewis replied in a public letter in an equally tempestuous manner. Dr Walters's bitterness was that of a disappointed man who was now the victim of 'strange delusions'. Lewis had simply wanted to pour ridicule on the delusion that 'in an assembly where nothing but English is spoken [the] ability to speak Welsh is essential to the successful advocacy of Welsh interests'. A letter by one 'Spectator' indicated the extent of Lewis's insensitivity to the Welsh language. Those who are 'conceitedly ignorant' of their own tongue, he wrote, but who 'cheer to the echo the rector's claptrap' should not believe that 'in his small sarcasm [they have] a strong tower of argument for their ignorance'. Lewis's comments, however well justified they may have seemed to him, could only be regarded by the Welsh *gwerin* clergy as further evidence of the gulf between the poor Welsh clergy and their wealthy English counterparts within the diocese. Henceforth Lewis stood as a marked man.[97]

Gladstone followed his usual custom when presented with a new name. First, he requested references from those who knew him, and secondly he put that new name on a shortlist with other candidates in the expectation that his advisors would compare and contrast their abilities and personalities.

Thomas Thirlwall, nephew of the late bishop and a Radnorshire rector, appears to have recommended Lewis as against Chancellor Phillips, but Bishop Campbell did not know Lewis well, for the archdeacon's sphere of duty was 'more remote from here than England'. Gladstone could have confidence, however, in the judgement of the bishop of St Davids. Lord Aberdare was not so enthusiastic as that bishop. It would be a respectable appointment, he advised, but 'nothing more, an inferior Basil Jones, with nothing like his learning, his abilities or general reputation . . .' Lewis would certainly be more acceptable to Llandaff than the dean of Bangor, but his Welsh was not so good. A subsequent letter added a characteristic aside: Lewis as 'a three quarters man' was still inferior to an English candidate.[98]

Gladstone by now had a second shortlist. Lewis of Dolgellau and the dean of Bangor (his claims now revived), were briefly on it,[99] but by 7 January there were but two names, Archdeacon Lewis and David Williams, vicar of Llanelli, who had previously held a chair at St David's College, Lampeter. Williams had been considered by Gladstone for St Asaph during the 1870 election. Aberdare was not too impressed by Williams, for while all spoke well of him, it took little ability to gain a high reputation in Wales. Nevertheless, he enclosed a letter from J. W. Wynne-Jones, the vicar of Aberdare, who wrote that Williams had done well in Llanelli, his social position was supported by his marriage into a good family, but he was not an attractive preacher in Welsh. On the other hand Williams was perhaps 'too gentle . . . to deal with the bullies of ecclesiastical life' and might not be equal to bold action. If he was appointed bishop he might shrink, as a man of peace, from any new departure. In all probability Williams had 'never fixed on a mitre' and would prefer to be the ruler of one rather than ten cities. Aberdare concluded by remarking that more was needed for a bishopric than being a good parish priest, making clear that the balance was against Williams.[100] Williams's brother-in-law, Rees Goring Thomas, hearing that Gladstone was anxious to hear the views of Welsh laymen, disputed the need for a Welsh speaker. If Gladstone still wanted such a man, he could recommend Williams, but presumably as he was his brother-in-law he suggested the premier should contact the bishop of Winchester, Harold Browne, who had been vice-principal of Lampeter during Williams's time there. His good opinion of him has already been related in a previous chapter.[101]

Gladstone's advisors were now asked to compare the two favoured candidates, Williams and Lewis. The bishop of St Davids found this task a difficult one as he was friendly with both parties, but in the end considered that while Williams would make a good bishop, he was still in second place to Lewis. He felt that Lewis was more fitted for a place of authority than Williams, and he carried more weight with the clergy. There could be no question about Williams's Welsh or Lewis's efficiency, but he had never heard Lewis preach in Welsh, although he knew he spoke Welsh with 'perfect facility'. Thomas Thirlwall put Lewis first, though he was not certain of his Welsh, and Williams second. Bishop Campbell, a little unfairly, considered that Williams was committed to rather an extreme party, was 'slow and somewhat ineffective in delivery', and was not half the man that Lewis was, 'who would suit the Diocese capitally'. Lord Aberdare's nephew, William Conybeare Bruce, felt Lewis was the man, and Lord Aberdare himself, though he noted that Lewis did not possess Williams's sympathetic piety, learning and his experience of a large parish, felt that Lewis had the other qualities needed in a bishop which Williams lacked.[102]

Gladstone was now about to make his decision. Writing to Aberdare he informed him he was 'nearer the necessary point of choice as a man afloat on the Upper St Lawrence gets nearer Niagara'. It was not the happiest of expressions, nor was it meant to be. Lewis, he pointed out, had questionable Welsh, but there was more evidence of energy and pastoral success in Williams than Lewis.[103] Many had noted Lewis's deficiencies in Welsh, and many repeated the advice of Bishop Hughes of St Asaph who had warned Gladstone that Lewis's Welsh was barely sufficient, even though he had passed an examination in it.[104] But Gladstone preferred Aberdare's advice that the diocese of Llandaff required not so much a fluent Welsh speaker as a good administrator. And it was upon such an understanding that Gladstone seems to have made his choice.[105]

On 12 January 1883 Gladstone wrote to Archdeacon Lewis offering him the see of Llandaff with the sanction of the Queen. Although he had not the honour of his personal acquaintance, 'I venture to give you the assurance that the selection of your name has rested on no other grounds than that of reputed fitness, [and] that it has been the result of no small inquiry and consideration.'[106] The letter was totally unexpected, both to Lewis and to the Church at large. Lewis later wrote that when this offer came, he was not aware that Gladstone knew of his existence. 'No letter,' he wrote, 'ever produced a week of more utter wretchedness. The mental pain and suffering which that letter caused me are known only to God and my own heart.'[107] A writer in *Yr Haul* suggested that when his name was mentioned as the new bishop, all asked who and what he was, but within twelve hours all was known, and more than known, about him, and every shoemaker was discussing him.[108] At first Lewis wished to decline the offer, being ten years older than Ollivant when he was appointed. He made his first ever visit to Llandaff where the dean assured him that he would be acceptable to the diocese, which news, said a reporter, 'seemed to inspire the venerable gentleman with some degree of confidence'. On the advice of Bishop Basil Jones and others whom he consulted, and who advised him that it was his duty to accept 'such a high and responsible office', together with the persuasion of his wife, Richard Lewis accepted the nomination of the Crown to the see of Llandaff.[109] It was an impartial choice. Lewis was no partisan in churchmanship, he was Tory rather than Liberal, and his appointment would probably not satisfy the aspirations of the Welsh party. Gladstone looked for the best man for the see, and refused to gratify the whims of particular pressure groups.

The *Church Times* assumed that it was his knowledge of Welsh that had gained him the appointment. That language, it suggested, was a *sine qua non* in his parish, and thus the new bishop possessed 'what has been so greatly insisted upon as absolutely necessary in a Welsh bishop'.[110] Others were not so sure. 'Cymro', writing in the evangelical paper, *The Record*, argued that the new bishop merely possessed an acquired and limited knowledge of the language. At a push he might be able to read and compose a sermon in Welsh, but he was certainly not a Welsh scholar. His appointment had come because he was a friend of some influential Liberal politicians in south Wales, and he was a high church man at a time when the prime minister was determined to exclude evangelicals from places of authority within the Church. 'Cymro' also took umbrage at some statements made in a *Western Mail* report on the election. The bishop, it said, was involved in all the amusements of a country gentleman; shooting and fishing were some of his pastimes, and he excelled as well as any curate in croquet and lawn tennis. But, he asked, were these the qualifications required in a bishop? The appointment was a snub to the Welsh clergy, and it indicated that the oldest see had been sacrificed to 'party exigencies'.[111] *The Record* also protested in an editorial that Lewis's promotion was but another of Gladstone's 'unbroken line' of high church appointments. The evangelical party was being excluded from Gladstone's episcopal patronage.[112] A *Yr Haul* correspondent alleged that this English appointment was not a kindness to the men of Gwynedd. All the Welsh dioceses were now ruled by men of the south, and this seemed to be a rule of law rather than an accident of fate. Had Dyfed some charm for Gladstone that he should choose yet another bishop from that region?[113]

But other voices were also heard. The *Western Mail* considered it a good appointment. Lewis had demonstrated the abilities needed in a bishop during his time as archdeacon. He favoured the National Society and temperance, and he possessed abilities which were badly needed in his diocese, such as a concern for church building and restoration as well as for clergy discipline.[114] A writer in *Yr Haul* defended Lewis's record as a preacher in both languages. He 'does not sprout like Jones Blaenannerch, or gestures like Rhys Davies, or sweat drops across the Bible as Hwfa Môn does' (they were prominent Welsh Nonconformist preachers), but despite these handicaps he could not be bettered: 'if in doubt go and hear him and be convinced in five minutes.' Lewis was not a high church man, rather his churchmanship was based on the Bible, the Book of Common Prayer and the Articles of Religion. At sixty-three he was not over age, for he had never overworked himself but instead had laboured quietly and persistently throughout life, leaving the results to God. All in all, he had been a very successful clergyman, in spite of his misfortune in being incumbent of a neighbourhood which was so Nonconformist and prejudiced.[115] Francis Jones in his essay on his life and episcopate regards him as a 'country priest writ large', an understanding given credence by Bishop Owen of St Davids who, in a memorial sermon to Lewis, said that his rural ministry had prepared him for the charge of a populous diocese.[116] That may be so. What is true is that he rose to the office entrusted to him and enhanced it.

Alfred George Edwards:
His Appointment to St Asaph, 1889

Joshua Hughes, the first 'Welsh' bishop of modern times, died aged eighty-two in January 1889. An August holiday to Crieff, Scotland, ended in tragedy when he was paralysed by a stroke. Helpless and almost unconscious, he was just able to sign a letter authorizing the bishop of Bangor to perform the episcopal functions of his diocese, but unable thereafter to sign his deed of resignation.[1]

His appointment to St Asaph by Gladstone in 1870 had been greeted with much favour throughout Wales. But although he continually moved in Welsh circles and was a pioneer in the revival of Welsh Church life, his tenure of the see of St Asaph was relatively undistinguished. In many ways this was the one diocese to which a person of his background should not have been appointed. There can be little doubt that Hughes was resented in a diocese whose leading clergy were well-educated members of the local gentry whereas he was a man without a university background and was an evangelical of humble birth. The *gwerin* clergy of the diocese found it equally hard to respect a person of their own background, such was their cultural conditioning.[2] His successor, referring to him as Lady Llanover's man, told John Owen that he had alienated the gentry from the Church and made them 'almost into disestablishers'.[3] However, Hughes built upon the administrative foundation laid down by his predecessor, Bishop Short; gave the diocese a pastoral ministry unknown since the days of Bishop Horsley; and handed to his successor a diocese so effectively run that Edwards was able to devote much of his time to the fight against disestablishment. Hughes's episcopate was thus a quiet interlude between two aristocratic regimes.

It was quite clear from the time of his stroke that Bishop Hughes would have to resign. The archbishop of Canterbury, Edward

White Benson, advised the prime minister, Lord Salisbury, that it might be necessary to nominate a coadjutor bishop for the diocese with the right of succession. Legislation permitted this, but the bishop's death ended the suggestion, though had this nomination taken place it might have become an interesting precedent for future appointments.[4]

Some criticism was expressed about the delay in the bishop's resignation, but few were aware of the difficulties involved. One correspondent in the local press even asked why the bishop had not retired earlier. How could a man of that age do his duty, he asked, especially when there were a number of ardent, able and zealous men of middle years available to take his place? This state of affairs was causing much injury to the diocese, particularly as clerical red tape prevented any other bishop or clergyman assuming the bishop's duties by proxy. Yet, he continued, the bishop's stipend was still being paid. In his eighteen years of office he had received over £80,000, unlike the poor incumbent of Llandegla who had to exist on an income of £95 per annum without the benefit of a parsonage house.[5]

The bishop's long incapacitating illness and his inability to resign meant that Lord Salisbury, the Conservative prime minister of the day, was given space to find the right man for a very difficult see; a see divided in terms of language and culture, and at an even more difficult time. For this was the time of the first intensive period of the disestablishment controversy, during which the tithe disputes were becoming increasingly problematic. Many churchmen believed that the 'final grand onslaught' of protestant Nonconformity and liberalism would be made against the Church of England in Wales within the next few years.[6] An appointment was needed, therefore, that would recognize these facts, and provide a leadership for the Church at this critical time in its history. Writing a fortnight before the bishop's death, Archbishop Benson informed the prime minister that to fill such a see, 'so as best to meet the difficulties of the Church in Wales is, I am aware, no easy task at present'.[7] Few would have disagreed with him.

Consequently, long before Hughes's death, the prime minister was 'overwhelmed with advice' as to the qualities required in the man he should appoint,[8] and with recommendations of possible candidates. Speculation was fuelled by the press, both local and national. In September, a month after Hughes's incapacity and four months before his death, the correspondent of *The Times* warned that 'controversialists' should be excluded,[9] and in the same month the *Wrexham Advertiser*, assuming the bishop would retire on a third of the see's income, £1,400, suggested a number of candidates: Dean Perowne of Peterborough, Dean James of St Asaph, who was soon to move to the headmastership of Rugby, and Canon Howell of Wrexham.[10] Benson had already submitted a number of names to Lord Salisbury: Canon Thomas Williams of Bangor; Frederick Edmondes of Llandaff (though he doubted he would accept despite possessing all the necessary qualifications); A. G. Edwards, vicar of Carmarthen and secretary to the bishop of St Davids, who though he was 'not quite ripe' might 'be a success'; D. R. Thomas of Meifod and J. Lewis Meredith of Gelligaer, who had been highly recommended by the bishop of Llandaff.[11]

It was almost universally accepted that the new bishop should be Welsh-speaking, and preferably a preacher who could draw large congregations.[12] The *Church Times* mentioned that a group of Welsh clergy, through a Welsh representative, had informed the prime minister that a strong man who was a Welsh speaker was needed in view of the attacks being made on the Church. The *Baner* attributed this more to the fear of the Welsh clergy that the premier would be in a hurry to fill the post and ignore the real needs of the diocese.[13] When the appointment of Archdeacon Watkins of Durham was rumoured, if not announced, the protests poured in to newspapers and to Downing Street. Whatever other qualities he possessed, it was argued, he lacked the primary qualification of one engaged in the work of spiritual oversight, that 'of being able to hold communication with his flock in their own language'.[14]

David Jones, rector of Llanfairpwllgwyngyll in Anglesey, and a noted historian of the Welsh Church, wrote to the archbishop on the assumption that Salisbury had passed on the appointment of the new bishop to the archbishop.[15] This was denied by the bishop of St Davids.[16] But more correctly Jones went on to assert that Welsh churchmen looked upon the appointment as an indication of the policy that the government intended to pursue in the future with regard to the Church in Wales. If an Englishman or an anglicized Welshman was appointed, the hopes of Welsh churchmen would be crushed. The only hope of regaining lost ground, humanly speaking, he added, was in having bishops who could effectively address the people in the vernacular. Canon Howell, he suggested, could fulfil these requirements. He thus requested the archbishop to use his influence to secure a 'really' Welsh bishop for the Church in Wales, 'at a time, and on the eve of a crisis, when her stability and strength will be put to the severest test'.

A more influential note came from Dr Jayne, vicar of Leeds and bishop elect of Chester, who was a former principal of St David's College, Lampeter, and brother-in-law to A. G. Edwards. Noting the difficulties the premier was having in finding a successor to Hughes from amongst the Welsh clergy, Jayne offered to exchange Chester for St Asaph if Salisbury thought that he could 'in virtue of my Welsh experience, interests and sympathy – do better service to the Church' than in Chester. This could not be seen as a 'promotion', though he felt there was one great obstacle to such a transfer. He wrote in explanation of this comment:

> No one can feel more strongly or how much more vividly than I do the disadvantages under which a merely English speaking or an imperfectly Welsh-speaking clergyman labours, if placed among the Welsh-speaking parts of Wales. He has to fight at all events with his left hand tied behind his back. My own work as Principal of Lampeter would in some important respects have been much more efficient and fruitful had I been at home in the mother-tongue, and more especially, the devotional tongue of the district. I am therefore deeply, because by experience, sensible of my inferiority and disadvantage in this respect.

Jayne held that there were qualified Welsh-speaking clergymen available, although he did not mention his brother-in-law, Alfred George Edwards, by name.[17]

Salisbury, argued the *Record*, could not reverse the precedent established by Gladstone in 1870, or commit the mistake of confusing an Englishmen resident in Wales with a Welshman born and bred. His appointment of Jayne to Chester, rather than a Welsh see, showed that he understood that position.[18]

If the new bishop should be Welsh speaking, a writer in the *Guardian* commented, he should also be a strong leader, one who could rally the clergy around him to face the Nonconformists' 'unscrupulous attacks' against the Church, instruct the Church people in the strong points of their case and take the initiative in recalling people to the Church.[19] The new bishop, suggested the evangelical *Record*, needed to be 'chosen with future contingencies no less than present necessities borne well in mind'. But the *Record* noted another requirement it considered indispensable for this see. An evangelical appointment was essential. Surely Salisbury would not send a high churchman, possibly a ritualist, to succeed Hughes, for that would be 'a blunder so obvious, so far-reaching in its effects, and so disheartening to a large body of English and Welsh Churchmen that we do not like to think the calamity possible'.[20]

Welsh speaking, a strong man, an evangelical; no wonder Salisbury was in difficulties. With St Paul he might well have echoed, 'who is sufficient for these things?' As already noted an enormous number of names was submitted to him or bandied about in the press. A typical example of the latter is found in a *Western Mail* letter column from 'a disinterested vicar of 36 years' standing'. There were not many suitable Welsh clergy to choose from, he wrote (though they all said that), but one was Dr Walters of Llansamlet, who was also a proctor in Convocation. If moderate in his views (he meant evangelical) he was yet sound and safe; a splendid organizer and administrator, an outstanding bilingual preacher who attracted the masses and unrivalled as a defender of the Welsh Church.[21] Similar letters addressed to the press or the prime minister could be repeated *ad infinitum*. It was stated too that four clergy of the diocese of St Asaph had been strongly recommended to the prime minister, but their cases were not pursued, as Salisbury followed previous practice and declined to consider the claims of non-graduates or of anyone connected with the vacant diocese in question.[22] In one instance, however, it appears that even if this was true, Salisbury was prepared to vary his practice.

This was the case of David Howell, vicar of Wrexham. The *Record* noted in early February that Salisbury, in accordance with the usual practice, had submitted two names to the Queen for the vacant see. These names, it was understood, were those of Howell and Canon Watkins, archdeacon of Durham.[23] Whether matters reached this far is impossible to say, but it is clear that both names received careful and serious attention, and that both men were regarded as clear possibilities for the vacant see.

We turn now to see the arguments for and against the appointment of these and other candidates.

The Candidates Assessed

David Howell, vicar of Wrexham, had been widely suggested as the man best qualified to succeed Bishop Hughes. Indeed, he had been considered for that see in 1870. An ardent Welshman, of the same rural and Welsh background as Hughes, an evangelical, a noted preacher in the Welsh tradition and a keen eisteddfodwr, his ministries at Cardiff and Wrexham had made him a man to be noted in the counsels of the Welsh Church. 'A thorough specimen of a Welsh Churchman and a most popular man among his brethren in the diocese, his appointment would give universal satisfaction . . .' declared the *Wrexham Advertiser*, understandably effusive of its local man.[24] This was written soon after the bishop had been taken ill, but after his death the editor's enthusiasm for Howell knew no bounds. His eloquence in both languages, his pastoral concern, his activity in many movements irrespective of sect or creed, had secured him the esteem of both churchmen and Nonconformists. Clearly, his long experience would make him the practical, working bishop that St Asaph needed.[25]

That doyen of Welsh women, Lady Llanover, once more added her support for Howell as she had done on former occasions. In his younger days Howell had been a member of her national stable and worn her colours. But she hinted darkly to Benson that Howell's character was being 'traduced' 'to the highest personage of the Realm', while the bishop of St Davids was promoting the claims of his secretary A. G. Edwards.[26] She appears to hint, in her deplorable handwriting, that her two allegations were somehow connected.

Joseph Cullin, one of the six preachers of Canterbury cathedral and a noted missioner who had worked extensively in Wales, argued that 'no one would have half the power with the Welsh people' as Howell. He was clearly writing to defend Howell against his detractors, for not only were men recommended, they were also critically appraised by the Queen and the prime minister's correspondents. If 'a want of culture' was one accusation against Howell, Cullin explained it arose from his lack of a university degree, but Howell had 'more literary culture' than nine-tenths of those who opposed his nomination. He was not a society man, but surely he was to be commended for 'the great . . . patriarchal simplicity of his life'. The opposition to his appointment arose from those who feared he would be over-active in requiring the Welsh clergy to do their work, and also because he was not a lover of advanced or ritualistic services and had made his feelings known in no uncertain manner about the necessity of reform within the Church. If Howell was appointed, Cullin thought, not only would he be a most able, willing and energetic diocesan, but he would also have as much individual influence as the four bishops of the Welsh Church had previously exercised collectively.[27]

Influential support for Howell came from another English source, the evangelical bishop of Exeter, Edward Henry Bickersteth. Writing with diffidence to Salisbury, and making it clear he was writing without Howell's knowledge, he enclosed an article in the *Standard* about the requirements needed in the new bishop of St Asaph. 'I could not help saying to myself', he wrote, 'why, Canon Howell . . . seems to possess every qualification the writer of this article claims'. He noted in particular his eloquence, the wide influence he possessed over his fellow clergy (which he had observed for himself), and a recent publication of his which showed 'a statesman like grasp of the position, and to mark him as a man who would lead others to victory. I am sure he is a man of faith and piety.'[28]

Both Lady Llanover and Cullen suspected that a powerful lobby to prevent Howell's candidature had been formed. At first Lady Llanover assumed this was because the bishop of St Davids was endeavouring to promote Edwards, and thus needed to eliminate any stronger candidate. But a month later she was writing to Salisbury having heard a rumour that the Queen had received some information 'which tended to injure his moral character', and had declined to consider her prime minister's recommendation of Howell for the see. The information, supplied from other sources, was that Howell's eldest son was born a month after he and his wife were married. It was probably a case of 'bundling' in the traditional Welsh manner of courtship. The matter was so delicate that her ladyship merely hinted at this, pointing out that when it had happened Howell was only nineteen years of age, and since then he had led an exemplary life. The matter, long since buried, and which had occurred, she believed, before Howell became a churchman, had been raised for an ulterior motive by those who wished to prevent his candidature.[29]

There is a strong suspicion that this information about Howell's past was made known to Benson, and possibly to others in authority, by Evan Jenkins, an Oxford graduate who had been vicar of

Manafon in Montgomeryshire since 1880. As Edwards made use of this information in order to disqualify Howell as an episcopal candidate on other occasions, there is an equal possibility that he, or his friends, also made use of it on this occasion to remove one of the strongest candidates from the scene.

The story gradually unfolds amongst the papers of Archbishop Benson at Lambeth Palace. The letters that concern us were written in 1893 but relate to this occasion. At Manafon, Jenkins had come into conflict with one Mrs Baynard, the wife of a former churchwarden, who complained to the archbishop that Bishop Hughes had made that wealthy parish a convalescent home for bachelor rectors and their housekeepers. Jenkins had made himself so obnoxious to his parishioners that she would not allow him over the threshold of her home. The Sunday services were shamefully neglected. He had even allowed the parish schoolmaster to preach instead of himself. Bishop Hughes noted there had been some irregularities at a children's service, but suggested that the real dispute was over the tithes, Jenkins only allowing an abatement to those in need of it, which probably did not include Mrs Baynard. Her accusations against previous clergy had been followed up by the bishop and the archdeacon of Montgomery and were found to be 'wild and inflammatory' (she had claimed that one lived in his kitchen in a drunken state, and another had attempted the murder of his wife and child) so that it seemed clear that she was motivated more by malice than truth.[30]

It should have been quite clear to those who read Jenkins's letters that his mind had become deranged, and part of the background to this story (which hardly emerges in the correspondence) is that having been found guilty in a local court of drunken and disorderly behaviour, he was suspended from, and later deprived of, his living. Being a bachelor his brother, Edward Jenkins, vicar of Lisworney near Cowbridge, took care of him, and brought him back to their childhood locality at Llantrisant. For a time Jenkins was committed to Bridgend Asylum, and was later sent to Fresherton near Salisbury, which he described as a place where people could 'be polished off speedily with the sanction of the law'. He accused these places of all kinds of 'diabolical barbarities', as he was later to accuse Bishop Edwards of endeavouring to murder him by starvation in order to put one of his favourites into his living, and of increasing the stipend of his curate whose wife 'was a prodigy of the foreigner the bishop had married'.[31]

Discharged in 1892, and writing mainly from London addresses, Jenkins informed the archbishop that he had distinguished himself as a clergyman before Edwards was a babe-in-arms, and then blamed himself that such a man should have been appointed to the see. Consequently, he wrote:

> David Howell of Wrexham was to be the man, but your grace was informed by me that Howell's first son, Taliesin, was born a month after marriage, and that it was Archdeacon Griffiths of Neath who was responsible for this man being in the ministry, who both married him and baptised his child in the space of two months, and yet persuaded him to enter the ministry of the Church. Though the insane cry for Welsh Bishops, he would have attained the mitre but for the intervention of the Queen herself.

He continued this theme in another letter. While he had some respect for Howell, he had none for Edwards. Indeed Howell was a saint compared to 'the reckless ruffian' who has been 'pitchforked' into the see of St Asaph.[32]

Was Howell's name mentioned to the Queen for this vacancy? It appears it was, for a letter among the papers of Queen Victoria in the royal archives at Windsor is endorsed 'Recommendation of Canon Howell to the See of St Asaph 1889'. Writing to the Queen's secretary, General Ponsonby, on 28 January, Salisbury noted in this letter the serious difficulty about Howell. He had seen an admission in his own hand that he had 'lived with his present wife before he married her, and the first child was born a good deal too soon'.[33] Sir Theodore Martin, the biographer of the Prince Consort who had a country house in north Wales, wrote deeply regretting this 'domestic scandal'. Had he known the circumstances he would never have recommended his name to the Queen, though Howell was 'regarded by high and low in the Principality as the fittest man'. A further letter from Martin, who had investigated the matter, pointed out that Howell was only eighteen when this happened and had no thoughts of being ordained. Ollivant had accepted him for ordination in full knowledge of these circumstances 'and did not think they were a bar to the admission to Holy Orders'. Should 'a juvenile transgression, followed by marriage, while the transgressor was a layman . . . operate against him after a long life of exemplary conduct and recognized efficiency?' If this rule was to be strictly applied, he continued, it 'would have stopped the career of many, who have proved themselves most valuable Churchmen'. Those who knew about Howell's transgression had 'forgotten and forgiven it, for the sake of the good he has done'.[34]

Salisbury was initially inclined to agree with Martin, but had to reconsider his position when he became aware that both the archbishop and the bishop of Exeter considered Howell's transgression to be a 'blot fatal'. Bishop Bickersteth thus wrote to Salisbury:

> I had not the faintest suspicion of any such bar sinister on the escutcheon of the Canon's past history. I deeply lament it, but feel how formidable, perhaps insuperable, an obstacle it is to his appointment, for 'a Bishop must be blameless, as the steward of God'.[35]

Salisbury was also advised that if the matter became public knowledge it would be exploited by the Welsh Nonconformist press to the disadvantage of the Church. He felt it impossible to recommend Howell to the Queen for this reason, while he wrote that he had received 'many (almost ferocious) denunciations of the appointment'.[36] It seems clear that Howell's claims had been carefully considered and sympathetically noted, and he appears to have been Salisbury's front runner for a time. Sadly he was damned by a tragic incident of his youth.

The archdeacon of Auckland in the diocese of Durham, the 45-year-old William Henry Watkins, was regarded as such a prominent candidate for the vacant diocese that an apparently unofficial announcement of his appointment was made. His name, said the papers, was a household one in England and Wales.

Watkins was a native of Breconshire, and a personal friend of Bishop Lightfoot of Durham, who when appointed to that see brought him into the diocese, gave him the archdeaconry, and desired to see him elevated to the bench. For personal reasons Watkins had asked not to be considered for the appointment to Llandaff in 1883. Although he was a moderate high churchman the *Western Mail*, in announcing his appointment, believed 'his views would be perfectly in touch with the clergy of St Asaph . . . and altogether he would be an ornament to the Church and the bench of bishops.' The premier has chosen wisely![37]

The south Walian *Western Mail* may have been happy with Watkins's rumoured appointment, even though his knowledge of

Welsh was not known, but the *Record* recorded a very different reaction. It commented that if Watkins was unable to preach in Welsh then his appointment was 'painfully inappropriate'. The high church papers had stressed that a knowledge of Welsh was of comparatively small importance. The *Record* thought otherwise, accusing the high church party of being more concerned with its own interests than with the prosperity of the Church in Wales or the peace of the Church of England. If some might conclude that this was an outburst of the evangelical school, the *Record* went on to quote remarks of Dean Edwards in the same vein, and he was a high churchman. Although Watkins had done good pastoral work at All Souls', Newcastle, where he was also vicar, he had signed Dean Church's memorial for the toleration of extreme ritual practices. His appointment meant the superseding of yet another evangelical dignity by a churchman of the opposite school, and besides this, Watkins's experience had been exclusively in England. It was not a happy appointment. Rather it was one that had been 'pushed' by the high church party to the exclusion of Welsh interests. If Lord Salisbury wanted to make the Church still less powerful in Wales then his wish would be gratified by the appointment of a non Welsh speaker.[38] *The Times* too, noting 'the annoying appointment of Archdeacon Watkins', said if the Church wished to hold its own in Wales it needed to retain the affections of the Welsh people. The appointment of a non Welsh speaker would not assist this process. The *Baner* commented that Lord Salisbury had appointed the next best thing to an Englishman, a man who was a stranger to the feelings of the Welsh people who had, in any case, turned their backs on the Welsh Church.[39]

Watkins was not appointed; he even denied he had been offered the see of St Asaph.[40] Was it simply speculation? Did the press infer that because Howell had been rejected then Watkins had been appointed? Or was a kite thrown into the wind, and hastily brought down when it was found that the opposition was too strong? And was the *Record* correct that the archbishop had strongly advised the nomination of Watkins? The official announcement, it continued, was premature as the Queen had not been consulted. She was so annoyed with this move against her prerogative that, as in the case of the late archbishop of Dublin (Trench) when Palmerston had offered him the see of Gloucester and Bristol without prior regal consultation, she positively refused to carry out the suggestion, even though it had been announced.[41] The *Western Mail* claimed the news had come from a senior cabinet minister, and added the moral that while it was an old story not to put one's trust in princes, 'it is the first time we have experienced the truth that the same rule applies to Ministers of the Crown'.[42]

The Final Choice

Most Welsh commentators were agreed on one thing about Watkins. His appointment to St Asaph would have been a disaster. It was a poor compliment to the Welsh Church, argued the *Western Mail*, when it possessed such men as David Howell and Alfred George Edwards, the vicar of Carmarthen: the selection of either of them would give satisfaction to most church people.[43] The hints were becoming clearer. The *Wrexham Advertiser* in early February suggested that the person being considered for the bishopric was well known as a scholar, platform speaker and preacher, and would stand side by side with the new bishop of Chester, Jayne. It was largely a clerical appointment (presumably made on the advice of the Welsh bishops), but it would give general satisfaction.[44] This was a fairly clear 'nod' in the direction of A. G. Edwards, for that was his reputation and he was a brother-in-law to Bishop Jayne at whose consecration he had preached.[45] Bishop Jones of St Davids was his great patron, stated the *Wrexham Advertiser*. If Howell, this paper suggested, had been disqualified through lack of a university degree (though he possessed all the other qualifications), and Watkins who, though he had high scholastic attainments, was found unsuitable because of his deficiency in Welsh, Lord Salisbury had found a man who combined both these qualifications in the person of the vicar of Carmarthen, A. G. Edwards.[46]

Edwards was aged forty and came from a distinguished clerical family. His grandparents had been strongly influenced by the Welsh Methodist revival. Henry, his elder brother, had been dean of Bangor, and a distinguished figure in the Welsh Church and in the movements to establish its national identity, but his reputation for controversy and instability had denied him episcopal office on three occasions. Edwards's first major appointment was as headmaster of Llandovery College. He later claimed that Lady Llanover's influence had been a determining factor in his ecclesiastical career, for he knew the Welsh word for butler, and she did not.[47] The inevitable clash followed, for while he brought the college into the mainstream of English public-school life, he effectively, perhaps inevitably, ended its role as a Welsh school, and totally ignored the terms of its trust deed. The issue came to public knowledge over the ending of the annual Welsh awards given by her ladyship. Her vented spleen was well advertised in the local press.[48]

As vicar of Carmarthen, Edwards followed a long evangelical succession (the *Church Times* described it as 'an extreme Puritan' place[49]), though he was a high churchman. But here, and in his concern for the Welsh people of the town, he appears to have adopted a sympathetic attitude, even establishing a new Welsh church, and managing to persuade the church people to accept a surpliced choir. Although he also served as rural dean and as the bishop's private chaplain or secretary, many believed his most important work had been in the sphere of Church defence. Nevertheless, it was felt by some that in his defence work he had adopted a too controversial tone when a conciliatory spirit was required.[50]

It was this 'dialectical calibre', to use K. O. Morgan's phrase,[51] evidenced by some challenging attacks on Nonconformist statistics in letters to *The Times* , together with his track record at Llandovery, which probably influenced Salisbury to nominate Edwards to the Queen for appointment to the see of St Asaph. It seems that the bishop of St Davids also pressed his claims,[52] while Davidson informed General Ponsonby at Windsor that 'Edwards will do well'.[53]

The Times, the *Guardian* and the *Standard* expressed gratification at Edwards's appointment. He would be a strong and acceptable bishop, and also a Welsh one. He had worked exclusively in Wales, and was familiar with the genius and circumstances of the Welsh people.[54] Even the *Record* greeted his appointment with some relief, writing that though he was a high churchman, 'he had not been at all conspicuous in its peculiar interests'. While it would have preferred a more evangelical appointment, it was at least thankful that the new bishop, like his brother the late dean, was more concerned for the Church at large than for the interests of any section of it.[55] The *Church Times*, however, was persuaded that he was a high churchman, but believed he would be a staunch upholder of the Church in Wales and would do much 'to retrieve the ground which the false policy of his predecessor lost to her'.[56] The *Western*

Mail, true to its Conservative bias, wondered how the Nonconformist press would take the appointment. This press had castigated the prime minister during the rumour of Watkins's appointment in order to discredit him, and wanted nothing better than the Church's downfall. It continued:

> We shall wait with some curiosity to hear what they will say now that the appointment has been given to a native Welshman, a man who speaks, writes, and preaches in the vernacular, a man in the full vigour of life, health, and activity, popular with his countrymen and friendly disposed beyond any cleric we know towards Nonconformists generally and the members of their ministry in particular. If these be qualifications, Welsh people of all classes and creeds will pronounce Bishop Edwards a *persona grata*, and the act of Lord Salisbury in recommending him to the favour of the Queen will be deemed worthy of all praise. There can be no doubt that, other things being equal, the advent to a Welsh episcopate of a powerful Welsh preacher like the whilom Vicar of Carmarthen is a distinct gain to the Church. If the common tradition be true, that the Welsh people were preached out of the Church, then will they, and must they, by parity of reasoning, be preached into it again. The preaching must, however, be of very a different type from that which obtains amongst the Nonconformists of the present day. It must be Gospel – purely and simply Gospel – none of that political tub-thumping which has already disgusted a great part of Wales and is daily disgusting an even greater one. Of this truth the new bishop is perfectly cognisant – none, perhaps, more so.[57]

The spiritual future of Wales lay with the Church, for, as Edwards frequently remarked, Nonconformity was unable to meet the religious aspirations of the Welsh people. Summarizing his position the *Record* proclaimed that while he held these views, 'it is clear that he does not regard with favour the notion that the Church should succeed and thrive by a partizan and factious spirit, but that its power and influence should depend upon its being the most spiritual body in the country'.[58]

The Welsh press provided the sour note. The nationalistic magazine, *Cymru Fydd*, was as representative of any in its annoyance at Edwards's elevation. Noting the rapidity of his promotion, it added: 'it is evidence that he has always grazed in green pastures.' It continued:

Can he preach? Not proven, we believe. Can so young a clergyman, who is so inexperienced in parochial duties administer the affairs of a diocese with discretion and success? It is uncertain . . . The Rev. A. G. Edwards only lately appeared above the horizon of Wales. About a year ago he wrote letters to the *Times* to prove that the Calvinistic Methodists were decreasing in numbers and influence, and he savagely attacked the vernacular press. He soon found out his mistake, and then advocated that a union should be formed between the Welsh Church and this declining denomination of Nonconformists . . . We have no fault at all to find with this latter proceeding, but the 'right about face', was so quickly done that we fear the appointment of the Rev. A. G. Edwards promises to supply Wales with a career of brilliant instability. Church people will rejoice in the new Bishop's energy, zeal, and talent, and be annoyed at his indiscretion and fickleness: Dissenters will be charmed with his affable pleasant manners, and exasperated by his random attacks; the world will be greatly amused, but nobody will trust him. May this young Bishop escape the danger indicated so plainly by the Apostle, 'A bishop, then, must be . . . not a novice, lest, being lifted up with pride, he fall into the condemnation of the devil.'[59]

What were the mechanics of Edwards's appointment? Hartwell Jones alleged that a group of ambitious clerics, with their head-quarters at Lampeter and Llandovery, had formed a 'conspiracy' to capture the highest offices on the Welsh Church, under the guise of being its defenders. Such men, he argued, had an anti-Welsh bias, and believed that 'the only hope of salvation for the Welsh Church lay in pandering to England' and thus losing the Welsh identity of the Church. The two leaders of this group, Edwards of St Asaph, and John Owen, later bishop of St Davids, managed to obtain a strong influence over the prime minister of the day, Salisbury. Furthermore, they had at their command 'a brood of sycophants from whose fangs no one's reputation was safe', who were 'employed to rake up incidents of the past which could be distorted to the detriment or disadvantage of victims'.[60]

Most readers of Hartwell Jones's autobiography, in which this passage occurs, would dismiss his allegations as over colourful at the best, and as occasioned by a frustrated ambition at the worst. But there is evidence to suggest that many of Jones's contentions were based on some degree of fact, and that he was aware of what was happening in the innermost counsels of the Welsh Church. Edwards made himself notorious over his reaction to the appointment of Lloyd to Bangor in 1890. He had wished for Owen. Some of the clergy of that diocese petitioned against the appointment of any bishop who might resemble Edwards and follow his methods of political intrigue and undercover operations. In his own diocese Edwards faced three major and public rows in the early years of his episcopate. One was with Howell, who had become archdeacon. This row, although outwardly about Howell's apparent endorsement of a disestablishment scheme, which he denied, was in reality about the way in which Edwards was conducting his campaign against the disestablishment of the Church, using political rather than spiritual weapons. Thereafter Edwards made continual use of the one discreditable episode in Howell's life to prevent his candidature for any Welsh bishopric.

A further row took place with another archdeacon, D. R. Thomas, who acted in partnership with a considerable number of the diocesan clergy. Although this was publicly said to be about the bishop's patronage (he was in fact promoting as dignitaries only those who agreed with his policy), it was once more about Edwards's policy on Church defence, which not only stressed the links with England at the expense of Welsh nationality, but also defended the Church by attacking Nonconformity. Edwards demanded the absolute loyalty and allegiance of his clergy to this particular policy. In the light of these 'rebellions', G. W. E. Russell's strictures against schoolmaster-bishops take on an added force. One even wonders if he had Edwards in mind when he wrote that 'the petty despotism of a head-mastership is, without exception, the worst possible training for any position where feelings have to be considered, and persuasion has to be used, and criticism anticipated, and even sometimes resistance encountered.'[61] And so it was, alas, with Edwards. There was a further row in 1898.[62] Significantly, the two senior men involved in these rows, Howell and D. R. Thomas, had been regarded as candidates for the see in 1889.

Through his involvement in the disestablishment campaign and the tithe disputes Edwards became as close to the prime minister as the most senior bishops of the Church of England. He used his position to good effect. As the *Carnarvon and Denbigh Herald*, a paper in the Liberal interest, suggested some years later, Edwards and Jayne's power in controlling the Welsh Church was considerable, for 'their influence in the highest political circles was very great'.[63]

For example, Edwards suggested that a baronetcy for Sir William Thomas Lewis of Aberdare would gratify Conservatives of all classes in Wales, and he later obtained financial help from the premier for Church defence work.[64] There is evidence that he endeavoured to take a prominent part in the election to Llandaff in 1905, so that Archdeacon Edmondes, having declined the appointment but called in to advise the then premier, Balfour, refused to do so until Edwards had left his Downing Street study.[65] Gladstone, still to serve his last terms of office as prime minister, was a resident of the St Asaph diocese, and Edwards frequently consulted him, asking him to use his influence, for example, in the tithe disputes;[66] persuaded him to support his desire for the Church Congress to meet at Rhyl, at a time when the Welsh Church was under special attack;[67] and corrected Gladstone's opinions on Nonconformist claims and statistics.[68] Clearly Edwards had an almost direct entry to the various governments of that period, and he made full use of his opportunities to obtain a Welsh episcopate sympathetic, or at least not hostile, to his plan of campaign.

Hartwell Jones's comments may well be applied to this St Asaph election, even though the policy was then in an elementary stage of its development. Jayne, ex-principal of Lampeter, and Edwards, ex-headmaster of Llandovery, worked together for the latter's appointment. There were ties of blood as well as of interest. Jayne wrote to Salisbury offering himself for St Asaph, yet virtually stating that his would not be a good appointment as he did not speak Welsh. This was written on 23 January, when Watkins, a non Welsh speaker, was still being considered, and just about the time when Howell had been dismissed on the grounds of immorality. The prime minister was clearly at his wits end to find a man acceptable to both the Welsh and English interests of the Church, let alone the diocese, and this pressure from Jayne and Bishop Jones of St Davids would have made him more sympathetic to Edwards's claims as the last eligible candidate in the race. It was not the first, nor the last time when a man was nominated because all his rivals had had their claims eliminated.

It would be absurd to claim a 'conspiracy' on this occasion, although the word might be used to describe the actions of Edwards and his 'syndicate' in later elections. Even then it must be remembered that these men shared a common view of the needs of the Church in Wales, though one found rather unacceptable by the older clergy. The younger and more ambitious men naturally gravitated to the strong leadership exercised by Edwards (he was probably one of the most decisive leaders the Welsh Church ever possessed), and were well rewarded for their support. Those who opposed him were left out of the running, as Edwards was prepared to use guile and cunning in an endeavour to discredit them and prevent their appointment to high office, as Hartwell Jones infers. None could deny Howell's unfortunate past, even though it could be excused. But what might be hard to excuse is the way in which Edwards and his friends used this and other similar information to discredit their rivals and advance their own candidates, if not their own candidature. But on this occasion Edwards's claims were strong, and at that time they were found acceptable by a large cross section of people within the Welsh Church. As the *Rhyl Advertiser* commented, it was hoped that the new bishop would find the courage to drive the engine and not sit forever in the brake-van, as was usual with the Welsh bishops. But it also suggested that his well-known principles might cause him a 'troublesome' future. And so it proved to be.[69]

~ 10 ~

The Levisian Maze:
The Election to Bangor, 1890

James Colquhoun Campbell, the Scottish-born bishop of Bangor, resigned his see in April 1890. His resignation was delayed because of an appeal against his judgement in a case involving the rector of Beaumaris. Declining to retain possession of the palace, as was his right, he accepted the pension of one-third of the income of the see, which meant that his successor had to manage on £2,800. Campbell was then in his late seventies and had held the see for over thirty years. He died at Hastings in 1895.[1] The news of his impending retirement enabled the prime minister to start the process of finding an eligible candidate, while it also offered the same opportunity to the many Welsh factions who wished to push forward their own men. The dean of Windsor and the Queen's ecclesiastical confident, Randall Davidson, felt quite sorry for the prime minister, who had had to face the St Asaph vacancy the previous year, 'having again to plunge into the levisian Jonesian and Evansian maze'. For his own part, he could never sort out 'as to which is which'.[2]

Dean Perowne of Peterborough was favoured by Lord Salisbury, the prime minister, but not supported by the ecclesiastical establishment. John Owen, dean of St Asaph, young and thus easily dismissed, was supported by Bishop Edwards of St Asaph and his friends, and later abandoned by them in favour of Watkin Williams, the then dean of St Asaph. David Howell, archdeacon of Wrexham, was supported by a number of English bishops as well as by the Welsh patriotic party, and Daniel Lloyd, headmaster of Christ College, Brecon, seems to have been supported by a party that had developed in opposition to Edwards. Bishop Jayne considered that in March the names under consideration were Howell, Lloyd and Owen,[3] later to be replaced, it was said, by Lloyd,

224

Perowne, Watkin Williams, and Rowland Ellis of Edinburgh, a former incumbent in the diocese of St Asaph.[4]

Obviously these were not the only names to be submitted to the prime minister for consideration or paraded in the public press for cosmetic purposes. The bishop of St Albans suggested D. J. Davies, rector of North Benfleet in Essex. As a Cambridge man he would offset the too many Oxford appointments to the episcopate, or failing him, Shadrach Pryce, compiler of a popular Welsh hymnal.[5] David Williams, rector of Llandyrnog in Denbighshire, was nominated by Bishop Ryle of Liverpool as a powerful Welsh preacher and a thoroughly evangelical clergyman, though not a university man.[6] The bishop of St Davids, hearing that Ryle and Howell had recommended Williams, probably on party grounds, wrote to Davidson that while he was not a bad sort of man he would do nothing to raise the character of the Welsh clergy.[7] Protheroe of Aberystwyth was also mentioned,[8] as were Archdeacon Edmondes of Llandaff ('a gentleman'); Canon Thomas Williams of Bangor, later archdeacon of Merioneth ('too young, much spoken of'); Archdeacon Pryce of Bangor ('desired by the present bishop, not by leading clergy'); and Canon Roberts of Llandaff, later dean of Bangor (who seemed promising but young): all these comments coming from the pen of Archbishop Benson. But, he warned Davidson, there were 'certain prominent persons to beware of', namely Howell of Wrexham, Llewelyn Thomas of Jesus College, and Rowland Ellis.[9] The bishop of St Davids was the source of his information here, warning that strict enquiry should be made as to their antecedents, and eliciting the comment that he knew the reason in the first case, but not for the others.[10]

The press was full of letters suggesting the names of possible candidates. This caused considerable distaste to several people, including one who wrote under the pseudonym of 'Offeriad'. These recommenders, he wrote, too often measured others by themselves. Should a sprat appear among the minnows such men 'magnify it to a whale'.[11] Another correspondent, 'A Lay Churchman', held that those who made such recommendations were curates or 'petty vicars' anxious to please.[12] The kind of line these men took is exemplified by a letter signed by 'Cymro Eglwysig' which appeared in the *Western Mail*. He wanted a further name added to a list provided by another correspondent. This name was that of the rector of Lampeter Velfrey, David Pugh Evans. His claims were that he had preceded the present bishop of St Asaph at Carmarthen and the present bishop of Llandaff in his present parish. As a born leader of men he had been appointed rural dean, and was almost idolized by the clergy of the two deaneries in which he had served. He was always courteous and good tempered even under provocation; qualifications that were indispensably necessary for the success of any Church dignitary. In the same issue 'Neader' of Glamorgan wrote of two clergymen, David Williams, vicar of Llanelli, Carmarthenshire, and Joseph Hughes, rector of Cwmdu, as men well adapted to fill the vacancy.[13] No doubt most of these letters and recommendations deserved the derision that was heaped upon them.

Other correspondents, if they did not suggest names directly, informed both the prime minister and the archbishop of the kind of man required for the bishopric of Bangor. The clergy, it was said, wanted a man of parochial experience who would be both a pastor and a preacher, thus effectively ruling out both Perowne and Lloyd.[14] But equally clear was the need for a Welsh speaker, ruling out Perowne again. 'A Welsh Priest', after complaining about the social bias of the Church against such men as Griffith Jones of Llanddowror who fulfilled their ministry, argued that 'baby bishops' were not required. He explained this term as meaning those bishops who attempted 'to master their "mother tongue" during the baby-hood of their prelatic existence'.[15] If the bishops of St Asaph and Llandaff had 'double duty to pay' in bilingual areas, another wrote that in Bangor the English were outnumbered ten to one by the Welsh, and the feeling for the language was extremely strong.[16] Yet another argued that Campbell had never been a strong bishop, for he was too quiet and unobtrusive for such a diocese. A new bishop would need to strengthen the Welsh Church at its weakest link. If he should prove a failure the Church in Wales was doomed! It was hopeless to look to the clergy of Bangor. There was not a man among them who stood a head taller than all his fellows. Rather a bishop was needed who was able 'to speak with his enemies in the gate', stimulate zeal in his clergy, and develop the moral and religious life of the diocese.[17]

This debate and acrimony was continued in letter column after letter column and in private conversation, while the prime minister got on with his task of finding the right man for the see. There was a lengthy delay in the procedure caused by the by-election in the

Caernarfonshire seat. Salisbury was advised that any recommendation he might make would offend a certain number of people, and so it would be better to postpone making a choice until the election was over.[18] By this time the four names mentioned earlier as the 'front runners' were either under active consideration or had been rejected. We look at each candidate in turn.

The First Offer

'I do not gather that you had yourself given credence to so utterly absurd a rumour as that the great Diocese of Bangor would be used as a place of exile wherein to confine a man "who is too strong to be kept in England" ', wrote Dean Davidson to one F. Gell in March 1890. 'You quote it, I imagine, as showing the length to which some men will go in such arguments.'[19] Nevertheless, Gell was nearer the truth than he may have realized, for such a man was seriously considered and even offered the see of Bangor.

This man was John James Stewart Perowne, a former chaplain at Lincoln's Inn, vice-principal of St Davids College, Lampeter (where he virtually ran the college through the incapacity of the principal), joint editor of Bishop Thirlwall's *Remains*, a member of the panel of translators of the revised version of the Bible, holder of a Cambridge chair and now dean of Peterborough. And he was offered the bishopric of Bangor by Salisbury in early March 1890,[20] even though Davidson advised that he had been considered to be too old for the 'most laborious and heavy diocese' of Ripon the previous January.[21]

Perowne was qualified in a number of ways for an episcopal appointment by a Conservative prime minister, apart, of course, from being a member of that party himself.[22] Having worked for a number of years in a part of Welsh-speaking Wales it was assumed that he had some knowledge of its language and its Church. Actually, as William Price, the historian of St David's College, mentions, he had little time for Welsh traditions or for its language which he thought should be removed from the syllabus at Lampeter. He was a genial person although a poor judge of men.[23]

If Perowne was more than surprised at the offer, and begged for time to consider it, the Welsh establishment, led by the bishop of St Asaph, was absolutely appalled by it. Bishop Jayne of Chester, a former principal of Lampeter, wrote to Davidson on 7 March claiming he knew more of Wales than did many. Bangor was the most Welsh of all the dioceses and a Welshman must be appointed to it. Perowne had been 'talked of' for Llandaff and St Asaph, but not for Bangor. To put him there would be a grievous mistake. Perowne was anything but a success at Lampeter and had never showed any capacity for ruling Welshmen; rather he was 'much the contrary'.[24] Bishop Edwards himself wrote the following day to Davidson, and begged him to use his interest to prevent Perowne's appointment (though he did not name him), for a non Welsh speaker at Bangor 'would be a crushing disaster to the Church in Wales'.[25] A further letter of Jayne to Davidson indicated that he had seen Lord Salisbury and informed him that Perowne's appointment would not suit Bangor at all, and those who knew the circumstances of the diocese felt it would be a disaster. Although he had suggested no names to the premier, he felt that Owen was the man for the job.[26]

Davidson was now in an awkward position. Both Perowne and those against his appointment were requesting his advice and assistance. As usual he played this tense situation coolly and with masterly diplomacy, without either side knowing about his dual intervention.

Perowne had consulted him on 7 March. Davidson, who was desperately trying to persuade him not to accept the see, advised him not to throw a decision back upon the prime minister but to make it himself. The next day Perowne wrote to him stating that he felt it would be better for him simply to tell Lord Salisbury that he could not conscientiously accept the see because of his lack of proficiency in the Welsh language.[27] A few days later Perowne had still not made up his mind. Although he felt he should decline the offer his letter seemed to indicate that he hoped Davidson would convince him otherwise. Perhaps he could reactivate the Welsh he had learnt at Lampeter, seventeen years before. This was what the bishop of St Davids had done, he claimed, though Basil Jones was not a good advertisement for that policy! But Perowne soon realized that this bishop was a Welshman born and bred. If an English appointment to Bangor would be unpopular and a hindrance to the bishop's usefulness, Perowne also believed that Gladstone's 'wonderful discovery' that Wales had not had a Welsh-speaking bishop for 200 years had set everything on fire. Gladstone, he asserted, had 'never inflicted a greater injury upon the Church when he encouraged – I might almost say created – the national sentiment in favour of Welsh Bishops'. Yet Perowne also accepted that Salisbury's choice was limited; because of origin and upbringing it was hard to find any 'scholars and gentlemen' among the Welsh clergy suitable for nomination to the see. Perowne thus concluded that bishops of Welsh sees, if they were Welshmen, must be 'on a far lower level than those of English sees'. The bishop of Winchester (Edward Harold Browne, a former vice-principal of Lampeter) had informed him that Bishop Hughes of St Asaph was a good man, 'but no one would have thought of making him a bishop in England'. And that was clearly true.

But was it really necessary for a bishop of Bangor to speak Welsh? asked Perowne in his agony of frustrated ambition and indecision. Did the Welsh parochial clergy need a Welsh-speaking bishop? Perowne replied to his own questions, clearly endeavouring to convince himself that he should accept Salisbury's offer of the see. No bishop addressed ordination candidates in Welsh, and it was not necessary to do so for confirmation candidates either, as all children were brought up to speak English in the board schools. Bishop Ollivant had once told him that he was hardly ever asked to confirm in Welsh in his latter days, while English services were now preferred to Welsh, even in Nonconformist churches. Indeed, when he was at Lampeter the Welsh shopkeepers of the town had asked him to conduct English services in the college chapel for them during the long vacation, though they had two Welsh services in the parish church. The churches in England and Wales needed to be drawn together, but this could not be done by lowering the status of the episcopate. If the position of the Church in Wales was to improve it had to keep pace with the Church of England, and this meant, Perowne concluded, that in this instance a non-Welsh-speaking bishop was required. And why shouldn't English bishops in Wales have Welsh-speaking suffragans? Welsh bishops, he reasoned, were no more necessary for Wales than Yorkshiremen for York or Ripon. Furthermore, he had trained well over 200 of the present Welsh clergy.[28]

Such sentiments could not stand the test of reality, and Perowne later admitted he had no knowledge of the diocese of Bangor whatsoever.[29] Salisbury seems to have made his mind up for him – one assumes urgent representations were made from Lambeth and

Windsor – and he thus wrote to Perowne stating that the appointment of any person but a native Welshman would be very unpopular, even though he personally considered that the home-rule sentiment was artificially excited. While Salisbury denied the validity of the claim for Welsh-speaking bishops, he was indicating very clearly to Perowne that he wished him to withdraw (probably unaware that he was about to make that decision), and was perhaps rather apologetic that he had offered him the see in the first place.[30] Dean Vaughan, who was called upon in an attempt to persuade Perowne to withdraw, wrote to Davidson that the business 'went to his heart' for Perowne greatly desired to be a bishop.[31] With such clear hints given him by Salisbury and others it is hardly surprising that Perowne eventually declined the nomination to the see. In signifying his intention to a relieved Salisbury, Perowne wrote that he had been influenced by the reasons the prime minister had given, the need for a Welsh bishop, and by his own lack of adequate Welsh, 'no longer what it once was'. He continued,

> With your Lordship I deplore extremely the 'Home Rule' sentiment which has taken possession of the Principality, but as it exists, I feel not only that my own usefulness would be seriously impaired by the acceptance of a Welsh bishopric, but that the Church might suffer through me at a time when it needs strengthening in every possible way. And I should indeed be sorry if the unpopularity of the appointment were in any measure to recoil upon your Lordship.[32]

The news that he had been offered the see, but declined it, was not generally known for some two weeks after his withdrawal. The press applauded Perowne's sacrifice. The *Western Mail* in an editorial regarded Perowne's refusal as a rebuke to 'whoever placed the vacant bishopric . . . at his option', but being a good Tory paper it declined to blame Salisbury for this nomination. Although Perowne was qualified to become bishop of a more important see than Bangor that 'but one thing I lack' was sufficient to disqualify him. And although the Welsh Church 'may have to put up with a man of lower intellectual stature' than the dean, a Welshman was needed. The editor concluded:

> if a man who would be an honour to any English diocese, possessing an acquaintance with the needs of the Welsh Church that is not enjoyed by

any member of the Government, rejects the tempting offer of one of its bishoprics on the sole ground that he does not know the Welsh language, surely we shall not have the offer repeated to any other dignitary who may possess [his] disqualification but not his spirit of abnegation.[33]

But the editor was probably unaware of the pressure placed on Perowne to decline the see by those who had offered it to him in the first place.

The Clique

There were many clergy who believed that a 'clique' was 'running' the youthful John Owen (whom Edwards had appointed dean of St Asaph[34]) for election to Bangor, reported Daniel N. Lewis in a letter to Dean Davidson. His letter in fact was one of support for the candidature of Daniel Lloyd who happened to be his brother-in-law. Lloyd, canvassing himself, was greatly discouraged, writing to his sister:

> It is difficult to ascertain the truth, but I believe that John Owen is pushed tremendously, but I do not know who his supporters are, save for Jayne, Edwards and the clique. It is a gross chance [?] if he succeeds. He was a Methodist 10 years ago and his father is a Methodist deacon now I am told, near Pwllheli. I have strong supporters, S. Walenham [sic], Cornwallis West, Kenyon, I think, and Walsh, but I feel sure the other side will do something to knock me over and I have made up my mind not to be disappointed, but it will be hard to see a fellow who has not done a tithe of my work put over me.[35]

What Lloyd wrote privately, Lewis wrote openly, indicating in his letter to Davidson that many considered that this St Asaph-based 'clique' had too much power. 'Even men of high character,' he argued, 'who generally speaking would be slow to find fault, view with regret the various influences exerted by the Bishop of Chester [Jayne] and his brother-in-law the Bishop of St Asaph and their friends in the matter of Church appointments in Wales.' It would be dangerous, he hinted, to let them gain another success.[36] Benson, however, felt that the suspicion held by the Welsh clergy that the two bishops and Owen had formed a 'ring' had 'not much in that'.[37]

Jayne and Edwards had managed to dispose of the prime minister's first choice by persuading Davidson and Salisbury that Perowne was the wrong man. His Welsh was probably no better or worse than Campbell's, but it was easy to point out that times had changed. Jayne, having managed to obtain a personal interview with the prime minister, wrote that he fancied Salisbury had been 'inundated with private, but powerful protests' about Perowne's appointment. As a result 'a storm had been averted'.[38] It was the wrong bishopric for the Conservative dean. The dean whom Salisbury wished to honour went instead to the more lucrative and pleasing pastures of Worcester in the following year.

Their task was now to push their man. Jayne, in writing to Davidson of his interview and correspondence with the prime minister, in which he had tried to avoid a 'dictatorial or intrusive tone', also mentioned that Owen was the fittest man. His youth was an obvious objection, while 'his utterance' was 'a little peculiar' as he spoke Welsh with a slight lisp, and he was from a humble and Nonconformist background, but all in all he was 'a very rare man'. His work at Lampeter where he had been the Welsh professor was 'singly invaluable'; moreover he was an outstanding man of influence, a born leader, full of enterprise and initiative who had taken into his capable hands the church press, parochial mission and the leadership of the younger clergy. Gladstone had called him 'a very remarkable man'; the bishops of St Davids and Llandaff had urged Edwards to appoint him to the deanery; Archdeacon Watkin Williams, Owen Evans (the warden of Llandovery) and Archdeacon Edmondes (a former principal of Lampeter) had said he was the man for Bangor, thus happily eliminating the names of quite a few possible rival candidates![39] There could be no comparison between Daniel Lloyd (now identified as the leading candidate) and Owen, Jayne wrote later,[40] almost echoing the claim of the *Church Times* that Owen was regarded as next to the bishop of St Asaph as the greatest figure in Church life in north Wales.[41]

Bishop Edwards also made clear his preference for Owen. In writing to Benson he argued that he was the best man for Bangor; his Welsh was better than any clergyman in Wales save Silvan Evans, and he was a man of the people, a north Wales Welshman. His appointment to Lampeter was largely on his recommendation. His work for the church press and missions, his educational work, and his influence over some of the clergy of the diocese, could only mean that his appointment to Bangor would be full of hope and promise for the Welsh Church. The leader of the Liberationist party was even quoted in support of his candidature. He had said that if 'Dean Owen was made Bishop of Bangor, he would render the Church in that diocese impregnable'.[42] In late March, when the choice was going against Owen, Edwards wrote again to Benson, who duly conveyed its contents to Lord Salisbury. Watkin Williams, he wrote, was *next* to Owen.[43]

Archbishop Benson, in a letter to Davidson reviewing the various candidates, wrote that he had formed a 'considerable' opinion of Owen. 'He is odd looking and small and only 37 years old – and looks 27.' Dean Vaughan had spoken of him and said that when he had preached at Llandaff Cathedral 'he had not recognised the language until near the end of the sermon – which was English'. Although the bishop of St Davids at first thought 'he would keep', Benson felt on the whole there was little doubt that Owen was the best candidate, a matter which had been confirmed by a letter from the bishop of St Asaph.[44] 'I am inclined to think he is the man', Benson wrote two days later, adding that his work in Wales will offset his 'being odd' in the House of Lords.[45] The difficulty of understanding Owen's English was obviously a major drawback to his candidature, for writing to Salisbury at a later date, Benson concluded that Owen's English could not 'be very bad considering his high distinction at Oxford'.[46] Davidson too noted him as 'a man with the oddest of Welsh utterance in speaking English and a most ineffective presence', but, he added, 'apparently a man of real power and likely to make an effective Diocesan whatever he might be elsewhere'.[47]

However, by the middle of March it must have seemed to Edwards that Owen's candidature was not advancing at all well, possibly because of his youth. Although Davidson considered that Owen and Watkin Williams seemed to stand at the head of the list,[48] Salisbury's letter to Ponsonby (Queen Victoria's secretary) of 13 April indicates that while Owen was strongly backed by Benson, Edwards and Jayne, his youth, bad manners and his father's status as an official in a dissenting church in the diocese of Bangor stood against him. Although these concerns would be modified by time, 'he had better wait'.[49]

Edwards, with his well-informed ear, had probably picked up this criticism, and consequently a new tactic was tried and Watkin Williams, archdeacon of St Asaph, was brought into the field as the

233

more acceptable candidate. Although Edwards made it clear that while Williams was not his first choice, the bishops of St Davids and Llandaff had heartily acquiesced in his nomination by Edwards, agreeing that both Howell and Lloyd, the other candidates, would not be desirable.[50] Edwards argued in a similar way to Benson. Williams was 'eminently strong' from a social and personal side as a member of the house of Wynnstay: he was a man of business, his views were evangelical and although his Welsh was not strong it was not unsatisfactory and practice would make him more efficient. His appointment to Bangor might not arouse any enthusiasm but it would be found generally acceptable.[51] Jayne, although he also regarded Owen as the better man, was still prepared to support Watkin Williams, though his Welsh was only passable and he was 'blundering' in his English public speaking; but on the other hand he was a most honourable gentleman of good family who had identified himself with the 'clergyhood' and had a most presentable wife.[52] By this time even the newspapers were regarding Williams as the probable new bishop.[53] Edwards was good at publicity too. Yet Williams's candidature came to nothing. It may be that this was because of the adverse statements made about him by two of the senior English bishops, Ryle of Liverpool and Bickersteth of Exeter, both Conservative supporters. Ryle considered Williams to be a thoroughly high churchman who had introduced the eastward position in the cathedral. This, he pointed out, was one of the principal accusations made against the bishop of Lincoln (whose trial for ritual practices was awaiting judgement) and evangelical churchmen were very sensitive about this matter. Bickersteth had made careful enquiries of Williams, and felt he possessed no pulpit or platform power and had a most imperfect knowledge of Welsh.[54] The letter was endorsed by Salisbury who wrote that while he was probably the best candidate he was not a good Welsh speaker.[55]

If the candidatures of Owen or Williams were to be pressed, the claims of other candidates needed to be suppressed. There was considerable support for Howell, now archdeacon of Wrexham, to be appointed the new bishop of Bangor. But Edwards knew of that one episode in his life that had already discredited him, namely the birth of his eldest son a month or so after his marriage.

Howell was supported by Bishop Ryle, leader of the evangelical group within the Church of England at that time, and Bishop Bickersteth of Exeter. Ryle, who expressed a hope that Salisbury's appointments would give much satisfaction to his supporters, counting himself amongst their number, had written to commend Howell. But Salisbury had replied by noting the objection mentioned above. Ryle withdrew his recommendation but expressed surprise at this fact: 'I had heard rumours that there was *some* shadow over an early period of his life. But I had no idea that it was so black . . .' His appointment as a bishop would be 'a disastrous mistake'.[56]

Bickersteth felt differently, however, and wrote to Salisbury that he had reconsidered his statement of the previous year, in which he held that the 'obstacle' was 'a grave barrier' to Howell's candidature. He continued:

> But I have more than once regretted that I too hastily regarded the barrier as insurmountable, for probably St Paul [whom he had previously quoted] meant a Bishop must be living and have *long* lived a blameless life – he would hardly in that state of society have demanded a stainless moral character from youth. And I think your Lordship named St Augustine as a signal proof of this in the judgment of the Early Church.

Howell's appointment as an archdeacon and examining chaplain 'may well seem to cover the sin of youth in the estimation of the Church'. He also argued that Howell's evangelical churchmanship, though there was nothing narrow about it, would 'in the present state of our beloved Church be a real advantage'. Furthermore, Howell's elevation to the episcopate would be an 'immense strength' to the Conservative party, for evangelicals were expressing much concern that Salisbury was not favouring their party in his church appointments.[57]

Salisbury, in his reply, challenged Bickersteth to find an alternative candidate who could combine ability with a perfect knowledge of Welsh and was also an evangelical. Bickersteth replied by dismissing all the candidates suggested by Salisbury, namely Lloyd, Williams and Protheroe, and argued that only one man possessed all these qualifications desired by the prime minister. That man was Howell. He was the man for the post; he had lived down the sins of his early manhood which had occurred long before he had any idea of entering the ministry. But the good bishop also had to deal on a wider front, and so he asked that if a high churchman was appointed to Bangor, then an evangelical man such as Moule or

Chavasse should be appointed to St Albans.[58] Dean Vaughan, in a letter to Davidson, also recommended Howell, whose by now famous sermon on the Welsh Church at St Margaret's, Westminster, had been bold, a 'too true utterance', and seemed to offer 'such a view of the real faults and perils of the Church in Wales . . . [that] he would be a man of real mark on the bench'. Nevertheless, Vaughan made it clear that he accepted that Welsh speakers who had been elevated to the bench would not be on a level with their English episcopal colleagues.[59] Such arguments seem to have appealed to Salisbury for a note in the royal archives headed 'names suggested for the see of Bangor', of 13 March, is endorsed by these words: 'Lord Salisbury thinks of Mr Howell for Bangor hoping that the scandal about him has been forgotten.'[60]

The support seemed so overwhelming for Howell that Edwards mounted a counteroffensive. Writing to Davidson, Edwards pointed out that he had not written to recommend anyone to Lord Salisbury and would not do so unless asked, but he added, 'I trust there is not the least danger of Canon Howell, Vicar of Wrexham, being thought of for the vacancy, and this for a reason which you probably already know.'[61] He also wrote to Benson noting that Howell was being favourably considered for Bangor:

I would not trouble your grace unless I knew this was authentic.

I. Your grace knows the blot upon his moral character. If the whole truth comes out, there will be found to be *two* blots of the same kind.

II. Impurity is one of the most prevalent sins in Wales – I mean impurity in the way of illegitimate children or children born just after a marriage is accelerated to make them legitimate in the eye of the law – If this sin is to be permitted in our Bishops, the effect will be morally disastrous.

III. But apart from this objection – which in my humble opinion ought to be absolutely implacable – Canon Howell is a man whom very few trust, he is simply shunned and disliked by a great number of the Welsh clergy and I firmly believe from what I know that his appointment to Bangor would even on personal *apart* from moral considerations, be an untold calamity in Wales. I fear that unless your Grace intervenes this calamity will befall us.[62]

Edwards's fellow bishops also wrote to Salisbury and other influential people, supporting his claim that Howell's appointment was not at all desirable.[63] The bishop of St Davids noted there was at least one reason that might alone excuse him, but felt that his would be a most undesirable appointment in other respects.[64] Bishop Jayne also ventured into the fray. Howell ought not to be considered. He had no solid claim except that of being a good preacher and platform speaker in both languages. He had notoriously neglected the interests of Welsh worshippers at Wrexham and had never been able to influence his own curates. He continued his character assassination with these words: 'he is an excellent and distinguished specimen of the type from which Wales has been grievously suffering and which it does *not* want. I had hoped we were free from all danger of him.'[65]

Archbishop Benson, replying to Davidson, wrote that he was already aware of this matter and had included Howell on his list of names 'to beware of'.[66] A further letter added the comment: 'You will remember that Lord Salisbury *at once* said when the Howell question was up before, that the facts rendered his appointment impossible. So that I think St Asaph must be mistaken – if not, Lord Salisbury must be reminded and warned.' But there were dangers. Canon Mason (a noted retreat conductor and friend of Benson) 'is very strong for Howell. And he sees much of Liddon [canon of St Paul's and one of the most influential clerics of his day], they may be a stream of influence setting that way.'[67]

Thus Howell was discredited. He had assumed Benson was his friend, but he forgot he was also an ecclesiastical politician. By mid-April Salisbury had accepted the judgement of Benson, Ryle and Lord Selborne that 'the blot' (as they termed it) was a fatal bar to Howell's claims. Surprisingly Salisbury noted that Edwards and Jayne had depreciated Howell's appointment on 'more general grounds'.[68]

The Choice of a Schoolmaster

When his appointment to the see of Bangor had been announced, Daniel Lewis Lloyd told his pupils at Christ Church College, Brecon, that his elevation was 'not of his seeking', but he was happy to put his services freely at the disposal of the Church wherever they might be of value.[69] In this respect Lloyd was being more than a little modest, for it is clear that he either ran his own campaign to obtain the bishopric or allowed members of his family and friends to do so for him. Benson suspected he had canvassed widely, noting he had written to a high sheriff stating he was a candidate and requesting a testimonial.[70] His sister, Sarah, was equally active on his behalf. Writing to the Liberal Unionist agent in north Wales, H. Tobit Evans, she asked him:

> Can you do anything for my Brother to get the Bishopric of Bangor. You can testify to the hard work done by him in Wales, and how he has assisted young men of talent to enter the Ministry of the Church whose parents could not afford them an University Education unless some person had given them a helping hand, if you can exercise any influence in his behalf in good quarters I shall *always* feel grateful.[71]

Lloyd's brother-in-law, Daniel N. Lewis, also wrote to Davidson commending Lloyd as an excellent schoolmaster, a sound divine, and warning the dean against the clique which was promoting Owen's appointment.[72] A brother, Charles Lloyd, writing from Maesycrugiau, wrote to Perowne's Welsh brother-in-law, Colonel David Evans, who did not even know Lloyd, asking him to use his influence on his behalf. 'Do be a good fellow and use all your personal influence on his behalf, and I believe if successful you will have done a good turn to the Welsh Church in North Wales,' he wrote. The letter eventually found its way to Davidson and is contained in his papers.[73] He also noted that Lloyd was supported by the then dean of Bangor, the tractarian Evan Lewis. Lloyd had served as Lewis's curate during the time when he was headmaster of Dolgellau Grammar School. He had moved from there to be head of Friar's School, Bangor, and thereafter to Brecon. Although a Cardiganshire man, Lloyd almost appears to have been the local candidate for the diocese of Bangor.

Apart from his family and friends few others appear to have supported his candidature. But Lloyd was a strong Conservative supporter. He later successfully recommended Llewelyn Thomas of Jesus College, Oxford, for a canonry at St Asaph which was then in the gift of the crown because of the appointment of Owen to the bishopric of St Davids, claiming that Thomas had done good work for the Conservative party, especially in Oxford. Likewise he recommended Ellis Nanny for a baronetcy, arguing that no man in north Wales had worked harder for the Conservative cause than he had.[74]

It may be that Lloyd had political friends who spoke for him in high places.

Like every other candidate, Lloyd had his detractors. Some were gentle. Bishop Bickersteth dismissed him as nothing better than a fairly successful schoolmaster who knew nothing of spiritual or pastoral work.[75] Davidson wrote to the Queen that his work had been confined to schoolmastering 'in rather second-class schools (which is much more serious and very delicate to say)' and that his wife was 'mentally affected'. This would be a major handicap as much was 'socially required' at Bangor. Nevertheless, he was a hard-working and popular man, and there was no reason why he should not be approved.[76]

Other correspondents were not so courteous. Generally speaking these were the men who wanted to push Owen, and thus had to discredit Lloyd. Jayne held he was quarrelsome, jealous and autocratic, a 'mere schoolmaster' who had never taken any marked interest in Church life and work.[77] Edwards said he was a good Welshman and able schoolmaster, but not a man who had shown any interest in Church work. Nor was he a man of religious earnestness. He was also deficient in tact and temper.[78] Lloyd, in his estimation, was better than Howell, but he was by no means the best man available.[79]

The bishop of St Davids thought Lloyd a good schoolmaster, his Welsh 'unimpeachable', but he certainly did not come up 'to his idea of what a Welsh bishop ought to be'. He had no parochial experience, he had seen nothing in him to indicate that he would ensure good spiritual leadership in the diocese, his confirmation candidates from Brecon were much lower in number than those of Llandovery, and his wife's mental condition would hinder him in the social duties of his office.[80] As it became more and more clear that Lloyd might be the new bishop, the bishop of St Asaph fired yet another warning shot. As a bishop Lloyd would be of no help to the Church in north Wales. While he was a member of the English Church Union his sermons and conversation suggested he had became distinctly Socinian in his views. But now, Edwards wrote, Lloyd had declared himself a high churchman, and the ritualistic party was sufficiently satisfied with his declaration that, headed by the dean of Bangor, it was pressing his appointment upon the prime minister. He would not mind his views so much if he thought there was any sincere conviction in them. He concluded: 'I should deplore the appointment of a man of his tone and temper to Bangor.'[81]

By 15 April Davidson noted that Lloyd had been recommended, and in a letter to 'Sir H. P.' (Ponsonby), he stated that Salisbury had already submitted his name for nomination to the Queen as bishop of Bangor some weeks before. He, Davidson, had pointed out to the Queen the objections against his appointment, namely that he was 'a second grade schoolmaster with no especial fitness for high office,' as well as his wife's mental incapacity. He had added that Lloyd was so identified with high churchmanship that he would be anything but acceptable to the evangelical sympathies of Wales. He believed that the Queen had put these facts before Lord Salisbury, and one thing was certain. Salisbury had said he wished to appoint an evangelical, but Lloyd was the very reverse. Davidson recommended that the Queen should suggest to the premier that the appointment would be on his own responsibility for recommending a man with these drawbacks, but he accepted that such disqualifications could not justify the Queen absolutely refusing her consent.[82] Salisbury, in a telegram to Ponsonby, expressed surprise about the Queen's objection and wondered about the source of her information. 'It would be difficult to find another equally fit,' he added.[83]

Lloyd's appointment to the bishopric of Bangor was announced in early May 1890. The *Carmarthen Journal* thought he was likely to make his mark as a bishop if he cooperated with 'the young and energetic Bishop of St Asaph',[84] but the evangelical *Record* wondered what his qualifications were for the high office to which he had been called. They did not appear to be obvious, as was also the case with Prebendary Festing whose elevation to the see of St Albans was announced at the same time. It was annoyed not only because Lloyd was not an evangelical, but also because evangelicals in general seemed to be excluded from the bench in Salisbury's appointments. The prime minister's appointment of high church bishops was driving into hostility 'thousands of hitherto staunch defenders of the Church and of the integrity of the Empire'. The *Baner* noted the surprise his appointment had caused at Bangor. Few thought he would be chosen as he was not a well-known preacher.[85] Yet Sir John Puleston, in a letter to John Owen recognizing the disappointment Lloyd's elevation would cause for him and Edwards ('the best of bishops who is so warmly your friend and mine'), could not remember an instance of such 'spontaneous applause over a bishop's appointment'.[86]

The *Western Mail*, in an editorial, noted that the Church did not need preachers and platform speakers so much as men who could lead and discipline their forces into meeting the needs of the age. Although Lloyd had no parochial experience, it was not always the parish priest who made the best bishop. If what Lloyd had done in Christ Church College could be taken as an earnest of what he would 'achieve in his more exalted capacity', Welsh Churchmen should be grateful for his appointment.[87] Lloyd himself took up the challenge, and speaking at a function said that one of the criticisms made against his appointment was that he would treat the clergy as he would treat schoolboys. 'He made bold to accept the challenge. If he were able to treat them in the way he had treated his boys, he should win from them their respect – their gratitude – and should he say? – their abiding affection.'[88] The English readers of the *Record*, where this appeared, must have shuddered with embarrassment at such self-publicity, while his comment on the same occasion that his motto would be 'Peace, not strife' must have caused some considerable anxiety to Edwards and his friends.

Much of what Edwards and others had written about Lloyd proved to be true: the diocese suffered much under him, but that was a later reflection. What was inexcusable, however, was Edwards's reaction.

A press release regarding Lloyd's appointment appeared in the local papers, including the *Western Mail*, in early May. An amazing eulogy about Lloyd was added to this paper's report, which was so exaggerated that, in the words of a royal memoranda, the newspapers left out 'most of the self flattering parts'. The press release stated that Lloyd, as a school-master, the Arnold of Wales, had given greater service to Welsh education than any other person during that century. Lord Salisbury could be congratulated on an excellent appointment, which would prove acceptable to both the clergy and laity of the diocese of Bangor. Lloyd, it added, would 'soon occupy as an ecclesiastic the position he has so long held as an educationalist'.[89]

Edwards alleged he had obtained a copy of this eulogy from the London correspondent of a local paper. Claiming it appeared that the original was in Lloyd's own handwriting, he accused the bishop-elect of writing his own publicity.[90] This was after the appointment had been announced but before Lloyd had been officially elected, so that if he could prove his assertion Edwards would probably have forced Lloyd to withdraw from the nomination, and bring himself into public speculation and dispute if not ignominy.

But Edwards was badly mistaken. The eulogy was not written by Lloyd, but by two of his Brecon friends, T. H. Hughes, then the Church Pastoral-Aid Society's secretary for Wales (it was in his hand), and E. O. Jones, a master at the college. Apart from answering questions put to him about his background, Lloyd strenuously denied he had had anything to do with it, though he admitted he had sent it to the papers himself.[91] By the time this denial was known and accepted, Edwards's claim had not only produced a scandal in high places, but had also been brought to the attention of archbishop, prime minister and Queen. Salisbury felt that there was nothing that could be done,[92] but Benson wondered if he could conscientiously perform the consecration ceremony under these circumstances.[93] As a result Benson had a personal interview with Lloyd about the matter, and wrote that he could not doubt his innocence. This information was relayed back to Salisbury. Edwards, informed, was glad to hear the news and was sure that 'good will result from this'.[94]

'This wretched Bangorian business', as Davidson described it to the archbishop, who had 'pricked the bubble', was a source of great embarrassment to the ecclesiastical world of Lambeth and Windsor. Lord Salisbury was highly annoyed and termed those involved 'a set of gobe-mouches who have listened to a wretched threepenny story which broke down the moment it was investigated'. Davidson burned with indignation against 'the culpable indiscretion' of the bishop of St Asaph and his 'own fervid imagination'. The Queen had had to be informed and had been put 'into the humiliating position of having practically to "climb down" and is not likely to be pleased thereat'. For Edwards's sake he had refrained from naming him, allowing the blame to rest 'upon ourselves', but he hoped Edwards would have to eat 'humble pie' in explaining this to the various peers. The matter, Davidson wrote in a concluding letter, was 'somewhat melancholy as showing the reckless unwisdom for which we have to be prepared in a man whom we had hoped to rely upon in coming controversies needing, above all else, judicial fairness and honesty and absence of bias'.[95] Benson was equally indignant. 'I asked again and again whether he was certain and even telegraphed. He was quite certain . . .' The Bishop of St Asaph, he continued, 'who was our hope and promise in Wales is discredited, in a way we cannot afford to have any bishop discredited . . . But there is left still on our hands a man, who looks what he is and is what he looks. "Poor little Wales." '[96]

Did Edwards take the matter to heart? Hardly! Speaking some months later at the opening of the new church at Llansilin, Denbighshire, he spoke about the necessity of confronting the disestablishment campaign in a charitable and peace-loving spirit. But, he added, it was not inconsistent with 'the character of a peaceful, peace-loving, and peacemaking bishop to contend for the truth', especially against distinct falsehoods circulated without contradiction by some place-hunters, who in the struggle for power and position found no weapon too mean or too contemptible to be used.[97] If Davidson or Benson ever read this report they might well have replied: 'Speak for yourself.'

Edwards and his group had access to some influential places. Benson obtained for him an interview with the premier in late March writing, 'he is a clever man and well acquainted with the situation and with all the people in Bangor'.[98] He was able to obtain that infamous press eulogy as well as other pieces of information which he would use in order to discredit those candidates he had no wish to see appointed. His influence certainly helped to prevent Perowne's appointment; his reminders ended Howell's chances, but he was still unable to prevent Lloyd's elevation. Possibly this was because Lloyd had better political allies than Edwards, who had only been bishop of St Asaph for one year. It took time to cultivate those friendships which stood Edwards in such good stead in later years. Equally, it may be that Edwards made a fateful mistake of pushing a man who, though eligible, was considered far too young, and then back-peddling too hastily with another candidate thought to be more presentable. Owen had as little parochial experience as Lloyd, but on paper Lloyd was probably the far stronger candidate and one who was far better known in Welsh-speaking Wales. Edwards's subsequent actions might only have clarified the wisdom of Salisbury's choice in the minds of the hierarchy.

Furthermore, there must have been many like Daniel Jones, vicar of Lampeter, who were grateful for Lloyd's appointment, as they believed it had been obtained on merit rather than by influence. He may have been right, but he was certainly not wrong in his other assertion, that many, even those in high places in Wales, rejoiced that in this appointment 'the power of the clique' had been broken.[99] His assertion was premature. The power of the clique had already stopped two candidatures, and only on the final choice had they been defeated. Its power was to become even more obvious in the future appointments to the Welsh bench.

But why was Edwards so bitter against Lloyd? It is true they were rival schoolmasters, but that could hardly have been the real reason. Was it because Lloyd was known to be anxious to live in harmony with Nonconformity, and to forward the good relationships with dissent developed by Bishop Campbell in his diocese?[100] Edwards's philosophy was probably well summed up by an editorial in the *Western Mail* of March 1890. It read: 'one very simple criteria which should go far to govern the appointment is the discovery of the individual whose choice would be least agreeable to the Liberationalists . . . To die gracefully crying "Kismet" may be highly spiritual; but we may be forgiven if we think that it will be more manful to fall wielding the weapons of reason, justice and persuasion.'[101] This may have been the crux of the matter. Edwards was convinced that the Church had to fight dissent. Lloyd preferred to live in harmony with it. His appointment would be a weak link in the defence of the Church which Edwards had reserved to himself. It was not a question of spiritual life but of practical concern for the future. As such Lloyd would not do. Prime ministers worked on different criteria, and thus Lloyd was appointed.

~ 11 ~

The True Welshman from the North: The Election to St Davids, 1897

Basil Jones, bishop of St Davids from 1874, died in the January of 1897. The *Western Mail* suggested in an obituary that in view of the scholastic nature of the last two appointments to that see, the new bishop should have won his spurs within the parochial rather than the academic field. The former bishop, it continued, had been appointed under the old system of governing Wales, 'when its distinctive nationality was ignored, and its language regarded as a peculiarity which was rapidly becoming extinct'. It still feared, however, that the prime minister, Lord Salisbury (an experienced bishop-maker, with twenty-one of the thirty-one bishops on the bench having been appointed by him) had yet to recognize the national spirit arising in Wales, or the need for a Welsh appointment in the diocese of St Davids.[1]

The diocesan missioner, Robert Camber-Williams, an influential figure in the diocese, summed up the local requirements while preaching at Carmarthen. The new bishop should be one who combined spiritual mindedness and intellect, genuine piety and manifold power; who embodied in his own life the virtues of faith, duty and sacrifice; a man who would not only enter into the feelings and understand the wants and characteristics of Welshmen, but who would realize that the Church is 'a true branch of the one holy, Catholic, and Apostolic Church'.[2]

The papers added their own comments. It is more difficult to prophesy who will be made bishop of a Welsh see 'than to foretell the winner of the Derby', argued the *Western Mail*. An editorial noted the difficulties. Both Gladstone and Salisbury had endeavoured in their appointments to Welsh dioceses to uphold the dignity and prestige of the English episcopate. St Davids was the largest diocese in the Kingdom and thus it needed an active young man who possessed considerable powers of organization. As the diocese was still moderate in terms of churchmanship, there was no advanced ritual in it as at Cardiff, this factor also had to be taken into consideration. On the other hand it claimed Welsh people would not care if their new bishop was high, broad or evangelical, with or without a reputation for pulpit power and scholarship, organization and leadership, as long as he was 'racy of the soil' and capable of performing his episcopal duties in Welsh.[3] The *Church Times*, which regarded Wales as a backwater, argued that there was real room for definiteness in Church life and teaching, even of moral reform, and commented that frothy eloquence did not make a good bishop; rather, a bishop was needed who would keep the clergy up to the mark in Church principles.[4] The evangelical *Record*, by comparison, criticized the *Manchester Guardian* for stating that the diocese of St Davids was the most backward diocese in Wales because of the evangelical tendencies of its late bishop. At least one half of the clergy and nine-tenths of the laity were distinctly evangelical. If Lord Salisbury as premier wanted to strengthen the Church in Wales he should appoint an evangelical Welshman to this see.[5] Nevertheless, the local paper, the *Carmarthen Journal*, quoted the late bishop's comment on the death of Archbishop Benson the previous year. He had suggested that people should refrain from speculation about his successor and should turn instead to prayer. The editor made clear that his paper, at least, would follow this advice, and avoid all speculation in its columns.[6]

Dean Vaughan of Llandaff, one of the most influential churchmen of his age, addressed the same concern in a letter to Randall Davidson, bishop of Winchester. Davidson was the Queen's advisor, and in the absence of an archbishop (Benson had just died) seems to have acted as Salisbury's confidant in this as in other matters. There was no doubt, Vaughan emphasized, that the new bishop must be a Welshman, 'for *hack* Welsh is useless and only a native can speak anything else. But again he must be able to speak *English*. You would scarcely believe the sort of English that is habitually uttered in our churches. One man, who would else be much thought of, Owen of Lampeter, is absolutely unintelligible in English.' A schoolmaster was not required. Two Welsh bishops from this category were sufficient. Nor was a fighting bishop needed, for one such bishop as the bishop of St Asaph 'is enough for us'. The real necessity was for a man of spiritual influence. 'You have no idea how keenly *religious* Wales yearns for the Gospel,' Vaughan observed, 'the Gospel preached with power and lived in charity. To count up increased services and churches, baptisms and confirmations, does not *touch* the people.' Vaughan recommended C. E. T. Griffith (not Griffith*s*, he pointed out, 'it needs the greatest care to make sure of the right man.') He was a gentleman, his wife a lady – a most attractive couple. A son of a former rector of Merthyr (John Griffith), he was a Welshman, a beautiful speaker and writer of English, an evangelical by birth and connection, but most gentle and courteous towards others.[7]

Rumours abounded. One was that the bishop of St Asaph had refused to be translated. At least this rumour was true. Bishop Edwards had been sounded out by Lord Salisbury.[8] The *Church Times* was grateful. It felt much the same about Edwards as did Dean Vaughan. The appointment of one already in episcopal orders would not be welcomed in the diocese or be conducive to the good will of the Church. A combative prelate was not needed as much as one who would build up the diocese in the catholic faith and devotion, and who would fully sympathize with his clergy in their isolation and difficulties.[9]

A further rumour suggested that Archdeacon Protheroe of Aberystwyth would be appointed.[10] Described as an advanced high churchman, a good English speaker and scholar, it was noted that Welsh was not his strong point.[11] Nevertheless, Bishop Lewis of Llandaff was asked to comment on his and John Owen's claims. Lewis suggested that Protheroe was a good Welsh scholar, preaching well in both languages, and was a successful parish clergyman. But he doubted if he had a sufficiently high tone of mind to exercise the influence required of a bishop. Lewis suggested two further names. One was his own archdeacon, Edmondes, a Welsh speaker and a man of deep piety. The other was Dean Watkin Williams of St Asaph. He was also a Welsh speaker (though the letter was endorsed in another hand: 'Sir J. Puleston though says "he speaks it badly"'). In addition Williams was a gentlemen of means and an able organizer. The bishop also expressed his shame at the 'wire-pulling' that was being employed.[12] Other names put forward and reported in the press were those of the Revd G. W. Gent, later principal of St David's College, and Hartwell Jones, vicar of Nuffield.[13] Canon Hughes of Hardingstone, Rowland Ellis, Thomas of Gainsborough (favoured by the archbishop of York), James, the headmaster of Rugby and Archdeacon Watkins of Durham were also noted as possible candidates.[14]

The names of two other men were put forward as eligible candidates by interested parties almost as soon as the death of Bishop Jones had been announced. These were Protheroe's father-in-law, David Howell, archdeacon of Wrexham, and John Owen, principal of Lampeter and a former dean of St Asaph.[15]

Howell's entitlement to episcopal office was regarded by his local paper as more substantial than of any other Welshman,[16] though it suggested that his wise and Christian method of dealing with Nonconformity was not regarded with much favour by the St Asaph school, which preferred to drive dissenters away by argument rather than win them back to the Church. Why are his claims overlooked? asked the *Record*. He is the *facile princeps* among the Welsh clergy. If the election was left to the Welsh clergy, he would be elected by a large majority.[17] The *Record* was not aware, however, as to how Edwards and others had used and were continuing to use information about Howell's pre-Christian past to prevent him obtaining episcopal office.

The Campaign for Owen

In many respects John Owen was the stronger candidate. The London *Times* regarded him as early as 1890 as 'that splendid Welshman', and the *Church Times* at the same time suggested he was next to Bishop Edwards as 'by far the greatest figure in Church life in the whole of North Wales'.[18] He had been born into a humble, Calvinistic Methodist and Welsh-speaking family in the Llŷn peninsula, and his rise to public notice had all the elements in it that gave such legendary character to the life of Sir Henry Jones. As a former warden of Llandovery, dean of St Asaph and professor and principal at Lampeter he was known to generations of younger clergy, and all the appointments he held, it was claimed, displayed his concern for Wales, as well as his administrative power and ability. Rumours abounded about his appointment and were as frequently denied. One rumour suggested that if Edwards was translated to St Davids, then Owen would be appointed to St Asaph.[19]

The bishop of Llandaff, Richard Lewis, however, told Salisbury that while he had the greatest respect and admiration for Owen as principal at Lampeter, he was unfitted for so great a diocese as St Davids, as he did 'not possess the highness of mind and of purpose required for a mitre', and he had no parochial experience. Furthermore, to appoint a third Welsh bishop from the ranks of schoolmasters would be disheartening to the parochial clergy. He might do well in the Welsh part of his diocese, but he could never influence the more serious-minded and deep-thinking men of the English areas.[20] Davidson, now bishop of Winchester, having noted the objections to Owen because of his strong links with Edwards, added others. These were his humble origin and his incapacity to speak clear English which made it difficult for some to understand him, though his written English 'could be beautiful'. Nevertheless, he added, no one could complain that this 'untutored Celt of a shaggy sort' was not Welsh enough, and his humble origin would be no obstacle with the Queen. It was not the case in which the Queen could cast her veto, even though the bishop of Llandaff and Dr Vaughan preferred a different type of person.[21] Commenting upon his likely election, the *Church Times* endorsed the general feeling that no man without parochial experience could make a good bishop of St Davids. The new bishop, it continued, though he would need to be Welsh speaking, would also have to make himself available to the non-Welsh population and speak to them intelligibly. It was a clear and unsubtle hint about Owen's pronunciation of English. He would also need to be a man of wide culture and breadth of view. This could never be gained in 'the narrow associations' of Lampeter.[22]

Owen's claims were promoted by Bishop Edwards, who seven years earlier had made Owen his favoured candidate for the see of Bangor. Writing to Salisbury, Edwards noted that he had seen Mr Gladstone who had authorized him to tell the prime minister that from personal knowledge he had formed a very high opinion of Canon Owen. If Lord Salisbury wished to refer to him, he would gladly reply.[23] This was Edwards's style all over. And one assumes there were the usual personal interviews with the politicians and others. Owen's daughter, in her hagiographical work on her father, notes that many people, old Llandovery boys, St David's College men, people who had read his articles or listened to his speeches, wrote commending him to Salisbury. She did her best to avoid any idea that this was an organized campaign, and is highly selective in the account she gives of his election.[24] Her father's papers, now available, reveal a very different story.

Davidson was fully aware that there was an organized campaign to get Owen elected, though he was more circumspect in his approach. Writing to the Queen through her secretary, A. J. Bigge, he noted that there was 'a great deal of hot Welsh blood boiling in this matter'. Owen, he continued, was an intimate friend of the bishops of Chester and St Asaph, and the 'trio are commonly known as the "mutual admiration society" '. The two bishops, especially Edwards, had been 'campaigning' for Owen's election to St Davids.[25]

John Owen's papers fill in the details of this campaign. Having failed to secure his appointment to Bangor in 1890, his friends rallied around his cause as soon as they heard of the seriousness of Bishop Basil Jones's illness. Led by Edwards, the leading members of this caucus consisted of Bishop Jayne of Chester, Owen Evans, warden of Llandovery College, and T. Llewellyn Williams, who was the organizing secretary of the Society for the Propagation of the Gospel (SPG) for Wales. On 12 January, when the serious condition of Basil Jones's illness was first known, Edwards was in London, and immediately saw 'Watkins' in his club, recording to Owen that 'everything I could put . . . was put', and also Balfour, the Conservative leader in the Commons, who 'was very civil'.[26] Two days later Edwards reported that he had written thirty letters and informed Owen how he read the 'situation'. Watkin Williams was the most formidable rival for he had Davidson's support, but he feared that Lord Emlyn might 'run' Archdeacon Protheroe as his second name, which would be very unfortunate. He still thought 'Old H.' (Howell) 'means it for himself and son-in-law [Protheroe] be hanged.' Having written this, Edwards added a footnote to the letter. He had just heard of the bishop's death, and Owen Evans had arrived at St Asaph by the late train. It would be better to make sure of two or three names, such as Emlyn, Davidson, Puleston and surprisingly Dilke, rather than trust too much to 'smaller people'.[27]

The day after the bishop's death a campaign meeting was held at St Asaph. In attendance were Owen, Owen Evans and Evan Roderick (vicar of Mold who had been Edwards's private chaplain). This meeting was known to some of the diocesan clergy for T. Ll. Williams hoped it would not 'get to the papers, otherwise some spiteful comments might be made on it'.[28]

At first Owen expressed some rectitude about this campaign, but T. Ll. Williams made it clear to him that if his claims were not pressed he would be excluded from consideration. Lloyd of Bangor, he claimed, had three-quarters of the clergy on his side and Edwards himself had large numbers. Though he himself did not like the plan, 'I simply state how things are done . . . and what carries weight.'[29] Nevertheless, Williams thought it expedient to wait until after the funeral before canvassing influential laymen.[30] His letter of 22 January expressed some concern. He had attended a clerical meeting at Wrexham and it had been alleged that Owen was 'working hard' for the bishopric. It is almost impossible, he continued, 'to impress on some of them that the office is not an object of ambition'.[31] Perhaps here was Owen's essential dilemma; could personal ambition be linked with his concern for the government of the Church?

By this time the campaign was in full swing. The day after the bishop's death Edwards wrote to Owen: 'have been hard at it all day, not outside the door and every clergyman in this diocese and Bangor who can be trusted will be asked to write before Tuesday to Lord Salisbury.' In this letter-writing Edwards was assisted by Tom Lloyd, vicar of Bala and diocesan missioner, 'Vicar Williams', probably the vicar of St Asaph and William Richardson of Corwen, later archdeacon of Wrexham. The hint is given that Tom Lloyd wrote a sample letter for the clergy to follow, noting the needs of the vacant diocese and the need of a bishop who possessed 'commanding powers of mind and endeavour'.[32] On the following day Edwards went to London, where he had arranged 'interviews' with Lord Emlyn and Davidson. He had accepted the advice 'of the three' not to see Lord Salisbury, for 'he must not think that I lay any special claim to speak'.[33] On 20 January, Edwards informed Owen that the bishop of Chester was with him and all was being done that could be done. Later that month, when things did not look too hopeful for Owen, he 'put everything aside' and once more travelled to London in order to 'interview' Emlyn and Davidson. On this occasion he persuaded the archbishop of York to 'write for you' to the archbishop of Canterbury and to Salisbury. York, he added, carried great weight with the premier.[34]

John Rhŷs, principal of Jesus College, Oxford, was one of several laymen who assisted in this campaign. Informing Owen that he had written a large number of letters in his support, he noted some of the recipients of his letters: Lord Cranbrook, Boscawen, Balfour and Lord Salisbury himself.[35] D. Morgan Jones advised Owen that

Lord Selborne was an important man and 'must be sounded from every quarter'.[36]

The group was well aware of the opposition to Owen. T. Ll. Williams wrote on 26 January that 'a great effort will be made for another besides you'.[37] Tudor Howell, David Howell's son and Conservative MP for Denbigh, was described as their leading opponent. He was 'tooth and nail' for his brother-in-law, Protheroe. There was also his enmity towards Edwards, so that even if Owen was appointed, reported Williams, he and his friends would never allow his vacant canonry at St Asaph to be awarded to Edwards's 'pet'.[38] Another correspondent also identified 'the Howell gang', and suggested that they dared not publicly proclaim what they had whispered in Lord Salisbury's ears, while Edwards believed that 'the Howell lot' were demurring Owen's candidature because of his lack of parochial experience.[39] William Nicholas, rector of Flint, believed that their expressions about Owen, such as 'a racy son of the soil' or 'son of a peasant', had rebounded back on them.[40] Writing to Owen on 27 January, Edwards noted an interview with Emlyn and Schomberg McDonnell, Lord Salisbury's secretary, when 'he certainly pushed back Protheroe'. He tried to remain as calm as possible when he was told that while Owen was favourite 'until the race is over you can never tell'.[41] It was not until later that Edwards discovered from Davidson that Owen's most determined opponents were the bishop of Llandaff and Dr Vaughan. Their opposition was the cause of the long delay in the appointment.[42]

This delay caused Edwards and his colleagues to alternate between hope and despair, while Edwards's paranoia became all too obvious. For him it was not so much a matter of personalities but of policies. He clearly believed that his policy alone could 'save' the Welsh Church from destruction. If, on the one hand, he could be elated when he heard from the Foreign Office (Salisbury also acted as Foreign Secretary) that Owen would be going to St Davids,[43] or that his name had gone to the Queen,[44] he could also write 'the delay, the delay, that dries up all my hopes'.[45] He wondered if Salisbury's handshake in the House of Lords was 'a civility' to make up 'for failure elsewhere',[46] and when he heard that James was absent from Rugby School, he jumped to the conclusion that he had been summoned to Hatfield House, Lord Salisbury's home.[47] Hearing from Vicar Williams that James had read a Welsh service, which indicated his ability in that language, he felt this might explain the delay in the appointment if it was known to Salisbury.[48] D. Morgan Jones was asked to contact the local MP and the Liberal agent at Rugby, both of whom were alienated from James, requesting them to write against his appointment.[49] Edwards's letters note his fear that Salisbury had a compromise candidate or that the Queen would not confirm Owen's appointment. He wrote to Owen that if he lost the appointment, 'they will know what manner of man they have passed over'.[50] Even Tudor Howell's remark that Owen would be appointed by 'the skin of his teeth' failed to satisfy him.[51] But Howell was in the know, and his statement was true.

John Owen accepted Salisbury's offer of the diocese of St Davids on 14 February, Salisbury having written to the Queen stating that Owen had been 'strongly recommended by an enormous number of clergy and laity in connection' with the diocese.[52] In his reply to the premier Owen wrote: 'I can only say that it shall be, all my life, my constant endeavour and prayer to be enabled to discharge faithfully the heavy responsibilities of the difficult office which I am now writing to accept.'[53]

The *Western Mail* announced Owen's appointment on 16 February. His name, it stated, had been keenly identified with the vacancy; a hardly surprisingly statement when that paper had continually advanced his claims. Owen's appointment had given great satisfaction. Welshmen of all creeds and classes knew his sterling qualities and indomitable energies, his manly outspokenness and his strong and inevitably fair advocacy of what he considered to be the truth. Although he had fought hard for the Welsh Church in press and on platform he had done so in a style that all respected. He and Edwards had driven the Church's enemies 'from every position at the point of a bayonet. Not a charge was left unanswered, not an argument went without an adequate reply.' But all this was done in such a way that Owen had fewer enemies 'than any other public man in the Welsh Church or out of it'. Although young, he knew the diocese of St Davids extremely well, and though his knowledge of pastoral work was not extensive, Owen had certainly not spent his days in a monastery unaware of the needs and difficulties of the parochial clergy. Above all, he was a Welshman. The appointment, the editor added, 'must impress all that the Church is still the most democratic institution in the kingdom'. It was a claim fully endorsed by the editor of the *Baner*, who congratulated 'our old friend' upon his elevation and suggested he would bring a new spirit to the diocese of St Davids.[54]

Even the *Record* welcomed Owen as one who was both Welsh and also a 'moderate' churchman with wide sympathies.[55] While his 'catholic principles' had not taken a very definite line, suggested the *Church Times*, it hoped that that influence 'overspreading' the Church would affect him as it had other bishops. Then he would be found 'as strenuous a defender of the Faith as of the possessions of the Church'.[56] The *Carmarthen Journal*, now released from its vow of silence, suggested that bishops had one weakness: they were unapproachable to many of their clergy because of their dignity and income. It hoped that Owen's Welsh background would make him a different kind of bishop to his clergy.[57]

A strong lobby endeavoured to persuade the new archbishop that Owen's consecration as a bishop should take place in Wales. Archdeacon Griffiths of Llandaff was the prime mover in this, suggesting Llandaff cathedral as the more central point. It could be a bilingual service, it was argued, with the three Welsh bishops deciding by lot as to which one preached. This, Griffiths argued, would indicate the importance of the Welsh language in the life of the new bishop and in the life of the Welsh Church.[58] This suggestion probably arose from a real concern to re-emphasize the importance of a language diminishing in value in many parts of Wales. Nothing came of this proposal although Owen's consecration at St Paul's Cathedral had to be delayed. This was because Dean Phillips of St Davids died in early March before the dean and chapter had proceeded to the election. A new dean had to be appointed before the formal election of Owen by the chapter could take place. The new dean, ironically, was David Howell. He was appointed by Salisbury as the gift of the deanery fell within his patronage during the vacancy of a see. It was a good consolation prize and many rejoiced. Owen did not. He would have preferred Archdeacon Bevan of Hay or Chancellor Davey, his vice-principal at Lampeter. But Salisbury ignored his recommendations.[59]

Bishop Lewis's concern about the shameless wirepulling in this and other appointments has been noted, although it is not easy to pick up such an atmosphere from the various newspaper accounts. That the public believed this was so is established by a letter from 'A Welsh Churchman' in the *Church Times* of 5 March which inaugurated a bitter controversy about this matter. A new danger faces the Church in Wales from within, this anonymous writer alleged, for her 'highest places' were being obtained by unqualified and unprepared men by the use of 'skilful manipulation'. This, he claimed, was bound to affect the spiritual tone of the Church. Many agreed with him.[60] The argument was continued in a more personal way by one 'Catholicus Menevensis'. His was a bitter attack on Owen as a fighting bishop and schoolmaster, though he wisely declined to name him. Are we to hold our peace, he wrote, 'in view of intrigue and wire-pulling of the most shameless kind, because it has been practiced before and elsewhere?' Nevertheless, he conceded that even if a popular election was held, in a climate when temporal prosperity had assumed too great an importance in the minds of the Welsh clergy, fighting bishops would continue to be elected.[61]

Other correspondents joined in the resulting paper battle. It is notorious, wrote 'A Welsh Churchman', that whenever there has been a 'good fat carcass, the birds have scented it, however far away, with almost telegraphic quickness'. And was it an accident that on the day of the late bishop's death there was an unseemly rush northwards as fast as steam could travel? Justifying his statements later he argued that the pattern of appointments of Edwards, Owen, and Jayne, bishop of Chester and a brother-in-law of Edwards, proved his point, and he further alleged that these men, with the addition of Owen Evans, warden of Llandovery and a close friend of Edwards, were 'together' in north Wales within three days of the bishop's death.[62] Only the timescale was wrong.

The general consensus of opinion was against him. It was felt that Owen would never allow himself to be a party to such 'wire-pulling' or would ask anyone to 'lift a finger' to put him into a bishopric.[63] Watkin Williams, writing from the deanery of St Asaph, once occupied by Owen, argued that if one doubted that Owen accepted this work in obedience to the divine will, or that the Church under him would prosper, then one must doubt the efficiency of the grace of God.[64] Owen's daughter, in her biography of her father, notes that her father vowed never to enter into competition for any preferment. But friends persuaded him otherwise in this instance, and he permitted his name to go forward. These friends were noted as Bishops Edwards and Jayne, Owen Evans and T. Ll. Williams, SPG secretary for Wales![65]

There was clearly truth in the rumour that Salisbury wished Edwards to be translated to St Davids, assuming that St Asaph would be an easier diocese to fill. There was clear substance in the general feeling that Edwards and his friends ran a campaign for Owen's appointment, and that Owen was aware of it. Many suspected, but had no evidence, that Edwards used every trick in his repertoire to advance his own candidate and to discredit his rivals. Although at first matched with Protheroe, Owen's experience of high office, the knowledge gained of him by prominent politicians during the tithe campaign, and his general ability, stood him in good stead. Edwards thus had little difficulty in 'running' his candidate, who had proved a loyal and trusty lieutenant to him in the disestablishment campaign. Thereafter, Owen described Edwards as his great and loyal leader. Yet was there an organized opposition to Owen as Edwards appears to have believed? Or were the two parties, described by Edwards as the 'Howellites and Asaphites', in total opposition to one another? There was certainly opposition to his overall policy and it is clear that other groups lobbied for their own candidates, but it hardly appears that the opposition was as organized as Edwards's campaign. T. Ll. Williams wrote that Owen's opponents were not so much his enemies as men who regarded the election as a political contest won by the person who got the most votes.[66] This may be so, but Tudor Howell, if he masterminded a campaign for Protheroe, appears to have done so in the more sedate spirit of the establishment, namely by mentioning names in the right places.

Paradoxically, for one appointed for the needs of a Welsh-speaking diocese, Owen was never known to have spoken to his clergy in Welsh.[67] Owen's episcopate was long, though not as long as that of Edwards, but it was a balanced episcopate, even though the political campaign against disestablishment took the time that should have been given to diocesan affairs. When disestablishment came, and with it the division of his diocese which had been mooted by a strong lobby during that vacancy of 1897,[68] Owen was a tired man. Death came early in 1926.

~ 12 ~

A Vacancy in Bangor:
The Episcopal Election of 1898

Daniel Lewis Lloyd, bishop of Bangor from 1890, resigned his see in November 1898, having been incapacitated by a long and trying illness. He had had a brain haemorrhage in February, but by July he was able to walk a little and understand what was said to him, but he was still unable to reply. The suffragan bishop of Swansea was taking confirmations and ordinations, but otherwise the episcopal work of the diocese was almost totally neglected.[1] If the clergy were attached to their kind-hearted bishop, wrote Archdeacon Pryce of Bangor to Archbishop Temple, they were not blind to the fact that he could not continue with his diocesan work. He felt, however, that if they suggested to the bishop that he should resign, it could induce another attack.[2] Temple, trying to ease the situation, considered the appointment of a suffragan bishop, but felt that only Lloyd's resignation could avoid an ecclesiastical scandal. But, he added, 'the bishop is poor, his wife is in an asylum, his family is large', and there was no certainty he would consent to such a step.[3]

Others were less charitable. Letters alleged that the situation in the diocese was deplorable. Thomas Lloyd, vicar of Abergele and later archdeacon of St Asaph, wrote to E. S. Talbot, bishop of Rochester, complaining about the lack of love and hope pervading the whole diocese.[4] Lord Penrhyn, one of its leading landowners, argued that during the eight years of his episcopate, even before Lloyd's illness, there had been a seeming want of attention to duty. The bishop had not held a visitation of the diocese since he was elected. Anxieties, cares and family illnesses, besides the deterioration of his own health, had afflicted him since his appointment, and these problems had frequently caused the postponement of ordinations and confirmations. He had lived effectively at Llanarth, his Cardiganshire home, for the previous year.[5] John Morgan, rector

257

of Llandudno, possibly asked for his comments, replied in much the same way. The whole work of the diocese had steadily declined since his appointment. The bishop was now totally incapable of discharging his office. In the last fortnight he was being taught the alphabet. Yet livings were still 'being filled up'. Should there not be an enquiry?[6]

This general if devastating impression was corroborated by others. Canon Fletcher of Wrexham, writing to the archbishop of York, alleged that 'no words can exaggerate the feeling of clergy and laity as to the present scandal' in the diocese of Bangor. Some in that diocese, he had heard, wanted a suffragan bishop and had suggested Grimaldi Davis, vicar of Welshpool, for that office. Some enquiry ought to be made of him from Lord Powis and Lord Penrhyn. In his opinion, however, the diocese required a new appointment, not a suffragan; in particular 'a high minded Christian gentleman' who would elevate the clergy and not be out of touch with the leading laity.[7] Harry Wace, a layman from Dolgellau, argued that the bishop should resign, for the work of the diocese was in absolute chaos and the clergy were indignant at his neglect.[8] The archdeacon of Merioneth, Thomas Williams, urged by the bishop of Llandaff 'to go straight to headquarters', voiced the same concern.[9]

The archbishop had little option in view of these and other statements save to request his suffragan's resignation. Lloyd's son, claiming that illness alone prevented his father from resigning, felt unable to lay Temple's letter before him, as it would only aggravate his condition and make him feel wholly unwanted.[10] The bishop eventually retired on a pension of a third of the diocesan income (which came out of the episcopal revenues) to his home at Llanarth. Here he died in August of the following year, in a state worse than 'childish simplicity'.[11]

The Diocesan Concern

The *Carnarvon and Denbigh Herald* in its issue of 7 October 1898 printed a circular said to have been produced by Thomas Williams, archdeacon of Merioneth, and some of the senior diocesan clergy of the now vacant see. A meeting had taken place of some of the rural deans and the archdeacon under the chairmanship of the dean of Bangor. As a result, it was suggested that the rural deans of the diocese should write to the prime minister and archbishop upon the lines of a memorandum agreed on at that meeting. In addition the meeting accepted the names of John Lloyd, the suffragan bishop of Swansea (who had been appointed in 1890 to assist the elderly Bishop Basil Jones of St Davids), and Archdeacon Edmondes of Llandaff, 'with practical unanimity', as possible successors.[12]

This memorandum, addressed to the prime minister, was seen as a strong and bitter attack on the bishop of St Asaph. His statements and actions had outraged many loyal churchmen who preferred a quiet and low-key approach to the Nonconformists (then canvassing for disestablishment) than the outright attack that Edwards promoted.[13] Edwards's attitude had already provoked two strong rebellions amongst his own clergy. The editor of the *Independent* newspaper wrote this about the bishop who had provoked this attack:

> Englishmen may perhaps be surprised at this blunt language, but Welsh Churchmen have long ago come to the conclusion that the Bishop of St Asaph, by his imperious temper and unscrupulous methods, is making the Anglican Church increasingly odious in the Principality . . . It was he who led a Welsh clergyman to write: 'This is but a sample of Episcopal doings which make us hang down our heads in sorrow.' It was he who provoked 75 out of the 206 incumbents in his diocese into signing a protest against his own use of patronage, the memorialists including one of his own archdeacons and his late chaplain. It was he, who, having surrounded himself with a platform of landlords, rated his clergy like schoolboys, and cowed them into silence. But the reckoning day has come at last, and the clergy of Bangor have amply avenged their ill-treated brethren of St Asaph.[14]

The memorial pointed out that: 'The appointment of any one coming to the diocese in the Spirit and pledged to the methods of what is known as "the St Asaph policy" would, in our opinion, be fatal to the peace and well-being of the Church in the diocese.' It requested Lord Salisbury to have regard to the following principles, which they believed were accepted by 'the whole Church throughout the Diocese':

> (A) That the man should be a man who has had long and varied experience of Church work from the inside; not one who, whether a schoolmaster or otherwise, has to learn his work after coming to the Bench . . .

(B) That the nominee should be one who by age no less than by experience would command the respect and confidence of his diocese. We need in a Bishop experience no less than energy, judgment not less than strength, self restraint no less than zeal and enthusiasm.

(C) That the nominee should be a man of known religious earnestness testified by all as a man of deep spirituality of life – no flippant political exploiter, no diplomatic trickster, no headstrong partisan, but one who in the calmness borne of faith accepts the Church as Christ's spiritual Body – a Body with Divine commission, dependent for her life and discipline upon spiritual sanctions and spiritual agencies; not a political engine to be worked by political methods for the accomplishment of political, or, worse still, personal designs.

Having suggested that the appointment should not be made from the diocesan clergy, they requested that either they, as the dean and chapter, should be allowed to make recommendations, or that the premier should consult them about the names he was considering for the appointment.[15]

The archdeacon and his friends, reported the *Carnarvon and Denbigh Herald*, had been bitterly attacked by the *North Wales Chronicle* for this memorial. For its own part, it felt that it was not to be wondered at that the clergy of Bangor had no wish to be brought under a 'yoke' that had proved intolerable to their colleagues at St Asaph.[16] The *Chronicle* had claimed that this 'low and scurrilous intrigue' was simply the continuation of some undercover work by the archdeacon, another dignitary, and a radical Nonconformist correspondent, against the bishop of St Asaph. In addition the memorial resembled in phrase and handwriting some of the anonymous letters sent to 'most editors in this district'. It accused the writers of the memorial of 'offering to the Bishop of Bangor the gratuitous insult which is implied in the devout prayer that no schoolmaster Bishop "who has to learn his work after coming to the Bench" – may be appointed to preside over the See of Bangor. To no other Bishop in Wales can the taunt apply . . .' It continued:

> The authors of this venomous 'Memorandum' were evidently too intent on tilting at the Bishop of St Asaph to have respect for common-sense and decorum . . . The whole thing breathes the atmosphere, not of religion, but the world: the low world of intrigue and cunning, which honourable laymen – not to speak of Ministers of the Church – eschew and avoid.[17]

The *Western Mail*, in alluding to this controversy, argued that it was a thinly veiled attempt to continue a policy adopted by various Welsh nationalists to hold up Lloyd 'as a model and pattern of what a Welsh prelate ought to be, with the intention of casting unfavourable light upon other Welsh bishops'.[18] Lloyd George in a speech at Bangor in late November was obviously following this nationalist argument when he stated:

> He had said strong things from time to time about bishops, but he could not recall a single instance in which he had said a harsh thing about Bishop Lloyd, and he would tell them why. The late Bishop of Bangor had always shown that he possessed the conscience of a true shepherd. He, at any rate, did not harry his flock like a mad dog. He was, moreover, a real patriot. Wales had a warm corner in her heart for all those in high places who cherished her ancient tongue . . . No one could rob Bishop Lloyd of the distinction of being the first member of the episcopal bench in Wales who in recent times departed from that fatuous [anti-national] policy. For all the good which he did, which he had episcopal precedent for despising, and for all the evil he did not, which he had equally exalted sanction for perpetrating, he was, and would be, honoured amongst all ranks and creeds of his country.[19]

Lloyd George's comments and the *Western Mail's* surmise may be the reason why Edwards's supporters found it necessary to turn the memorial around and suggest it was an attack on Lloyd himself.

As a result of this outburst of concern, if not of fear, from the senior clergy of Bangor, a furious row developed. The dean of Bangor, Evan Lewis, endeavoured to explain that the meeting had been called simply to consider what, if anything, could be done to secure the selection of the best available man for the diocese. All were impressed by the solemnity of the occasion during which special prayers had been composed for the vacancy. He was incorrect, however, in his assertion that both archdeacons supported the meeting. It soon became clear that Archdeacon Pryce of Bangor had refused to attend. The meeting, the dean went on to assert, then considered the memorandum which had been produced for discussion by a participant. He much regretted that the unrevised rough draft of the memorandum had been published without authority by 'some false friend' or one hostile to their concern.[20] The archdeacon of Merioneth, obviously under considerable pressure, denied there was any desire to attack Bishop Lloyd, whom he personally had served loyally and continued to trust, love and honour. The archdeacon also argued in a letter to the *Manchester Guardian*, in response to the persistent attacks made on him, that the primary task of the meeting was to devise intercessions for the vacancy. He clarified the fact that as his fellow archdeacon had declined to attend, only the rural deans of his own archdeaconry had been invited, although others, namely members of the chapter, were also present, and other clerics had written in to support the draft of that memorandum.[21] One suspects that the memorialists were surprised by the adverse publicity they had received, horrified that Edwards's supporters had suggested they were attacking their former bishop, and were now endeavouring to back-pedal as fast as they could. In fact the memorandum seems to have been accepted with little thought of its implications.

One correspondent who described himself as a priest 'grown venerable in the service of the Church', who had been absent from the meeting, had written to the archdeacon saying he could not 'see why Dr Edwards or anyone outside the diocese should foist upon us, just to please themselves, a man of whom we do not approve'. Another, a rural dean in the archdeaconry of Bangor, had written to him in this 'present painful crisis', stating that the St Asaph policy, which he once supported, had been disastrous to the Church, and he prayed that no supporter of that policy should be appointed. A layman, writing in the same paper, agreed with the archdeacon that the meeting was no 'intrigue', and expressed his regret that the choice of a new bishop should rest in the hands of the 'clerical denizens of that diocese' (St Asaph). The election should take place without the interference of 'impertinent and mischievous . . . agitators or wirepullers belonging to any other diocese'.[22]

Those who attacked the memorandum and its authors were not numerous, but were highly vocal. A number of the clergy of the diocese, 48 out of 147 incumbents and 20 of the 70 curates, including J. W. Wynne Jones, vicar of Caernarfon and a rural dean, John Morgan, rector of Llandudno, Canon Robert Williams of Llanfaelog, and Chancellor Silvan Evans, protested against this memorandum in a memorial of their own to Salisbury. It was neither conducive to the well-being of the Church in their or any other diocese, they alleged, and they deplored the attempt to discredit 'by imputation the bishop of another diocese'. But it was pointed out by others that while the diocese had been 'carefully canvassed', the promoters of this memorial had failed to obtain the support of even one third of the diocesan clergy. Only four dignitaries had signed, compared to eleven out of thirteen rural deans who had expressed themselves in agreement with the principles of the memorandum and half the cathedral chapter who had been present at the meeting. Most of those who had signed this memorial to the prime minister were young incumbents and curates. The clergy, it was alleged, were consequently against any pro-Edwards appointment. And those who had signed the memorial were in turn accused of making 'their salvation sure . . . in anticipation' of the election of 'an adherent of the "anti-national policy" '.[23]

Chastened by the strong reaction of the press and Church leaders against them, the so-called 'conspirators' held a further meeting on 24 October at the chapter house. In all probability the same people attended this as the previous one. On the same day the dean wrote to the archbishop. Their only motive in holding such meetings and devising the memorandum was the good of the Church. Turning their collective thoughts into a prayer he prayed that the Holy Spirit would guide the archbishop and those in authority 'to make choice of a man who is known to possess spiritual power, with practical knowledge gained by experience, of the difficulties which surround the Church in Wales so that, as our Bishop, he may be a trusted leader and guide in our Spiritual work having a view only to the glory of God, and the salvation of souls'. However, there was one fact he desired to place before the archbishop:

> it is well known that there are two parties, small in numbers but strong in position, who are doing their utmost to promote the selection of their respective friends. There are circumstances, however, which could render the selection of either an unfortunate thing for the diocese. These we do not enter into now, but are prepared to do so, if desired.[24]

One party is clearly identified, namely that of the bishop of St Asaph and his friends. Was the other that of the archdeacon of Merioneth, as was hinted by the *Manchester Guardian*? If so, his plans seriously misfired. In all probability his candidate was Bishop Lloyd, the suffragan bishop of Swansea in the diocese of St Davids, but, regretfully, the records are silent. The whole of the running appears to have been done by Edwards and his group. His contacts with the politicians were far too powerful to admit the name of any newcomer on to the list of eligible candidates.

The Public's Recommendations

The usual letters of recommendation poured into Lambeth and Downing Street. Daniel Morgan, rector of Llantrisant in Anglesey, suggested Archdeacon Pryce, describing him as no extreme man, a good scholar, firm yet affable.[25] Sir William Priestley of Horsham noted the merits of the vicar of Warnham in Sussex, Richard Bowcott, a Welshman and a Welsh speaker. As a former curate of Llanover one assumes he might have satisfied Lady Llanover's requirements (though she had died two years earlier).[26] The *Record* suggested A. A. Mathews, a former vicar of Holy Trinity, Swansea, and a noted athlete in his day.[27] It later suggested the names of Bishop Lloyd, David Howell, dean of St Davids, Watkin Williams, dean of St Asaph, Archdeacon Protheroe of Cardigan, Archdeacon Bruce of Monmouth, Walter Thomas of Holyhead, N. T. Hughes of Hardingstone, Nottinghamshire, Canon Thompson of Cardiff and Owen Evans the warden of Llandovery.[28] Correspondents in the *Carnarvon and Denbigh Herald* suggested Watkin Williams, Archdeacon Protheroe or Owen Evans, and later Alexander Goldwyer Lewis, vicar of Aldford, in Chester, and Archdeacon Williams of Merioneth, as suitable candidates.[29] The *Liverpool Post* equally entered the fray and mentioned the strong possibilities of either Owen Evans or Rowland Ellis, then serving in the Scottish Episcopal Church in Edinburgh.[30] The latter's name was highly recommended by Stephen Gladstone, vicar of Hawarden and son of the former prime minister. A former vicar of Mold, he wrote, a Welshman, a perfect gentleman, one of the same type as Bishop Walsham How, and yet, most unusual for a Welshman, he was a man without ambition.[31]

Bishop Richard Lewis wished to promote his archdeacon, Frederick Edmondes. Writing to Bishop Davidson of Winchester, still the Queen's ecclesiastical advisor as well as the intermediary between Windsor, Lambeth and Downing Street, he pointed out that Edmondes was 'far and away' the fittest of all the Welsh-speaking clergymen to succeed Lloyd. Edmondes, he added, had been secretary of the two Welsh Church Congresses which had been held in Wales, clerical secretary of the diocesan conference, chairman of the Bridgend Board of Guardians, and rector of a bilingual parish, Coety. Furthermore, he was a first-class adminis- trator and the best man of business he knew. But the good bishop, unlike his contemporaries, would not approach the prime minister due to his horror of wirepulling.[32] Davidson encouraged him to write to Salisbury. This Lewis did, pointing out that he was the senior Welsh bishop, and, after stressing Edmondes's good family background, his considerable means and moderate church views, alleged he was not a person who would put himself forward for preferment.[33]

Bishop Edwards's Man

Bishop Edwards had his man, although he may have had to change his choice in the light of the Bangor protest, as we note later. This was his own dean, Watkin Williams, even though the *Record* had suggested that he had no ambition for the job.[34] So confident was Edwards of his appointment, it was alleged, that he happily left for a holiday at Lisbon.[35] Had he been in doubt, the paper reported, he would not have put the Bay of Biscay between himself and Downing Street! A strong lobby of support for Williams developed. Canon Fletcher of Wrexham wrote to his friend, the archbishop of York. He rejoiced that there was every prospect of some real episcopal oversight in the diocese of Bangor. If the archbishop of Canterbury consulted him, Fletcher asked, would he mention the eminent merits of 'our good dean of St Asaph'. He was a man of good birth, son of a baronet and a nephew of Sir Watkin Wynne of Wynnstay, and much given to generosity and hospitality. His London flat was the rallying point for the Welsh members of both Houses of Convocation in London. A plain, practical and original preacher, he was equally a man of business. Even though he was a man of considerable wealth (a matter of some importance as one third of the diocesan income would be allocated as a pension for Bishop Lloyd), he nevertheless lived simply. Indeed, when he came to the deanery he even sold his horses and carriages in order to devote the whole of his official and private income to good works.[36] Clearly, good hospitality and holy poverty were still regarded as apostolic requirements for a bishopric.

John Owen, bishop of St Davids and one of Edwards's most loyal disciples, urged the necessity of a quick appointment. The diocese had lacked leadership for two years, and some of its dignitaries who might have given it a spirit of 'dignified calmness and self control' had instead set an example 'just the reverse'. Yet even Owen's loyalty to Edwards, who had almost obtained Owen's bishopric for him, could not for the time being overcome his primary loyalty to his nation. The dean, he noted, was not a fluent Welsh speaker, though his presence would strengthen the Welsh bench, and he was a gentleman of wide culture and of a chivalrous Christian character.

Dismissing the claims of the bishop of Swansea, his own suffragan, Owen noted the stronger claim of Owen Evans, warden of Llandovery, as a candidate for the vacant diocese. If a fluent Welsh speaker was required then the warden was the man, but Owen made clear he still preferred the dean, for the warden held the same post as he and the bishop of St Asaph had held. Consequently, he continued: 'if three successive wardens of Llandovery were elevated to the Welsh Bench in succession the capacity of the Welsh imagination for suspecting some imparity of influence has to be taken into account.' There was also that dislike of schoolmaster-bishops. Evans had been the favoured candidate of Edwards, but by this time he was being used as a strawman in order to highlight Watkin Williams's candidature.[37]

A further letter from Owen wholeheartedly recommended the dean. If all doubts in his mind were removed, he yet warned the prime minister that he should expect statements of the most damaging character to be made against the dean, 'for one of the most unpleasant features of Welsh episcopal vacancies is the extraordinary recklessness with which Welsh clergy – who are as a rule worthy men enough – will write against persons whose appointment they may not personally like'. Owen by now had discovered that Williams had taken Welsh services in his former parish, Bodelwyddan, and for Owen this was sufficient proof of his competence in that language. Besides, he and his family were sympathetic to all that was good in Welsh life.[38]

Laurence A. Brodrick, a layman of Coed Coch, Abergele, was persuaded to use his own influential connections in favour of Williams's candidature. The previous appointment to Bangor, he wrote to his father (Viscount Midleton), was a disaster and had weakened the Church in that diocese. The bishop of St Asaph had begged him to write to the bishop of Winchester (Davidson) and bring the dean's name to his notice.[39] This Brodrick did in a letter of 24 September, requesting the bishop to use his influence for the dean if such an opportunity arose. The dean's hospitality to the diocesan clergy was well known. He helped, for example, those men of slender income who had to think twice before they could incur the expense of a day's absence from home. Mrs Williams too was beloved by all classes for her tact and goodness. It was most necessary for the new bishop to be of a good social position, for he needed to 'better if possible the stamp of men who seek ordination in North Wales'. Williams's appointment would be welcomed by many of the leading laity of the diocese as a pledge that the 'Church would be quickened and her deficiencies made good'. The dean had taken the lead in pacifying the St Asaph clerical revolt, and his willingness to accept the leadership of the bishop of St Asaph would also be an advantage as the two dioceses lacked the resources to go it alone in such matters as church defence and a training college for the clergy. Such cooperation between the two bishops would give widespread encouragement to the churchmen of both dioceses.[40]

A further letter, noting that many of the most prominent laity in the diocese of Bangor had written to the prime minister in warm support of Williams, added that several people had sought to discredit the dean by making a 'determined attempt' to connect him with the agitation of the previous year. While the bishop had summoned a meeting at Wrexham of the diocesan clergy which was attended by the leading laity, from the duke of Westminster down, the dean had adopted a different technique. With much tact he had gathered together a large number of the malcontents at the deanery and took 'them over to the Palace where a formal reconciliation took place'. Such agitation, coming from a small group who traded on the ignorance and poverty of their clerical brethren, was equally illustrated by the action of the senior clergy of Bangor with regard to the present vacancy. These groups, he added, endeavoured to show they had more support than was warranted in fact, and no prominent layman had supported their intrigues, which had discredited the Church and provided fuel for her enemies. Under these circumstances the appointment of a man of peace, such as the dean, would be a distinct advantage. His social position would enable him to disregard any personal attacks which might be made on him, and his influence would turn the minds of his clergy away from 'such pitiful and unworthy agitation to the earnest prosecution of their spiritual duties'.[41]

There were others too who wrote in favour of Williams. Bishop Talbot of Rochester, though he thought Williams was not 'great things' to look at, testified he was nevertheless a gentleman and his wife, although deaf, a lady. Above all, the dean was a man of peace and a good sound churchman.[42] Arthur Lyttelton thought that underneath Williams's unassuming manner there lurked a strong man. He possessed character and individuality so that he would take his own line as bishop and would not 'follow the gang'.[43] That may have been the clinching argument.

Lloyd George, in what the *Western Mail* was pleased to call an 'extravagant speech' accompanied by much laughter, said this:

> An unscrupulous and ambitious neighbouring potentate wishing to annex the vacated dominion to his empire, knowing that he could not very well occupy the Throne himself, endeavoured to thrust one of his own creatures into possession of it, in order to rule through him. Those wars had always been fierce and prolonged, and the contest for the See of Bangor had in that respect the characteristics of every conflict of its kind in history. It had accomplished, at any rate, one good object: it had shown that there was a deep-rooted dissatisfaction amongst the best men of the Church with the present state of things . . .

Lord Salisbury, he concluded, 'would, in all probability, appoint another bishop of the Asaph brand, possessing none of the qualities which history had repeatedly proved to be the only passports to the Welsh heart'. The reason for this was quite clear. The Church, placed in a false position by its claim to be the national Church, did not need for its defence a preacher and a spiritual man, but rather 'a person who fulfilled the description which St. Paul regarded as a positive disqualification for the sacred office of Bishop, namely, a striker'.[44]

No doubt this was political rhetoric by a man who was then totally opposed to the Church and all that it stood for, but even such rhetoric as this needed some foundation in truth for it to be remotely credible.

A Compromise Candidate?

Edwards and the leading laity of north Wales were almost exclusively supporters of Salisbury's Conservative government, and such a noise for one man, well arranged, and the demand for haste, clearly secured the election of Watkin Williams to the see.[45] The embarrassing fact of the Bangor protest was glossed over by cleverly coupling it up with an entirely different incident, that of the St Asaph clergy revolt. The laity who helped to suppress the latter were clearly concerned about upholding the authority of a Tory bishop, whereas the clergy were concerned about the cause of national identity. Edwards's political churchmanship was well supported in influential places, even though it was mistrusted by many apart from the Bangor clergy. Yet at the end of the day these men and their protest were marginalized by Edwards's tactics. One wonders if at least they knocked Edwards's favourite candidate out of the running. This was probably Owen Evans, warden of Llandovery, who clearly answered the Bangor description of the man they did not want. He was young, a schoolmaster, pastorally inexperienced, and a close friend and supporter of both Edwards and Owen. Might it be that by their action the Bangor clergy obtained a compromise candidate; one who would be reasonably acceptable to both them and the prime minister, but one who if he would not promote Edwards's schemes and policies would at least not frustrate them? Williams was no schoolmaster, no slavish follower of Edwards, and he certainly fitted the bill provided by the Bangor clergy in their job description for their new bishop. His leadership may never have been brilliant, but at least it brought the diocese together.

Did Edwards thus change his candidate mid-stream, realizing the opposition against his appointment? If so, then it shows the agility and subtlety of his mind; the mind of a politician, rather than the mind of a bishop.

This interpretation is endorsed by the subsequent correspondence between Bishop Owen and Salisbury regarding the deanery of St Asaph, for it was customary for the prime minister to claim the right of presentation to the ecclesiastical preferments vacated by a newly appointed bishop. Salisbury now claimed this right. Edwards was clearly concerned to get his own man appointed. He begged (through John Owen) that the prime minister would postpone an appointment until he had returned from Portugal. It was an important question for the bishop as he had to work so closely with the dean, added Owen.[46] Edwards wrote to Salisbury from Lisbon on the same day with a similar request.[47] Another request followed, again submitted by Owen, as it appears Salisbury was biding his time with the appointment. It would be most unfortunate, he wrote, for anyone to be appointed dean who had taken part in 'a most unworthy attack' recently made on the bishop. Though that 'trouble' was happily over, Owen hoped that the influence of the two north Wales bishops would prevent the possibility of a further reoccurrence of the 'most disgraceful . . . event which I have ever known in connection with the Church in Wales'.[48]

Salisbury was happy to comply with this request, and accordingly consulted Edwards about acceptable candidates. Edwards, in replying, noted a number of names. Archdeacon Llewellyn Wynne-Jones was the man preferred by the diocese. Though great objections had been made to his appointment as archdeacon, it was to his credit that that feeling had now passed away and he was most popular with, and trusted by, the clergy. Besides this, he had 'large private means'. Canon Fletcher was also noted with favour. A subsequent letter warned against some other people whose names might have come to the prime minister's attention. Archdeacon Protheroe would not be acceptable. As a son-in-law of Dean Howell of St Davids, who was involved in that 'painful incident' which had taken place in the diocese the previous year, his appointment would be hurtful to the well-being of the diocese; indeed it could be calamitous. The Hon. Hugh Mostyn would undoubtedly accept the deanery if offered it, but he was disqualified by being unable to speak a word of Welsh. Edwards later suggested such names as W. H. Hutton of St John's College, Cambridge, and Francis Chavasse, later bishop of Liverpool, but seems to have forgotten that his objection to Mostyn would also apply to them.[49]

Salisbury also wrote to Owen asking if the name of Owen Evans, warden of Llandovery, would be acceptable to the bishop of St Asaph. Owen replied to this query. Evans was a capital man, an examining chaplain to the bishop of Chester, a close personal friend of himself and Bishop Edwards, and a strong Welsh-speaking clergyman. To this letter McDonnell (Salisbury's secretary) added an endorsement for his chief's attention: 'He is a capital man but I understand the Bishop of St Asaph would not recommend him, as he wanted to run him for the next Bishopric.'[50]

In these words 'he wanted to run him for the next bishopric' we have an adequate reply to both Owen's and Edwards's comments about the senior clergy of Bangor, and which may be summed up in that proverb about the pot calling the kettle black. But a comment arises: why did Edwards not run Owen Evans for Bangor in 1898? The answer must be that the opposition was too great and a compromise candidate had to be found, one acceptable to both Edwards and the Bangor clergy. Watkin Williams was therefore brought forward, even though all seem to have agreed that his Welsh was hardly sufficient for that most Welsh speaking of dioceses. Edwards and his group, however, preferred policy to patriotism and pastoral care; his Welsh would simply have to do.

When news of Williams's appointment was released, the *Church Times* noted his good work in the diocese of St Asaph. He had improved the tone of the cathedral services. It added, significantly, that he was probably a stronger Tory than either Edwards or Owen.[51] The *Record* thought he was more sympathetic to the high church movement, having brought in Gore, Scott Holland and Canon Mason to lecture in the cathedral. It further claimed that this appointment was yet another triumph for the anglicizing policy in the Welsh Church favoured by Salisbury and a further indication of the prime minister's sympathies with the high church party.[52]

The *Carnarvon and Denbigh Herald* claimed that his appointment had been received with mixed feelings. Williams's friendship with the bishops of St Asaph and St Davids, wrote a London correspondent, would lead to a common policy of ecclesiastical administration in Wales. The paper had suggested as early as September that if Williams was appointed then the whole of Wales would be merged into the diocese of St Asaph and Edwards would have a new dignity as archbishop of that see. It now feared that Edwards wished to control the Welsh Church. This common policy, some thought, would also commit Williams to an anti-national policy in Church matters and would lead to an increased bitterness between churchmen and Nonconformists. If his connections meant that he could appeal to the aristocracy for financial support for the diocese, and his own considerable means supplement the episcopal income, nevertheless his Welsh was less than perfect and he had no reputation as a preacher. His appointment, it was alleged, showed the prime minister's absolute indifference to the clerical memorandum.[53] Alleging that the appointment of this 'aristocrat to the

271

tips of his fingers'[54] had been occasioned by the advice of Lord Penrhyn and the bishop of St Asaph, assisted by the fact that the new bishop was a sound Tory, this Liberal paper suggested that the dean and chapter now had the opportunity of informing the world that their recent agitation was not a farce. It advised the chapter to decline to elect the new bishop, but the editor significantly added that he feared they were 'not compounded of martyr-stuff'.[55] The *Western Mail* was more sympathetic, being conducted in the Conservative interest, and welcomed his appointment. The new bishop, it claimed, would revitalize the diocese. Although his appointment was anticipated, it was known that Williams would never have taken any steps to bring himself to the premier's notice. Though he was no preacher he yet brought other, more needed, qualities to the diocese, especially in being a man of peace able to bind together those who differed.[56]

Williams continued in the tranquil possession of his see, almost imitating his beloved bees in their steady and peaceful pursuit of labour, until his resignation in 1924. Throughout his years as a diocesan bishop he took an independent line on most things, to the exasperation of his colleagues. The fears of those who believed he would simply be a pawn in the hands of Edwards were never justified. After his resignation Watkin Williams lived on for another twenty years, and acquired a rather different kind of fame, that of being the oldest living bishop in the Anglican Communion.

~ 13 ~

The Last State Appointment:
The Appointment of Joshua Pritchard
Hughes to Llandaff, 1905

Richard Lewis, bishop of Llandaff since 1883, died after a long and lingering illness on 24 January 1905. If the *Western Mail* commented that 'nothing but his unselfish devotion to his duty and his love for the diocese kept him from retirement long ago',[1] the *Church Times*, with less charity but more honesty, regretted that he had not resigned as his advanced age had made him unequal to the needs of a diocese and a Church passing through a time of crisis.[2] The bishop was sixty-two when he was nominated to the see, and was even then diffident about accepting it at such an age. Nevertheless, he remained in office until his death at the age of eighty-three. His workload was substantial; he wrote, it was estimated, more letters a day in his own hand than most dock clerks, and this was in addition to a heavy round of engagements. The *Baner* suggested that he was the most hard-working bishop ever seen in Wales.[3]

A year before his death Lewis, realizing his now unequal strength, endeavoured to obtain the appointment of a suffragan bishop for the diocese, claiming that the population of his diocese was more than one million and that the number of his clergy had increased by 120 since 1883. With the help of a suffragan he could continue at his post.[4] The archbishop (Randall Davidson, elected in 1903) replied as tactfully as he could that there was a rule, 'unfailingly observed', that any temporary difficulty arising from the illness or advanced years of any bishop 'must not be met by the creation of a new suffragan bishopric', though he was personally keen to help him.[5] Lewis replied, perhaps a little hurt, that he did not require a suffragan because of his own advanced age, but because of the increase in the episcopal work of the diocese. His case was similar to that of the diocese of St Davids, where the suffragan bishopric of Swansea had been established.[6] He was answered by polite words:

'I know', wrote the archbishop, 'how much we all owe to you for your loving and effective service to our Church.'[7] The gentle hint about retirement was simply ignored.

If Lewis's closing years had been one of failing strength, his twenty-one-year episcopate had allowed him to build on the foundation of his predecessor, Alfred Ollivant. Lewis's example, encouragement and leadership had enabled the Church to expand in the industrial valleys and had manifestly improved the diocese's moral tone and spiritual life. Only the Welsh language periodical of the Church, *Yr Haul*, provided a discordant note. He should have made more of the Welsh language in his diocese, it suggested, and given more support to his bilingual clergy. His attitude here, together with the growing and pervading English influence of the day, had meant that the number of flourishing Welsh congregations in his diocese had been reduced to twelve.[8]

Surprisingly, there was little newspaper speculation about his successor compared to previous vacancies. One reference was by Canon Beck of Roath, who in a pulpit tribute to the late bishop, hoped for a similar apostolic bishop, rather than a great scholar, 'a renowned schoolmaster, or a man of worldly command and diplomacy'.[9] The *Western Mail*, however, noted various rumours. Owen Evans would be appointed or the bishop of St Asaph translated, and it added that the claims of possible and impossible candidates were being fully discussed in the church at large.[10]

There were, however, as usual, more subtle pressures. One of Hartwell Jones's supporters indicated that another syndicate was running its own man, so that there was a fierce if quiet battle for supremacy going on.[11] Even before the bishop's death the lines were being drawn. W. S. de Winton, a leading tractarian and an influential Welsh Church figure, made his feelings clear in a letter to one Talbot, who remains unidentified. Winton claimed to know Wales thoroughly, having had banking experience throughout south Wales. He was not a ritualist, but his absorbing desire was to keep the 'old Church together'. The bishop would either die or be forced into retirement, he wrote. It was essential that a Welsh speaker be appointed because of the pressure of the disestablishment campaign. He himself considered that if this was not possible then a first-rate Englishman would be an ideal appointment, who could then have a Welsh-speaking suffragan such as Dean Roberts of Bangor.

The disestablishment campaign, Winton advised, was a real battle for the Church in Wales. It would be fought and won in Glamorganshire. A successful appointment to Llandaff was essential as the whole Church in Wales looked to that diocese for leadership. 'The only really brilliant Welsh-speaking Churchman is the Bishop of St Davids', he advised – an assertion which might have been contested in St Asaph! Owen, he continued, was not only capable of inspiring enthusiasm among the Welsh, he was also strong, trustworthy, level headed and tactful, and a man as much appreciated by Lord Cawdor as by the small-land farmer. Furthermore, he was able to hold his own against the Nonconformists without offending them. Nevertheless, Owen would have to sacrifice £300 per annum if he was translated to Llandaff, and this would be hard for a man without private means. But he ought to be urged to take such an appointment. If all this was to the credit of Owen, it was by reflection to the discredit of Edwards, bishop of St Asaph. Indeed, Winton added a warning note. If the premier thought he could transfer Bishop Edwards to Llandaff, he should note that he was not level-headed or tactful and as unpopular with Nonconformists as Owen was popular.

If Owen felt unable to accept, or the prime minister to appoint, then Winton suggested some other names for consideration. Archdeacon Edmondes of Llandaff was the first: 'Bishop Lewis, I *know*, would like him to be his successor. He is strong, level-headed, absolutely straight and just to all sections of Churchmen . . . but he would not be a leader such as Bishop Owen and he would inspire no enthusiasm.' C. A. H. Green, vicar of Aberdare, had been mentioned by Lewis as one who would be a bishop one day, but he was a little young. Owen Evans, archdeacon of Carmarthen, would do for another see, but not for Llandaff, and Dean Roberts of Bangor would be an excellent suffragan but not a diocesan bishop.[12] When Winton discovered that Edmondes had declined the nomination he pressed Green's name strongly. A good man, he would be better for Llandaff than St Davids; since his marriage to 'a lady of means' he had a private income, and he was strong, wise, straight, methodical and hard working, a clever man, a good preacher and organizer. Of course, he was Winton's brother's brother-in-law, who was also Green's churchwarden, but you know me well enough, he added, to realize that under such circumstances he would be more critical of his qualifications than he would otherwise be. Bishop Lewis had told him that Green would be a Welsh bishop one day.[13] He was to follow A. G. Edwards as archbishop of Wales.

But there was one contender Winton had no wish to see appointed. This was Hartwell Jones, then rector of Nuffield and a prominent figure in Welsh cultural circles. 'I have never heard anyone say that they thought him fit to be a Bishop, but he is said to be rather fond of self-advertisement and his name may be suggested by his friends,' he wrote with warning malice.[14] He knew all the men he had mentioned, he wrote in a further letter, save Hartwell Jones, whom he had no wish to know. 'He is I fancy a respectable man with no particular qualifications,' but, he added, 'a wire-puller, at least he is reputed to be.'[15]

Clearly Balfour, the Conservative prime minister, had no easy choice. As Davidson wrote: 'Clearly nobody can be appointed with universal acclaim.'[16] Winton's suggestion of an English bishop with a Welsh suffragan may well have seemed an attractive option to the premier as it considerably widened the choice of men for the see. Balfour, through his secretaries and possibly through the archbishop, sounded out a number of people about this possibility. One reply was received from A. C. Legard of Cardiff, an Etonian and a former government inspector of education in Wales. He argued that a Welsh-speaking bishop was not a necessity. The percentage of Welsh speakers in Glamorgan had decreased in one decade from 21.8 per cent to 6.6 per cent, though many English speakers still attended a Welsh chapel on Sundays. It would be a happy day for Wales if 'an Englishman of liberal views with something of the Celtic enthusiasm' was appointed who was also a good academic man.[17]

Others thought differently. Chancellor J. Richards of Bangor wrote, admittedly later, that the influence of the revival then going on necessitated a bilingual appointment as well as a man of parochial experience. 'Pobun' (everyman) writing in Y *Llan* argued that while one third of the population spoke Welsh, and even more understood it, it was as necessary for a bishop of Llandaff to speak the language as an incumbent in a bilingual parish. The bishop, he argued, existed for the people, and in a time of revival new life was being breathed into the Welsh language. If the Church did not provide for the spiritual needs of the Welsh people then it had forfeited its right to be a National Church.[18]

The revival, mentioned by Richards, had broken out in November 1904. Although it was not confined to Wales, its main impact was in that country. While it mainly affected Welsh Nonconformity, it also influenced the Welsh-speaking churches of the four dioceses. Timothy Rees, then a monk of the Community of the Resurrection, Mirfield, but a Welsh speaker, and later bishop of Llandaff 1931–9, was released by his order to assist those churches affected by the revival in the diocese of Llandaff. The revival had finished its course by the end of 1905.

The *Church Times* also took up this issue. Gladstone's policy of appointing Welshmen to Welsh dioceses had debarred many loyal Englishmen working in the Church in Wales from episcopal honours. These men were often drawn from a higher social class than the native Welsh clergy, and gave a far higher standard of churchmanship and of parochial duty, being men of a distinctive Catholic emphasis. Surely it was a pity to debar such men from office. This was not to belittle the Welsh tongue, but the need for it could be over-emphasized and so allow it 'to obscure far more important qualifications'.[19] But the argument of the editor of the *Church Times* was one of expediency rather than of dogma. The rumour was announced in its pages that an Englishman, ignorant of the Welsh language, would be appointed. Just what was needed for the diocese of Llandaff, the paper argued, as 'the diocese needs a tonic not a soporific'. The Welsh clergy had not produced such men and would never do so until the Welsh language – as the language of religion if not of commerce – was respected and maintained by those in authority in the Church.[20] Strangely, Bishop Owen almost concurred in this judgement. He wrote to Davidson that 'a weakness in Welsh [in the new bishop] is undesirable, without the compensation of a strong *distinction* of some kind'.[21]

The *Western Mail* argued not only for a Welsh speaker but also for a person who could bring new life into the diocese and a spirit of unity and organization. It also challenged the *Church Times* in its assertions. If colonial missionaries learnt the language of their people, so a new bishop of Llandaff needed to understand Welsh. If Balfour ignored the previous trend pursued by both Gladstone and Salisbury and appointed an Englishman he would perpetrate an act of discourtesy which would be seen as an insult to the Welsh people.[22]

Such publicity may well have made the advisors of the premier re-think the advice given to them by Winton.

The Popular and Self-appointed Candidates

In every Welsh episcopal election there were a number of men who recommended themselves. One was John Parry, vicar of Hammersmith in London, who wrote soon after he had heard of Lewis's death. Bishop Hughes of St Asaph had persuaded him to go to Cambridge and had then advised him to gain experience in a large London parish, expressing his hope that he would return to Wales and put this experience to good use. He believed that the time had now come for him to do this and so he 'delicately' offered himself for service as the new bishop, hoping that if he was appointed he, as a Welsh speaker, could improve relations between the Church and Nonconformity. Surprisingly his letter was followed up and the bishop of London, while expressing dismay that Parry had applied for such a post, wrote that he was a good organizer and a man of power.[23]

There was, as Winton hinted, a clear lobby for Hartwell Jones. If rumour was true it was a lobby he himself had engineered to put forward his own claims to the vacant bishopric. Jones, the son of a Welsh clergyman, had held a chair in Latin at University College, Cardiff, and had taken a prominent part in the work of Welsh Church defence.

Benjamin Thomas, rector of Nelson, believed that if Hartwell Jones was appointed to the vacant see, he would bring the dignity and spiritual power of the English episcopate to the diocese, as well as scholarship, culture and religious fervour. His appointment would be an asset to the whole Church.[24] Clement Davies, vicar of Northop, argued another way. It would be a calamity if Wales was deprived of his usefulness and influence at a time when these qualities were so much needed.[25] Morgan Owen, a former education inspector and speaker at Church congresses, then living at Welshpool, endeavoured to persuade the archbishop that Jones was a man the Welsh people had learnt to respect, trust and look to for spiritual guidance, wise counsel and material aid. Both the late bishop and Dean Vaughan had respected him. He pointed out that Jones had served under the archbishop (when he was bishop of Rochester) as rector of Nuffield and as an assistant inspector of schools. He had been greatly influenced by the archbishop, and thus in a sense he had been prepared by the archbishop for holding such an important office as a bishop in the Anglican Church.[26] Robert Owen, vicar of Bagillt, Holywell, also wrote to the archbishop commending his name,[27] as did Andrew Hyslop, vicar of All Saints and Welsh chaplain at Cardiff. Jones had served as an honorary curate to that parish while he held his Cardiff chair, and thus Hyslop felt able to inform the archbishop of the hard work he had done and the respect in which the diocese held him. When he was a candidate for the principalship of Lampeter in 1897, Dean Vaughan had written a testimonial for him. In it he wrote: 'I hear him mentioned for all the offices (in succession) which fall vacant in the Principality, from Bishoprics downwards, and it is evident he occupies a foremost place in public estimation . . .'[28]

Other members of the laity also wrote to support Jones's candidature, from William Williams, a Cardiff solicitor,[29] to Sir J. H. Puleston, a banker and former Tory member of Parliament. Jones's appointment, he argued, was one desired by the clergy of the diocese, and he went on to inform the archbishop that when he was at Rochester he (Davidson) had expressed his admiration for the way in which Jones had got over certain difficulties. He hoped that the archbishop would therefore support the representations being made to the prime minister for his appointment. Bishop Owen managed to marginalize Puleston by writing to Davidson that he was unrepresentative of Welsh opinion and had little influence in Wales.[30]

But Morgan Owen almost gave the game away by writing about a 'syndicate running another man'. It would be an evil day if this other man was appointed rather than Hartwell Jones.[31] It was a clear hint that there was a syndicate running Hartwell Jones, and it is interesting to note that all the letters supporting his candidature were written around the first week in February. One assumes that Balfour and other political figures received similar letters, as Puleston indicates, but these have not survived.

The bishop of St Asaph, A. G. Edwards, enclosing a letter from Lord Abergavenny supporting Hartwell Jones, added that in his opinion, 'Mr Jones is *not* a man who would at all [be] fitted for such a post.'[32] It was obviously an opinion shared by those in authority, for Hartwell Jones's campaign soon fizzled out like a damp squib.

Offers and Rejections

Balfour seems to have paid little attention to the numerous recommendations he was receiving from all quarters. Instead he was quietly finding his own candidates. He first approached Dr H. A. James, headmaster of Rugby and a former dean of St Asaph. The approach was made through the archbishop, who wrote to James on 4 February, a time when Hartwell Jones's campaign was at its full strength. The archbishop wrote that he was well aware that James had made it clear he would decline the offer of the see, but he now begged him to reconsider his decision. Llandaff was the most important of the Welsh bishoprics and the holder of it needed to be a man of power, a leader and a spokesman. It is most important, he added, that at this present juncture it is filled by one accustomed to leadership. James, he pointed out, had both the moral qualifications and experience needed, and he anticipated that he also had a sufficient knowledge of Welsh. 'I can think of no other man now alive who could so effectively as yourself promote at the present time the great interests which are at stake.' Although he might prefer to be a great schoolmaster rather than a bishop, his appointment to Llandaff might do much to promote the religious welfare and progress of the country. 'May God guide you aright,' he concluded.[33]

In his reply James stated that Balfour's offer had come as no surprise, for the bishop of St Asaph had approached him about it even before Bishop Lewis had vacated the see by death. But he had declined to allow his name to go forward, for his experience as dean of St Asaph had convinced him that he had neither vocation nor aptitude for episcopal work, and he had made up his mind neither to seek nor accept such preferment. Although he was willing to make a sacrifice in order to serve Wales, his appointment to a see would be a disservice. Besides this his knowledge of Welsh was slight, and though he could pronounce and read it, he could not converse in that tongue. In a further letter to Bishop Edwards, who passed it on to Davidson, James noted that he had already declined an invitation to be bishop suffragan of Manchester and also Bishop Lewis's suggestion that he should be nominated as his successor. It was not simply the thought of being a bishop in Wales which worried him; it was the very thought of being a bishop. James also claimed that his age (he was sixty) was against him.[34] He had forgotten that Bishop Lewis was even older when he accepted the see.

Ironically, James died in 1931 in possession of another post of distinction, president of St John's College, Oxford. He thus absolutely declined the offer.[35]

The prime minister's thoughts were now with the man whom Winton had intimated was the one Bishop Lewis wished to succeed him, his friend, Frederick Edmondes, archdeacon of Llandaff. Bishop Lewis had mentioned his name and his circumstances to the archbishop the previous year when he had suggested Edmondes might be appointed his suffragan. Edmondes, he wrote, belonged to one of the old Glamorgan county families, his brother had been a distinguished principal of St David's College, Lampeter, and he was a nephew of a principal of Jesus College, Oxford. A widower, aged sixty-five, Edmondes possessed an ample fortune (said to be £3,000 per annum from coal royalties) and was regarded as a good scholar, an excellent man of business, a moderate churchman and a Welsh speaker. He was popular with all schools of thought in the diocese, and if the clergy of the diocese were able to vote for a new bishop, added Lewis about the man he hoped would become his suffragan bishop, 90 per cent would vote for him.[36] Davidson felt the appointment of Edmondes would be a 'very happy solution' though Winton wrote that while he would be a good and useful successor to Bishop Lewis in 'quiet times' the present situation demanded something more.[37] Arthur Lewis, registrar of the vacant diocese and the late bishop's son, requested Owen to urge him to accept the appointment when they met at Convocation, and he later wrote that the 'strongest possible pressure' had been placed on him.[38] Edwards too, after James's refusal, felt Edmondes was the candidate who would be preferred by the clergy and the laity of the vacant diocese.[39]

The prime minister, possibly unaware of Edmondes's feelings, clearly considered he was the most eligible candidate. As a result, the bishop of St Davids was asked about him by the archbishop. Although he replied suggesting that the archbishop had got Edmondes mixed up with his brother (the principal), he believed he spoke Welsh and had studied Welsh with a well-known Welsh scholar.[40] It was sufficient. Edmondes was formally offered the bishopric of Llandaff and promptly declined it. Writing to the archbishop he said that he was not unaware of the gravity of the position or of the difficulty of filling the vacancy. But he felt on personal grounds that his faults of character, 'of which my numerous kind friends know nothing', made it impossible for him to under-take the office of bishop. 'It is a bitter thing to have to say; but your Grace recognizes in your letter that there may be in a man's life facts which are insuperable obstacles to his acceptance of a bishopric of which he alone can judge.' Did Davidson know more than others about something in Edmondes past and gave him a hint to desist from his candidature or were his protests genuine? We do not know. The *Baner* expressed surprise that he had turned the office down, and wondered who would be the next to be offered this 'sinecure'.[41]

More Suggestions

Balfour was now in some difficulty with both his nominees declin-ing the bishopric. The archbishop, who was later to write about the vast correspondence he had had on this subject,[42] was appealed to again. He thus wrote to the three Welsh bishops, various of the Welsh peers (Tredegar, Cawdor, Kenyon and Windsor), Archdeacon Edmondes and Mr Oliver Jones of Fonmon (a leading churchman in the diocese of Llandaff), as well as to English dignitaries, asking for comments about various people whose names had been recom-mended to him for the vacancy. Their names were as follows: Owen Evans, archdeacon of Carmarthen; Dean Griffith Roberts of Bangor; Dean Pryce of St Asaph; Bishop Lloyd, the suffragan bishop of Swansea; and Archdeacon Bruce of Monmouth.[43] H. A. James's recommendations of Pritchard Hughes of Llantrisant and Thomas Lloyd of Rhyl were also the subject of some enquiry at the same time.[44] The names of Llywelyn Wynne-Jones, archdeacon of Wrexham, and C. A. H. Green, vicar of Aberdare, appear to have been added later. It is interesting to compare this list with one compiled about the same time by the *Church Times*.[45] It suggested that the names being mentioned in public circles were those of Owen Evans, Hartwell Jones, Principal Bebb of Lampeter, Dr James of Rugby, Rowland Ellis of Edinburgh, Bishop Lloyd and Archdeacon Watkins of Durham, who had already been considered for two previous Welsh vacancies.

Winton's suggestion about translating the bishop of St Davids, John Owen, to Llandaff was also considered. It was strongly backed by the diocese, especially after Edmondes's declension. Dean

Davey, Archdeacon Bruce and Arthur Lewis all urged Owen to accept the offer of Llandaff if it was made to him, and probably wrote in the same tenor to the premier. Edmondes also recommended this move for not one of the names suggested was really satisfactory. Bishop Owen would be well received and he had done a good job for St Davids which could be repeated in Llandaff, while 'a man of less ability and mark' could continue his work in St Davids.[46] It is not known whether Owen was approached, but if he was, he declined nomination. His replies to those who urged him to accept a translation were carefully crafted letters of anguish and hesitation. While he would do his duty if called, he had no wish to start afresh in another diocese. He was probably grateful to Davidson who advised against a translation.[47]

As we turn to look at the names of those placed on the archbishop's list, it is useful to note that the eventual result showed a clear north-south split. Bruce was put first by most south Walians, but last by those from north and west Wales.

Griffith Roberts, dean of Bangor since 1903, had previously been diocesan missioner at Llandaff. Lord Kenyon, who had consulted with Principal Reichel of Bangor, wrote that he liked him decidedly, but he was not an able man and stood below his predecessors in the deanery. He was also an inferior man to Dean Pryce of St Asaph and the present bishops of St Asaph and St Davids. He might be classed 'with our Bishop', Watkin Williams, though if he was inferior to him in personality he had much more openness of mind and was much more energetic. Rumour credited him with the 'singularly wise pastoral letter' which the bishop had issued at the beginning of the revival. This he believed was true. His goodness, energy and cordiality could go a long way, but Llandaff needed a man with more intellectual power.[48] Although the bishop of Bangor supported his candidature,[49] as did Lord Cawdor (a good holy man and a good Welshman, he wrote),[50] others endorsed Lord Kenyon's opinion. Oliver Jones reported that while he was popular with the clergy and knew Welsh, his wife would not be much good in that position, and while worthy he was not strong. This was an opinion repeated by Edmondes, who also felt that Roberts would not be able to inspire much enthusiasm.[51] Pryce, Robert's fellow dean at St Asaph, was barely noted.

John Lloyd, the suffragan bishop of Swansea, was regarded by the archbishop as a good suffragan, active, keen, capable and thoroughly

Welsh, but not really of sufficient calibre for a diocesan appointment.[52] Edmondes agreed; he was a quiet and amiable man, but no leader of men. His background was of rural areas and he had no knowledge of large towns and colliery districts, though such a statement could have been equally well written of Bishop Lewis before his elevation.[53] Thomas Lloyd of Rhyl, wrote Owen about Dr James's recommendation, was a successful parish priest and a good preacher in both languages, but was not up to the requirements of Llandaff in 'depth, solidarity and strength'.[54]

Owen Evans, archdeacon and vicar of Carmarthen, was the son of a Cardiganshire farmer, aged 52, and a great friend of Bishop Owen, who supported his candidature, as he had done during the 1898 Bangor vacancy. In fact Bishop Owen was deeply troubled and hurt by the 'injustice' done to Owen Evans by his detractors, who, it appears, had written to Balfour protesting against his possible appointment. What worried Owen in particular was the 'temperate condemnation' of 'responsible men', of whom Edmondes was one. While Owen made clear to Davidson that he would refrain from comment because of his 'intimacy' with him, nevertheless he suggested that he was the leading candidate. If he was appointed, he wrote to Edwards, they would be accused of 'wire-pulling'; 'but let them say what they may say' he added in a later letter.[55] Owen also endeavoured to dismiss an idea the archbishop had been given that Bishop Lewis disliked the thought that the archdeacon might be his successor. This, he argued, was simply from a fear that Evans's friends 'might push him'.[56] Cawdor, however, held he was a poor man of business, he was not a leader of men and was constitutionally lazy.[57] Cawdor's claim that two sound judges of men who knew him well had said he would not do for either St Davids or Llandaff was not one shared by the Welsh bench, at least if Edwards was to be believed. For he claimed that both his two fellow Welsh bishops supported Evans, and he would be happy to welcome him as a colleague to the Welsh episcopate and help him as much as he could, though he added, rather damningly, that some people in the diocese would strongly object to him.[58] Evans belonged to the St Asaph circle, and this circle may possibly have been this other 'syndicate' which was mentioned earlier as trying to 'run' their own man. Edmondes stated, however, that he had given no proof of any competency, and his appointment would be ill received,[59] though Lord Kenyon supported Evans, adding, rather naively, that he was beloved of his pupils at Llandovery, 'and I always think schoolboys are good judges of character'.[60]

Llywelyn Wynne-Jones, like Owen Evans, was a product of the St Asaph stable. Edwards had promoted him from a virtual curacy at Wrexham into the archdeaconry of that name in 1897 after eleven years in orders. He later gave him the deanery in 1910. Kenyon dismissed him cutely: his wife had some money so he is independent 'as far as that goes'.[61] Edmondes was more forthright; there was no evidence of fitness, but 'it seems probable that he would be a mere creature of the Bishop of St Asaph'.[62] Cawdor reckoned he would not do at all. There was much dissatisfaction when he was made archdeacon.[63]

William Conybeare Bruce, archdeacon of Monmouth (then in the diocese of Llandaff), was recommended by many, including the dean of Windsor and Lords Tredegar and Windsor.[64] He had been archdeacon since 1885. A pupil of Temple at Rugby, he was a nephew of the first Lord Aberdare, a former home secretary and Gladstone's intimate advisor during the Welsh elections of 1870 and 1882. Oliver Jones, who had discussed matters with Lord Windsor, thought that the bishop of St Davids should be translated, but failing that, the order of nomination should be Bruce, then the dean of Bangor and finally the bishop of Swansea. Bruce was far superior to the dean; he had power, vigour and initiative, and he was a gentleman whose wife 'would take her place well'. He was of the same churchmanship as Dean Vaughan, who had thought highly of him. His weak point was his temper and his cutting tongue which had made him unpopular with some clergy, although he might still be acceptable to most of the clergy and laity of the diocese. Oliver Jones also believed Bruce 'could get up enough Welsh' to perform his episcopal functions, though he did not speak Welsh. He had, however, large private means so he could probably afford to pay for a Welsh suffragan out of his own pocket. Yet he had not sought office and Jones felt he would only accept it reluctantly,[65] though Lord Windsor wrote that he would place pressure on Bruce, so that he would 'not . . . refuse the responsibility under the present difficult circumstances'.[66]

There were more disparaging voices, however, as well as a warning about the character of those who would oppose Bruce's nomination. Edmondes wrote that his appointment would offend the Welsh national sentiment, and he confirmed Jones's fears about his temper, for he was often harsh to his inferiors.[67] Cawdor wrote the same: he knew no Welsh, was unpopular with the clergy, had an impulsive temper, and 'if anything, upholds the dignity of anything a little *too* much'.[68] Some support for Bruce, whether requested or unsolicited is not known, came from William A. Edwards, rector of Llangan and a nephew of Bishop Edwards, who noted his own friendship with the archdeacon. Vaughan, he wrote, had considered Bruce as eminently fit for the episcopate, and he was also sympathetic to the present government. He knew that many strong representations had been made to the prime minister for his appointment, and he believed that Bruce would accept the nomination if he was offered it.[69] A further letter from the same source noted other and less welcome representations to the prime minister and to others 'in high quarters' against Bruce's appointment. These were being made by certain 'small groups of clergymen in Wales with their lay friends who were always ready to take these steps'. One wonders if this was a reference to Hartwell Jones or the bishop of St Asaph? These people represented no solid or weighty opinion, but there was a 'great danger that their energetic agitation' could be over-estimated. The diocese would welcome the archdeacon who would be a great centre of unity; his churchmanship which had been inspired by the late Dean Vaughan 'is just what we want'.[70]

Bruce seems to have been offered the see, but declined it.[71] The *Church Times*, not always accurate and as malicious as ever, reported this was so, and said that the announcement that he had declined the see had been received with a certain sense of relief as he was not Welsh speaking and his appointment would be controversial.[72]

Archdeacon Bruce's refusal, if that was the case, placed the prime minister in an even greater dilemma. His name, it appears, was the only one regarded as generally acceptable on that original list by the appointed 'selectors', even though such acceptability was limited to the diocese itself.

The Final Name

When Dr James of Rugby was asked his opinion of two candidates, Archdeacon Wynne-Jones and Bishop Lloyd, he replied with a third name, which he bracketed with Lloyd. 'The man however whom above all others I should like to see appointed is Pritchard Hughes,' he wrote. 'I believe he would be an admirable appointment. He is a man of a great deal of culture, a fervid Welsh preacher, and a man I believe of deep religious feeling; an evangelical I suppose, but of an enlightened type, and broad minded enough to get on with all classes of people.' Though he could not speak of his work at Llantrisant, where he was vicar, he could speak of his personality. Although such an appointment would be unexpected, he yet believed it could prove to be the best possible one.[73]

Bishop Edwards, apparently consulted, agreed with Dr James. He would place Pritchard Hughes first, though he had earlier preferred Wynne-Jones, his protégé, Owen Evans and the dean of Bangor, in that order. When the chips were down Edwards could move very fast. Pritchard Hughes was a thorough Welshman and a gentleman, a combination which Edwards probably considered was rare enough to be noted, who had done excellent work in a parish with a population of 20,000 for over twenty years. Moreover, his wife was a lady who would be of great help to him. Besides, he could have added, he was not unused to episcopacy, for he was a son of Edwards's predecessor as bishop of St Asaph, Joshua Hughes. A further letter of Edwards again endorsing Hughes managed to dismiss all other possibilities. It was not acceptable to translate the bishop of St Davids, and Bishop Lloyd was not on the same level. Hughes's appointment would be one in which all schools and sections 'would quietly acquiesce'; a not untypical example of one of Edwards's left-handed compliments.[74] Bishop Owen was a little more hesitant, and doubted if he was strong enough for the diocese.[75]

Hughes was an evangelical, and it was thought this could create difficulties. J. J. Sanders, the prime minister's secretary, wrote to the archbishop, who also seemed to favour the appointment, that 'the experiment of Hughes is well worth making. I expect I shall be able to convince the Prime Minister than in view of what we are doing in Gloucester and Rochester it is prudent to incline to a Churchman of Hughes's stamp.'[76] The need for a judicial balance in churchmanship in these episcopal appointments was obviously working in Hughes's favour, even though Arthur Lewis had advised against either a high churchman or an extreme evangelical.[77]

The way was opening for Hughes's appointment, although it appears he had less of a vetting than any other candidate, the advantage, no doubt, of being at the end of the queue. On 9 March

Joshua Pritchard Hughes wrote to the archbishop, thanking him for his 'most kind, encouraging and helpful letter of yesterday . . . I hope I have not been too presumptuous in venturing to accept the grave responsibility of the post that has been offered me. I certainly did not seek for it and did not expect it.'[78] Preaching at Llantrisant Church, after the appointment had been announced, Hughes said that the call was unsought, undesired and unexpected, but he felt, after consulting others, he was not justified in refusing to face the great responsibilities and difficulties of such an office.[79] Many others echoed his sentiments. Bishop Owen of St Davids noted that his selection had taken people by surprise but it was kindly received as Hughes was respected for his hard work. Nevertheless, the high churchmen in Llandaff and the authorities of St Michael's College were a little doubtful about his appointment.[80] Others felt his appointment was a recognition by the prime minister of the pastoral work he had accomplished and of the respect in which he was held by Nonconformists.[81] Many of them attended his Sunday evening services when he preached in Welsh after their own services, and he was welcomed by them as a man of toleration.[82]

The evangelical *Record* welcomed his appointment, for while he was not strongly identified with the evangelical school of thought, he was a moderate churchman and a loyal supporter of the evangelical societies, such as the Church Missionary Society and Church Pastoral-Aid Society.[83] Its opposite number, the *Church Times* noted Pritchard's character and concern for temperance, but felt that too little was known about him for any definite opinion to be made about Balfour's choice. Its next issue was a little more sarcastic about him. It hoped that the numerous congratulations the bishop-elect had received would not mislead him into thinking that a busy parish priest could necessarily become a good diocesan bishop. Though he was known to be tolerant and generous in his estimation of men of all schools of thought, it required much moral courage to thwart the tendency to neglect and disparage the work of men who were not of the safest school. It equally hoped that he would not follow the policy of freely admitting the 'derelicts and failures of Dissent' into the sacred ministry.[84]

Edwards's Syndicate?

There are many hints recorded that the bishop of St Asaph was 'running his own man' for Llandaff, though this talk mainly came from the supporters of Hartwell Jones. Perhaps they recognized that Edwards was their chief opponent. T. Morgan Owen talked about 'a syndicate',[85] and Thomas Jones, chaplain of the Epping Union, wrote that 'the pugnacious Bishop of St Asaph has had too much of his way in the past'.[86] Daniel Lewis, rector of Llanenddwyn in Merioneth, a rural dean and a future proctor in Convocation, wrote supporting either Dr James or Hartwell Jones, but he added that Archdeacon Owen Evans and Archdeacon Morgan of Bangor belonged to a group of friends who already had too much control of the Welsh Church in their hands.[87] Owen Evans was a very close friend of Edwards and Owen of St Davids, and was initially sponsored by them for the bishopric of Bangor in 1898. A further comment is supplied by T. T. L. Morgan, a noted Welsh exile who was vicar of Milton near Sittingbourne. He believed that all the Welsh names being talked about for the appointment were the result of 'wire-pulling . . . But things are done in Wales, in high ecclesiastical circles, which are utterly unknown and undreamed of in England.' He was all but naming Bishop Edwards, a matter confirmed by his notice of the successful opposition launched against Perowne's appointment to Bangor, similar in style to the agitation against Vaughan becoming dean of Llandaff. Neither was a genuine Welsh movement. Rather it was the action of a few Welsh clergy, acting together, 'who were themselves English in all their instincts' although they could speak Welsh.[88]

Edwards had actively corresponded with Archdeacon Edmondes and Dr James about the appointment, damned Hartwell Jones while enclosing a letter supporting him, and endeavoured to whip up some support for his own archdeacon, Wynne-Jones, who was regarded by Edmondes as being simply his 'creature'.[89] Edmondes himself wrote in his diary that when he went to Downing Street at Balfour's invitation to give an opinion on the six candidates who were then under consideration, he discovered Edwards 'closeted' with him. He refused to give an opinion until the bishop had left the room.[90] It must have marked the end of their friendship.

Edwards was never able to live down his reputation as a man of sinister intrigue, and this was often reflected, so it was believed, in the role he took in these episcopal elections. One can certainly understand his dislike of Hartwell Jones. By all accounts he would have made a poor bishop, although his failure to achieve that distinction enlivened his personality and writings for the remainder of his long life. At first Edwards supported Dr James, a former dean of St Asaph but never dean to Edwards, then Wynne-Jones, and finally Hughes, who as a new man might well be prepared to lean on Edwards's guidance as the senior Welsh bishop.

Two significant points remain to be said regarding Hughes's appointment. First, it was a departure from the hitherto clear rule that an appointment would not be made from within the vacant diocese. This change may well indicate the difficulties Balfour faced in making a nomination to the see of Llandaff. Secondly, Hughes was Welsh speaking. The other candidates considered were not although all had some knowledge of that tongue. It is a strong indication that the ecclesiastical world no longer regarded an ability to speak Welsh as being one of the requirements for a bishop of that diocese, although it seems to have been agreed that a Welsh-speaking suffragan might be needed. Hughes's appointment to Llandaff may have seemed a victory for the patriotic group of Welshmen who for nearly a century had campaigned for Welsh-speaking bishops. But in reality it was a technical victory; the final triumph had eluded them.

~ 14 ~
Conclusion

The episcopal appointments described in this book took place over a short period of time, for some people within the span of their own lifetime, and yet the election of Thirlwall to St Davids in 1840 seems to be a world apart from that of Hughes to Llandaff in 1905. Wales was no longer the appendage of England, nor were bishops the inevitable straw men of politicians. Bishops also tended to remain in one diocese rather than being translated to other sees. This was because of the equalization of episcopal incomes by the Ecclesiastical Commission and the new Victorian concept of episcopacy allegedly introduced by the Sumner brothers and Bishop Wilberforce.

I have noted the considerable difficulties prime ministers faced in nominating a person to the Crown for a vacant bishopric, especially for a Welsh see. A fine balance had to be found between the conflicting claims of the Church parties, the ancient universities, and political and ecclesiastical considerations. Pritchard Hughes benefited in 1905, for example, because the other nominations on the table were of high churchmen, and he was the evangelical who, as it were, balanced the books. To give a further illustration, this time of the university claim, his father, Joshua Hughes, was assumed to have had a Cambridge degree, and Gladstone was probably put out when he realized this was not so. Furthermore, the supporters of the prime minister's party assumed, as a matter of course, that he would use his patronage as a means of enhancing his own party, either by strengthening his support in the House of Lords, or by rewarding political families in an age during which it became respectable for younger sons to be ordained. Thirlwall is an obvious example of that first concern, while both Disraeli and Salisbury received letters of recommendation for particular candidates, emphasizing their political credentials, from their supporters. Salisbury, to his credit, was prepared to spread his net wider than that of mere political considerations, but even he had no wish to appoint a known sympathizer of the opposite party who might speak against his government's proposals in the House of Lords.

These considerations remained true, by and large, throughout the period under consideration. But there were two other elements which became increasingly important in the course of time. One was the Queen herself. Her wide political experience, her ability to obtain good advisors and her concern for the Church of which she was supreme governor, meant that she also began to take an active part in the process of selection. As a result Howell was dropped from the shortlist of eligible candidates during a number of elections because of the moral blemish of his earlier days, and Watkins possibly failed to become bishop of St Asaph in 1889 as Salisbury did not observe the proper protocol which the Queen required, namely that she be consulted and her consent obtained before an appointment was announced.

The major element, however, in the appointments to Welsh sees, was the desire of the Welsh speakers of Wales to see Welsh-speaking bishops elected. At first this desire was manifested by the use of public meetings, petitions and deputations to meet the prime minister. It was perhaps inevitable this should be so. The Welsh Church, especially in the north, was well organized in the task of petitioning as a result of the long campaign to save the threatened north Wales see from extinction in order to establish a new bishopric in Manchester. The same techniques were followed in the agitation for the repeal of the Corn Laws. By the 1870s, however, these techniques of influence had been replaced by the newspaper columns. Within their columns, especially the correspondence columns, the claims of the vacant see to have a Welsh-speaking bishop were announced, or denounced, as the case may be, and the names of likely candidates proclaimed or dismissed. These columns became a public arena of vitriolic debate and patriotic fervour. Downing Street probably paid little attention. It received the same sort of correspondence more directly, and on one occasion this correspondence left an unpleasant impression on the mind of at least one cabinet minister who had been permitted to read it.

The appointments to Welsh sees followed a threefold pattern. Thirlwall and Short were appointments of Englishmen and followed the classic pattern of eighteenth-century patronage. Thirlwall, challenged by David James (whose son declined the offer of the see of Llandaff in 1905), learnt Welsh in a fashion, whereas Short, although equally challenged by R. W. Morgan, simply became hostile and defamatory to the Welsh language and those who spoke it. The second stage of appointments was of the so-called 'half and half' bishops, whom we may describe as Anglo-Welsh, men who had acquired a smattering of the Welsh tongue but were not too confident in using it outside the set text of the liturgy. Both Campbell and Ollivant came into this category, and probably Basil Jones, whose elevation by Disraeli to St Davids in 1874 reversed the policy pioneered by Gladstone four years earlier. Salisbury's offer of the see of Bangor to Perowne in 1890 would have been a throwback to this earlier policy, but by that date even the English ecclesiastical advisors to the Queen expressed alarm and concern at this nomination. The final stage was the appointment of native Welsh bishops, typified by the nomination of Joshua Hughes to the see of St Asaph in 1870. Gladstone's concern was to obtain a preaching bishop, one able to outpreach Nonconformity and win back its adherents to the Church. The expectations were too high in any case, but there was also the major difficulty of finding suitable native Welsh speakers who also held the other necessary qualifications for episcopal office.

This was not a question of language so much as a problem about society, and this in turn reflected a further consideration which was never satisfactorily faced, namely, what was the essential role of a bishop of the Church of England? If the bishop was to be pastor of his clergy and leader in his diocese then the question of social background was not so important, though he still needed to be able to win the confidence of his gentrified and university educated clergy. But if he was also a member of the House of Lords and a peer of the realm, then other considerations came into play. Such a bishop needed to be able to take his place there with poise and ability, to act as a courtier as well as an ecclesiastic, and to be able to feel at ease with the manners and customs of high society. It is interesting to note that this problem was not confined to ecclesiastical appointments. There was often a problem in finding suitable people to act as magistrates, while Salisbury found great difficulty in nominating a lord lieutenant for Cardiganshire in 1888, although part of his problem was to find an eligible member of his own party.[1] On the other hand, Archdeacon John Williams of Cardigan, Archdeacon Bruce Knight of Llandaff and Thomas Thomas of Caernarfon would undoubtedly have been appointed had they been the right political colour or lived long enough. But men of this calibre were in short supply.

The basic problem was a simple one. Most native Welsh speakers came from a milieu that was deprived, through poverty, of the benefits of education and of mixing in so-called good society. The skills of living well were denied them. It meant, so their detractors claimed, that they lacked poise and charm, were unable to appreciate the finer points of scholarship, and perhaps spoke with the rougher accents of honesty rather than the refined speech of their betters. They were simply disadvantaged. And such people, so the argument would have run, needed to be kept in their places of inferiority.

For the members of the upper classes Gladstone's appointment of Hughes in 1870 was an attack upon their privileged status in society, and their right to govern in Church and country. Hughes's lack of a university education and his assumed humble background were regarded as minus points in society's scale of valuation. It needed a second generation of such appointments to make them more respectable, by which time and for various reasons the universities were more accessible to such men. Edwards's father, for example, was a clergyman of some repute. His grandparents were of the same stock as Bishop Hughes. Lloyd had earned his position through educational advantages and by his successful mastership of some minor public schools. The same applied to Owen, in spite of his accent. Quaintness has the habit of making a person a society-pet. Besides, it was realized that the growing menace of disestablishment meant that the Church in Wales needed native bishops who could disprove the taunt that it was an alien Anglicized institution.

By the end of this study, with the election of Hughes to Llandaff in 1905, it seems clear that the pressure to appoint a Welsh-speaking bishop was diminishing, or, to put it another way, that those who had opposed such appointments in the first place were winning the argument. The reasons for this are complex, and are much more complicated than the suggestion that by this date the growing Anglicization of Wales (often furthered by the deliberate policy of Church and state schools) meant that the need was less urgent than before. It was probably not unconnected with the obvious failure of Gladstone's hope that such bishops could out-preach Welsh

Nonconformity. However, paradoxically, this process was taking place against the background of the growing marginalization of the bishops in the House of Lords (which in turn reflected the position of the house itself), and was accompanied by the growing realization that bishops were meant to be pastoral and diocesan figures rather than peers of the realm. The first two episcopal appointments made by the disestablished Church in Wales were of men who were not native Welsh speakers. Green of Monmouth was able to speak an academic form of Welsh, which was not understood, and Bevan of Swansea and Brecon spoke no Welsh at all. If it is argued that these were dioceses where little Welsh was spoken in any case, then it also needs to be said that the case for an entirely Welsh-speaking episcopate in Wales had been defeated.

This was a point forcibly made by a 'Welsh Nationalist Priest' in an article which appeared in *The Welsh Outlook* during 1929. Entitled 'Episcopal Appointments in Wales', the writer accused the Electoral College of an Anglicizing policy which would alienate still further the Welsh-speaking Church people of 'Yr Hen Fam'. He concluded that 'unless our Bishops see to it that the Church adapted itself to the national needs of Wales, many a true Nationalistic Welshman will forsake her rather than desert the phalanx of Welsh Nationalism.' The wheel had turned full circle.[2]

There was another aspect of these later episcopal elections which needs exploring. This was the existence of pressure groups established to further the claims of a particular candidate. Griffiths, at first the choice of Gladstone for St Asaph in 1870, Lloyd, the eventual victor in the Bangor election of 1890, and Hartwell Jones, an unsuccessful contestant in 1905, were all suspected of running their own campaigns. It was not an unjustified suspicion. Edwards, as has been noted, masterminded the campaign for Owen to be elected to St Davids in 1898. We may also note the claim of Owen in 1898 and Hughes in 1905 that they had never *actively* sought elevation to the Episcopal bench. The 1890s brought in more subtle pressures still, with claims of pressure groups, 'wirepullers', 'cliques' and 'syndicates' mentioned in the press columns and in the letters of respectable advisors to the prime minister. A number of such 'syndicates' have been identified. One was established in favour of Hartwell Jones, but another, and far more important one, was linked with Bishop Edwards of St Asaph. He was regarded by one correspondent as the 'King-maker in Wales in matters ecclesiastical', who had already made two Welsh bishops by 1904, and expected to make the third at the next vacancy. One of his archdeacons, D. R. Thomas, himself an episcopal candidate, alleged that he had established 'a syndicate for working ecclesiastical promotions in Wales'.[3] Such reports were correct. Edwards managed to dismiss the leading contender for the diocese of Bangor in 1890, David Howell, on grounds of morality, although the real reason was undoubtedly because Howell would not subscribe to his policy of attacking Nonconformity in order to defend the Church, and of emphasizing the links with England in an attempt to prevent disestablishment. Failing to get his own candidate in at that election, Edwards attacked the prime minister's nominee, Lloyd, in such a way that had his allegations been correct, it would have resulted in public ignominy for Lloyd. Again, Lloyd would not subscribe to Edwards's views on church defence. In 1898, unable to get his own man elected to the see of Bangor, he accepted a compromise candidate who would not harm his campaign, or so he believed, but when asked if he wanted his first nominee, Owen Evans, to be appointed dean of St Asaph, he replied to the prime minister's secretary, McDonnell, with the amazing statement that he wished to run him for the next bishopric instead. And in 1905, Edwards was noted exercising his authority within the prime minister's study by Edmondes, who had declined the nomination, but had been called in to advise.

We know that both Gladstone, and Benson as archbishop, felt very diffident about men pushing their own claims; Benson even argued that Lloyd was unfit for a bishopric by reason of his activity in this direction. One wonders, however, how they felt about these pressure groups? Were they a uniquely Welsh institution, to be excused by the assertion that the Welsh Church was still relatively uncivilized, as Dean Vaughan and others alleged, or did they have their English counterparts? In all probability there were pressure groups in England, which were conducted with more decorum in the lobby of the house, the club library, or at the weekend house party. By comparison, the Welsh pressure groups were uncivilized and uncouth, but not ineffective, so far as Edwards was concerned with his own political entrees, although there seems to be no record that he was ever invited to these house parties. Yet McDonnell appears to have accepted his statement of intent for Owen Evans without demur.

The real test of these appointments must be the track record of those elevated as bishops of Welsh sees. Thirlwall would have been a failure as a pastoral bishop in any diocese. To have been placed in a Welsh diocese simply made that failure more acute. But he was appointed, after all, as a spokesman in the House of Lords for the Liberal party. It is even open to question if he accepted this role either. Short was a difficult character, and yet in many ways he built up an administration in the diocese of St Asaph which could stand comparison with that model of episcopal efficiency allegedly established by Wilberforce at Oxford. Ollivant was an outstanding success at Llandaff, even though his later years might have been better spent in graceful retirement than in active work. Campbell, though a diligent bishop, lacked imagination, but on the other hand was prepared to allow others to take the lead for him. Hughes was a disappointment, so far as the brief given him by Gladstone for his appointment was concerned. He did not, and could not, outpreach Nonconformity. But he did raise the hopes and aspirations of many Welsh clergy that elevation to the highest office in the Church would not be denied them. Alas, as explained earlier, he was in the wrong diocese for his episcopate to have been appreciated, and many accepted that he would never have risen beyond a rural deanery in an English diocese. Basil Jones was a competent but not an exciting bishop, though he had all the credentials required, of education, breeding and manners. Lewis of Llandaff was a lesser Basil Jones, but would certainly never have become bishop of an English diocese, as Basil Jones might have done. Edwards was a politician, never a statesman, a schemer rather than a planner. Thankfully, through the work of Short and possibly Hughes, his diocese could run without him as he concentrated on wider issues, but in these matters his inability to think constructively led him, and the Church in Wales, into narrow alleyways of bitterness and shame. Furthermore, Edwards determined that his policy alone could be correct, and so he ruthlessly cast aside men of imagination, compassion and justice, who might have achieved reconciliation and accommodation with Nonconformity. In England, had he become a bishop, he would have been contained by a wider Church, but, paradoxically, it was his antagonism to Nonconformity which caused Salisbury to consider him for the vacant bishopric. Lloyd was a nonentity, a man of the moment and little else. Owen's accent would never have allowed him to achieve any high position in English circles, but he was a good diocesan, and a man who might have done much to bring healing to the Welsh churches had not a misplaced loyalty to Edwards stood in the way. Watkin Williams would have made an amiable squarson happily receiving a cathedral prebend as a reward for long country service in England. It was his misfortune that he spoke Welsh. And Hughes, the last of the bunch, might have found an English archdeaconry more to his taste than a Welsh bishopric. Yet most of these men rose to the challenge and if they were not in the same league as the 'professional' bishops in the English sees, they gave a leadership to their dioceses that was pastorally motivated and spiritually acute. This applied especially to Lewis, Owen and Pritchard Hughes.

Most of these bishops were good men, only one obviously malicious, but each of the groups noted suffered the limitations of their position. The earlier bishops were never able to grasp the peculiar structures of the Welsh Church, its ethos, and its understanding of itself. Thirlwall, Short and even Ollivant were unable to see that in many ways the Church and Nonconformity were almost identical in doctrine and methods of piety. Very often the clergy came from Nonconformist backgrounds, and retained such allegedly Nonconformist activities as preaching meetings, *seiadau* and so forth. Too often this was frowned upon by the bishops, whose vision of Nonconformity was circumscribed by their belief in the establishment of the Church. The Church in Wales became as a result even more alienated from its roots. The situation was exasperated by the latter breed of bishops, led by Edwards. His vision of the Church was limited to its role as a structure of the English establishment. He had neither faith nor courage to go beyond that picture, as Howell did, to see a Church that was real and pure because it was divested of its state trappings. As a result, he condemned the Welsh Church to an all-out war of attrition, in which both sides lost heavily in terms of spiritual life and vitality. What might have been, if others had been selected instead, is a dream still being pursued by that Church today.

Notes

1. In Pursuit of a Welsh Episcopate

1 John S. Peart-Binns, *Edwin Morris* (Llandysul, 1990), pp. 108–9, quoting J. R. Lloyd Thomas. See also Hensley Henson's strident comments on this subject quoted by Owen Chadwick in his *Hensley Henson* (Norwich, 1994), p. 146.

2 Quoted in *Annual Report of Lambeth Palace Library*, 1988, pp. 18–19. John S. Peart-Binns, in his biography of Archbishop Joost de Blank, *Joost de Blank* (London, 1987), p. 87, notes that in the South African episcopal elections bishops were appointed after a long process of balloting. Two outstanding candidates would cancel each other out, thereby allowing an indifferent candidate to be elected.

3 Dot Jones, *Statistical Evidence relating to the Welsh Language 1801–1911* (Cardiff, 1998), pp. 222–3.

4 Geraint H. Jenkins (ed.), *A Social History of the Welsh Language: The Welsh Language and its Social Domains 1801–1911* (Cardiff, 2000), p. 34.

5 Ibid., p. 9.

6 Ibid., pp. 12, 19, 23, 26, 104–5, 432, 462–4.

7 Ibid., p. 146.

8 Ibid., pp. 34–5, 39, 81.

9 Edward Copleston, *A Charge to the Clergy of the Diocese of Llandaff* (London, 1836), pp. 23–4, and H. A. Bruce's letter in CMG (12 January 1850), p. 3.

10 Roger L. Brown (ed.), *The Letters of Edward Copleston, Bishop of Llandaff, 1828–1849* (Cardiff, 2003), pp. 20–5.

11 Jenkins, *Welsh Language*, pp. 228–9.

12 J. H. Davies (ed.), *The Letters of Goronwy Owen* (Cardiff, 1926), p. 65, translated by W. W. Davies in his *Wales* (London, 1930), pp. 233–4.

13 Quoted by E. D. Evans, 'John Evans, bishop of Bangor 1702–16', *Transactions of the Honourable Society of Cymmrodorion*, NS 7 (2000), 52, 55.

14 J. A. Bradney, *Llandaff Records* (Cardiff, 1912), vol. IV, p. 18n.

Dugdale (in VI-A-1303) suggests that John Thomas (1691–1766), thought to have been born in Dolgellau, was elected bishop of St Asaph in 1743 but not consecrated to that see as he was almost immediately translated to Lincoln. He was later bishop of Salisbury. His fluent knowledge of German commended him to George II.

15 See, for example, *The Depositions: Arguments and Judgments in the Case of the Churchwardens of Trefdraeth* (London, 1773), against Dr Bowles; and the views of William Jones, of Llangadfan, who felt that English bishops encouraged English clergy in Welsh parishes to promote the English language: G. H. Jenkins, ' "A Rank Republican (and) a Leveller", William Jones, Llangadfan', *Welsh History Review*, 17 (1995), 374.

16 Richard Watson, Jnr, *Anecdotes of the Life of Richard Watson* (London, 1818), I, pp. 384–5.

17 A. H. Johnes, *On the Causes which have Produced Dissent from the Established Church in the Principality of Wales* (2nd edn, London, 1870). Although care needs to be exercised in accepting all Johnes's statements, there is a basic truth in his assertions. But these matters were not confined to Wales, see, for example, R. M. Beverley, *A Letter on the Present Corrupt State of the Church of England* (Beverley, 1831), pp. 10–13.

18 K. O. Morgan, *Wales in British Politics* (Cardiff, 1970), pp. 36–7; *Report*, 1854, pp. 27–9. See also M. E. Jones, ' "Wales for the Welsh?" the Welsh county court judges', *Welsh History Review*, 19 (1999), 643–78.

19 A. J. Johnes, *A Letter to Lord John Russell on the Operation of the Established Church Bill* (London, 1836), p. 8. A similar debate took place in 1833 in the House of Lords when a petition was presented protesting about the inconveniences experienced 'in consequence of the bishops appointed to sees within the Principality, and a portion of the inferior clergy, being ignorant of the Welsh language': *Monmouthshire Merlin* (6 April 1833), p. 4.

20 Letter of John Griffith to the Lord Chancellor, printed in *John Bull* (29 April 1848), p. 273.

21 *Hansard's Parliamentary Debates*, XXXV (1836), 1138–40, cf. an earlier debate, ibid., 150–7.

22 6 & 7 William IV, chap. 77, repealed by the Pluralities Act 1838 (1 & 2 Vict, chap. 100). See Roger L. Brown, 'Pastoral problems and legal solutions', in Norman Doe (ed.), *Essays in Canon Law* (Cardiff, 1992), pp. 13–14.

23 Johnes, *Letter to Lord John Russell*, p. 6 (in which he quotes Hall); and see pp. 3–4, 13–14 for their protests about the failure of this clause.

[24] John Williams, *On the Inexpediency, Folly and Sin of a 'Barbarian Episcopate' in a Christian Principality* (London, 1858), pp. 13, 18; John Williams to David James, 27 September 1849, *Letters*, p. 24. I have been unable to trace this promise in *Hansard*, though one may note Lord John Russell's remarks on the omission of the amendment rejected by the House of Lords (*Hansard*, xliv (1838), 844 of 31 July 1838). A letter from J. B. Bruce to Lord Bute of 7 October 1838 (NLW Bute Papers, L79/126) notes that Bruce had heard Mr Guest, MP, say that Lord Melbourne had asserted that at the next vacancy of a Welsh bishopric 'it could be filled up by a Welshman', with John Williams of Edinburgh as the probable candidate.

[25] The full text of this meeting and a similar one at Manchester is found in *Diwygiad yr Eglwys Sefydledig yn Nghymru* (Liverpool, 1837).

[26] *Report*, 1855, pp. 24–5. See Roger L. Brown, *The Association of Welsh Clergy in the West Riding of Yorkshire* (Welshpool, 2001). Its members included Joseph Hughes (Carn Ingli), E. O. Phillips, later dean of St Davids, and David James, rector of Panteg. They also campaigned for Welsh-speaking judges and for a university for Wales.

[27] Joseph Morgan, *The Rev. David James of Panteg* (Pontypool, 1925), pp. 12–20.

[28] Ibid., pp. 13–14, 19.

[29] *Report*, 1855, p. 26.

[30] *Report*, 1852, p. 6. Some activity took place in 1843, according to a letter of Joshua Walmsley MP to David James, 21 October 1843, in *Letters*, p. 5, while many such as W. H. Owen noted they had been long-term supporters of the movement: see Owen to an unknown correspondent, 22 October 1849, *Letters*, p. 27.

[31] *Report*, 1852, pp. 30–2.

[32] *Report*, 1853, pp. 17–18.

[33] Lady Hall (later Lady Llanover) to Mrs Richards, 7 May 1855, *Letters*, p. 154.

[34] Daniel Jones, *Welsh Bishops for Wales. An Essay on the National and Scriptural Claims of the Established Church in Wales to be Governed by Welsh Bishops* (Llandovery, 1851), pp. 15–16, 22–3, 26, 28.

[35] *Haul* (1844), pp. 351–3.

[36] *Haul* (1852), pp. 170–1. Translated by Phyllis Brown.

[37] Roger L. Brown, 'The Copleston Memorial', *Morgannwg*, 41 (1997), 38–50.

[38] CDH (3 November 1849), p. 6. Russell replied that he would give full consideration to the remarks contained in the letter.

[39] CMG (1 November 1856), p. 7.

[40] Perowne to Davidson, 10 March 1890, DP, 28/16.

[41] Lady Hall to David James, 28 March and 2 June 1851, to Thomas

James, 5 November 1851, to Joseph Hughes, 30 March 1851, *Letters*, pp. 8, 41, 44–9, 82–3, cf. Lady Hall to Thomas James, 15 April 1851, *Letters*, p. 50.

42 Lady Hall to Joseph Hughes, 27 April 1851, *Letters*, p. 52.

43 D. W. R. Bahlman, 'Politics and church patronage in the Victorian era', *Victorian Studies*, 22 (1979), 267–73; J. S. Reynolds, *The Evangelicals at Oxford, 1735–1871* (Oxford, 1975), pp. 133–4; Michael Henning, *Sons of the Prophets* (London, 1979), pp. 56–65; Georgina Battiscombe, *Shaftesbury* (London, 1974), pp. 250, 262–5; Bernard Palmer, *High and Mitred* (London, 1992), p. 36. For a study of Palmeston's bishops see Nigel Scotland, *Good and Proper Men* (Cambridge, 2000).

44 Harriet Thomas, *Llewelyn Thomas: A Memoir* (London, n.d.), pp. 22–3.

45 Benson to Gladstone, 23 July 1883, GP, 44109/37.

46 David James writing in *Report*, 1855, pp. 26–7.

47 Morgan, *David James*, pp. 14–15; cf. *Report*, 1855, pp. 27–9, where David James argued that the origin of dissent lay within the Church, as did John Griffith in a letter to the Lord Chancellor (CMG [15 April 1848], p. 3), and R. W. Morgan (*Maynooth and St Asaph*, (London, 1845), pp. 39–40). See also *Golifer, The Diocese of Llandaff: Proposed New Churches. A Letter to Lord John Russell* (London, 1850), pp. 4–5.

48 *Report*, 1855, pp. 26–9.

49 *Report*, 1856, pp. 55–6.

50 Johnes, *Letter to Lord John Russell*, pp. 13–14.

51 Morgan, *David James*, p. 15; cf. *Report*, 1855, p. 28.

52 *Report*, 1852, p. 31.

53 Ibid.

54 *Report*, 1856, p. 56.

55 Jones, *Welsh Bishops for Wales*, pp. 18–20.

56 *Report*, 1854, pp. 38–9.

57 *Report*, 1854, pp. 41–2. Such confirmations were known to some as 'dumb shows': *Report*, 1855, pp. 20–1.

58 R. O. Roberts, 'David Griffith', *Province*, XII (1961), 66.

59 *Report*, 1856, pp. 57–8; Morgan, *Maynooth and St Asaph*, pp. 36–7.

60 Jones, *Welsh Bishops for Wales*, p. 17.

61 CDH (3 November 1849), p. 5.

62 *Report*, 1852, p. 32; cf. Jones, *Welsh Bishops for Wales*, p. 16.

63 Johnes, *Letter to Lord John Russell*, p. 15.

64 Williams to James, 26 October 1849, *Letters*, pp. 35–6.

65 Writing as *Ordovicis* in *John Bull* (6 March 1847), p. 150, and in CMG (4 November 1848), p. 4: cf. Griffith writing as *Cambro Sacerdos* in ibid. (7 November 1846), p. 3.

[66] John Griffith writing in *John Bull* (12 February 1848), p. 103.

[67] *Report*, 1856, pp. 27–8.

[68] *Report*, 1856, p. 57.

[69] See O. W. Jones, *Glyn Simon* (Llandysul, 1981), p. 27.

[70] E. E. Owen, *The Later Life of Bishop Owen* (Llandysul, 1961), pp. 490–5.

[71] Christopher Bethell, *A Letter to the Clergy of the County of Anglesey* (not published, London, 1837).

[72] Ibid., pp. 5, 8.

[73] Ibid., pp. 7–8. Bishop Beaw of Llandaff used a similar argument in 1699: Craig D. Wood, 'The Welsh response to the Glorious Revolution', *Journal of Welsh Religious History*, NS 1 (2001), 29.

[74] Bethell, *A Letter to the Clergy of the County of Anglesey*, pp. 11–13.

[75] Ibid., pp. 13–14.

[76] Ibid., pp. 15–17.

[77] Ibid., p. 16.

[78] Ibid., pp. 17–19. Bethell had said much the same in his *Second Charge to the Clergy of the Diocese of Bangor* of 1834, p. 28. He then expressed the hope that his diocese would receive no injury from his appointment for want of his knowledge of its language and his 'English partialities and prejudices'.

[79] Copleston, *Charge* of 1836, pp. 23–4.

[80] Ibid., pp. 25–7.

[81] David Evans, *Atgofion* (Lampeter, 1904), p. 142. A similar suggestion was made by 'A Montgomeryshire Man' in *The Principality: or the Wants of Wales Considered* of 1851, quoted by Matthew Cragoe, *An Anglican Aristocracy* (Oxford, 1996), p. 204. He argued that to make a knowledge of the Welsh language indispensable would be to bar the claims of the majority of the most erudite scholars of the universities to Welsh sees. This policy would reduce the Welsh Church to stagnation.

[82] D. W. R. Bahlman, 'Politics and church patronage', 253.

[83] Ibid., 278, 280. The Queen disliked Disraeli's eccentric and politically inspired appointments: D. W. R. Bahlman, 'The Queen, Mr Gladstone, and church patronage', *Victorian Studies*, 3 (1960), 361.

[84] C. K. F. Brown, *A History of the English Clergy* (London, 1953), p. 123.

[85] Bahlman, 'The Queen', 355–6.

[86] Ibid., 357.

[87] D. W. Bebbington, *William Ewart Gladstone* (Michigan, 1993), pp. 152–3, quoting Morley's life of Gladstone, Vol. 1, p. 431. Gladstone, writing to Lord Acton, suggested that bishops needed to possess some of the qualities of saints, theologians, pastors, preachers, philosophers, gentlemen and men of business: Brown, *History of the English Clergy*, p. 123.

[88] *Report of the Cambridge Church Congress*, 1861, pp. 64–5. Lindsay wanted bishops to be elected by the clergy and communicants, cf. 'D.C.L.', *Letters on Church Matters Reprinted from the Morning Chronicle* (London, 1851), Vol. I, p. 105, Vol. II, p. 244. H. C. G. Matthew, *Gladstone 1809–74* (Oxford, 1986), p. 211, quotes Lord John Russell's dictum: 'No talents, no learning, no piety, can advance the fortunes of a clergyman whose political opinions are adverse to those of the governing party.'

[89] Bahlman, 'The Queen', 350. But Longley had warned Melbourne that if he required his subservience in the Lords on church reform questions he could not accept the bishopric of Ripon offered him: in letter of 29 February 1836, LPL, Longley Papers, 1/68.

[90] Bahlman, 'Politics and church patronage', 270.

[91] Ibid., 255. He wished to make 'merit' the passport to the bench: Bahlman, 'The Queen', 359–60.

[92] Bahlman, 'Politics and church patronage', 256–7, and Bahlman, 'The Queen', p. 359.

[93] Bahlman, 'Politics and church patronage', 257–8, 265.

[94] Ibid., 255, 257, 260–5.

[95] Ibid., 259.

[96] Ibid., 266, 277–8.

[97] Ibid., 260.

[98] Ibid., 253–4, 279. He was later dean of Ripon.

[99] Ibid., 266–8, 273–5.

[100] Quoted by CMG (17 April 1869), p. 8.

[101] Stuart Rendel, *Disestablishment in Wales: A Remonstrance: Addressed to the Bishop of St Asaph* (Oswestry, 1885), p. 9. The bishop had suggested that the proposals for disendowment were akin to robbery.

[102] Bahlman, 'Politics and church patronage', 260–1. It was easily argued, therefore, that bishops should not have such parliamentary privileges. Many thought that these duties hindered their diocesan and pastoral work and made them live in a too fashionable and aristocratic style: WM (22 July 1873), p. 2; *Monmouthshire Merlin* (22 March 1834), p. 3; Joyce Coombs, *George Anthony Denison, The Firebrand* (London, 1984), pp. 80–2.

[103] Brown, *History*, pp. 111–3, 122; David Edwards, *Leaders of the Church of England 1828–1978* (London, 1968), pp. 112–13.

[104] Bahlman, 'Politics and church patronage', 254.

[105] Ibid., 296.

[106] Owen Chadwick, *The Victorian Church* (London, 1972), vol. 2, pp. 336–8. The evangelical party became more assertive about demanding their 'fair share' of episcopal appointments by the 1880s.

[107] Bahlman, 'Politics and church patronage', 270, 286–8, 291–5. In his foreword to his *Regina v Palmerston* (London, 1962), B. Connell notes the brutal frankness between them, and added, 'I have been advised not to embarrass their descendants by reproducing some of the passages.'

[108] Bahlman, 'The Queen', 362.

[109] A. C. Benson, *Edward White Benson* (London, 1899), Vol. 2, p. 293; F. Hardie, *The Political Influence of Queen Victoria* (London, 1963), pp. 133–7; and Bahlman, 'The Queen', 352–4.

[110] Bahlman, 'Politics and church patronage', 287.

[111] Ibid., 287.

[112] Queen Victoria's secretary to Gladstone, 24 December 1882, RA VIC, D8/200.

[113] Bahlman, 'The Queen', 361; G. K. A. Bell, *Randall Davidson* (Oxford, 1952), pp. 61, 164–5; Peter Hammond, *Dean Stanley of Westminster* (Worthing, 1987), p. 178; Palmer, *High and Mitred*, pp. 40–1, 89–91; and see especially O. Chadwick, *The Spirit of the Oxford Movement* (Cambridge, 1992), pp. 247–55, and his *Victorian Church*, Vol. 2, pp. 328–40.

[114] Bahlman, 'Politics and church patronage', 282, 285, 289–90, 295. The Queen also unsuccessfully attempted to veto the appointment of Percival to Hereford in 1895 as he supported disestablishment: Chadwick, *The Victorian Church*, Vol. 2, p. 334. Davidson wrote that he himself 'never scrupled to advise her to veto nominations if they were really unsuitable or bad, and during my years of advising her the veto was exercised a great many times': Stephen Taylor (ed.), *From Cranmer to Davidson: A Miscellany* (Church of England Record Society 7, 1999), pp. 397–8. See also Bell, *Davidson*, p. 176.

[115] The Queen to Gladstone, 17 January 1870, quoted by Philip Guedella, *The Queen and Mr Gladstone* (London, 1933), p. 215 (no. 194). For the Queen's interest in Wales and the Welsh Church see A. P. Stanley (ed.), *Letters to a Friend by Connop Thirlwall* (London, 1882), pp. 22–3, 130, 342.

[116] Palmer, *High and Mitred*, p. 89, quoting a letter of Gladstone to his daughter Mary.

[117] Though the political advantage of such nominations declined after 1832, R. A. Solway in his *Prelates and People* (London, 1969, p. 7) notes that twenty-three of the 100 bishops appointed between 1793–1852 had close family connections with the aristocracy.

[118] William Ceidrych Thomas, *The Church in Wales: Shall we End it or Mend it?* (London, 1893), p. 10. Their appointments were resented as they had no parochial experience and only a second-rate reputation as preachers.

[119] Note letters of W. Davies to Benson, 26 April 1890, BP, 82/26; and Archbishop Longley to his son Henry, 6 May 1860, LPL, Longley Papers, 1838/49.

[120] Jones, *Welsh Bishops for Wales*, p. 25.

[121] Article (allegedly by Wilberforce), 'The Church and her Curates', *Quarterly Review*, 123 (1867), 227.

[122] Jayne to Selbourne, 3 January 1899, SP.

[123] Ponsonby to Queen Victoria, 16 May 1874, RA VIC, D4/49.

[124] Vaughan to Davidson, 13 March 1890, DP, 522/95.

[125] WM (27 January 1897), p. 5.

[126] See the letter of Archbishop Whately of Dublin to a clergyman, who, asking for advice about whether he should apply to the government for a bishopric, was warned against accepting such political patronage and told that the archbishop objected to such soliciting: LPL, MS 2164, fol. 73.

[127] Hartwell Jones, *A Celt Looks at the World* (Cardiff, 1946), pp. 69–75. The quotation cited is on pp. 74–5.

[128] Roberts to John Owen, 20 May 1898, JOP, box 2, file regarding the appointment to the principalship of Lampeter.

[129] Ryle to John Owen, 2 June 1898, JOP, box 2, file as above.

[130] Davidson to A. J. Bigge, 5 February 1897, RA VIC, D12/112.

[131] CDH (21 January 1896), p. 6.

[132] NLW, D. R. Thomas papers, SA/DR/52, fol. 34, a cutting from the *Schoolmaster* (10 December 1904), p. 1158.

2. The Last Political Appointment

[1] CJ (10 July 1840), p. 3. Jenkinson was buried at Worcester Cathedral admid scenes of great solemnity: CMG (25 July 1840), p. 3.

[2] CJ (10 July 1840), p. 3.

[3] *Haul* (1840), pp. 250–2.

[4] CMG (18 July 1840), p. 3.

[5] CDH (25 July 1840), p. 117, quoting the *Sun*. The editor had in mind those who denied the necessity of a Welsh bishop being Welsh speaking, quoting Bishop Burgess as an example: see *Welshman* (17 July 1840), p. 2, and (7 August 1840), p. 2.

[6] CDH (18 July 1840), p. 115, cf. CJ (24 July 1840), p. 3.

[7] Hall to Melbourne, 11 July 1840, RA MP, 74/109.

[8] CDH (25 July 1840), p. 119; *Welshman* (7 August 1840), p. 2.

[9] E. N. Lewellin (Mrs Nares), *Pleasant Memories of Eminent Churchmen* (Carmarthen, n.d.), pp. 8–9.

[10] CJ (31 July 1840), p. 3.

11 *Morning Herald*, quoted by CMG (25 July 1840), p. 3.
12 Lady Hall to David James, 2 June (1851?), *Letters from Llanbadarnfawr Parish Chest* (NLW typescript), p. 9.
13 CMG (25 July 1840), p. 2.
14 CMG (18 July 1840), p. 3, and (25 July), pp. 2–3.
15 CDH (18 July 1840), p. 115.
16 CMG (25 July 1840), p. 3.
17 CJ (7 August 1840), editorial, pp. 2–3.
18 J. B. Bruce to Lord Bute, 7 October 1836, NLW, Bute Papers, L79/126.
19 CJ (10 July 1840), p. 3.
20 CMG (18 July 1840), p. 3. It noted a rumour that he had been offered it.
21 Knight was also mentioned with Archdeacon Davies of Brecon as possible candidates by 'Veritas' in CMG (11 July 1840), p. 3.
22 Maxwell Fraser, 'Sir Benjamin and Lady Hall in the 1840s', *NLW Journal*, 14 (1965), 35. Compare a letter of J. B. Bruce to Lord Bute of 7 October 1836 (NLW, Bute Papers, L79/126). The writer claimed that Lord Melbourne had asserted that the next vacancy in a Welsh bishopric would be filled by a Welshman. Although John Williams was spoken of as the probable candidate, the writer mentioned that most men in Glamorgan and the adjoining counties believed Williams's claims to promotion could not be compared to those of Bruce Knight.
23 Davies to Melbourne, 18 July 1840, RA MP, 74/72. The testimonials and note have not survived.
24 CDH (25 July 1840), p. 119.
25 Lisburne to Melbourne, no date, RA MP, 74/149.
26 Merewether to Melbourne, 9 and 10 July 1840, and draft reply, RA MP, 74/154–6. Merewether had suggested as an alternative the vacant deanery of Durham. The curt if polite reply of 18 July noted that the bishopric had been determined, and that the appointment to the deanery was complicated by reason of its connection with the university there. See also Bernard Palmer, *High and Mitred*, (London, 1992), p. 34. Merewether, for all his egotism, was a reforming dean of Hereford.
27 CJ (24 July 1840), p. 3; John Griffith writing in *John Bull* (12 February 1848), p. 103, said that Knight was not only a Welsh-speaking man but also one who had actually discharged the duties of a Welsh see.
28 CMG (25 July 1840), p. 2, and (1 August 1840), p. 3.
29 CMG (25 July 1840), p. 2, and CDH (25 July 1840), p. 119. The CMG doubted the Whig *Morning Post's* assertion of 23 July about this appointment on the basis of what Melbourne had said to the Liverpool delegation.
30 Melbourne to Merewether, 18 July 1840, RA MP, 74/156.

31 CJ (7 August 1840), p. 2.

32 Ibid., (24 July 1840), p. 3, (31 July 1840), p. 3, and (7 August 1840), p. 2, editorials. An editorial in CDH (25 July 1840), p. 119, suggested that the apathy of the Welsh had ensured Thirlwall's appointment, but also claimed that the Welsh clergy, as Tory adherents, 'had done all in their power to render themselves obnoxious to a Liberal administration'.

33 J. C. Thirlwall, Jr, *Connop Thirlwall*, (London, 1936), pp. 108–9.

34 Ibid., pp. 66–85, 108–12; WM (1 June 1874), p. 5; Melbourne to Howley, 5 July 1840, RA MP, 76/108. Thirlwall in his biography (pp. 110–12) quotes one Alexander Bain who suggested that Melbourne may well have asked these two bishops for another opinion on Thirlwall's orthodoxy, which they could not deny. This move had been instigated by a Cambridge friend of Thirlwall, Charles Buller, who thus paved the way for his appointment to St Davids. Furthermore, when Melbourne suggested that Thirlwall was not orthodox in his preface to that translation, he and Buller spent the morning in Melbourne's library searching for precedents for Thirlwall's opinions.

35 J. J. S. Perowne and L. Stokes, *Letters Literary and Theological of Connop Thirlwall*, (London, 1881), p. vii.

36 WM (1 June 1874), p. 5. *Farley's Bristol Journal* suggested this too, 'for reasons of state infinitely more cogent than the efficiency of the Church', though it anticipated that the dean of Bristol, John Lamb, would be appointed, presumably because he was a relative of Melbourne: quoted CMG (8 August 1840), p. 3.

37 Howley to Melbourne, 14 July 1840, RA MP, 76/107.

38 Melbourne to Howley, 15 July 1840, RA MP, 76/108.

39 Thirlwall, *Connop Thirlwall*, p. 110.

40 Ibid., quoting Mrs Brookfield, *The Cambridge Apostles*, p. 177.

41 WM (1 June 1874), p. 5.

42 Melbourne to Thirlwall, 15 July 1840, RA MP, 78/149.

43 Thirlwall to Melbourne, 21 July 1840, RA MP, 78/150.

44 Thirlwall, *Connop Thirlwall*, p. 112.

45 Ibid., pp. 113–14, quoting J. A. Froude, *Carlyle in London*, I. p. 159. Thirlwall (pp. 113–14) relates a strange story of himself accepting Melbourne's offer in the premier's bedroom, surrounded by folio volumes of the Fathers; 'excellent reading and very amusing' said Melbourne. Showing a copy of Thirlwall's edition of Schleiermacher to him, Melbourne pointed out the copious marginal notes made in it by the archbishop: 'He does not concur in all your opinions; but he says there is nothing heterodox in your book.' This comes from W. A. Torrens's *Memoirs of Lord Melbourne*, and may be the source of DNB's assertion that Thirlwall accepted Melbourne's offer at a

personal interview. But this is highly unlikely in view of his letter of acceptance, already quoted.

46 Hall to Melbourne, 27 July 1840, RA MP, 74/110; J. Richards to an unknown correspondent, 28 June 1850, noting that Archdeacon John Williams had made the 'discovery' that Hall had supported Thirlwall's candidature, *Letters*, p. 39.

47 Lady Hall to David James, 2 June (1851?), in *Letters*, pp. 8–9.

48 *Welshman* (24 July 1840), p. 2.

49 Quoted by Michael Hennell, *Sons to the Prophets*, (London, 1979), p. 56.

50 Quoted by Thirlwall, *Connop Thirlwall*, pp. 114–16.

51 Copleston to J. M. Traherne, 5 September 1840, in Roger L. Brown (ed.), *The Letters of Edward Copleston, Bishop of Llandaff, 1828–1848* (Cardiff, 2003), p. 251.

52 O. W. Jones, *Isaac Williams and his Circle*, (London, 1971), p. 98, and *idem, Rowland Williams*, (Llandysul, 1991), pp. 54–5.

53 *Record* (20 August 1840), p. 3, though a 'beneficed clergyman within the diocese of St Davids' protested at this interference and stated that these allegations were untrue: ibid. (3 September 1840), p. 3.

54 *Haul* (1840), quoted in D. M. James, 'Some Social and Economic Problems of the Church of England in the Diocese of St Davids, 1818–74' (unpublished MA thesis, University of Wales, 1972), pp. 264–6, and *Haul* (1840), pp. 281–3.

55 CMG (1 August 1840), p. 2.

56 *Record* (27 July 1840), p. 4.

57 *Report*, 1852, pp. 13–24.

58 *Record* (6 August 1840), p. 3.

59 Quoted by CMG (15 August 1840), p. 3.

60 *Farley's Bristol Journal*, quoted CMG (15 August 1840), p. 3. Richard Davies's reply in ibid., (8 August 1840), p. 3, suggested it was time that the agitation ceased and the gospel mandate of peace on earth be respected.

61 Quoted CMG (15 August 1840), p. 3. James was briefly warden of Llandovery and later rector of Panteg, Monmouthshire.

62 Joseph Morgan, *David James, Panteg* (Pontypool, 1925), pp. 32–9. The original appeared in many papers, such as CDH (8 August 1840), p. 126, and CMG (8 August 1840), p. 3. Thirlwall did not hold this letter against James, and in fact offered him the living of Llanbadarn Fawr in 1860: Morgan, *David James*, p. 40.

63 Writing to a friend, Milnes, quoted by Thirlwall, *Connop Thirlwall*, pp. 122–4. See also W. T. Gibson, 'Fresh light on Bishop Connop Thirlwall of St Davids', *Transactions of the Honourable Society of Cymmrodorion* (1992), 142–4; *Haul* (1842), pp. 126–7; *Haul* (1901), pp. 206–8.

[64] James, 'Some Social and Economic Problems', p. 267, quoting *Cambrian* (17 October 1840). *Haul* (1840, pp. 347–9) suggested that Thirlwall's speech at this eisteddfod – his knowledge of Welsh being his 'most important and most sacred obligation' – should mean that the uncomfortable feelings between him and the Welsh should be ended, for clearly he would be a blessing to his diocese.

[65] WM (29 July 1875), pp. 4, 6; and see Gibson, 'Fresh light', pp. 143–4.

[66] David Evans, *Atgofion*, (Lampeter, 1904), pp. 142–3.

[67] John Morgan, *Four Biographical Sketches*, (London, 1892), pp. 72–3.

[68] Lady Hall (later Lady Llanover) to Gladstone, 14 November 1869, GP, 44423/118.

[69] Thirlwall to Gladstone (writing of J. J. S. Perowne), 17 January 1870, GP, 44424/20. But he did not believe that a knowledge of Welsh was a *sine qua non* for an episcopal appointment to a Welsh diocese.

[70] WM (1 June 1874), p. 5, and CJ (5 June 1874), pp. 4–5. Lord Palmerston commented that while he had been chosen for his learning he was 'insufficient' as a diocesan bishop: quoted by Nigel Scotland, *Good and Proper Men* (Cambridge, 2000), p. 27.

[71] Rees Goring Thomas to Sir Stephen Glynne, 26 February 1870, GP, 44425/139, and cf. George Huntington, *Random Recollections* (London, 1896), pp. 86–8.

[72] A letter by a 'Welsh Clergyman', printed in the *Cambrian* (29 August 1840), suggested that Thirlwall should be translated to Chichester, whose bishop, Otter, had just died, so that one who understood 'the language of those over whose immortal souls he is expected to watch' could be appointed to St Davids in his place.

3. The Alien Bishop in the North

[1] William Carey (1769–1846) was educated at Westminster and Christ Church, and through the support of the dean of the latter, Dr Cyril Jackson, became headmaster of Westminster in 1803, together with other sinecures and royal appointments. Although he was a country parson between 1814 and 1820, in that later year he was elevated to the bishopric of Exeter, where his energy and administration redressed what had been a sorry situation. In 1830 he was translated to the wealthier bishopric of St Asaph. He bequeathed a large sum of money for the benefit of his diocese.

[2] See my *Lord Powis and the Extension of the Episcopate* (Cardiff, 1989).

[3] D. R. Thomas, *The History of the Diocese of St Asaph* (three volumes, Oswestry, 1908–13), Vol. I, p. 184. *North Wales Chronicle* (27 October 1846), p. 3, suggests that Short only acted during 1844 while

the bishop of Bangor held a few confirmations and consecrated two burial grounds in 1845. The bishop, it added, though confined to a sofa, 'had to the last the charge of his diocese'.

4 V. Spencer Ellis, 'Thomas Vowler Short', *Province*, 2 (1955), 118–24.

5 CDH (26 September 1846), p. 154.

6 The material quoted here is from PLD, 509 and 513, (Bethell to Powis, 21 September and 22 October 1846); Hansard 89 (1847), 271; cf. *English Churchman*, (1843), p. 133, which quoted statements that both bishops would decline to accept the other see.

7 Russell to Howley, 18 September 1846, LJRP, 5c/185.

8 Parliamentary Papers 1851, XLII, 343–5, esp. 344. This recited the previous arguments for the episcopal income for the joint see (of £5,800 as against £4,200 each for the two individual sees). G. F. A. Best in his *Temporal Pillars* (Cambridge, 1964), p. 436, suggests that this formula was in order to keep open the option of having a united see.

9 *Record* (24 September 1846), p. 4; W. H. Owen to Viscount Clive, 18, 19 and 22 September 1846, PLD, 507–8, 511; Clive to Owen, 21 September 1846, PLD, 510; Russell to Powis, 4 November 1846, PLD, 514.

10 Wood to Russell, 1 September 1846, LJRP, 5c 174. Writing to the Queen, proposing the retention of the diocese of St Asaph, Russell added, 'it must be retained for the present, subject to the future decision of Parliament': Russell to the Queen, 18 September 1846, RA VIC, J44/69.

11 Russell to Howley, 18 September 1846, LJRP, 5c/185.

12 *Record* (24 September 1846), p. 4, (12 October 1846), p. 3, cf. 'Verus's' letter, ibid., (19 October 1846), p. 3 (he regarded it as a temporary measure).

13 Wood to Russell, 1 September 1846, LJRP, 5c/174.

14 Maltby to Russell, 19 September 1846, LJRP, 5c 194 and also letters of 9 October 1846, LJRP, 5d 130, and 26 September 1846, LJRP, 5c/318.

15 Draft of Russell to Sumner, 21 September 1846, LJRP, 5c/230; Russell to the Queen, 3 October 1846, RA VIC, D15/58.

16 Wood to Russell, 30 September 1846, LJRP, 5c/388.

17 *English Churchman* (1846), p. 629; *Record* (29 October 1846), p. 4. This idea fell to the ground when Archdeacon Shirley was appointed bishop of Sodor and Man.

18 Maltby to Russell, 26 September 1846, LJRP, 5c/318.

19 Russell to Short, 5 October 1846, LJRP, 5d/76.

20 *Sketch of the Life of Bishop Short* attached to the 9th edition of his *Sketch of the History of the Church of England* (London, 1875), pp. lxi, lxv–vi.

21 Ibid., pp. xlv–lxi; R. A. Soloway, *Prelates and People* (London, 1969) p. 323.

22 Short to Longley, 29 October 1841, LPL, Longley Papers, I/198. Their friendship is well attested in this correspondence.

23 Short to Longley, 29 July 1841, Longley Papers, I/186.

24 S. Gray to Russell, 21 October 1846, LJRP, 5d/258, cf. *Sketch of the Life of Bishop Short*, pp. lxiii–v.

25 R. W. Morgan, *The Church and Its Episcopal Corruptions in Wales* (2nd edn, London, 1855), pp. 66–7. He was not alone as these sentiments are also expressed by a correspondent, 'Gwilym Avan', in CDH (24 October 1846), p. 167, who called it 'an artful dodge'.

26 Owen to Clive, 18–19 September 1846, PLD, 507–9, and 22 September 1846, PLD, 511; Clive to Owen, 21 September 1846, PLD, 510.

27 Grosvenor to Russell, 3 October 1846, LJRP, 5d/48, and Denbigh to Grosvenor, enclosed in LJRP, 5d/52.

28 John Williams, *On the Inexpediency, Folly and Sin of a 'Barbarian Episcopate' in a Christian Principality* (London, 1858), pp. 13, 18.

29 Owen to Clive, 18, 19 and 22 September 1846, PLD, 507–8, 511.

30 Letters of 'S. D.' of Pendre Isa, CDH, (3 October 1846), p. 159; (31 October 1846), p. 175.

31 CDH (26 September 1846), p. 154.

32 CDH (7 November 1846), p. 179; cf. *English Churchman* (1847), p. 473, and *Record* (19 October 1846), p. 3. 'Verus' writing in the latter, felt that the need for Welsh-speaking bishops was more important than the need to retain the two Welsh sees. He was a pioneer in requesting that Wales should have its own archbishopric.

33 Hansard, 3rd Series, cxi (1850), col. 901.

34 Thomas Vowler Short, *Primary Visitation Charge to the Diocese of St Asaph*, 1847, pp. 14, 21.

35 *Report of the Manchester Church Congress*, 1888, p. 73.

36 CDH (24 November 1849), p. 2.

37 J. H. Davies (ed.), *The Life and Opinions of Robert Roberts* (Cardiff, 1923), see p. 450.

38 Ibid., p. 378.

39 R. W. Morgan, *Correspondence and Statement of Facts connected with (his) Case and (Bishop) Short of St Asaph* (London, 1855), p. 20. For a life of Morgan see my *Parochial Lives* (Llanrwst, 2002), pp. 131–64.

40 R. W. Morgan, *Scheme for the Reconstruction of the Church Episcopate and its Patronage in Wales* (London, n.d.).

41 Ibid., p. 4, cf. *Report*, 1855, p. 18.

42 Morgan, *Scheme*, pp. 40–2.

43 R. W. Morgan, *The Church and its Episcopal Corruptions in Wales* (2nd edn, London, 1855).

44 Ibid., pp. 71f.

45 Morgan, *Correspondence and Statement*, p. 36.

46 Ibid., p. 29.

47 *Sketch of the Life of Bishop Short*, pp. lif.

48 *Correspondence between the Archbishop of Canterbury and R. W. Morgan* (London, 1855).

49 *Report*, 1852, pp. 39–41, cf. *Report*, 1855, pp. 18–22.

50 Williams, *Barbarian Episcopate*, pp. 9–17, 28.

51 Ibid., note especially p. 58.

52 NLW, Church in Wales Records, SA/MISC/1723. Williams, in his *Barbarian Episcopate* (p. 6), is quite scathing of these 200 clergy whose propositions 'virtually make void the Scripture testimony'. The CDH (25 July 1857), p. 5, described the letter of Archdeacon Clive and eight other clergy, including his two curates, requesting clerics in the diocese to sign the counter-petition as full of 'trashy tricky' paragraphs. None of these men, it concluded, would wish to get rid of Short who had given most of them some of the best livings in the diocese. See also CDH (6 June 1857), p. 4, and (4 July 1857), p. 4, and *Eddowes Salop Journal*, (5 August 1857), p. 6.

53 Williams, *Barbarian Episcopate*, p. 11. He argued that many of the clergy signed this petition not because they approval of Short's episcopate, but rather in order to 'strengthen his hand for the performance of his episcopal duties'.

54 Short to Longley, 29 July 1841, Longley Papers, I/186.

55 *Sketch of the Life of Bishop Short*, p. lxviii.

56 Ellis, 'Thomas Vowler Short', *Province*, 2 (1955), 122.

57 See Longley Papers, I/61 (of 1828) and II/62–6 (1848).

58 T. V. Short, *Charge delivered to the Clergy of St Asaph* (1853), pp. 8–12, 19, 29–31; *Sketch of the Life of Bishop Short*, p. lxviii; Ellis 'Thomas Vowler Short', pp. 118–24.

59 David Evans, *Adgofion* (Lampeter, 1904), pp. 145–6.

60 He gave up his London home, in which he entertained on a generous scale, in order that more of his clergy could have decent parsonages of their own: *Sketch of the Life of Bishop Short*, pp. lxxf.

61 CDH (24 November 1849), p. 2.

4. The Deceit of Lord John

1 Roger L. Brown, *The Letters of Edward Copleston, Bishop of Llandaff, 1828–1849* (Cardiff, 2003), pp. 5–47; CMG (20 October

1849), p. 2; *Record* (18 October 1849), p. 3, and (25 October 1849), p. 3.

2   He had taken it on the assumption that the diocese of Bristol was to be united with that of Llandaff.

3   Williams to James, 27 September 1849, *Letters*, p. 24.

4   Williams to James, 18 October 1849, *Letters*, pp. 25–6. This 'promise' is also mentioned in John Williams, *On the Inexpediency, Folly and Sin of a 'Barbarian Episcopate' in a Christian Principality* (London, 1858), pp. 13, 18.

5   CDH (3 November 1849), p. 8. He was answered by a number of correspondents and an editorial in the same paper: (3 November 1849), p. 5 and (10 November 1849), p. 8.

6   *Report*, 1852, p. 30.

7   CDH (3 November 1849), pp. 4–5. The paper had also campaigned for Welsh-speaking school inspectors.

8   *Principality* (26 October 1849), p. 3.

9   CDH (10 November 1849), p. 8.

10 CMG (27 October 1849), p. 4.

11 *Life and Letters of Rowland Williams* (London, 1874), Vol. 1, pp. 138–9. The memorial was too late, but it was sent in the expectation that on the next occasion the premier 'would give due consideration to these wishes'.

12 CDH (3 November 1849), pp. 4–5.

13 *Principality* (26 October 1849), pp. 3–4; CDH (3 November 1849), p. 6; CMG (27 October 1849), p. 4; *Haul* (1849), p. 370; *Monmouthshire Merlin* (27 October 1849).

14 CDH (3 November 1849), p. 6.

15 Ibid., p. 4.

16 Ibid., pp. 4–5.

17 Quoted by E. T. Davies in David Walker (ed.), *A History of the Church in Wales* (Penarth, 1976), p. 132.

18 *Monmouthshire Merlin* (27 October 1849), editorial; CMG (8 December 1849), p. 3: in reply to a letter of 'Giraldus' of (1 December 1849), p. 3.

19 CMG (8 December 1849), p. 3.

20 CMG (10 November 1849), p. 4; CJ (25 March 1870), p. 6.

21 Williams to David James, 18 and 26 October 1849, *Letters*, pp. 25–6, 35–6; Owen to David James (?), 22 October 1849, *Letters*, p. 27; Williams to an unknown correspondent, 27 October 1849, *Letters*, p. 29; Parry to David James, 24 October 1849, *Letters*, pp. 30–1. But Lady Hall in a letter to Thomas James (14 November 1851, *Letters*, p. 90) noted his 'weak belief' that he could stand well with both parties. His Conservative alignment is noted by CMG (20 July 1840), p. 3.

NOTES

22 Lady Hall to David James, 2 June 1851, *Letters*, pp. 9–10.
23 Richards to an unknown correspondent, 29 June 1850, *Letters*, p. 39. He noted that Hall declined to take part in a deputation. Williams was still hoping for a bishopric in the 1850s, but his supporters felt that his published indiscretions were harmful to his cause. They recognized, however, that these and his former 'backslidings' were due to his concern for his large family, his lack of riches, and the problems of filling his school at Llandovery (Lady Hall to Thomas James 14 November 1851, *Letters*, pp. 87–91). Williams died in 1858 before the next episcopal vacancy.
24 CMG, letter by 'M. A.' of 27 October 1849, p. 4; cf. 20 October 1849, p. 3; Sumner to Russell, 20 October 1849, LJRP, 8b/123.
25 Sumner to Russell, 19 October 1849, LJRP, 8b/119.
26 Williams to Lansdowne, 16 October 1849, LJRP, 8b/91.
27 Sumner to Russell, 22 October 1849, LJRP, 8b/135.
28 Sumner to Russell, 19, 20 and 27 October 1849, LJRP, 8b/119, 123, 171; and see C. J. Blomfield to Russell, 27 October 1849, LJRP, 8b/173 for Blomfield's recommendation. He was bishop of London.
29 Letter of 'Hwntw' in CDH (10 November 1849), p. 8.
30 CMG (3 November 1849), p. 2, and (10 November 1849), p. 3.
31 CDH (3 November 1849), p. 5.
32 Lord John Russell's letter to the Queen recommending Ollivant is dated 24 October 1849: RA VIC, A20/98. Russell's letter to Prince Albert of 21 October 1849 enclosing correspondence relating to the see of Llandaff might suggest that the Prince had some interest in the appointment: RA VIC, D20/55. Bernard Palmer, *High and Mitred* (London, 1992), p. 36, notes the friendship of Russell with the Prince Consort, who often influenced his appointments.
33 CMG (10 November 1849), p. 3.
34 Williams to James, 18 October 1849, *Letters*, pp. 25–6.
35 E. T. Davies in Walker, *History*, p. 132: *Record*, 25 October 1849, p. 4. Lord Auckland (Robert John Eden) became bishop of Bath and Wells in 1854.
36 It suggested his appointments were so bad that the Church ought to give up and cast off its state connection.
37 WM (18 December 1882), p. 3.
38 *Record* (29 October 1849), p. 4.
39 CDH (24 November 1849), p. 2; CMG (8 December 1849), p. 3; *Haul* (1849), pp. 400–1.
40 Quoted by CDH (17 November 1849), p. 6.
41 *Report*, 1852, p. 36. This is possibly why an obituary of Ollivant in *Yr Haul* (1883, pp. 70–1) suggested that Ollivant owed his appointment to the Yorkshire Welsh clergy.

NOTES

42 Williams to James, 27 October 1849, *Letters*, p. 37 (cf. ibid., 26 October 1849, p. 36). Hughes was John Hughes, vicar of Aberystwyth and later archdeacon of Cardigan and a noted evangelical leader. By 'Lampeter men' Williams meant a group led by Colonel Harford and his nephew and heir's father-in-law, Baron Bunsen, an intimate friend of the Prince Consort. They wished to obtain a bishop sympathetic to St David's College: Williams to James, 10 November 1851, *Letters* pp. 84–5.

43 'A Welshman' writing to CDH (10 November 1849), p. 8.

44 E. T. Davies writing in Walker, *History*, p. 133; Lady Hall to David James, 28 March 1851, and to Thomas James, 5 November 1851, *Letters*, pp. 41, 82–3. She added that Russell had admitted he had endured so much subsequent agitation for Welsh bishops that he felt Ollivant's appointment had not been worth *'the rows kept up since'*. Her anti-Ollivant feelings were strongly expressed in other letters in the same collection (see pp. 52–3, 87).

45 Lady Hall to Thomas James, 5 November 1851, *Letters*, pp. 82–3.

46 *Principality* (9 November 1849), p. 4.

47 'Hwntw' in CDH (10 November 1849), p. 8.

48 CMG (23 March 1850), p. 4.

49 See Roger L. Brown, 'Laying the foundation stone of Lewis' School, Pengam', *Gelligaer*, 13 (1990), 12–17; Ollivant's reply to these allegations, indicating his limitation in conversational Welsh, is in CMG (13 July 1850), p. 3.

50 WM (18 December 1882), p. 3. cf. the letter of a 'Welsh layman' in CDH (30 April 1859), p. 6.

51 'A Welshman in Yorkshire', CDH (24 November 1849), p. 2.

52 CMG (8 December 1849), p. 3.

53 'Hwntw' in CDH (10 November 1849), p. 8.

54 *Record* (22 December 1882), p. 1013.

55 Sumner to Russell, 19 October 1849, LJRP, 8b/119.

56 Ollivant was not conspicuous for his use of the Welsh language, possibly because of the earlier controversies about his ability in it.

5. *The Scotch Bishop*

1 See, for example, his *Sermons Preached at the Cathedral Churches of Chichester, Gloucester and Bangor* (London, 1857), pp. vii–ix: *Reflections on the Proceedings of an Association calling itself the Church Protestant Defence Society, and on the Pretensions and Position of those Clergymen in the Church of England who call themselves*

Evangelical (London, 1857); his *Fifth Charge to the Diocese of Bangor*, 1843, pp. 11–12, 27–30; and *Eighth Charge*, 1852, pp. 8–18: *Record* (23 April 1859), p. 3.

2 CDH (30 April 1859), p. 4 (its editor was hostile to Bethell's high church theology): *Record* (29 April 1859), p. 2.

3 *Record* (9 May 1859), p. 2, cf. (6 May 1859), p. 2.

4 CDH (30 April 1859), p. 6. He stated further that he believed the man most qualified for the post was ignorant of the Welsh language. This was possibly Dean Thomas Williams of Llandaff.

5 CDH (30 April 1859), p. 6. This may be regarded as an attack on both Thirlwall and Short whose inability to realize that religious enthusiasm was part of the Welsh character, and not simply a Nonconformist trait, are clearly described in this report.

6 CDH (30 April 1859), p. 6. Morgan wanted the same principle extended to all public appointments in Wales. Derby's secretary simply acknowledged his letter.

7 CDH (30 April 1859), p. 4; Derby to Powis, 4 May 1859, DerP. 188/1, fols 40–1.

8 CDH (30 April 1859), p. 6.

9 *Record* (29 April 1859), p. 2. In the next issue (6 May 1859), p. 2, the *Record* argued that the English policy in the Welsh Church meant that its bishops 'rarely came across the undercurrent' of Welsh feeling, which, in turn, caused an alienation between Church and dissent.

10 CJ (25 March 1870), p. 6.

11 Derby to J. P. Williams, MP, 19 April 1859, DerP. 187/2, fol. 192.

12 Derby to Sir William Joliffe, 21 April 1859, DerP. 187/2, fols 207–8; and Derby to Powis, 5 May 1859, DerP, 188/1, fols 50–2.

13 *Record* (2 May 1859), p. 2.

14 Harriet Thomas (ed.), *Llewelyn Thomas: A Memoir* (Bangor, 1897), pp. 22–3; *Record* (29 April 1859), p. 2; (9 May 1859), p. 2.

15 *Record* (29 April 1859), p. 2; (9 May 1859), p. 2.

16 Derby to Newport, 25 April 1859, DerP, 188/1, fols 3–4.

17 Derby to Bishop Ollivant of Llandaff, 25 April 1859, DerP, 188/1, fols 9–12; Derby to Lord Tredegar, 25 April 1859, ibid., fol. 7; Derby to J. P. Williams, 24 April 1859, Der, 187/2, fols 210–1; Derby to Lord Emlyn, ibid., fols 208–9.

18 CDH (7 May 1859), p. 5.

19 Derby to Lady Williams-Wynn, 25 April 1859, DerP, 188/1, fols 5–6.

20 CDH (28 May 1859), p. 6, quoting Morgan's letter of 3 May to Derby. That Bonnor was offered the see was denied in the CMG (28 May 1859, p. 5), though another correspondent gave him credit for declining it on the ground of his lack of Welsh: CDH (21 May 1859), p. 3. Bonnor's lack of Welsh was partly refuted by *Presbyter* in CDH (4 June 1859), p. 6.

21 CDH (7 May 1859), p. 5. There is no evidence for this assertion in Lord Derby's papers.

22 CDH (28 May 1859), p. 6, quoting his letter to Derby of 26 April. Denying that he was a claimant for the see he alleged that the premier's advisors were prejudiced in their belief that there was no clergyman in Wales suitable for episcopal office.

23 Derby to Newport, 25 April 1859, DerP, 188/1, fols 3–4. Writing to Lord Emlyn about Dean Williams of Llandaff, Derby asked him to state his qualifications 'as a Clergyman and a Preacher, the character of his Church opinions, his familiarity or otherwise with the Welsh language, and the bias of his political views, if he has any': Derby to Emlyn, 24 April 1859, DerP, 187/2, fols 208–9.

24 Derby to Ollivant, 25 April 1859, DerP, 188/1, fols 9–12. The junior bishops did not have a seat in the House of Lords.

25 Derby to Cairns, 25 April 1859, DerP, 188/1, fols 4–5.

26 Derby to Ollivant, 25 April 1859, DerP, 188/1, fols 9–12.

27 Derby to Powis, 2 and 4 May 1859, DerP, 188/1, fols 36–7, 40–1.

28 Derby to Patten, 28 April 1859, DerP, 188/1, fols 24–5.

29 Derby to Hall, 24 April 1859, DerP, 187/2, fol. 211.

30 Derby to Jolliffe, 25 April 1859, DerP, 188/1, fols 1–3.

31 Derby to J. P. Williams, 21 April 1859, DerP, 187/2, fols 198–9. He added that he was in no hurry to fill up the vacancy, and 'doubt not that I shall have (indeed I have already) a numerous List of Candidates to select from'. Williams was recommending one Mr Herbert.

32 Derby to J. P. Williams, 24 April 1859, DerP, 187/2, fols 210–1.

33 Derby to J. P. Williams, 19 April 1859, DerP, 187/2, fol. 192.

34 Derby to Jolliffe, 25 April 1859, DerP, 188/1, fols 1–3.

35 Derby to J. P. Williams, 21 April 1859, DerP, 187/2, fol. 198.

36 Derby to Patten, 28 April 1859, DerP, 188/1, fols 24–5.

37 Derby to Dungannon, 2 May 1859, DerP, 188/1, fols 35–6.

38 Derby to Campbell, 2 May 1859, DerP, 188/1, fols 39–40.

39 Derby to the Queen, 4 May 1859, DerP, 188/1, fols 41–2, and RA VIC, A27/62. By 'Wesleyans' Derby meant Calvinistic Methodists, probably unaware of the differences between the two denominations.

40 Derby to Campbell, 5 May 1859, DerP, 188/1, fols 45–6.

41 Derby to Powis, 5 May 1859, DerP, 188/1, fols 50–2.

42 Wilton D. Wills, 'The Revd John Griffith and the revival of the Welsh Church in the nineteenth century', *Morgannwg*, 13 (1969), 88–9.

43 CMG (28 May 1859), p. 5; (11 June 1859), p. 8; and (5 November 1859), p. 5; *Haul* (1896), pp. 1–4.

44 *Record* (18 May 1859), p. 2.

45 *Record* (29 June 1874), p. 2.

46 CMG (14 May 1859), pp. 5–6. Even Ab Iolo Morganwg, son of the more famous Iolo, spoke of the 'extent and accuracy of his attainments' in

the Welsh language, which was probably received in a less guarded sense than was originally contemplated: *Llandaff Church Extension Society: Substance of Speeches*, 1850, p. 20.

47 CMG (5 November 1859), p. 5.

48 CDH (21 May 1859), p. 4, cf. (28 May 1859), p. 6. The tone of this editorial was bitterly reproved by the editor of CMG (28 May 1859, p. 5). William Bruce was another brother-in-law of Campbell, and he had been forced to decline one of the more lucrative benefices in the diocese of St Asaph because of his inability to speak Welsh.

49 CDH (9 July 1859), p. 5.

50 CDH (18 June 1859), p. 6; cf. CDH (28 May 1859), p. 6, a letter of 'J. W. J.'.

51 CDH (21 May 1859), p. 3.

52 CDH (4 June 1859), p. 6; and (11 June 1859), p. 6.

53 CDH (4 June 1859), p. 6. Morgan's political views seem to have changed over the years.

54 CDH (28 May 1859), pp. 4, 6.

55 CMG (25 June 1859), p. 8.

56 Quoted by W. A. Westley, *Bishops of the Four Welsh Dioceses* (Manchester, 1912), p. 28.

57 CDH (21 May 1859), p. 4.

58 *Haul*, (1896), p. 1.

59 *Church Times* (24 December 1869), p. 510.

60 WM (28 February 1890), p. 3. The comment was somewhat unfair. Campbell had helped establish the first diocesan conference within the Church of England and had encouraged a vigorous lay association in his diocese.

6. 'Wales for the Welsh'

1 Bruce to Gladstone, 25 January 1870, GP, 44086/107.

2 The most important of these is Matthew Cragoe, 'A question of culture: the Welsh Church and the bishopric of St Asaph, 1870', *Welsh History Review*, 18 (1996), 228–54.

3 Short to Archbishop Tait, 4 January 1870, TP, 167/28; Tait to Short, draft reply, TP, 88/8.

4 Bishop Campbell to Bruce, 18 January 1870, GP, 44086/98; CJ (14 January 1870), p. 2. Short, however, went to live with his brother-in-law, Archdeacon Wickham, at Gresford, where he died in April 1872.

5 Memoir in T. V. Short, *Sketch of the History of the Church of England* (9th edn, London, 1875), p. lxv–xx; T. V. Short, *Charges delivered to the Diocese of St Asaph* (1847), pp. 6, 21, (1859), p. 9.

NOTES

6 Gladstone to Archbishop Thomson, 12 January 1870, GP, 44424/90.
7 The Queen to Gladstone, 17 January 1870, quoted by Philip Guedella, *The Queen and Mr Gladstone* (London, 1933), p. 215 (no. 194).
8 Cragoe, 'A question of culture', p. 240.
9 Henry Richard, *Letters on the Social and Political Condition of the Principality of Wales* (London, 1866), pp. 2–3, 22–7, 36, 70, 88–92.
10 R. I. Parry, *Henry Richard* (Aberdare, 1968), p. 2 of text.
11 Edwards may well have had another motive for writing this letter, knowing he was a strong candidate for the vacant see: K. O. Morgan, *Wales in British Politics 1868–1922* (Cardiff, 1970), p. 33. The letter was included in H. T. Edwards, *Wales and the Welsh Nation* (London, 1889), pp. 94–178. Gladstone was unaware of this letter until Lady Llanover pointed it out to him: Gladstone to Lady Llanover, 26 January 1870, GP, 44424/181.
12 Edwards, 'The Church of the Cymru: A Letter to the Rt. Hon. W. E. Gladstone, MP, in *Wales and the Welsh Nation*, pp. 134–5, 148–9, 157, 160–6, 171–8.
13 William Hughes, *A History of the Church of the Cymry* (London, 1916), pp. 390–1.
14 Quoted CMG (1 November 1856), p. 7.
15 Philip Magnus in his biography of Gladstone (London, 1973, p. 96) suggests that by the 1850s Gladstone had abandoned his previous belief that a revived Church of England would be able to win back vast numbers of Nonconformists into her fold. He may well have believed that Wales was in a different category.
16 Gladstone to Tait, 7 January 1870, GP, 44330/144 and TP, 88/3; Gladstone to Bruce, 12 January 1870, GP, 44086/82; Gladstone to Bishop Ollivant, 30 January 1870, GP, 44424/212.
17 Gladstone to Wellesley, 2 February 1870, GP, 44339/136. Wellesley wondered if the Established Church had become a lost cause in most of the diocese of Bangor, but hoped that a good Welsh bishop might save the position in St Asaph: Wellesley to Gladstone, 4 February 1870, GP, 44339/137.
18 Gladstone to Thirlwall, 5 and 12 January 1870, GP, 44538/40–1 (quoted by Matthew, *The Gladstone Diaries*, VII, p. 213), and 44424/88.
19 Gladstone to Thirlwall, 12 January 1870, GP, 44424/88.
20 See the comments by Sir Stephen Glynne in his letter dated the Feast of the Annunciation 1870, to Gladstone, in GGC, 837, and also quoted by A. G. Veysey in his 'Sir Stephen Glynne', *Journal of the Flintshire Historical Society*, 30 (1981–2), 162. 'It is almost hopeless', he wrote, 'to expect those of the higher families to be really Welsh in language, for they are educated, and live wholly amongst the English, & unless

320

they lived chiefly amongst servants and peasants would never speak Welsh as vernacular.'

[21] Reprinted in the CJ (4 March 1870), p. 7, and other local papers, and copied in GP, 44425/127.

[22] WM, 12 March 1870, p. 7. A manuscript copy is in GP, 44086/137f with Bruce's endorsement: 'an able man, but injudicious'.

[23] CT (25 February 1870), p. 78.

[24] Gladstone to Tait, 7 January 1870, TP, 88/1.

[25] CMG (11 December 1869), p. 8; WM (17 February 1870), p. 2.

[26] Gladstone to Mrs Tait, 9 February 1870, TP, 103/279.

[27] Quoted from the diaries of Edward Hamilton and the memoirs of George Leveson Gower by Bernard Palmer, High and Mitred (London, 1992), pp. 85–7.

[28] Quoted by CMG (20 November 1869), p. 8.

[29] CMG (5 February 1870), p. 5.

[30] Matthew, The Gladstone Diaries, VII, pp. 213–53. Gladstone also records reading a great deal of material relating to the Welsh Church.

[31] Gladstone to Llanover, 13 November 1869, NLW, MS 16343E/123; and Llanover to Gladstone, 12 November 1869, GP, 44423/97, and 24 January 1870, GP, 44424/166.

[32] Llanover to Gladstone, 19 February 1870, GP, 44425/25.

[33] Llanover to Gladstone, 24 and 28 January 1870, GP, 44424/166 and 191. In the latter she alleged that Basil Jones was 'a wolf in sheep's clothing'.

[34] Gladstone to Llanover, 21 January 1870, NLW, MS 16343E/127.

[35] Thirlwall to Gladstone, 24 February 1870, GP, 44425/117.

[36] Gladstone to Wellesley, 2 February 1870, GP, 44339/136.

[37] Tait to Gladstone, 10 February 1870, TP, 167/26. Gladstone found the same difficulty regarding the appointment of low churchmen to episcopal office, see Gladstone to Wellesley, 20 August and 13 September 1869, GP 44339/107 and 114, and Palmer, High and Mitred, pp. 88–9.

[38] Gladstone to Jacobson, 18 January 1870, GP, 44218/187.

[39] Gladstone to Ollivant, 18 January 1870, GP, 44424/115.

[40] Gladstone to Bruce, 12 January 1870, GP, 44086/82.

[41] Gladstone to Lady Llanover, 22 February 1870, NLW, MS 16343E/133.

[42] Gladstone to Bruce, 18 February 1870, GP, 44086/123.

[43] Gladstone to Bishop Browne, 24 February 1870, GP, 44115/16; cf. Gladstone to Bruce, 12 January 1870, GP, 44086/82.

[44] Llanover to Gladstone, 17 November 1869, GP, 44423/165.

[45] Bruce to Gladstone, 8 January 1870, GP, 44086/70. He acknowledged that the late Archdeacon Williams of Cardigan had requisite learning and ability but he was 'sus atque sacerdos'.

[46] Bruce to Gladstone, 14 January 1870, GP, 44086/86.

[47] Thirlwall to Gladstone, 7 January 1870, GP, 44424/20. He added that the appearance of Phillips's name on Gladstone's list of possible candidates should indicate 'the great need of careful enquiry as to the others'.

[48] Thirlwall to Gladstone, 14 January 1870, GP, 44424/102.

[49] Campbell to Bruce, 14 January 1870, GP, 44086/92.

[50] Glynne to Gladstone, 10 and 13 March 1870, GGC, 689.

[51] Gladstone to Thomson, 12 January 1870, GP, 44424/90.

[52] Gladstone to Cawdor, 13 January 1870, GP, 44424/92.

[53] George Dagnall to Gladstone, 26 January 1870, GP, 44424/176. It was agreed he was too old at seventy-four, was a thorough-going Tory and his efforts would be anti-Liberal.

[54] Bruce to Gladstone, 8 January 1870, GP, 444086/70: 'a cultivated and able man'.

[55] Glynne to Gladstone, 26 January 1870, GGC, 689.

[56] Campbell to H. A. Bruce, 14 January 1870, GP, 44086/92; Bruce to Gladstone, 15 and 20 January, 2 March 1870, GP 44086/90, 107, 130; Llanover to Gladstone, 17 November 1869, GP, 44423/165. Bruce was anxious to let it be known that neither he nor his family had any share in Campbell's elevation. Derby's offer had come as much as a surprise to them as to the bishop.

[57] Llanover to Gladstone, 9 January 1870, GP, 44418/96.

[58] Llanover to Gladstone, 14 November 1869, GP, 44423/118. Jones, she wrote, is not one of the sham confraternity who said on receiving a good Welsh living, 'I thought I must refuse it, as I could not do Welsh duty, but the Bishop told me he should not require it.'

[59] Llanover to Gladstone, 17 November 1869, GP, 44423/165: Wellesley to Gladstone, 4 February 1870, GP, 44339/137: Campbell to Bruce, 14 January 1870, GP, 44086/92.

[60] Llanover to Gladstone, 17 November 1869, GP, 44423/165.

[61] Cawdor to Algernon West, 28 February 1870, GP, 44425/145.

[62] Llanover to Gladstone, 17 November 1869, GP, 44423/165.

[63] Llanover to Gladstone, 17, November 1869, GP, 44423/165, and 24 January 1870, GP, 44424/166.

[64] Gladstone to Bruce, 12, 14 and 18 January 1870, GP, 44086/82, 92, 98.

[65] Gladstone to Jacobson, 18 January 1870, GP, 44218/187, and Jacobson's reply, 20 January, GP, 44218/188; Ollivant to Gladstone, 13 and 20 January 1870, GP, 44424/97 and 129.

[66] Wellesley to Gladstone, 4 February 1870, GP, 44339/137; Llanover to Gladstone, 14 November 1869, GP, 44423/118, and 9 January 1870, GP, 44418/96; Thirlwall to Gladstone, 7 and 31 January 1870, GP, 44424/20, 218.

67 Mrs Williams to Chance, 15 January 1870, GP, 44424/135; Evans to Gladstone, 28 February 1870, GP, 44425/147; Campbell to Bruce, 14 and 18 January 1870, GP, 44086/92 and 98; Bruce to Gladstone, 20 January 1870, GP, 44086/104; Glynne to Gladstone, 19 January 1870, GGC, 689.

68 Llanover to Gladstone, 17 November 1869, GP, 44423/165; Ollivant to Gladstone, 13 January 1870, GP, 44424/97; Morgan to Gladstone, 19 January 1870, GP, 44424/121; Richard to Gladstone, 8 March 1870, GP, 44425/226; Bruce to Gladstone, 13 and 15 February 1870, GP, 44086/84 and 90.

69 Thomson to Gladstone, 9 November 1869, GP, 44423/60, and 11 January 1870, GP, 44424/80; Tait to Gladstone, 10 January 1870, GP, 44330/146, and an undated draft reply, TP, 88/7.

70 Llanover to Gladstone, 17 November 1869, GP, 44423/165 and 18 February 1870, GP, 44425/25. She also noted that he had been rejected at Llandovery by the trustees due to his lack of Welsh.

71 Thirlwall to Gladstone, 17 January 1870, GP, 44424/20, cf. Wellesley to Gladstone, 4 February 1870, GP, 44339/137, and Glynne to Gladstone, 10 March 1870, GGC, 689.

72 Bruce to Gladstone, 11, 13, 14 and 28 January 1870, GP 44086/78, 84, 86, 107.

73 WA (29 January 1870), p. 5; Record (24 January 1870), p. 2.

74 Quoted by Record (24 January 1870), p. 4, and Welshman (28 January 1870), p. 8.

75 Record (26 January 1870), p. 2.

76 Morgan to Gladstone, 24 January 1870, GP, 44424/172, and note ibid., 19 January 1870, GP, 44424/121, in which he recommended Griffiths of Neath and Basil Jones.

77 A. P. Stanley (ed.), Letters to a Friend by Connop Thirlwall (London, 1882), pp. 254–5.

78 Llanover to Gladstone, 14 and 17 November 1869, GP, 44423/118 and 165. But Howell was not mentioned in her letter of 19 February (GP, 44425/25) as being on her list of candidates, possibly because, as she had written on 14 November, that while an 'indefatigable' clergyman, who might make an 'incomparable bishop', she thought him too young at the present time.

79 Kinnaird to Gladstone, 8 January 1870, GP, 44424/30.

80 Gladstone to Bruce, 12 January 1870, GP, 44086/82, and Gladstone to Ollivant, 12 January 1870, GP, 44424/87.

81 Ollivant to Gladstone, 14 January 1870, GP, 44424/97. This is wrongly attributed to Thirlwall by Matthew in The Gladstone Diaries, VII, p. 219, footnote 2.

82 Ollivant to Gladstone, 31 January 1870, GP, 44424/214.

83 Richard to Gladstone, 8 March 1870, GP, 44425/226.

84 Bruce to Gladstone, 8, 11 and 13 January 1870, GP, 444086/70, 78, 84.

85 Bruce to Gladstone, 28 January 1870, GP, 44086/107.

86 Kinnaird to Gladstone, 8 January 1870, GP, 44424/30. Although the clause is not in Kinnaird's hand it belongs to the letter and is not an endorsement by another.

87 Gladstone to Wellesley, 2 February 1870, GP, 44339/136.

88 *Haul* (1889), pp. 1–4, 36–8.

89 Gladstone to Cawdor, 13 January and 1 February 1870, GP, 44424/92 and 221; Gladstone to Ollivant, 18 January 1870, GP, 44424/115. At least one person, D. V. Pugh, refused Griffiths a testimonial as he considered canvassing improper (Pugh to Tait, 15 February 1870, GP, 44424/318). The comment regarding Hervey is quoted in GGC, 2101. Charles Wordsworth was also accused of canvassing for the bishopric of St Andrews in 1852. In spite of protests he was elected: see Arthur Burns, 'W J Conybeare: "Church Parties" ', in S. Taylor (ed.), *From Cranmer to Davidson*, Church of England Record Society, 7 (1999), p. 330n.

90 Griffiths to Llanover, 10 January 1870, GP, 44424/67: Llanover to Gladstone, 11 January 1870, GP, 44424/65.

91 Llanover to Gladstone, 14 and 19 November 1869, GP 44423/118 and 165.

92 Llanover to Gladstone, 18 January 1870, GP, 44424/111.

93 Griffiths to Campbell, 17 January 1870, GP, 444086/102.

94 Cawdor to Gladstone, 17 January 1870, GP, 44424/62.

95 Cawdor to Gladstone, 4 February 1870, GP, 44424/234, and cf. ibid., 6 February 1870, GP, 44424/252.

96 Wellesley to Gladstone, 4 February 1870, GP, 44339/137.

97 Gladstone to Mrs Tait, 9 February 1870, TP, 103/279.

98 Ollivant to Gladstone, 20 January and 7 February 1870, GP, 44424/129, and 256.

99 Thirlwall to Gladstone, 26 January 1870, GP, 44424/182.

100 Bruce to Gladstone, 28 January 1870, GP, 44086/107.

101 Ollivant to Gladstone, 8 February 1870, GP, 44424/262.

102 Gladstone to Ollivant, 9 February 1870, GP, 44424/268.

103 Tait's secretary, C. W. Sandford, to Gladstone, 14 February 1870, GP, 44424/297.

104 Bruce to Gladstone, 18 February 1870, GP, 44086/119.

105 There is no record of an interview with Gladstone noted in Gladstone's diaries: H. G. Matthew (ed.), *The Gladstone Diaries* (Oxford, 1982), VII, 241–4.

106 Thomas to Tait, 11 February 1870, GP, 44424/299; to Gladstone, 22 February, GP, 44425/86; to Glynne, 19 and 26 February 1870, GP,

44425/49 and 139; Bruce to Gladstone, containing extracts from Thomas's letter, 18 February 1870, GP, 44086/119.

[107] Though denied by D. V. Pugh (to Tait, 23 February 1870, GP, 44425/111) it was confirmed by Henry Richard in a letter to Gladstone of 8 March 1870: GP, 44425/226.

[108] Bruce to Gladstone, 19 February 1870, GP, 44086/124. Walters was probably Dr Thomas Walters, later vicar of Llansamlet. The letters are noted by Bruce in his letter but their contents are not disclosed. They appear to have been forwarded to him by Gladstone: Gladstone to Bruce, 15 February 1870, GP, 44086/123.

[109] Thirlwall to Gladstone, 14 February 1870, GP, 44424/302.

[110] Bruce to Gladstone, 18 February 1870, GP, 44086/119.

[111] Ollivant to Gladstone, 16 February 1870, GP, 44424/310.

[112] Kinnaird to Gladstone, 16 February 1870, GP, 44424/308.

[113] P. Phillips and Robert Smith to Venn, both 16 February 1870, GP, 44425/51 and 55.

[114] John Thirlwall to Thirlwall, 15 February 1870, GP, 44424/323.

[115] T. Thirlwall to Thirlwall, 25 February 1870, GP, 44425/138.

[116] Noted by C. W. Sandford in a letter to Algernon West, 25 February 1870, GP, 44425/128.

[117] Gladstone to Wellesley, 28 February 1870, GP, 44339/144: Gladstone to Ollivant, 28 February 1870, GP, 44425/152.

[118] *Haul* (1889), p. 37.

[119] WM (6 June 1874), p. 6.

[120] Gladstone to Browne, 24 February 1870, GP, 44115/16; Browne to Gladstone, 25 and 27 February 1870, GP 44115/17 and 22.

[121] Thomas to Gladstone, 23 February 1870, GP, 44425/105.

[122] Thirlwall to Gladstone, 24 February 1870, GP, 44425/117.

[123] Nicholl to Bruce, 1 March 1870, GP, 44086/132; Bruce to Gladstone, 2 March 1870, GP, 44086/130.

[124] Thirlwall to Gladstone, 24 February 1870, GP, 44425/117; Browne to Gladstone, 27 February 1870, GP, 44115/24.

[125] Thomas to Gladstone, 23 February 1870, GP, 44425/105; Nicholl to Bruce, 1 March 1870, GP, 44086/132; Thirlwall to Gladstone, 24 February 1870, GP, 44425/117.

[126] George Borrow, *Wild Wales* (Nelson Classics, London, n.d.), pp. 497–8, 501–2.

[127] Ollivant to Gladstone, 7, 8, 22 February and 2 March 1870, GP 44424/256, 262 and 44425/78, 168, 176. The pamphlet concerned the projected union between St David's College, Lampeter, and Christ Church, Brecon.

[128] Thirlwall to Gladstone, 7 March 1870, GP 44425/205.

[129] Richard to Gladstone, 8 March 1870, GP, 44425/226.

[130] Llanover to Gladstone, 17 November 1870, GP, 44423/165.
[131] Bruce to Gladstone, 22 March 1870, GP, 44086/139.
[132] Tait to Gladstone, 10 February 1870, TP, 167/26–7.
[133] Wellesley to Gladstone, 1 March 1870; Gladstone to Wellesley, 2 March, GP 44339/146 and 148; Gladstone to Glynne, 12 March 1870, GGC, 22.
[134] Gladstone to the Queen, 8 March 1870, RA VIC, D2/57.
[135] Gladstone to Hughes, 11 March 1870, GP, 44425/237.
[136] Hughes to Gladstone, 12 and 14 March 1870, GP 44425/247 and 252.
[137] Hughes to Tait, 17 March 1870, TP, 88/72.
[138] *Haul* (1889), pp. 66–9, 103–6; WM (22 January 1889), p. 5; *Record* (25 January 1889), pp. 85, 88; David Evans, *Atgofion* (Lampeter, 1904), pp. 150–1.
[139] *Record* (16 March 1870), p. 2, and (18 March 1870), p. 3; CT (18 March 1870), p. 118 (neither of these papers states Hughes had graduated). The WA in its obituary (26 January 1889), p. 3, stated he had gained a scholarship at Queen's College, Cambridge.
[140] Gladstone to the Queen, 8 March 1870, RA VIC, D2/57.
[141] Williams to Gladstone, 18 March 1870, GP, 44425/283.
[142] Gladstone to Hughes, 19 March 1870, GP, 44425/288. For the distribution of episcopal patronage between the universities see D. W. R. Bahlman, 'The Queen, Mr Gladstone and church patronage', *Victorian Studies*, 3 (1960), 359n. Of Gladstone's twelve other episcopal appointments between 1868 and 1870, including translations, eight were Oxford men, three Cambridge men and one a Dublin man.
[143] Hughes to Gladstone, 20 March 1870, GP, 44425/291.
[144] G. Hartwell Jones, *A Celt Looks at the World* (Cardiff, 1946), p. 51.
[145] WM (29 December 1882), p. 4.
[146] CJ (18 March 1870), p. 5.
[147] CMG (26 March 1870), p. 5.
[148] WA (19 March 1870), p. 5.
[149] *Welshman* (18 March 1870), p. 5.
[150] Glynne to Gladstone, Feast of the Annunciation 1870, GGC, 837, and 3 March 1870, GGC, 689.
[151] Llanover to Gladstone, 16 and 18 March 1870, GP, 44425/266 and 271; Gladstone to Llanover, 17 March 1870, GP, 44425/268 and NLW, MS 16343E/135.
[152] *Baner* (2 April 1870), p. 2.
[153] WM (6 April 1870), p. 2, quoting the *Daily News*.
[154] Quoted in R. B. Knox, *Wales and 'Y Goleuad' 1869–79* (Caernarfon, 1968), p. 122.
[155] DNB; *Haul* (1889), pp. 66–9; WM (22 January 1889), p. 5; *Record* (25 January 1889), p. 88.

156 *Record* (25 January 1889), p. 85.

157 WM (16 June 1874), p. 7.

158 Gladstone to Ollivant, 9 February 1870, GP, 44424/268.

159 F. D. How, *Bishop Walsham How* (London, 1899), p. 114.

160 Church Pastoral-Aid Society, *Abstract of Report*, 1886, pp. 20–3.

161 WA (2 February 1889), p. 7, and see his obituary in WA (26 January 1889), p. 3.

162 Hartwell Jones, *A Celt Looks at the World*, pp. 51–2. Nevertheless, A. G. Edwards, Hughes's successor, though an Oxford man, faced 'the standard of rebellion' several times in his diocese.

7. Mr Disraeli's Choice

1 CT (5 June 1874), p. 280, suggested he would resign in September, 'being in a state of great prostration at Bath'.

2 WM (12 June 1874), p. 5.

3 Walsh to Corry, 28 May 1874, DisP, 247. Unless otherwise mentioned, the Disraeli papers (DisP) are in the Badleian Library, Dep Hughenden 157/4.

4 Memorial to Disraeli by the St David's College Board, 3 June 1874, DisP, 261. They wished to see a gentleman of Welsh 'extraction' appointed who, as visitor to the college, would be able to determine the tone of the ordinands in the college. The memorial was more than a subtle hint that Basil Jones should be appointed, and Llewelyn Lewellin, the principal, wrote to Corry in his favour on the same day: Lewellin to Corry, 3 June 1874, DisP, 259.

5 Dynevor to Lord Barrington, 26 June 1874, DisP, 299.

6 Ibid., 17 June 1874, DisP, 281, and see Corry's comment, DisP, 295.

7 WM (1 June 1874), p. 5, (10 June 1874), p. 8: an alternative proposal was to place Swansea in the diocese of Llandaff.

8 WM (1 June 1874), p. 4.

9 *Record* (29 June 1874), p. 2.

10 Wynne to Lord Penrhyn, 27 June 1874, DisP, 309.

11 WM (27 June 1874), p. 6.

12 Dynevor to Barrington, 26 June 1874, DisP, 299.

13 WM (23 June 1874), p. 7.

14 Cawdor to Corry, 17 May 1874, DisP, 243.

15 WM (16 June 1874), p. 7; cf. letter of 'Spectator' in ibid., (22 June 1874), p. 6.

16 WM (27 June 1874), p. 6.

17 Inglis-Jones to Corry, 17 June 1874, DisP, 277.

18 WM (25 January 1897), p. 5.

[19] WM (18 June 1874), p. 6.
[20] WM (19 June 1874), p. 8.
[21] CJ (8 July 1874), p. 3.
[22] WM (22 June 1874), p. 6.
[23] WM (11 June 1874), p. 8.
[24] WM (16 June 1874), p. 7.
[25] WM (1 June 1874), p. 4, and (16 June 1874), p. 7; *Wrexham Guardian* (6 June 1874), p. 2.
[26] WM (10 June 1874), p. 8, (16 June 1874), p. 7; Dynevor to Barrington, 26 June 1874, DisP, 299.
[27] WM (1 June 1874), p. 6, and (16 June 1874), p. 7. Although his appointment was rumoured, the *Baner* suggested that some 'inspired' friend must have written it: *Baner* (1 July 1874), p. 1.
[28] WM (16 June 1874), p. 7; CJ (5 June 1874), p. 5.
[29] WM (16 June 1874), p. 7.
[30] WM (27 June 1874), p. 6.
[31] Morgan to Disraeli, 18 May 1874, DisP, 245; Dynevor to Barrington, 24 June 1874, DisP, 297.
[32] Bonnor to Sir Watkin Wynne, 26 May 1874, DisP, 157/2/147–8.
[33] Dynevor to Barrington, 17 June 1874, DisP, 281.
[34] Dynevor to Barrington, 26 June 1874, DisP, 299; Bonnor to Wynne, DisP, 157/2/147–8.
[35] WM (6 June 1874), p. 6, and (12 June 1874), p. 8.
[36] Edwards to Manners, 27 May 1874, DisP, 253 and Lord John Russell to Corry, 30 May 1874, DisP, 251. *Baner* expressed its gratitude that this 'hypocrite' was not appointed: *Baner* (1 July 1874), p. 1.
[37] *Wrexham Guardian* (6 June 1874), p. 2; WM (1 June 1874), p. 4 and (16 June 1874), p. 7; Dynevor to Barrington, 24 June 1874, DisP, 297.
[38] WM (11 June 1874), p. 8, (16 June 1874), p. 7: Dynevor to Barrington, 17 June 1874, DisP, 281.
[39] WM (19 June 1874), p. 8; Barrington's memorandum, 10 June 1874, DisP, 265; Dynevor to Barrington, 12, 17 and 26 June 1874, DisP, 269, 281, 299.
[40] Barrington's memorandum, 10 June 1874, DisP, 265; Dynevor to Barrington, 26 June 1874, DisP, 299.
[41] WM (11 June 1874), p. 8; Barrington's memorandum, 10 June 1874, DisP, 265; Inglis-Jones to Corry, 17 June 1874, DisP, 277; Talbot to Corry, 14 June 1874, DisP, 273; Tilly to Talbot, 13 June 1874, DisP, 275.
[42] WM (16 June 1874), p. 7; Dynevor to Barrington, 12 and 17 June 1874, DisP, 269 and 281; cf. WM (11 June 1874), p. 8. It was rumoured he had been appointed: *Guardian* (10 June 1874), p. 723.
[43] WM (10 June 1874), p. 8, (11 June 1874), p. 8; (16 June 1874), p. 7,

(27 June 1874), p. 6; Woolcombe to Tait, 24 June 1874, LPL, Tait Papers, 93/60f; Barrington's memorandum, 10 June 1874, DisP, 265; Inglis-Jones to Corry, 17 June 1874, DisP, 277; Wain to Inglis-Jones, no date, DisP, 279; Dynevor to Barrington, 24 June 1874, DisP, 299; Hughes to Perowne, LPL, Perowne MSS, no. 34; Latimer Jones to Perowne, 22 June 1874, ibid., no. 37; Lumby to Perowne, ibid., no. 35.

44 CJ (26 June 1874), p. 5; *Baner* (27 June 1874), p. 2; Lord Powis to Corry, 19 June 1874, DisP, 157/2/151.

45 D. W. R. Bahlman, 'Politics and church patronage in the Victorian age', *Victorian Studies*, 22 (1979), 287, 289. His suggestion that Disraeli drew his name from that list is probably wrong, but the fact that it was there may well have influenced his choice.

46 WM (1 June 1874), p. 4, (16 June 1874), p. 7, (5 July 1874), p. 4, (10 July, 1874), p. 4, (15 January 1897), p. 5; CT (22 January 1897), pp. 90–1; *Baner* (15 July 1874), p. 13; Wynne to Penrhyn, 27 June 1874, DisP, 309; Dynevor to Barrington, 24 and 27 June 1874, DisP, 299; Lewellin to Walsh, 23 May and 3 June 1874, DisP, 249 and 259. Basil Jones had presumably changed his political alliance, for in 1865 he was a member of Gladstone's committee at Oxford: Bahlman, 'Politics and church patronage', p. 289. Or did Disraeli get it wrong? Dean Wellesley, writing to Queen Victoria in 1875, stated that Disraeli regarded 'the Church as the great state-engine of the Conservatives', and would never willingly propose a clergymen with Liberal sentiments for high office: Robert Blake, *Disraeli* (London, 1969), p. 507.

47 Quoted in WM (9 July 1874), p. 5.

48 Disraeli to the Queen, 1 July 1874, RA VIC, D4/81. Dean Wellesley considered the appointment 'very proper': Wellesley to the Queen, 2 July 1874, RA VIC, D4/82.

49 Basil Jones to Disraeli, 4 July 1874, DisP, 313.

50 Tait to Thirlwall, 19 Aug 1874, LPL, Tait Papers, 93/298; Thirlwall to Tait, 20 August 1874, ibid., 93/302.

51 *Pall Mall Gazette*, quoted by WM (9 July 1874), p. 5.

52 *Record* (13 July 1874), p. 2.

53 WM (9 July 1874), p. 5.

54 WM (15 January 1897), pp. 5–6; (18 January 1897), p. 6; (25 January 1897), p. 5; CT (22 January 1897), pp. 90–1.

55 Dynevor's memorandum, 9 June 1874, DisP, 263.

56 Barrington to Corry, 13 June 1874, DisP, 267.

57 Edward Neville to Corry, 11 April 1877, DisP, 157/3/81.

58 Inglis-Jones to Corry, 17 June 1874, DisP, 277.

8. Unexpected and Unknown

1 Aberdare to Gladstone, 21 December 1882, GP, 44087/139.
2 G. K. A. Bell, *Randall Davidson* (Oxford, 1952), p. 165.
3 Gladstone to Lightfoot, 28 December 1882, GP, 44478/271.
4 K. O. Morgan, *Wales in British Politics: 1868–1922* (Cardiff, 1970), p. 60.
5 G. Hartwell Jones, *A Celt Looks at the World* (Cardiff, 1946), p. 50.
6 Roberts to Gladstone, 22 December 1882, GP, 44478/172–4.
7 Edwards to Morris, 26 December 1882, GP, 44315/108.
8 WM (22 December 1882), p. 3.
9 Bell, *Randall Davidson*, p. 74.
10 NWG (27 January 1883), p. 8; cf. WM (2 January 1883), p. 3.
11 WM (22 December 1882), p. 3.
12 WM (26 December 1882), p. 2, cf. (23 December 1882), p. 3.
13 WM (19 December 1882), p. 3.
14 WM (22 December 1882), p. 3.
15 *Baner* (13 January 1883), p. 5; WM (29 December 1882), p. 4; (12 January 1883), p. 2; (13 January 1883), p. 2.
16 Grosvenor to Gladstone, 31 December 1882, GP, 44315/102.
17 Gee to Gladstone, 22 December 1882, GP, 44478/160.
18 Queen Victoria's secretary to Gladstone, 24 December 1882, RA VIC, D8/200.
19 Gilbertson to Gladstone, 21 December 1882, GP, 44478/154.
20 WM (19 December 1882), p. 3.
21 Lady Llanover to Gladstone, 24 December 1882, GP, 44478/188.
22 Ibid., 24 January 1883, GP, 44479/121.
23 Ibid., 16 December 1882, GP, 44478/112; 24 December 1882, GP, 44478/188.
24 Ibid., 16 December 1882, GP, 44478/112; cf. Hussey Vivian, to Gladstone, enclosing a letter of Lady Llanover, 20 December 1883, GP, 44478/141.
25 Hughes to Gladstone, 22 December 1882, GP, 44478/164.
26 Quoted by WM (19 December 1882), p. 3.
27 WM (22 December 1882), p. 3; cf. WM (26 December 1882), p. 2.
28 Aberdare to Gladstone, 21 December 1882, GP, 44087/139.
29 Ibid., 3 January 1883, GP, 44087/124.
30 Ibid., 19 December 1882, GP, 44087/135.
31 Ibid., 21 December 1882, GP, 44087/139.
32 Ibid., 24 December 1882, GP, 44087/151.
33 Ibid., 19 December 1882, GP, 44087/135.
34 Campbell to Gladstone, 6 January 1883, GP, 44479/86; and see ibid., 2 January 1883, GP, 44479/28.

35 Thomas to Gladstone, 10 January 1883 GP, 44479/99.

36 WM (23 December 1882), p. 3.

37 WM (26 December 1882), p. 2; (27 December 1882), p. 2.

38 WM (9 January 1883), p. 2 (an editorial), and see letters (27 December 1882), p. 2.

39 Lightfoot to Gladstone, 25 December 1882, GP, 44478/197.

40 WM (29 December 1882), p. 4.

41 WM (26 December 1882), p. 3 (letter of 'Welshman').

42 WM (22 December 1882), p. 3.

43 WM (26 December 1882), p. 3.

44 W. H. Fowler to Gladstone, 21 December 1882, GP, 44478/151.

45 Rees Goring Thomas to Gladstone, 10 January 1883, GP, 44479/99.

46 Aberdare to Gladstone, 19 December 1882, GP, 44087/135; WA (30 December 1882), p. 3; WM (28 December 1882), p. 2. Vaughan was excluded, however, on the grounds of his alleged homosexual relationship with a Harrow pupil: B. Palmer, *High and Mitred* (London, 1992), p. 55.

47 Grosvenor to Gladstone, 31 December 1882, GP, 44315/102. A cutting in D. R. Thomas's scrapbook (Church in Wales Records, NLW, SA/DR/49, f. 72, stated to be from the *Christian Commonwealth* of 16 June 1892), alleges that he was close to being selected by Gladstone for the see of Llandaff; cf. *Montgomeryshire Collections*, 38 (1918), 272. This is mere gossip.

48 Grosvenor to Gladstone, 31 December 1882, GP, 44315/102; G. S. Talbot to Gladstone, 26 December 1882, GP, 44478/211; Hughes to Gladstone, 26 December 1882, GP, 44478/224; WM (29 December 1882), p. 4; (3 January 1883), p. 2; *Record* (5 January 1883), p. 7.

49 Lady Llanover to Gladstone, 16 December 1882, GP, 44478/112; and 25 January 1883, GP, 44479/165; WM (23 December 1882), p. 3; (26 December 1882), p. 3; (29 December 1882), p. 4.

50 Aberdare to Gladstone, 3 January 1883, GP, 44087/124; WM (29 December 1882), p. 4.

51 Hughes to Gladstone, 26 December 1882, GP, 44478/224.

52 Vivian to Gladstone, 22 December 1882, GP, 44478/181; G. S. Talbot to Gladstone, 26 December 1882, GP, 44478/211; Sinclair to Lord Sudeley, 24 December 1882, GP, 44478/240; Aberdare to Gladstone, 18 December 1882, GP, 44087/129; Richard's draft to Gladstone in NLW, MS 20395c (it refers to this election and not the Bangor election as the catalogue suggests).

53 NWG (6 January 1883), p. 5.

54 Lady Llanover to Gladstone, 16, 24, 25, 26 December 1882, GP, 44478/112, 188, 201, 232. Henry Richard said much the same about Howell's parochial ministry: Richard to Gladstone, 1 February 1883, GP, 44479/36.

55 WM (23 December 1882), p. 3; (26 December 1882), pp. 2–3; (2 January 1883), p. 3.

56 Grosvenor to Gladstone, 31 December 1882, GP, 44315/102.

57 RA VIC, D8/208.

58 Gladstone to Campbell, 25 December 1882, GP, 44478/195.

59 WM (20 December 1882), p. 2.

60 Richard to Gladstone, 1 January 1883, GP, 44479/36; Gee to Gladstone, 22 December 1882, GP, 44478/160; Hughes to Gladstone, 22 and 24 December 1882, GP, 44478/164 and 224; Richard's draft to Gladstone, NLW, MS 20395c.

61 WM (20 December 1882), p. 2.

62 Lady Llanover to Gladstone, 16 December 1882, GP, 44478/112, cf. 141; and 14 January 1883, GP, 44479/121.

63 Aberdare to Gladstone, 19 and 22 December 1882, GP, 44087/135 and 145.

64 Hughes to Adam Farrar, 29 December 1882, GP, 44478/285.

65 Farrar to Hughes, 1 January 1883, GP, 44479/34; Sinclair to Sudeley, 24 December 1882, GP, 44478/240; Hughes to Gladstone, 29 December 1882, GP, 44478/283; Gladstone to Lightfoot, 28 December 1882, GP, 44478/271; Lightfoot to Gladstone, 29 December 1882, GP, 44478/289; Gladstone to Campbell, 1 January 1883, GP, 44479/3. Benson thought that Watkins ran the diocese of Durham for Lightfoot (Bell, *Randall Davidson*, p. 169). Watkins never made the episcopate, though it was felt he should have become the first bishop of Newcastle when that diocese was separated from Durham: cutting in SA/DR/54, fol. 241, which also alleged he declined the see of Llandaff because of his attachment to Bishop Lightfoot.

66 Quoted by WM (19 December 1882), p. 3. Had Perowne changed his political allegiance?

67 Aberdare to Gladstone, 18 December 1882, GP, 44087/129; Gladstone to Aberdare, 22 December 1882, GP, 44087/149 (quoting Campbell); Hughes to Gladstone, 1 January 1883, GP, 44479/9; Sinclair to Sudeley, 24 December 1882, GP, 44478/240; Gilbertson to Gladstone, 31 December 1882, GP, 44478/303.

68 Gladstone to Aberdare, 22 December 1882, GP, 44087/149; Campbell to Gladstone, 31 December 1882, GP, 44478/301, and 2 January 1883, GP, 44479/28; Gladstone to Campbell, 1 January 1883, GP, 44479/3; Vaughan to Gladstone, 4 January 1883, GP, 44479/79.

69 Gladstone to Campbell, 25 December 1882, GP, 44478/195; Grosvenor to Gladstone, 31 December 1882, GP, 44315/102.

70 Grosvenor to Seymour, 2 January 1883, GP, 44315/104; Morris to Grosvenor, 28 December 1882, GP, 44315/106; Edwards to Morris, 26 December 1882, GP, 44315/108.

[71] Jacobson to Gladstone, 3 January 1883, GP, 44218/233; Williams to Jacobson, 21 December 1882, GP, 44218/235.

[72] Biscoe to Gladstone, 19 December 1882, GP, 44478/137.

[73] WM (23 December 1882), p. 2.

[74] NWG (27 January 1883), p. 8; WM (22 December 1882), p. 3.

[75] Roberts to Gladstone, 26 December 1882, GP, 44478/207.

[76] Hartwell Jones, *A Celt Looks at the World*, p. 51.

[77] Richard's draft to Gladstone, NLW, MS 20395c.

[78] Richard to Gladstone, 1 January 1883, GP, 44479/36; Vivian to Gladstone, 22 December 1882, GP, 44478/181; Talbot to Gladstone, 26 December 1882, GP, 44478/211; Howell to Gladstone, 2 January 1883, GP, 44474/4; Wynne Jones to Aberdare, GP, 44087/161.

[79] WM (20 December 1882), p. 2.

[80] WM (21 December 1882), p. 4.

[81] Aberdare to Gladstone, 19, 24, 26 and 31 December 1882, 7 January 1883, GP, 44087/135, 145, 151, 165, 181. Gladstone asked Bishop Campbell if he could confirm Aberdare's remarks about Edwards's sanity. He replied it was so; he needed a man to take care of him: Gladstone to Campbell, 1 January 1883, GP, 44479/3; Campbell to Gladstone, 2 January 1883, GP, 44479/28.

[82] Hughes to Gladstone, 26 December 1882, GP, 44478/224, and 1 January 1883, GP, 44479/9.

[83] Gladstone to Aberdare (quoting Campbell), 1 January 1883, GP, 44087/149; Campbell to Gladstone, 31 December 1882, GP, 44478/301, and 8 January 1883, GP, 44479/92.

[84] Gladstone to Campbell, 25 December 1882, GP, 44478/195, and 7 January 1883, GP, 44479/90; Gladstone to Aberdare, 22 December 1882, GP, 44087/149; Campbell to Gladstone, 8 January 1883, GP, 44479/92.

[85] Gladstone to Campbell, 26 and 28 December 1882, GP, 44478/219 and 269: Aberdare to Gladstone, 24 December 1882, GP, 44087/151; Campbell to Gladstone, 27 and 31 December 1882, GP, 44478/254 and 301; 5 January 1883, GP, 44479/81; *Record* (5 January 1883), p. 7; H. C. G. Matthew (ed.), *The Gladstone Diaries*, (Oxford, 1990), 10, p. 384.

[86] WM (8 January 1883), p. 2.

[87] Aberdare to Gladstone, 3 January 1883, GP, 44087/124; Gladstone to Campbell, 1 January 1883, GP, 44479/1; Campbell to Gladstone, 2 January 1883, GP, 44479/28; the Queen to Gladstone, 10 January 1883, RA VIC, D9/10.

[88] Gladstone to Campbell, 1 January 1883, GP, 44479/3.

[89] Aberdare to Gladstone, 24 December 1882, GP, 44087/151, 162. The letter of the bishop of St Davids, dated 19 December 1882, is enclosed.

[90] Ibid., 24 December 1882, GP, 44087/151.

[91] Jones to Gladstone, 27 December 1882, GP, 44478/265.

[92] Francis Jones, 'A Victorian bishop of Llandaff', *Journal of the National Library of Wales*, 19 (1975), 32–7.

[93] WM (18 January 1883), p. 3. He spent much time with David Evans, vicar of Aberafan and Baglan.

[94] WM (18 January 1883), p. 3; CJ (19 January 1883), p. 3.

[95] WM (17 January 1883), p. 3; (18 January 1883), p. 3; CT (19 January 1883), p. 42–3; *Record* (19 and 26 January 1883), pp. 49, 81.

[96] WM (30 January 1905), p. 5.

[97] WM (12 May 1874), p. 6; (14 May 1874), p. 8; (19 May 1874), p. 7; (21 May 1874), p. 6.

[98] Thomas Thirlwall to Gladstone, 29 December 1882, GP, 44478/275; Campbell to Gladstone, 30 December 1882, GP, 44478/299; Aberdare to Gladstone, 31 December 1882, 5 January 1883, GP, 44087/165, 177.

[99] Gladstone to Campbell, 1 January 1883, GP, 44479/3.

[100] Aberdare to Gladstone, 3, 5 and 7 January 1883, GP, 44087/124, 177, 181 (the date of 3 January is wrongly given in the letter as 1882); letter of Wynne-Jones of Aberdare, no date, GP, 44087/126.

[101] Thomas to Gladstone, 10 January 1883, GP, 44479/99.

[102] Basil Jones to Aberdare, 1 January 1883, GP, 44479/17; Thomas Thirlwall to Gladstone, 1 January 1883, GP, 44479/22; Campbell to Gladstone, 5 January 1883, GP, 44479/81; Aberdare to Gladstone, 4 and 7 January 1883, GP, 44087/173 and 181.

[103] Gladstone to Aberdare, 4 January 1883, GP, 44087/175.

[104] Hughes to Gladstone, 1 January 1883, GP, 44479/9.

[105] Gladstone to Campbell, 7 January 1883, GP, 44479/90.

[106] Gladstone to Lewis, 12 January 1883, GP, 44479/110; the Queen to Gladstone, 10 January 1883, RA VIC, D9/10.

[107] C. H. Dent, *Distinguished Churchmen* (London, 1902), pp. 1, 4–5.

[108] *Haul* (1883), pp. 90–1; Hartwell Jones, *A Celt Looks at the World*, p. 50–1.

[109] WM (18 January 1883), p. 3; CJ (19 January 1883), p. 3; Lewis to Gladstone, 18 January 1883, GP, 44479/139; Crystal Davies, *Mother's Union Alive* (Cowbridge, 1993), p. 14.

[110] CT (19 January 1883), p. 42–3.

[111] *Record* (26 January 1883), p. 81; WM (18 January 1883), p. 3.

[112] *Record* (19 January 1883), p. 49.

[113] *Haul* (1883), pp. 129–31.

[114] WM, (19 January 1883), p. 3.

[115] *Haul* (1883), pp. 92–3.

[116] Jones, 'A Victorian bishop', p. 56; WM (30 January 1905), p. 5.

9. Alfred George Edwards

1 McKenny Hughes to Archbishop Benson, 23 October 1888, BP, 55/35; Lord Powis to Benson, 4 December 1888, BP, 55/73, asking if the archbishop could supply episcopal help to the diocese; Bishop Campbell to Benson, 18 November 1888, BP, 55/41.

2 WA (26 January 1889), p. 5; WM (22 January 1889), p. 5; and a letter, 'A Disinterested Vicar', WM (1 February 1889), p. 4.

3 A. G. Edwards to Owen, 30 April 1889, JOP, box 1.

4 Benson to Salisbury, 11 January and 14 January 1889, SP. The legislation was 32 & 33 Vict, chap. 111, sections 4–5, of 1869. This was entitled 'An Act for the Relief of Archbishops and Bishops, when Incapacitated by Infirmity'.

5 Letters of 'A Layman' in WA (10 November 1888), p. 2, and (28 December 1888), p. 2. Lady Llanover said much the same, Llanover to Benson, 29 January 1889, BP, 55/77.

6 WM (16 February 1889), p. 4: letter of 'A Churchman'.

7 Benson to Salisbury, 11 January and 14 January 1889, SP.

8 *Record* (22 February 1889), p. 176. In his book of recommendations (entitled 'Bishopric and Clerical Appointments 1885–1887' (*sic*), now at Hatfield House), Salisbury noted the names of those who had been mentioned for the bishopric and their proposers: A. G. Edwards by Col. Sackville-West and Lord Emlyn; Archdeacon Edmondes by the Revd T. Hughes Jones; Canon Howell by Lord Herris, Lord Mostyn and the Revd M. B. Moorhouse; Dean James of St Asaph by Col. Sackville-West and the Revd T. Lloyd Williams; Evan Lewis by the dowager Lady Harlech; the Revd D. Lewis Lloyd by Mr John Hughes; Archdeacon Watkins of Durham by Sir Michael Hicks Beach, Mr J. D. Llewellyn and Sir R. Ellis, MP; and Watkin Williams by the Revd T. Lloyd Jones and Mr Swetenham, MP.

9 *The Times* (29 Sept 1888), quoted in K. O. Morgan, *Wales in British Politics: 1868–1922* (Cardiff, 1970), p. 82.

10 WA (29 September 1888), p. 8.

11 Benson to Davidson, 29 January 1889, DP, 17/166. A cutting from *The Christian Commonwealth* in D. R. Thomas's scrapbook suggests it was believed he was close to being appointed (Church in Wales Records, NLW, SA/DR/49, f. 72), while his obituary stated that it was no secret that he wished to succeed Hughes: *Montgomeryshire Collections*, 38 (1918), 273.

12 WA (23 January 1889), p. 3; (26 January 1889), p. 5: WM (1 February 1889), p. 4.

13 CT (25 January 1889), p. 75; *Baner* (30 January 1889), p. 8.

14 WM (16 February 1889), p. 4.

NOTES

16 WM (4 February 1889), p. 3.
17 Jayne to Salisbury, 23 January 1889, SP.
18 *Record* (25 January 1889), p. 85.
19 *Guardian* (20 February 1889), pp. 265–6.
20 *Record* (25 January 1889), p. 85.
21 WM (1 February 1889), p. 4.
22 *Record* (22 February 1889), p. 176. The WM in an editorial (23 January 1889), p. 2, disputed the need for a university graduate 'under the present circumstances' of the Welsh Church.
23 *Record* (8 February 1889), p. 123.
24 WA (29 September 1888), p. 8.
25 WA (26 January 1889), p. 5.
26 Llanover to Benson, 29 January 1889 and 5 February, 1889, BP, 55/77 and 89; Llanover to Salisbury, 20 September 1888, SP.
27 Cullin to Benson, 7 February 1889, BP, 55/93.
28 Bickersteth to Salisbury, 24 January 1889, SP.
29 Llanover to Salisbury, 5 February 1889, SP. C. G. Edmundes, a professor at St David's College, Lampeter, and a Vale of Glamorgan man, was also aware of Howell's past. While this incident was better forgotten he believed it debarred him from episcopal preferment: Edmundes to John Owen, undated, JOP, box 1, file of 1890 papers.
30 Mrs Baynard to Benson, 11 August 1885, 25 November 1887, 4 June 1888, BP, 49/15, 33, 45; Bishop Hughes to Benson, 17, 21 and 24 November, 1885, 1 December 1887, BP, 49/24, 28, 30, 37; Jenkins to Benson, 22 November 1887, BP, 49/32; Benson to Mrs Baynard, 15 December 1887, BP, 49/43.
31 Jenkins to Benson, 28 March, 26 April, 30 June, 3 and 8 July, 4 August, 1893, BP, 116/289, 291, 296, 117/72, 77; Bishop Edwards to Benson, 1 April 1893, BP, 117/75. For a life of Evan Jenkins see my article in *Montgomeryshire Collections*, 83 (1995), 177–88.
32 Jenkins to Benson, 8 and 15 July 1893, BP, 116/296 and 306.
33 Salisbury to Ponsonby, 28 January 1889, RA VIC, D13A/90.
34 Martin to Ponsonby, 30 and 31 January 1889, RA VIC, D13A/91–2.
35 Bickersteth to Salisbury, 26 January 1889, SP. By the next vacancy he had changed his mind and urged Howell's appointment in spite of this past: ibid., 17 March 1890, SP.
36 Salisbury to Ponsonby, 2 February 1889, RA VIC, D13A/93.
37 WA (9 February 1889), p. 7; WM (8 February 1889), pp. 2–3; Stephen E. Gladstone to Canon Mason, 13 February 1889, BP, 55/101, earnestly hoping that the appointment was not true.
38 *Record* (8 February 1889), pp. 121, 135; (15 February 1889), p. 157.
39 *The Times* (8 February 1889), p. 9 *Baner* (30 January 1889), p. 8; (9 February 1889), p. 4; (16 February 1889), p. 1.

40 WA (9 February 1889), p. 7.
41 *Record* (22 February 1889), p. 176; *Baner* (20 February 1889), p. 5.
42 WM (18 February 1889), p. 3.
43 WM (8 February 1889), p. 2.
44 WA (2 February 1889), p. 5.
45 CT (15 February 1889), p. 150.
46 WA (23 February 1889), p. 6. Davidson wrote to Benson to inform him of the appointment, a telling point on the relationship between Lambeth and Downing Street: 12 February 1889, DP, 18/5.
47 A. G. Edwards, *Memories* (London, 1927), pp. 88–9.
48 Robert Lucas, *A Gower Family* (Lewes, 1986), pp. 92–3; W. G. Evans, *A History of Llandovery College* (Llandovery, 1981), pp. 44–8.
49 CT (22 February 1889), p. 170.
50 WM (18 February 1889), p. 3; *Record* (22 February 1889), p. 176.
51 Morgan, *Wales in British Politics*, p. 82.
52 Llanover to Benson, 5 January 1889, BP, 55/89.
53 Davidson to Ponsonby, 12 February 1889, RA VIC, D10/87.
54 *Record* (22 February 1889), p. 176; *Guardian* (20 February 1889), pp. 265–6.
55 *Record* (22 February 1889), p. 183.
56 CT (22 February 1889), p. 167. This was probably a reference to Hughes's good relationship with Nonconformists.
57 WM (18 February 1889), p. 2.
58 *Record* (22 February 1889), p. 176.
59 *Cymru Fydd*, II (1889), 156–8. The *Baner* was equally sceptical, assuming that his appointment was due to the influence of Basil Jones of St Davids and as a reward for his polemical writings against Nonconformity: *Baner* (20 February 1889), p. 5.
60 Hartwell Jones, *A Celt Looks at the World*, pp. 69–70, 74. He claimed that he had been ostracized by them and prevented from becoming a Welsh bishop.
61 G. W. E. Russell, *The Household of Faith* (London, 1902), p. 398.
62 For these controversies see George Lerry, *Alfred George Edwards* (Oswestry, 1939), pp. 57–76, and my *David Howell: A Pool of Spirituality* (Denbigh, 1998), pp. 211–34.
63 CDH (30 Sept 1898), p. 7. An example of this 'power' is illustrated by Edwards's letter to Salisbury of 4 Mar 1897 (SP). Having heard that Buckley Jones, warden of Ruthin, had been recommended to the prime minister for a canonry, he wrote that if this was the case 'then there are some facts which I think it my duty to lay before you'.
64 Edwards to Salisbury, 18 September 1890 and 4 December 1893, SP.
65 Hartwell Jones, *A Celt Looks at the World*, pp. 74–5.
66 Edwards to Gladstone, 28 June and 25 September 1890, GP, 44510/122 and 44511/54.

[67] Ibid., 23 September 1890, GP, 44511/34.
[68] Ibid., 27 February 1891 and 6 March 1891, GP, 44512/132 and 153.
[69] *Rhyl Advertiser* (23 February 1891), in NLW, SA/DR/46, fol. 639.

10. The Levisian Maze

[1] Archbishop Benson to Lord Salisbury, 29 April 1890, SP; WA (17 May 1890), p. 3; *Record* (7 March 1890), p. 227; WM (28 February 1890), p. 3; (14 April 1890), p. 2.
[2] Davidson to Benson, 10 March 1890, DP, 18/7.
[3] Jayne to Davidson, 14 March 1890, DP, 28/45.
[4] Bishop Bickersteth of Exeter to Salisbury, 26 March 1890, SP. He felt that Ellis, though a devout and spiritually minded man, was too much a 'high churchman'. The bishop of St Davids, writing to Davidson (12 April 1890, DP, 28/69), called him an extreme ritualist, 'a party man', whose claim was both his strength and weakness.
[5] Bishop Claughton of St Albans to Salisbury, 24 April 1890, SP.
[6] Ryle to Salisbury, 4 March 1890, SP. His first choice was Howell.
[7] Bishop Basil Jones of St Davids to Davidson, 29 April 1890, DP, 28/80.
[8] Bickersteth to Salisbury, 26 March 1890, SP.
[9] Benson to Davidson, 13 March 1890, DP, 28/33.
[10] Jones to Benson, 13 March 1890, BP, 82/16.
[11] WM (6 March 1890), p. 4.
[12] WM (5 March 1890), p. 4.
[13] WM (4 March 1890), p. 4.
[14] WM (14 March 1890), p. 2.
[15] WM (8 March 1890), p. 3.
[16] WM (28 February 1890), p. 3.
[17] WM (28 February 1890), p. 3.
[18] Salisbury to H. F. Ponsonby, secretary to Queen Victoria, 13 April 1890, RA VIC, D13a/137. David Lloyd George won the election.
[19] Quoted in G. K. A. Bell, *Randall Davidson* (Oxford, 1952), p. 178.
[20] Perowne to Salisbury, 6 March 1890, SP.
[21] Davidson to Ponsonby, 24 January 1890, RA VIC, D10/133.
[22] Perowne to Salisbury, 22 April 1891, SP.
[23] D. T. W. Price, *A History of St David's University College, Lampeter* (Cardiff, 1977), Vol. I, p. 104.
[24] Jayne to Davidson, 7 March 1890, DP, 28/5. Davidson noted this correspondence in a letter to Benson of 10 March 1897: DP, 18/7.
[25] Edwards to Davidson, 8 March 1890, DP, 28/7.
[26] Jayne to Davidson, 11 March 1890, DP, 28/23.

27 Perowne to Davidson, 8 March 1890, DP, 28/9.
28 Perowne to Davidson, 10 March 1890, DP, 28/16.
29 Perowne to Davidson, 13 March 1890, DP, 28/40.
30 Salisbury to Perowne, 11 March 1890, SP; Perowne to Davidson, quoting Salisbury's letter, 12 March 1890, DP, 28/31. A letter expressing similar sentiments was sent by Davidson to Perowne on the same date (draft at DP, 28/22). He suggested that Perowne should add a footnote to his letter of withdrawal stating that Bangor was the most Welsh of the four dioceses and it was essential that it had a bishop who knew the Welsh language thoroughly. Salisbury was probably unaware as to how far Bangor differed from Llandaff. He had received some correspondence which had startled him, indicating how much Welsh was needed in Bangor. Indeed, the diocesan conference was mainly conducted in that language. Such remarks, Davidson added, 'will not commit you or anybody to the Gladstonian theory as to Welsh Bishops, but merely says that whatever force there is in the argument, it is specially at Bangor that it holds good'.
31 Vaughan to Davidson, 13 March 1890, DP, 522/95.
32 Perowne to Salisbury, 12 March 1890, SP. A *Times* obituary of Perowne (8 November 1904, in a book of press cuttings in the Perowne papers at LPL, MS 1963, fol. 3) states that Lord Salisbury asked him to withdraw his acceptance of the see 'explaining that the circumstances of the case required the appointment of one who could speak both languages'. Salisbury, it continued, probably felt that this 'regrettable incident' entitled Perowne to a claim to future preferment, and he was offered the diocese of Worcester in 1891. His son, in a reply (ibid., fol. 13), said this was incorrect. His father had written, but never posted, his letter of acceptance, knowing the feeling in the Principality that a Welshman should be appointed.
33 WM (27 March 1890), p. 2, cf. *Record* (28 March 1890), p. 289.
34 In his letter offering Owen the deanery, Edwards made clear it was upon the condition that he made up his emoluments to £1,000 per annum, and that he came as a colleague 'in the fullest sense': Edwards to Owen, 18 February 1889, JOP, box 1.
35 NLW, T. G. G. Herbert bequest, 1969, part 1, box 10, bundle 66, dated 20 March 1890. I owe this reference to Mr Bill Gibson.
36 Lewis to Davidson, 6 March 1890, DP, 28/1.
37 Benson to Davidson, 13 March 1890, DP, 28/33.
38 Jayne to Davidson, 15 March 1890, DP, 28/51.
39 Ibid., 11 March 1890, DP, 28/23.
40 Ibid., 14 March 1890, DP, 28/45.
41 CT (25 April 1890), p. 415.
42 Edwards to Benson, 13 March 1890, BP, 82/10; Edwards to Davidson,

11 March 1890, JOP, box 1, in which he described Owen as the 'pre-eminent candidate'.
[43] Benson to Salisbury, 25 March 1890, SP.
[44] Benson to Davidson, 13 March 1890, DP, 28/33.
[45] Benson to Davidson, 15 March 1890, DP, 28/49. Vaughan wrote to Davidson on 13 March 1890 (DP, 522/95) confirming Benson's sentiments. He hoped to see him a bishop, and felt that Owen with Edwards could yield a real influence in north Wales.
[46] Benson to Salisbury, 25 March 1890, SP.
[47] Davidson to Benson, 13 March 1890, DP, 18/8.
[48] Davidson to Ponsonby, 18 March 1890, RA VIC, D10/149.
[49] Salisbury to Ponsonby, 13 and 22 April 1890, RA VIC, D13A/137 and 142. Sir John Puleston wrote to Owen hoping he was not too disappointed. His name had held a high place and his youth would enable him to look forward to the future with confidence: Puleston to Owen, 3 May 1890, JOP, box 1, file of 1890.
[50] Edwards to 'my dear brother', 18 March 1890, DP, 28/61; Edwards to Davidson, 20 March 1890, DP, 28/ 63; Bishop Jones to Davidson, 29 April 1890, DP, 28/80.
[51] Edwards to Benson, 25 March 1890, BP, 82/20 and see fol. 22 attached.
[52] Jayne to Davidson, 14 March 1890, DP, 28/45.
[53] WM (25 March 1890), p. 3; *Record* (28 March 1890), p. 289, suggested Williams would not push himself forward.
[54] Ryle to Salisbury, 5 April 1890, and Bickersteth to Salisbury, 17 March 1890. SP.
[55] Salisbury to the Queen, 20 March 1890, RA VIC, D13a/133; Salisbury to Ponsonby, 20 March and 13 April 1890, RA VIC, D13a/136 and 137.
[56] Ryle to Salisbury, 4 March 1890, SP.
[57] Bickersteth to Salisbury, 17 March 1890, SP.
[58] Bickersteth to Salisbury, 26 March 1890, SP.
[59] Vaughan to Davidson, 13 March 1890, DP, 522/95. In the same letter he warned against Constable Ellis and Dean Lewis of Bangor, who were the real enemies of the Church in Wales, for unlike Howell and Griffiths they were churchmen first and Christians second.
[60] RA VIC, D10/148.
[61] Edwards to Davidson, 13 March 1890, DP, 28/38.
[62] Edwards to Benson, 14 March 1890, BP, 82/18.
[63] Noted in Edwards to Davidson, 20 March 1890, DP, 28/63.
[64] Jones to Benson, 19 March 1890, DP, 28/65.
[65] Jayne to Davidson, 14 March 1890, DP, 28/45. The allegations about the Welsh at Wrexham and his influence over his curates were totally untrue.
[66] Benson to Davidson, 13 March 1890, DP, 28/33.
[67] Benson to Davidson, 14 March 1890, DP, 28/43.

NOTES

68 Salisbury to Ponsonby, 13 April 1890, RA VIC, D13a/137. In a letter of 22 April 1890 Salisbury accepted that the support for Howell was substantial: ibid., 22 April 1890, RA VIC, D13a/142.

69 WM, 3 May 1890, p. 4. Lloyd had been previously headmaster at Dolgellau and Friar's School, Bangor, and revived the fortunes of all the schools he served.

70 Benson to Davidson, 13 May 1890, DP, 18/16.

71 Sarah E. Lloyd to Evans, 5 April 1890, in NLW, MS 20962E.

72 Lewis to Davidson, 6 March 1890, DP, 28/1.

73 Lloyd to Evans, 10 March 1890, DP, 28/57.

74 Lloyd to Salisbury, 10 March 1897 and 7 July 1892. SP.

75 Bickersteth to Salisbury, 26 March 1890, SP.

76 Davidson to Ponsonby, 20 March 1890, RA VIC, D13a/134.

77 Jayne to Davidson, 14 March 1890, DP, 28/45.

78 Edwards to Benson, 25 March 1890, BP, 82/20 and see fol. 22 attached.

79 Edwards to 'my dear Bishop', 18 March 1890, DP, 28/61.

80 Jones to Benson, 19 March 1890, DP, 28/65.

81 Edwards to Davidson, 12 April 1890, DP, 28/69.

82 Davidson, draft to 'Sir H. F.', 15 April 1890, DP, 28/75.

83 Salisbury to Ponsonby, 17 April 1890, RA VIC, D13a/141. Salisbury wrote that the only other candidates who received any similar support from Welsh authorities were Howell and Owen. But, for reasons already noted, he could not recommend them: Salisbury to Ponsonby, 22 April 1890, RA VIC, D13a/142.

84 CJ (9 May 1890), p. 8.

85 Record (30 May 1890), pp. 536–7. Baner (10 May 1890), p. 6. The Record suggested that Howell had been rejected because of his lack of a university qualification and the Baner argued it was because he had not been energetic enough in hounding Nonconformity.

86 Puleston to Owen, 3 May 1890, JOP, box 1, file for 1890.

87 WM (2 May 1890), p. 2.

88 Record (18 July 1890), p. 702.

89 WM (2 May 1890), p. 2 (a ms. copy is in BP, 82/34); memoranda of 19 May 1890, RA VIC, D10/155.

90 Draft note of Benson regarding T. H. Hughes, BP, 82/41; Davidson to Benson, 16 May 1890, BP, 82/43; Benson to an unknown correspondent (possibly T. H. Hughes), draft of 21 May 1890, BP, 82/49.

91 Draft note of Benson, BP, 82/41; Major Bigge to the Queen, 16 May 1890, RA VIC, D13a/144, and note at D13a/146. Lewis's acceptance of the eulogy was so embarrassing that it was totally ignored by the establishment.

92 Salisbury's telegram to Ponsonby, RA VIC, D13a/145, and memoranda of 19 May 1890, ibid., D10/155.

[93] Memoranda of 19 May 1890, RA VIC, D10/155. Benson commented to Davidson, 'I presume that nothing could make such a man resign, and nothing could bring home to him the state of his unfitness. I believe he has *canvassed* widely': Benson to Davidson, 13 May 1890, DP, 18/16.

[94] Edwards to Benson, 15 May 1890, BP, 82/39; Benson to Salisbury, 16 May 1890, BP, 82/41f and also SP; Salisbury to Davidson, 7 May 1890, BP, 82/45; T. H. Hughes (Brecon) to Benson, 22 May 1890, BP, 82/50.

[95] Davidson to Benson, 16 May and 19 May 1890, BP, 82/43 and 47. The Queen's comment may possibly be that found in a note at the royal archives: 'if the matter were not so serious, it would be very ludicrous' (RA VIC, D13a/144a).

[96] Benson to Davidson, 16 May 1890, DP, 18/17.

[97] *Record* (13 June 1890), p. 579.

[98] Benson to Salisbury, 25 March 1890, SP.

[99] Jones to John Lloyd, 3 May 1890: T. G. Herbert papers, bundle 332.

[100] NWG (10 May 1890), p. 3; *Record* (7 March 1890), p. 227.

[101] WM (11 March 1890), p. 2.

11. *The True Welshman from the North*

[1] WM (16 January 1897), p. 5, quoting, in part, the *Liverpool Mercury*.

[2] WM (21 January 1897), p. 6.

[3] WM (22 January 1897), p. 4.

[4] CT (22 January 1897), p. 89.

[5] *Record* (22 January 1897), pp. 77, 90.

[6] CJ (29 January 1897), p. 8.

[7] Davidson to Salisbury, quoting a letter of Vaughan to him, 19 January 1897, SP.

[8] Edwards to Salisbury, 22 January 1897, SP; *Baner* (30 January 1897), p. 1.

[9] CT (22 January 1897), p. 91.

[10] WM (29 January 1897), p. 6; *Baner* (3 February 1897), p. 13.

[11] WM (28 January 1897), p. 5; *Record* (29 January 1897), p. 101.

[12] Lewis to Salisbury, 30 January 1897, SP.

[13] *Baner* (3 February 1897), pp. 8, 13.

[14] Edwards to Owen, 11 February 1897, and T. Ll. Williams to Owen, 13 February 1897, JOP. Unless otherwise stated, JOP in this chapter refers to box 4, file 10.

[15] WM (16 January 1897), p. 5, quoting the *Liverpool Mercury*.

[16] WA (30 January 1897), p. 5.

[17] *Record* (29 January 1897), p. 101; (5 February 1897), p. 138; *Baner* (3 February 1897), p. 8; cf. CT (2 April 1897), p. 383.

[18] CT (25 April 1890), p. 415.

[19] WA (30 January 1897), p. 5. It was noted, surprisingly, by the *Baner* (30 January 1897), p. 1, that it was thought Dean Williams would take his place as bishop. This, the editor thought, would provide an excellent arrangement to promote disestablishment.

[20] Lewis to Salisbury, 30 January 1897, SP.

[21] Davidson to A. J. Bigge (one of the Queen's secretaries), 5 February 1897, RA VIC, D12/112.

[22] CT (22 January 1897), p. 89.

[23] Edwards to Salisbury, 28 January 1897, SP.

[24] Eleuned E. Owen, *The Early Life of Bishop Owen* (Llandysul, 1958), pp. 209–10.

[25] Davidson to Bigge, 5 February 1897, RA VIC, D12/112.

[26] Edwards to Owen, 12 January 1897, JOP.

[27] Ibid., 14 January, 1897, JOP.

[28] Williams to Owen, 22 January 1897, JOP, and Owen Evans to Owen, 12 April 1897, JOP.

[29] Williams to Owen, 15 January 1897, JOP.

[30] Ibid., 18 and 20 January 1897, JOP.

[31] Ibid., 22 January 1897, JOP.

[32] Edwards to Owen, 15 January 1897, JOP.

[33] Ibid., 16 January 1897, JOP.

[34] Ibid., 20 and 27 January 1897, JOP.

[35] John Rhys to Owen, 22 and 25 January 1897, JOP.

[36] D. Morgan Jones to Owen, no date, JOP, ibid.

[37] Williams to Owen, 26 January 1897, JOP.

[38] Ibid., 4 and 8 February 1897, JOP.

[39] D. Morgan Jones to Owen, 12 February 1897, JOP; Edwards to Owen, 2 February 1897, JOP.

[40] Nicholas to Owen, 30 January 1897, JOP, ibid.

[41] Edwards to Owen, 27 January 1897, JOP.

[42] Ibid., 12 March 1897, JOP.

[43] Ibid., 24 January 1897, JOP.

[44] Ibid., 3 February 1897, JOP.

[45] Ibid., 9 February 1897, JOP.

[46] Ibid., 1 February 1897, JOP.

[47] Ibid., 8 February 1897, JOP.

[48] Ibid., 11 February 1897, JOP.

[49] D. Morgan Jones to Owen, 8 February 1897, JOP, box 4, file 10.

[50] Edwards to Owen, 2, 8, 9, 10, 13, February 1897, JOP.

[51] Ibid., 3 February 1897, JOP.

[52] Salisbury to the Queen, 3 February 1897, RA VIC, D12/111.

[53] Owen to Salisbury, 14 February 1897, SP.

[54] WM (16 February 1897), pp. 4–5; Record, (19 February 1897), p. 9; Baner (17 February 1897), p. 9, cf. (20 February 1897), p. 4.

[55] Record (19 February 1897), p. 173.

[56] CT (19 February 1897), p. 191.

[57] CJ (19 February 1897), p. 5.

[58] WM (12 March 1897), p. 6.

[59] Owen to Salisbury, 8 March 1897, SP; Owen, Early Life, p. 213; Roger L. Brown, Dean Howell: A Pool of Spirituality (Denbigh, 1998), pp. 239–42. There is much correspondence in JOP regarding the deanery and on the assumption that the appointment lay with Owen many recommendations were made to him. Edwards thought Howell's appointment undeserved, though he was prepared 'to spare him to you': Edwards to Owen, 12 and 22 March 1897, JOP. W. H. Davey suggested that Howell had been appointed as a 'sop' to the Protheroe family, a recognition of Tudor Howell's services, and as a means of satisfying both the Welsh and the evangelical lobbies: Davey to Owen, 31 March 1897, JOP.

[60] CT (5 March 1897), p. 253; (12 March 1897), p. 284.

[61] CT (19 March 1897), p. 317. The temporal prosperity related to the disestablishment campaign.

[62] CT (9 April 1897), p. 412; (23 April 1897), p. 490; (7 May 1897), p. 545.

[63] CT (2 April 1897), p. 399.

[64] CT (9 April 1897), p. 412.

[65] Owen, Early Life, pp. 209–10.

[66] Williams to Owen, 8 February 1897, JOP; cf. Edwards's own concern that the episcopate was being seen as 'prizes for the winners' or factor fights, and McDonnell's comment that the election was a 'race' between rival candidates: Edwards to Owen, 27 January 1897, JOP.

[67] D. Parry-Jones, A Welsh Country Parson (London, 1975), p. 83. He equally conversed with his Lampeter students in English: Young Wales, 5 (1898), 7, quoted by D. Densil Morgan, The Span of the Cross (Cardiff, 1999), p. 35.

[68] WM (22 January 1897), p. 6; CT (22 January 1897), p. 89.

12. A Vacancy in Bangor

1 Dean Evan Lewis to Temple, 8 June 1898, TP, 8/403; Dr D. Rowland Jones to Archdeacon Pryce of Bangor, 23 July 1898, TP, 8/407; Lord Salisbury to the Queen, 4 October 1898, RA VIC, D12/113. He was having to learn to write with his other hand: CDH (16 September 1898), p. 7. There are no references to this election in the papers of Bishop John Owen at the National Library of Wales.

2 Pryce to Temple, 19 July 1898, TP, 8/409.

3 Temple to Salisbury, 22 August 1898, SP; Henry Wace to Temple, 29 August 1898, TP, 8/426.

4 Lloyd to Talbot, 20 September 1898, SP.

5 Penrhyn to Temple, 8 July 1898, TP, 8/414.

6 Morgan to Temple, 6 August 1898, TP, 8/416.

7 Fletcher to Archbishop Maclagan, no date, TP, 8/422 and 424.

8 Wace to Temple, 29 August 1898, TP, 8/426.

9 Williams to Temple, 28 September 1898, TP, 8/432.

10 Dean Lewis to Temple, 1 and 9 September 1898, TP, 8/428,430; D. R. L. Lloyd to Temple, 18 November 1898, TP, 8/440.

11 D. R. Lewis to Temple, 5 February 1900, TP, 8/443.

12 CDH (7 October 1898), p. 8.

13 CDH (30 September 1898), p. 7.

14 *Independent* paper quoted by CDH (7 October 1898), p. 8.

15 CDH (7 October 1898), p. 8.

16 Ibid., p. 4.

17 Ibid., p. 8; cf. *Llan* (4 November 1898), p. 3.

18 WM (10 December 1898), p. 4.

19 Quoted WM (24 November 1898), p. 5.

20 CDH (7 October 1898), p. 8; *Llan* (4 October 1898), p. 5, (18 November 1898), p. 4.

21 *Manchester Guardian*, quoted in CDH (14 October 1898), p. 8. One such letter of support for the dean and chapter came from 'A Priest in the Diocese of Bangor' in *Llan* (21 October 1898), p. 3; cf. the letter of J. R. Robert, ibid., (21 October 1898), p. 5, and letters in ibid., (11 November 1898), p. 3, and (18 November 1898), pp. 6–7.

22 CDH (14 October 1898), p. 8.

23 CDH (11 November 1898), p. 8; and (18 November 1898), p. 4: *Llan* (11 November 1898), p. 5. The question of the relative strength of those who signed the initial petition and the eighty who signed the protest was so bitterly argued in the letter columns of the *Llan* that the editor closed the correspondence as it had become so unseemly: *Llan* (25 November 1898), pp. 6–7; (2 December 1898), p. 8.

24 Dean Lewis to Temple, 24 October 1898, TP, 8/448. The cutting of the dean's letter in the *Manchester Guardian* follows in the archbishop's papers.

25 Morgan to Temple, 26 October 1898, TP, 8/446.

26 Priestley to Temple, 26 November 1898, TP, 8/455.

27 *Record* (16 September 1898), p. 898.

28 *Record* (23 September 1898), p. 922.

29 CDH (16 September 1898), p. 7; (23 September 1898), p. 8; (30 September 1898), p. 7.

30 Quoted in the *Record* (25 November 1898), p. 1163.

31 Stephen Gladstone to Talbot, 26 September 1898, SP. Ellis became bishop of Aberdeen in 1906.

32 Lewis to Davidson, 14 and 19 September 1898, DP, 51/170 and 172.

33 Lewis to Salisbury, 23 September 1898, SP.

34 *Record* (16 September 1898), p. 898. He later denied the rumour of his appointment: *Record* (16 December 1898), p. 1242.

35 WM (20 November 1898), p. 5: CDH (2 December 1898), p. 4.

36 Fletcher to Archbishop Maclagan, 20 September 1898, TP, 8/451, 453. The *Baner* commented that it appeared that a rich man was needed at this time and that Williams had a lot of this world's goods about him: *Baner* (10 December 1898), p. 3.

37 Owen to Salisbury, 2 November 1898, SP; letter of J. R. Roberts in *Y Llan* (21 October 1898), p. 5.

38 Owen to Salisbury, 18 November 1898, SP.

39 Brodrick to his father (Viscount Midleton), 11 October 1898, DP, 51/178.

40 Brodrick to Davidson, 24 September 1898, DP, 51/180.

41 Brodrick to Davidson, 11 October 1898, DP, 51/188.

42 Talbot to Salisbury's secretary, McDonnell, 20 September 1898, SP.

43 Lyttelton to Salisbury, 26 November 1898, SP.

44 WM (24 November 1898), p. 5.

45 Williams accepted the appointment the day after he was offered it by Salisbury: Williams to Salisbury, 9 December 1898, SP.

46 Owen to Salisbury, 9 December 1898, SP.

47 Edwards to Salisbury, 9 December 1898, SP.

48 Owen to Salisbury, 5 January 1899, SP.

49 Edwards to Salisbury, 2 January, 4, 8, 17 February 1899, SP. Howell was not involved in that clerical revolt.

50 Owen to McDonnell, 11 January 1899, SP. A further letter of 16 January stated that Evans would not accept nomination. Eventually Hugh Jones, rector of Llanrwst since 1868, a former fellow of Jesus College and a son-in-law of Dean Bonnor, was appointed.

51 CT (16 December 1898).

52 *Record* (16 December 1898), p. 1242.

53 CDH (16 December 1898), p. 8; (16 September 1898), p. 7; cf. (30 September, 1898), p. 7.

54 CDH (2 December 1898), p. 4.

55 CDH (16 December 1898), p. 4.

56 WM (10 December 1898), p. 4. A biography of Watkin Herbert Williams, *A Genial, Kind Divine*, written by Raymond Renowden, was published by Gwasg Gee, Denbigh, in 1997.

13. The Last State Appointment

1 WM (25 January 1905), pp. 4–5. Search among the Balfour papers at the British Library has indicated that nothing of value regarding this election has been retained. Search was made within the following volumes of manuscripts, MS 49857 and 49763, political correspondence, MS 49788, correspondence with the archbishop of Canterbury, and MS 49790 with the bishop of St Davids.

2 CT (27 January 1905), p. 99.

3 WM (25 January 1905), pp. 4–5, and (30 January 1905), p. 6; *Baner* (20 January 1905), p. 8. The paper expressed some amazement that Gladstone should have appointed such a staunch Tory to this position. See also ibid., (28 January 1905), p. 4.

4 Bishop Richard Lewis to Archbishop Davidson, 11 February 1904, DP, 95/336.

5 Draft: Davidson to Lewis, 19 February 1904, DP, 95/340.

6 Lewis to Davidson, 24 February 1904, DP, 95/344.

7 Davidson to Lewis, 3 March 1904, DP, 95/347.

8 Quoted by WM (22 February 1905), p. 4.

9 WM (30 January 1905), p. 6.

10 WM (16 February 1905), p. 4. The editor, William Davies, writing to Bishop Owen on 24 January 1905 about the imminent death of Bishop Lewis, added that the 'usual crop of correspondence will break out and wires be pulled in all directions': JOP. Unless otherwise stated, JOP refers in this chapter to box 6, file 12.

11 T. Morgan Jones to Davidson, 1 February 1905, DP, 95/379. William Davies, noted above, in a letter to Owen of 9 February 1905 referred to 'our northern friend' running Dr James of Rugby: JOP.

12 Winton in two letters to Talbot, 22 January 1905, DP, 95/348, 352. The recipient is probably not E. G. Talbot, then bishop of Rochester.

13 Ibid., 18 February 1905, DP, 95/415. Lord Cawdor later considered that being high church Green would not hold an even balance, and

being young and inexperienced his would be an unpopular appointment: Cawdor to Davidson, 23 February 1905, DP, 95/466.

14 Winton to Talbot, 22 January 1905, DP, 95/348.

15 Ibid., 22 January 1905, DP, 95/352.

16 Davidson to Bishop Owen, 21 February 1905, JOP.

17 Legard to 'My dear Lord', 28 January 1905, DP, 95/363.

18 Richards to Davidson, 1 March 1905, DP, 95/481 (he recommended Canon Williams of St Davids); *Llan* (10 February 1905), editorial, and (24 February 1905), p. 1.

19 CT (3 February 1905), p. 156, cf. (10 February 1905), p. 167.

20 Ibid., (10 February 1905), p. 163.

21 Owen to Davidson, 22 February 1905, JOP.

22 WM (4 February 1905), p. 4, and (6 February 1905), p. 4; cf. *Llan* (24 February 1905), p. 1.

23 Parry to Davidson, 26 January 1905, DP, 95/357; Bishop of London (Winnington-Ingram) to Davidson, note only, DP, 95/359. Parry resigned in the following year and retired to Ilfracombe.

24 Thomas to Davidson, 30 January 1905, DP, 95/369.

25 Davies to Davidson, 1 February 1905, DP, 95/381.

26 Morgan Owen to Davidson, 4 February 1905, DP, 95/387; Ernest Brown, rector of Montgomery to Davidson, no date, DP, 95/371.

27 R. Owen to Davidson, 4 February 1905, DP, 95/389.

28 Hyslop to Davidson, 6 February 1905, DP, 95/395. The Vaughan testimonial, which is enclosed, is also noted in G. Hartwell Jones's memoirs, *A Celt Looks at the World* (Cardiff, 1946), p. 74.

29 Williams to Davidson, DP, 95/399.

30 Puleston to Davidson, 31 January 1905, DP, 95/377; Owen to Davidson, 24 February 1905, JOP.

31 Morgan Owen to Davidson, 1 February 1905, DP, 95/379.

32 Edwards to Davidson, 13 February 1905, DP, 95/406.

33 Davidson to James (copy), 4 February 1905, DP, 95/391.

34 James to Davidson, 6 February 1905, DP, 95/393; Edwards to Davidson, 30 January 1905, DP, 95/373, enclosing James's letter to Edwards, 28 January 1905, DP, 95/375.

35 Davidson to Daniel Lewis, 8 February 1905, DP, 95/409.

36 Lewis to Davidson, 11 February 1904, DP, 95/336, and a note relating to candidates in DP, 95/498.

37 Davidson to Owen, 20 February 1905; Winton to Owen, 29 January 1905, JOP.

38 Arthur Lewis to Owen, 15 and 20 February 1905, JOP.

39 Edwards to Davidson, 30 January 1905, DP, 95/373.

40 Owen to Davidson, 7 February 1905, DP, 95/400.

41 Edmondes to Davidson, 20 February 1905, DP, 95/421; *Baner* (11

March 1905), p. 4. The WM (22 February 1905, p. 4) said he had declined to give reasons why he had turned down the see, but the CT (24 February 1905, p. 252) and Y Llan (24 February 1905, p. 1) suggested it was on the grounds of age – he was 65 – or because he felt daunted by the high qualifications insisted upon by others as a qualification for the office. *The Llandaff Diocesan Magazine* (October 1913, p. 65) noted, 'to but few is given the opportunity, strength of character and grace to say "nolo episcopari" '.

42 Davidson to T. T. L. Morgan, 11 March 1905, DP, 95/492.
43 Oliver Jones to Davidson, 21 February 1905, DP, 95/430; Windsor to Davidson, 21 February 1905, DP, 95/427. The lists are found at DP, 95/429, 432, 438.
44 Davidson to Bishop Owen, 20 February 1905, JOP.
45 CT (17 February 1905), p. 219.
46 Edmondes to Davidson, 22 February 1905, DP, 95/446.
47 Arthur Lewis to Owen, 11 and 20 January 1905; Owen to Edwards, 22 February 1905; Winton to Owen, 29 January 1905; Bruce to Owen, 30 January 1905; Davey to Owen, 31 January 1905; Owen to Bruce, 2 February 1905; Owen to Winton, 2 February 1905; Davidson to Owen, 21 February 1905: all JOP. Both Bruce and Davey emphasized that Cardiff was the centre for Wales and a strong man was needed.
48 Kenyon to Davidson, 21 February 1905, DP, 95/425.
49 Bishop Williams to Davidson, 21 February 1905, DP, 95/436.
50 Cawdor to Davidson, 23 February 1905, DP, 95/466.
51 Oliver Jones to Davidson, 21 February 1905, DP, 95/430; Edmondes to Davidson, 22 February 1905, DP, 95/446.
52 Davidson to J. J. Sanders (Balfour's secretary), undated, DP, 95/410.
53 Edmondes to Davidson, 22 February 1905, DP, 95/446.
54 Owen to Davidson, 24 February 1905, JOP.
55 Owen to 'my dear Lord' (Edwards), 31 January 1905; Owen to 'my dear Bishop' (Edwards), 20 February 1905; Owen to Davidson, 22 February 1905: JOP.
56 Owen to Davidson, 22 and 27 February 1905, DP, 95/457 and 472.
57 Cawdor to Davidson, 23 and 25 February 1905, DP, 95/466 and 476.
58 Edwards to Davidson, 24 February 1905, DP, 95/470.
59 Edmondes to Davidson, 22 February 1905, DP, 95/446.
60 Kenyon to Davidson, 22 February 1905, DP, 95/452.
61 Kenyon to Davidson, 17 February 1905, DP, 95/417.
62 Edmondes to Davidson, 22 February 1905, DP, 95/446.
63 Cawdor to Davidson, 23 February 1905, DP, 95/466.
64 Memoranda at DP, 95/429, 451 and 455.
65 Oliver Jones to Davidson, 21 February 1905, DP, 95/430, 433 (two letters of the same date).

[66] Windsor to Davidson, 21 February 1905, DP, 95/427.

[67] Edmondes to Davidson, 22 February 1905, DP, 95/446.

[68] Cawdor to Davidson, 29 February 1905, DP, 95/476.

[69] W. A. Edwards to Davidson, 22 February 1905, DP, 95/444.

[70] Ibid., 25 February 1905, DP, 95/474.

[71] T. T. L. Morgan to Davidson, 6 March 1905, DP, 95/486.

[72] CT (10 March 1905), p. 322.

[73] James to Davidson, 17 February 1905, DP, 95/419.

[74] Edwards to Davidson, 22 and 23 February 1905, DP, 95/460, 462.

[75] Owen to Davidson, 21 February 1905, JOP.

[76] Sanders to Davidson, 28 February 1905, DP, 95/480. Gibson of Gloucester and Hamer of Rochester were regarded as high church appointments.

[77] Arthur Lewis to Owen, 24 January 1905, JOP.

[78] Hughes to Davidson, 9 March 1905, DP, 95/488.

[79] *Record*, (17 March 1905), p. 248.

[80] Owen to Davidson, 14 March 1905, DP, 95/495.

[81] WM (13 March 1905), p. 5.

[82] WM (9 March 1905), p. 5.

[83] *Record* (10 March 1905), pp. 222, 229.

[84] CT (10 March 1905), pp. 303, 322, and (17 March 1905), p. 357.

[85] T. Morgan Owen to Davidson, 1 February 1905, DP, 95/379.

[86] Jones to Davidson, 1 February 1905, DP, 95/385.

[87] Daniel Lewis to Davidson, 7 February 1905, DP, 95/402.

[88] Morgan to Davidson, 6 March 1905, DP, 95/486. The *Church Times* (10 February 1905, p. 163) significantly noted, 'we have no time for the wire pulling and plotting so dear to the Celtic temperament'.

[89] Edmondes to Davidson, 22 February 1905, DP, 95/446.

[90] Recorded in Hartwell Jones, *A Celt Looks at the World*, pp. 74–5.

14. Conclusion

[1] K. O. Morgan, *Modern Wales* (Cardiff, 1995), pp. 226–7.

[2] *Welsh Outlook*, 16 (1929), 14–15.

[3] Cutting from D. R. Thomas's scrapbooks in the NLW, Church in Wales records, SA/DR/49, fol. 138, cf. SA/DR/52, fol. 34 (from *The Schoolmaster*, 10 December 1904).

Bibliography

Manuscripts

Bodleian Library, Oxford
Disraeli Papers

British Library, London
Gladstone Papers

Hatfield House
Papers of the 3rd marquess of Salisbury

Lambeth Palace Library, London
Benson Papers
Davidson Papers
Longley Papers
Tait Papers
Temple Papers

Liverpool Records Office
Letter Books of the 14th earl of Derby

Llandaff Cathedral Archives
Copleston Correspondence

National Library of Wales, Aberystwyth
Church in Wales Records
Bishop John Owen Papers
Miscellaneous Manuscripts
Powis Letters and Documents relating to the Proposed Union of the
Dioceses of St Asaph and Bangor

Public Record Office, London
Papers of Lord John Russell

Windsor Castle
Papers of Lord Melbourne
Correspondence of Queen Victoria

Theses and Typescripts

D. A. James, 'Some Social and Economic Problems of the Church of England in the Diocese of St Davids' (unpublished MA thesis, University of Wales, 1972).
'Letters from the Llanbadarnfawr Parish Chest', typescript, NLW.

Newspapers

Baner ac Amserau Cymru
Carmarthen Journal
Carnarvon and Denbigh Herald
Cardiff and Merthyr Guardian
Church Times
Cymru Fydd
English Churchmen
Guardian
Yr Haul
John Bull
Y Llan
Llandaff Diocesan Magazine
North Wales Chronicle
North Wales Gazette
The Record
Welshman
Western Mail
Wrexham Advertiser

Books and Articles

Bahlman, D. W. R., 'Politics and church patronage in the Victorian era', *Victorian Studies*, 22 (1979), 254–96.

Bahlman, D. W. R., 'The Queen, Mr Gladstone and church patronage', *Victorian Studies*, 3 (1960), 349–80.

Bell, G. K. A., *Randall Davidson* (Oxford, 1952).

Bethell, C., *A Letter to the Clergy of the County of Anglesey* (not published, London, 1837).

Bethell, C., *Charges to the Diocese of Bangor*, 1834, 1843 and 1852.

Bethell, C., *Reflections on the Proceedings of an Association calling itself the Church Protestant Defence Society* . . . (London, 1857).

Bethell, C., *Sermons Preached at the Cathedral Churches of Chichester, Gloucester, and Bangor* (London, 1857).

Bradney, J. A., *Llandaff Records* (Cardiff, 1912).

Brown, Roger L., *David Howell: A Pool of Spirituality* (Denbigh, 1998).

Brown, Roger L., 'Laying the foundation stone of Lewis' School, Pengam', *Gelligaer*, 13 (1990), 12–17.

Brown, Roger L., *Lord Powis and the Extension of the Episcopate* (Cardiff, 1989).

Brown, Roger L. (ed.), *The Letters of Edward Copleston, Bishop of Llandaff, 1828–1849* (South Wales Record Society, Cardiff, 2003).

Copleston, Edward, *A Charge to the Clergy of the Diocese of Llandaff*, 1836.

Davies, J. H. (ed.), *The Life and Opinions of Robert Roberts* (Cardiff, 1923).

Dent, C. H., *Distinguished Churchmen* (London, 1902).

Edwards, A. G., *Memories* (London, 1927).

Edwards, H. G., *Wales and the Welsh Nation* (London, 1889).

Ellis, V. Spencer, 'Thomas Vowler Short', *Province*, 2 (1955), 118–24.

Evans, W. G., *A History of Llandovery College* (Llandovery, 1981).

Foot, M. R. D. and Matthew, H. C. G. (eds), *The Gladstone Diaries* (Oxford, 1982–90).

Gibson, W. T., 'Fresh light on Bishop Connop Thirlwall of St Davids', *Transactions of the Honourable Society of Cymmrodorion*, 1992, pp. 141–58.

Gibson, W. T., 'Gladstone and the Llandaff vacancy of 1882–3', *Transactions of the Honourable Society of Cymmrodorion*, 1987, pp. 105–12.

'Golifer', *The Diocese of Llandaff: Proposed New Churches: A Letter to Lord John Russell* (London, 1850).

Guedella, Philip, *The Queen and Mr Gladstone* (London, 1933).

Hansard's Parliamentary Reporter.

Hennell, M., *Sons to the Prophets* (London, 1979).

How, F. D., *Bishop Walsham How* (London, 1899).

Hughes, William, *A History of the Church of the Cymru* (London, 1916).

Johnes, H., *A Letter to Lord John Russell on the Operation of the Established Church Bill* (London, 1836).

Johnes, H., *On the Causes which have produced Dissent from the Established Church in the Principality of Wales* (2nd edn, London, 1870).

Jones, Daniel, *Welsh Bishops for Wales: An Essay on the National and Scriptural Claims of the Established Church in Wales to be governed by Welsh Bishops* (Llandovery, 1851).

Jones, Francis, 'A Victorian bishop of Llandaff', *National Library of Wales Journal*, 19 (1975), 33–8.

Jones, G. Hartwell, *A Celt Looks at the World* (Cardiff, 1946).

Knox, R. B., *Wales and 'Y Goleuad' 1869–79* (Caernarfon, 1968).

Lerry, George, *Alfred George Edwards* (Oswestry, 1939).

Lewellin, E. N., *Pleasant Memories of Eminent Churchmen* (Carmarthen, nd.).

Morgan, J., *The Revd David James of Panteg* (Pontypool, 1925).

Morgan, K. O., *Wales in British Politics 1868–1922* (Cardiff, 1970).

Morgan, R. W., *Correspondence and Statement of Facts connected with (his) Case and (Bishop) Short of St Asaph* (London, 1855).

Morgan, R. W., *Correspondence between the Archbishop of Canterbury and R. W. Morgan* (London, 1855).

Morgan, R. W., *Scheme for the Reconstruction of the Church Episcopate and its Patronage in Wales* (London, nd.).

Morgan, R. W., *The Church and its Episcopal Corruptions in Wales* (2nd edn, London, 1855).

Owen, E. E., *The Early Life of Bishop Owen* (Llandysul, 1958).

Owen, E. E., *The Later Life of Bishop Owen* (Llandysul, 1961).

Parry, R. I., *Henry Richard* (Aberdare, 1968).

Palmer, Bernard, *High and Mitred* (London, 1992).

Peart-Binns, J. S., *Edwin Morris* (Llandysul, 1990).

Perowne, J. S. and Stokes, L. (eds), *Letters Literary and Theological of Connop Thirlwall* (London, 1881).

Price, D. T. W., *A History of St David's University College, Lampeter* (Vol. 1: Cardiff, 1977).

Reports of the Association of Welsh Clergy in the West Riding of Yorkshire.

Richard, Henry, *Letters on the Social and Political Condition of the Principality of Wales* (London, 1866).

Russell, G. W. E., *The Household of Faith* (London, 1902).

Short, T. V., *Sketch of the History of the Church of England* (London, 1875).

Short, T. V., *Primary Visitation Charge to the Clergy of the Diocese of St Asaph*, 1847.

Solway, R. A., *Prelates and People* (London, 1969).

Stanley, A. P., (ed.), *Letters to a Friend by Connop Thirlwall* (London, 1882).

Thirlwall, Jr, J. C., *Connop Thirlwall* (London, 1936).

Thomas, D. R., *The History of the Diocese of St Asaph* (3 vols., Oswestry, 1908–13).

Thomas, Harriet, *Llewelyn Thomas: A Memoir* (London nd).

Thomas, W. Ceidrych, *The Church in Wales: Shall we end it or mend it?* (London, 1893).

Walker, David, (ed.), *A History of the Church in Wales* (Penarth, 1976).

Westley, W. A., *Bishops of the Four Welsh Dioceses* (Manchester, 1912).

Williams, John, *On the Inexpediency, Folly and Sin of a 'Barbarian Episcopate' in a Christian Principality* (London, 1858).

Williams, Rowland, *Life and Letters of Rowland Williams* (London, 1874).

Wills, Winton D., 'The Rev. John Griffith and the revival of the Welsh church in the nineteenth century', *Morgannwg*, 13 (1969), 75–102.

Index